PROVOKING AGENTS

Provoking Agents

GENDER AND AGENCY IN THEORY AND PRACTICE

EDITED BY

Judith Kegan Gardiner

University of Illinois Press

URBANA AND CHICAGO

© 1995 by the Board of Trustees of the University of Illinois
Manufactured in the United States of America
1 2 3 4 5 C P 5 4 3 2 1

This book is printed on acid-free paper.

Library of Congress Cataloging-in-Publication Data

Provoking agents : gender and agency in theory and practice /
edited by Judith Kegan Gardiner.
     p.   cm.
Includes bibliographical references and index.
ISBN 0-252-02132-0. — ISBN 0-252-06418-6 (pbk.)
1. Feminist theory. 2. Gender identity. 3. Agent (Philosophy)
I. Gardiner, Judith Kegan.
HQ1190.P76   1995
305.42—dc20   94-18086
                                                            CIP

For my colleagues
in the Women's Studies Program
at the University of Illinois at Chicago
and for women activists everywhere.

Contents

Introduction

JUDITH KEGAN GARDINER

Provoking Agents takes responsibility for inciting action through feminist writing. The essays gathered here discuss women's agency, report feminist activity, intervene in contemporary critical debates, analyze obstacles to women's progress, and encourage progressive social change. At a time when conservatives rebuke feminists for destroying home, family, nation, and culture, and women activists chide feminist academics for careerist quiescence, these essays take on the difficult task of connecting theory with other forms of action to enhance their mutual effectiveness.

In the past few years, agency has become a central problem in feminist theory. This collection advances that discussion and also transcends its limits. The essays in this book define agency with relation to a variety of activities from writing to maternal surrogacy, from feminist consciousness-raising to AIDS activism. They clarify contemporary arguments about subjectivity, identity, and practical politics by showing their dependence on beliefs about agency and the related concepts of action and of performance, and they demonstrate that definitions of agency are not as important as the social uses of such concepts.

The title *Provoking Agents* evokes a dominant Western tradition that wants women to be passive and that suspects active women to be *agents provocateurs*, manipulators who incite others to harm. The essays in this volume repossess such negative terms for feminist uses, revaluing women's agency so that it can benefit women and advance other liberatory agendas. The essays repeatedly raise the question "Who benefits?" from theoretical formulations; their urgency springs from a desire to further a progressive feminist movement that is hampered by theoretical splits and political factions, confusion, and even despair. Many of the contributors to this volume, myself included, became committed to second-wave feminism in the 1960s and 1970s and saw our political activism, personal change, and scholarship as coherent, progressive, and hopeful. During the 1980s and up till now, such feminist activism has fragmented and diverged from the academy, although many of us in universities continue organizational and institutional as well as theoretical political activity. Other contributors to this volume who are more attuned to postmodernist theoretical perspectives may see such humanistic and utopian second-wave feminism as an impediment to feminist progress. To them, the idea of "provoking" or "calling forth" suggests the process that Louis Althusser dubbed "interpellation," in which prevailing discourses "call" or "hail" each of us to assume a place with respect to them.[1] Although no one can be entirely outside of social and discursive systems, both postmodernist and second-wave feminists agree that as agents within, we can and should answer back and, as Ellen Messer-Davidow suggests, act "otherwise" than in conformity to the status quo. At the same time, these essays are themselves provocative with regard to contemporary commonplaces among feminists, for example, doubting the powers of motherhood and authorship and finding some good news for women even in pornography and the decline of the middle-class family.

GENDER AND AGENCY
"I Do"

Gender has a conflicted relationship to agency. North American second-wave feminists noted that postwar academic theories mimicked popular Western stereotypes in holding that male is to female as active is to passive. For example, Sandra Gilbert and Susan Gubar contrasted the passive Angel in the House heroine of European fairy tales like Snow White or Sleeping Beauty with her artful and active stepmother, who turned against other women.[2] Whereas men were considered autonomous agents both of their own interests and of the social order as a whole, women were to be responsive to men, waiting to consent to marriage, and responsive to nature, spontaneously caring for children. They were patronized for being unable to act at all and condemned as selfish if they acted independently; they could transcend while fulfilling their womanliness only as altruistic agents of the divine. For men, agency was assumed to be a unified attribute of maleness, combining sexual potency, self-confidence, labor power, personal capabilities, and political and psychological autonomy.[3] For women, however, agency was disabled and dispersed according to social roles: the desiring female sexual subject was reviled, the maternal agent celebrated and circumscribed, and the woman laborer all too often exploited and ignored.

The situation was clearly more complicated than one of active men oppressing passive women. There were passive men and active women, anomalies that the dominant ideologies attempted to dislodge, in part, by assigning agency and passivity differential moral value according to gender: male activity was good and passivity bad; female passivity was good and activity bad, and deviations from this model were "perverse." Feminists pointed out the ways that this ideology harmed women through childhood socialization for learned helplessness.[4]

Psychoanalytic feminist theorists also showed how women raised in patriarchy might fail to develop agency. Struggles for recognition and self-confirmation, Jessica Benjamin believes, turn into relationships of domination if they are not premised on mutuality and equality. Daughters raised by devalued mothers will lack autonomy, and sons will repudiate dependence. "The idealization of motherhood," Benjamin argues, "is an attempt to redeem woman's sphere of influence. . . . by idealizing woman's desexualization and lack of agency," leaving freedom and desire as an unchallenged male domain.[5] This theory explores how social imbalances of power become psychologically internalized; it could also apply to the psychological repercussions of other oppressions such as racism, classism, and heterosexism.[6] Other psychoanalytic feminists and psychologists corroborate the idea that psychological autonomy and a child's sense of agency are still differentially gendered in this society.[7]

One reason some feminists may accept the paradigm that male activity pervasively confronts female victimization is an impulse within feminism to assign women only positive characteristics, thus revaluing traditional femininity. This approach awards women moral superiority over male oppressors as a counterweight to the traditional masculinist moralism that disparages women as sinful.[8] It also excuses women's apparent powerlessness. If we feminists have failed to change the world into an altogether better place, the reason must be the strength of sexist oppression. Few feminists want to minimize women's pain and suffering, the devastations of sexual violence, or the maldistribution of economic resources. Women produce much of the world's food and clothing but do not benefit in proportion to their labor.[9]

Current scholarship admits that women's agency can work either in behalf of or against individual women or groups. Judith Newton and Deborah Rosenfelt remind us that at any moment of history, women are "simultaneously . . . victims and . . . agents."[10] Micaela di Leonardo underscores the importance of "a crosscultural and historical perspective that stresses divisions among women on the basis of class, color, era, and culture" in correcting the tendency to assume female moral superiority.[11] Patriarchal structures reward individual women for upholding prevailing power hierarchies, often by undercutting other women's agency, as happens with "the new veiling" in some Islamic countries, according to Arlene Elowe MacLeod. "Although women are clearly assertive actors who struggle for better conditions for themselves and for their families, their efforts often seem to produce limited or ephemeral results," and women's subordination persists. To explain this situation, MacLeod argues that women are "both active subjects and subjects of domination"; women "always play an active part that goes beyond the dichotomy of victimization/acceptance, a dichotomy that flattens out a complex and ambiguous agency in which women accept, accommodate, ignore, resist, or protest—sometimes all at the same time." "Agency" is always embodied in power relations, MacLeod claims, and women's continued subordination results from women's as well as men's actions.[12] Western feminists should not patronize these veiled women, she warns, but rather ask how their viewpoints might lead to alternative discourses and effective political actions, a path that Patricia Stamp's essay in this volume follows with regard to women and the contemporary African state.

"We Shall Overcome"

While some feminists traced women's psychological oppression through fairy tales like Snow White, such stories were not necessarily the most powerful myths for today's feminists. The children's stories I remember with more pleasure preached action, willpower, and self-reliance to children growing up in the United States between World War II and the start of the second-wave women's movement. There was the Little Engine That Could, a paragon of positive thinking, who repeated, "I think I can, I think I can" until, huffing and puffing with effort, she completed her mission to deliver toys to children on the other side of the mountain.[13] Another childhood hero was the Little Red Hen, a mother whose barnyard pals refused to help her plant, grow, or grind wheat or bake bread, so that she repeatedly announced, "then I will have to do it myself." Smugly and apparently competently, she did, sharing her food with her chicks but not with her lazy friends. Then there was the record that sang, "Scientists say, and science can't lie, that the bee, the bee, the bee can't fly." I remember the bee as female, and she did fly, disproving those arrogant scientists. All of these stories used the magic and music of words to enforce their moral insistence on the necessity, and therefore the possibility, of individually motivated and effective action.

Like the authors of these children's books, Julie Nelson-Kuna and Stephanie Riger in this volume stress the importance of "efficacy beliefs," that is, of thinking one can do whatever is to be done, in shaping the different expectations that boys and girls in our society have about their own actions. Miriam Johnson places such expectations historically, speculating that the frustrated hopes for meaningful careers of postwar middle-class white American women fueled the second wave of the women's liberation movement. Many of the essays that follow question the attitudes of liberal individualism and of competitive capitalism seen in these children's stories. However, the rhythms of these tales also imply other possibilities, not only of ideologies that shape us before we are aware of them but also of the affective and unconscious dimensions to our sense of agency about which Ellen Messer-Davidow writes. Furthermore, narrative—storytelling in itself—seems to create subjects capable of action, although Carla Kaplan complicates this optimistic view of authorial agency in particularly oppressive conditions, for example, when the author is a woman slave.

Meditations on gender and agency raise some of the same questions as these childhood stories, particularly the meaning of autonomy and the inflection that individual psychological traits take from each child's socialization into a gendered, classed, and racialized society. The engine, the hen, and the bee stress the importance of beliefs about one's abilities. The plucky little critter who saves or helps others, however, still performs as an individual. For me as a middle-class white activist, fables of community or collective agency developed later, along with goals of institutional and social change. I became a member of groups that sang to encourage ourselves, "you can't scare me, I'm working for the union," "we will not be moved," and "we shall overcome," New Left groups that partly modeled themselves on, and sometimes joined in campaigns with, socialist labor organizations and African American civil rights demonstrations. These anthems shared the voluntarism of the children's homilies, their emphasis on sheer willpower, but the actions they sought were by and in behalf of groups validated by belief in shared goals and by histories of struggle. Through these collective actions, workers, black citizens, and antiwar protesters built organizations that achieved agency and renegotiated power structures, and they required and expected long-lasting commitments for their members to accomplish their goals.

The women's liberation movement, too, successfully mobilized women to think of themselves as agents both for themselves and in behalf of women as a group, as Margaret Strobel describes in her analysis of the Chicago Women's Liberation Union of the sixties and seventies. Patrocinio P. Schweickart also considers the project of feminism and grapples with the subject of "collective will-formation," and Patricia S. Mann elaborates a concept of interpersonal agency.

Whether focusing on the individual or the group, feminist activism of the women's liberation movement was action personalized and personified. Rejecting cultural and personal histories of women as devalued and as victims, feminist activists encouraged women's self-esteem and organized women to act for change. The feminist theorist bell hooks says, "Let's talk about why we see the struggle to assert agency—that is, the ability to act in one's best interest— as a male thing."[14] Second-wave feminism in the United States encouraged women to believe they could act in their collective "best interest" exactly because it was collective, the other members of one's consciousness-raising or work group affirming through resonant "clicks" of empathic understanding that one woman's realizations about what was and wasn't good for her were also the group's, that the individual and collective were implicated in one another, and therefore that the personal was political. In the materialist feminist groups to which I belonged, women insisted that the enemy wasn't individual men but patriarchy as a system, even though we saw that men as a group were advantaged by sexism and male privilege. This analysis clarified patriarchy's pervasive yet often unobtrusive power; it was enormously illuminating. However, it sometimes led to abstraction, perhaps through analogy with Marxist ideas about class, perhaps because we were turning the tables on a system that had seen only men as individuals while consigning women to be the interchangeable and intermittent objects of male attention. Thus some varieties of 1970s women's liberation saw women not as victims but as heroes of activism and as agents acting in behalf of other women, but at the same time they reified and so simplified the opposition by calling it patriarchy, as though that was a single transhistorical entity.

Nineteen seventies feminism led to definitions of common cause that seemed to hinge on the assertion of a common identity among all women. In the 1980s and into the 1990s, other feminists criticized seventies-style "sisterhood" for buying into a liberal ideology based on the bourgeois white male's image of himself as autonomous, unified, and paradigmatically human. Chéla Sandoval points out in this volume that women of color in the United States first criticized middle-class white feminism for assimilating all other women into its definitions. Then postmodernists charged that humanist and Marxist feminists were repeating errors committed by male liberals: the categories of "Woman," then of "women," were as erroneous as that of liberal "man" because they implied an invariant human essence and an essential, presumably natural and invariant, gender division.[15] Some radical feminists replied that women were fortunately not like Enlightenment conceptions of men, and some liberal feminists reaffirmed that women were, after all, more similar than different from "man," an identity that needed to be retained.[16] The question of "subjects and agents," as Susan Hekman puts it, continues to be a point of contention among feminists in which the issue of agency has become crucial. However, as Sandra Bartky points out, "one is not born but becomes a feminist"; the category of the essential woman is not a precondition for feminism.[17]

"Shit Happens"

Between the women's liberation movement and the present fell the Reagan-Bush years, a period of conservative backlash against feminist gains and U.S. losses and more generally against broad changes in the country's economy, demographics, family structures, values, and beliefs. I sketched second-wave feminism's analysis of postwar North America under the rubric "I do" to highlight its criticism of the ways a patriarchal past constructs women as passive through dominant institutions like marriage. But "I do" is also a first-person-singular performative in the present, one that reminds us the bride actively takes part in an institution she thinks is in her best interest. In contrast, the first-person-plural watchwords "we shall overcome" create a collective subject of group action that is committed to a common future. As used by materialist feminists, the borrowed refrain is also a reminder of the independent importance of movements by women of color before, outside of, and overlapping predominantly white feminism.[18] But if feminists analyze the past in order to change the future, conservatives mystify agency to protect the established order, often through a combination of fatalism and projection. Despite upholding male authority, conservatism encourages an ideology of passivity and resentment, especially for women and the working classes. The vulgar bumper sticker "shit happens" acknowledges no human agency. The slogan implies rather that the car's polluting exhaust, like an abusive father or a bad day at work, is a fact of fate or nature to be resented but endured in a perpetual present about which nothing can be done. Such an ideology effaces responsibility and denies accountability about who makes society's messes, though it confers blame—often on have nots who are portrayed as trying to steal privileges from the haves.

In the face of the conservative climate of the eighties and early nineties, both feminist activists and academic feminists express concern that they have drifted apart, and both call for theory that serves social change. Within academic feminism, the debate about agency is now taking shape in a confusing context of both social progress and backlash. Old formulae seem inadequate because they have not improved women's lives and those of other oppressed groups enough, yet feminist activists count some successes and are unsure of the advantage of switching to new formulations. hooks explains a comparable dilemma for progressive African-Americans who wish to "create a liberatory space to construct radical black subjectivity. This identity has to do with resistance, with reconstructing a collective front to re-vision and renew black liberation struggle."[19]

All feminists believe that feminism must be a movement for social change that will improve the lives of women, especially the most oppressed and disadvantaged. However, many feminists are uneasy about whether current theories render such positive changes more or less likely. Do attacks on liberal human identity and essence disable the concept of agency, and therefore do they inhibit feminist action? The Marxist critic Terry Eagleton worries that "a certain provisional stability of identity is essential not only for psychical well-being but for revolutionary political agency." He thus makes political agency the necessary core of his theory. From this standpoint he charges that various postmodernisms contain "no adequate theory of such agency, since the subject would now seem no more than the decentered effect of the semiotic process" in them.[20] Similarly, Stephanie Riger, a psychologist, argues that "to assume that the multiple voices of women are not shaped by domination is to ignore social context and legitimate the status quo. On the other hand, to assume that women have no voice other than an echo of prevailing discourses is to deny them agency and, simultaneously, to repudiate the possibility of social change."[21] The theorist Judith Butler also worries that "if we fail to recuperate the subject in feminist terms, are we not depriving feminist theory of a notion of agency that casts doubt on the viability of feminism as a normative model?"[22]

Thus within feminist theory making, the idea of agency has become a prerequisite around which other concepts are defined. The assumption behind these quotations appears to be that any theory that denies women "agency" retards the changes in patriarchal social structures for which feminism strives, because it denies the existence of an entity to attack those structures. Of course, one might believe, as Marxists hoped would be the case for capitalism, that patriarchy will fall apart through its own internal contradictions; however, no feminist I know believes that patriarchies will simply wither away but rather that they will adapt to new historical circumstances unless feminists act to alter them. Both sides in the debate between postmodernist deconstructionists and humanist or materialist feminists accuse each other of determinism. Both sides allege that the other's position hampers practical politics for feminist ends. The deconstructionist says that the humanist misunderstands real constraints on human action and falls into repeating old dominations. The humanist says that the deconstructionist sees a universe only of discourses and hence dismantles agency by disabling the concept of a human agent. Each places agency lopsidedly on only one side of an equation. For the materialist or humanist feminist, active women face oppressive social structures; for the narrow deconstructionist, discourses are social actors while people fragment into divided entities called into place by conflicting discourses.

The 1990 debate between the historians Joan Scott and Linda Gordon indicates an apparent impasse that the writers of the present collection address.[23] In a review of Gordon's book about social service agencies, Scott objects that "Gordon wants to insist that welfare clients are active agents" who "negotiate power among themselves" rather than passive victims of dominating social controls. Scott suggests that "a different conceptualization of agency might have avoided the contradictions" she finds in Gordon's work, a conceptualization that would define agency not as a trait of autonomous individuals, but as a specific, context-dependent "discursive effect, in this case the effect of social workers' constructions of families, gender, and family violence." Poststructuralist theory is politically necessary for feminists, Scott claims, in order to help us "understand how, in all their complexity, collective and individual differences are constructed, how, that is, hierarchies and inequalities are produced." In response, Gordon rejects Scott's "determinist perspective" for emphasizing gender as "'difference' marked by the otherness and absolute silencing of women," whereas she defines gender as "a power system in which women are subordinated" but "take choices and action despite constriction."

This publicized debate about women's agency took as its occasion a study of welfare "agencies." "When I hear agency I think bureaucracy, when I'd like to think travel," Nancy K. Miller notes wryly.[24] The word "agency" encapsulates the ambiguities of the arguments between Scott and Gordon: were the "agencies" the means by which dominant discourses shaped the behavior of poor women, or were the poor women themselves the agents? The word implies both: agency is action that cannot arise from a single, individual source but is always mediated and preceded by other actions and must always take place within a field of power relations, including those among women. Agency also always involves theory, as an angry welfare rights activist told a NOW convention: "We are an organization. We have an agenda. We have a theory around this stuff. And we are not going to stand up and say what you have done for us."[25]

"Act Up"

Who acts—people or discourses? The choice is a false one. "After all, activity is activity within recognized oppressive circumstances, and oppression is oppression of conscious human beings capable of action," according to one feminist collective.[26] On all sides of battles among patriarchal and feminist forces are human actors constrained and enabled by social structures, ideologies, and discourses upheld by human actors. Action and structure, freedom and constraint operate in individuals, in institutions, and in discourses. Patriarchal structures require constant human activity, just as emancipatory actions are themselves socially constructed. The essayists in this volume do not see agency as simply a "discourse effect"; nor do they validate the old-fashioned liberal construction of the autonomous human male as their model. They do demonstrate, however, that definitions of agency are still contested, as are the political consequences of differing approaches. Chéla Sandoval suggests that a new democracy of oppression has created the possibility for a new "oppositional consciousness" capable of actions of resistance, whereas Valerie Hartouni shows the resistance to changing gender definitions in both liberal and conservative legal discourses. Katie King defines feminism "from the activism up," where political agency defines identity rather than the reverse. The lesbian and gay liberation slogan "Act Up" insists on present action to create new identities, new human agencies, and new activities in the future. It is both playful and deadly serious, unlike the psychoanalytic dismissal of counterproductive behavior that is merely "acting out" unconscious directives. In contrast, "Act Up" is an imperative that reaches out to all its auditors—we, you, they—creating a present community of those hailed by its command to perform in one's own and the group's best interests.

Can an agent be separate from its actions? English-speaking feminists have learned to distrust the gendered categories implied by traditional pronoun usage like the generic "he." However, much of the debate about agency seems to accept categories of English nouns and verbs as descriptors of reality, whereas current knowledge about nature and society tells us that no entity exists without motion and change, that, therefore, agents are coextensive with their actions.

Outside a binary debate between defensive positions, postmodernist approaches can illuminate our current understandings of gender and agency. As society is increasingly pervaded by postmodern social relations, more influenced by images and representations in making purchasing or voting decisions or decisions about careers or lovers or family formation, representation becomes society's favored medium of action, and gender and agency are simultaneously reconfigured. In the industrial capitalism of the past, men appeared as political subjects and as economic producers; women, especially of the bourgeois classes, as consumables, sexual trophies and aesthetic objects to be exchanged among men, and also as consumers for themselves and their families and as custodians of democratic market values to be passed along to the next generation. However, now that the postindustrial United States is becoming more sluggish as an economic power and more dominated by a culture of consumption, the relation between gender and agency is altered. Both men and women work more hours for wages, often in situations in which they have little control over the product of their labor or of their conditions of work and in which they fear unemployment. Both men and women spend leisure time shopping in malls and switching channels with their television remote controls. I speculate that, in addition to the severe burdens of economic distress, such leisure activities attenuate people's sense of personal agency, particularly among men to whom this culture still represents anachronistic and elitist ideals of commanding, efficient labor and of personal athletic prowess. This gap between ideology and experience, in turn, may spur some men's cravings for more and more powerful representations of action, for example in movies in which violent and grandiose heroes blow away cars, buildings, and people, and perhaps also in political actions, like the U.S. war against Iraq, which can be represented in similar terms. Because these actions are hollow and unconvincing, however, the ante continually rises for better special effects and for more persuasive and more spectacular real and vicarious violence. In this situation of economic stagnation and representational equivocation, I surmise, masculinity no longer guarantees a man psychological assurance of agency or autonomy, an assurance he may try to heighten by devaluing women. Furthermore, as more social attention focuses on the advertised bodies of women, woman's status as body not for herself but for others compromises and complicates actual women's sense of their personhood, an ambivalence that Marianne Hirsch discusses in terms of women's family photographs, and Linda Williams in terms of pornography.

At the same time that producing images becomes a privileged form of production and consuming them a major form of leisure in contemporary America, many women, particularly United States women of color and Third World women, have moved from predominantly service occupations like paid domestic labor to an increasingly large share of factory production. These jobs have declined from unionized, high-earning men's jobs providing wages that could supposedly support a family to less-regulated jobs in alternative workplaces with fewer benefits, conditions that affect a large proportion of women and their children and so depress family wages. As sexual harassment and violence against women increasingly become public knowledge, moreover, some radical feminists return to a polarized rhetoric of female victimization and passivity in the face of evil male activity. On the other hand, conservatives agree with organized feminism in seeing feminism as an active and effective social force, although one contrary to their values.

With these complex reconfigurations of gender, it is not surprising that agency also takes on new and contradictory manifestations. As the essays in this volume demonstrate, discussion of such issues is important now, especially to academic feminists. At the same time, many of these authors indicate an impatience with academic feminism and validate their theories through other forms of political activism. The urgency many of these essays express may spring from a specific historical moment in which the women's liberation movement of the 1960s has apparently become fragmented in the 1990s into separate academic and activist wings, themselves divided among many tendencies, and opposed by a well-organized backlash that appropriates many feminist issues for its own purposes.

Martha Nussbaum describes a new feminist economics in which "abilities to take action, and not resources, are the primary goods." In this context Nussbaum sees that "capability" has become "by now a standard term in the literature of economics and development," meaning "that condition in virtue of which one is *able* to do something," including both internal and external conditions. Thus citizens' "capability" of voting, for example, would include their internal capacity for making choices as well as external conditions permitting voting to occur in a state where voting is meaningful political activity.[27] This concept of "capability," with an added moral dimension of personal and social responsibility, resembles the comprehensive sense of agency developed in the following essays.

"Sexuality is to feminism what work is to marxism," Catharine MacKinnon memorably announced, "that which is most one's own, yet most taken away."[28] I suggest that agency names the desirable qualities common to both sexuality and labor, and the conviction that agency is or should be "most one's own" is not the result of a natural essence but is a feminist belief about human fulfillment. The denial of agency is a denial of personhood that polarizes power relations. The definition of agency restricted to capitalist male autonomy denies the personhood not just of women but of other subjected groups. Such a definition provides the rationale for privileged male rule, since the rulers claim that the oppressed have no legitimate desires of their own, no abilities or motives or even interest in acting responsibly for themselves, and, conversely, that the actions they do take are self-destructive and destructive of social order. Popular representations of the drug trade fully fit this model: foreign or "underclass" pushers criminally parody market agency while their customers are passive zombies mindlessly endangering their families, including their fetuses, and the public at large. Feminists join other oppositional groups in contesting such definitions. They claim that the capacity to become an agent is potentially available to all people, but that such capacities are shaped in interpersonal and discursive fields of power that may inhibit or enable them. Each person's potential for activity will also be shaped throughout life as behaviors are repressed, rewarded, learned, and transformed in the practice of organizations and institutions from the family to the state, from the university to the feminist consciousness-raising group.

Taken together, the essays in this book explore gender, agency, and oppression at many levels, including the social denial of women's ability to act, the inhibition of women's inclination to act, the deflection of women's ability to act from self-interest, and the contrary premises required for more satisfactory female agencies and more satisfactory institutions and societies in which to act. These positive factors range from child-rearing practices to literary representations that encourage female autonomy as well as interdependence. They include beliefs that responsible and effective agents of change can and do exist. They also require social movements that confirm the need for and the possibility of change and encourage people to join them, changing their identities as they change their activities. And they must include processes of change that can advance the self and the group, negotiating conflicts among them, and thus advance feminist goals for a more just society for both men and women.

THE ESSAYS

Agents for Change

This volume begins with four essays that focus on women's activism and analyze its conditions and effects. What enables women to be agents in behalf of themselves and other women? The first two essays address how the women's liberation movement of the 1960s and 1970s changed women, and women changed their worlds. In "Acting Otherwise," Ellen Messer-Davidow analyzes feminist consciousness-raising groups to see how they changed what women felt and thought and did, and why they did not change broader social structures. Two major concepts in this essay advance the theory of agency: affect attunement and articulatory practices. The first emphasizes emotional as well as cognitive factors in feminism; the second connects individual with social and institutional change. Next, in "Consciousness and Action: Historical Agency in the Chicago Women's Liberation Union," Margaret Strobel examines an explicitly socialist-feminist organization that emphasized action rather than consciousness-raising. Quoting extensively from interviews, she describes how the organization moved women to become activists in behalf of women, encouraging individual and collective effort through specific institutional practices. For example, in the Speakers Bureau, women prepared one another to speak in public.

In comparison to these studies of American feminism, Patricia Stamp's "Mothers of Invention: Women's Agency in the Kenyan

State" argues that Kenyan "women's agency resides in their communal endeavors and is constantly reinvented in the context of political and social change," particularly as they contest the meanings of motherhood, "custom," and "tradition" against neocolonial and patriarchal practices. Katie King, too, stresses the international variety and specificity of oppositional practices in "Local and Global: AIDS Activism and Feminist Theory." No unitary homosexual "identity," she argues, grounds AIDS activism and the specific lesbian and homosexual formations she describes in Japan, Mexico, and the United States.

Reproductive Agendas

The essays in this section turn from organized feminist activism to contests over women's maternal and reproductive roles and their social meanings. A woman's power as mother in her family is so great that women need no other power, some traditionalists have argued. Motherhood makes the mediate nature of agency especially clear, since this maternal power was predicated on the woman being a conduit, not an independent agent, who shaped her children according to the dictates of God, nature, the state, and her husband, and who achieved heroism only when she was an agent not for herself but in behalf of her fetus or child. Late twentieth-century politics and technology appear to have disrupted such mythologized meanings of maternity and reproduction, but Valerie Hartouni demonstrates their continuing prominence in "Reproductive Technologies and the Negotiation of Public Meanings: The Case of Baby M." Despite the complexities of surrogacy, she shows, both conservative and liberal interpretations of the case construed "natural motherhood" to support male prerogative and paternal rights. In "Cyborgean Motherhood and Abortion," in contrast, Patricia S. Mann takes a more optimistic view of the liberatory potential of new reproductive technologies. Asserting that mere biological pregnancy is no longer a sufficient ethical basis for bearing a child, she argues that children today be seen as "social offspring" for whom particular adults must take conscious responsibility from the beginning. Instead of the surrogate or the cyborg, Miriam M. Johnson argues in "Maternal Agency vs. the Brotherhood of Males" for the independent power of maternal agency to bring about gender equality. She contrasts white middle-class feminists' ambivalence about motherhood and maternal values with the more positive evaluation given these as bases for community building by some African-American feminists and sees the rise of diverse and voluntary maternally oriented associations as creating the structural conditions for social transformation.

Enacting Theories

The contributors to this volume engage one another and a wide range of other theorists. The essays in this cluster locate their own feminist interventions with regard to the issues of agency and subjectivity as framed by competing theorists. Julie Nelson-Kuna and Stephanie Riger review "Women's Agency in Psychological Contexts," looking particularly at the gendering of action, emotion, and self-efficacy beliefs. Sandra Lee Bartky asks, "Agency: What's the Problem?" and decides that Foucault's later theories are compatible with people's being moral agents even though his early work apparently "denies the possibility of agency, autonomy, and liberation from domination." However, long before Foucault, she reminds us, feminists had already produced critical analyses of the micropolitics of everyday life and of oppressive regimes of knowledge and power. For Susan Hekman, in "Subjects and Agents: The Question for Feminism," the solution to dichotomies other theorists perceive between essentialist and social constructionist views of the subject can be resolved by dropping both in favor of a deconstructionist position and a "discursive subject" capable of agency and creativity. Chéla Sandoval, too, offers an advance beyond current feminist debates in her already influential concept of "oppositional consciousness," which she explicates here in "Feminist Forms of Agency and Oppositional Consciousness: U.S. Third World Feminist Criticism." This new form of historical consciousness, outside of dominant white feminism, operates through a "differential" organization that can align beyond gender with worldwide movements for social justice and decolonization.

Representation in Action

The last set of essays in this book pays special heed to the importance of modes of representation in contemporary culture—writing, reading, photography, film, pornography, and performance art. Patrocinio P. Schweickart begins by asking questions: "What Are We Doing? What Do We Want? Who Are We? Comprehending the Subject of Feminism." In answer, she employs the metaphor of feminism as a collectively written text-in-progress, a definition that includes the moral and the political. Her challenging theory foregrounds the necessary interaction between individual and political agency. The young women that Marianne Hirsch considers in "Resisting Images: Rereading Adolescence" alter family photographs to remove themselves from socially constraining scripts, creating spaces within which they can develop personal autonomy. Through the written and visual work of Jamaica Kincaid, Marguerite Duras, Lorie Novak, Valerie Walkerdine, and herself, Hirsch decides that ruptures with the past are necessary to women's future agency and change. Carla Kaplan is more cautious about the liberatory potentials of reading and writing as well as of legal contracts. In "Recuperating Agents: Narrative Contracts, Emancipatory Readers, and *Incidents in the Life of a Slave Girl*," she shows that under oppressive conditions, writing is not intrinsically subversive and the heroine's "efforts to avoid consent or participation in her own nearly overwhelming disempowerment lead her to refusals of engagement or contract that can look like passivity," although "what counts as fighting back" is exactly what is at stake.

Patrocinio P. Schweickart is optimistic about the project of writing for feminism; Marianne Hirsch is optimistic about readings resistant to the representations of others, and Carla Kaplan is skeptical that reading and writing are inherently subversive. This anthology concludes with Linda Williams's essay, "A Provoking Agent: The Pornography and Performance Art of Annie Sprinkle," which resists categorical statements about what is liberatory and what is oppressive for women. Williams sees Sprinkle's work as both art and strategy, her sexual agency putting theory in practice. Despite the "sexual saturation of 'woman,'" Williams concludes, U.S. women today can join men in the self-control and agency of contemporary sexual life.

NOTES

The essays in this volume spring from a context of current controversy among feminists and other thinkers, but I am the agent of their appearance here. I asked people from many disciplines whom I knew either personally or by reputation to submit papers on this topic. Although several had preemptive obligations, those who chose to contribute are intellectually committed and diverse. Their essays were substantially revised as the volume took shape, often in relation to the other essays. Together the essays range across and between the fields of philosophy, literary criticism, history, political science, sociology, psychology, anthropology, legal theory, and film, cultural, African, women's, and lesbian-gay-bisexual studies. I'm delighted with the variety of approaches and the synthesis of insights in this volume and thank all of the contributors for their vision and their revisions. I also thank Nancy K. Miller, Joan Wallach Scott, and Paul Smith for generously joining an earlier stage of this project and the readers for the University of Illinois Press for their comments.

1. Louis Althusser, "Ideology and Ideological State Apparatuses. . .", in *Lenin and Philosophy and Other Essays* (London: New Left Books, 1970), 123–73.

2. Sandra Gilbert and Susan Gubar, *The Madwoman in the Attic: The Woman Writer and the Nineteenth-Century Imagination* (New Haven: Yale University Press, 1979), 37–44. Also see Louise Bernikow, *Among Women* (New York: Harmony Books, 1980).

3. "Men" in this tradition implicitly refers to men of the dominant group, that is, upper- or middle-class white males. For one example of differently figured masculinity, see Ana Maria Alonso, "Gender, Power, and Historical Memory: Discourses of *Serrano* Resistance," in *Feminists Theorize the Political*, ed. Judith Butler and Joan W. Scott (New York: Routledge, 1992), 404–25.

4. See Lyn Mikel Brown and Carol Gilligan, *Meeting at the Crossroads: Women's Psychology and Girls' Development* (Cambridge, Mass.: Harvard University Press, 1992). Gender is only one of the axes of domination in our culture. In the contemporary U.S. race/class system, the activity of "underclass" black men is often stigmatized as criminal; the activity of "underclass" black women—who have not been socialized to passivity—as overly sexual and inadequately maternal, whereas the poor in general are blamed for passively refusing to "help themselves" become middle class.

5. Jessica Benjamin, *The Bonds of Love: Psychoanalysis, Feminism, and the Problem of Domination* (New York: Pantheon Books, 1988), 92.

6. For example, see Elizabeth Abel, "Race, Class, and Psychoanalysis? Opening Questions," in *Conflicts in Feminism*, ed. Marianne Hirsch and Evelyn Fox Keller (New York: Routledge, 1990), 184–204.

7. The most influential theorists in this regard are Nancy Chodorow, *The Reproduction of Mothering: Psychoanalysis and the Sociology of Gender* (Berkeley: University of California Press, 1978); and Carol Gilligan, *In a Different Voice: Psychological Theory and Women's Development* (Cambridge, Mass.: Harvard University Press, 1982). In this volume Julie Nelson-Kuna and Stephanie Riger discuss nonpsychoanalytic psychology.

8. Patricia Stamp reminds us in this volume that "tradition" is always an interested construction of the present, and that is true too of my uses to contrast it to feminism.

9. See Marilyn Waring, *If Women Counted: A New Feminist Economics* (Harper and Row, 1989).

10. Judith Newton and Deborah Rosenfelt, "Introduction: Toward a Materialist-Feminist Criticism," in *Feminist Criticism and Social Change: Sex, Class and Race in Literature and Culture*, ed. Judith Newton and Deborah Rosenfelt (New York: Methuen, 1985), xxii. Even this formulation apparently opposes victims and agents, obscuring the possibility of largely pas-

sive oppressors, like those perpetuating institutional racism, and of active victims.

11. Micaela di Leonardo, "Contingencies of Value in Feminist Anthropology," in *(En)Gendering Knowledge: Feminists in Academe*, ed. Joan E. Hartman and Ellen Messer-Davidow (Knoxville: University of Tennessee Press, 1991), 147.

12. Arlene Elowe MacLeod, "Hegemonic Relations and Gender Resistance: The New Veiling as Accommodating Protest in Cairo," *Signs* 17, no. 3 (Spring 1992): 533–34.

13. A current version is Watty Piper, *The Little Engine that Could* (New York: Platt and Munk, 1991). The publishers have trademarked the phrase "I think I can."

14. bell hooks, *Yearning: Race, Gender, and Cultural Politics* (Boston: South End Press, 1990), 206.

15. Among those who discuss this issue are Judith Butler, *Gender Trouble: Feminism and the Subversion of Identity* (New York: Routledge, 1990); Diana Fuss, *Essentially Speaking: Feminism, Nature and Difference* (New York: Routledge, 1989); and Denise Riley, *"Am I That Name?": Feminism and the Category of "Women" in History* (Minneapolis: University of Minneapolis, 1988).

16. The best-known radical feminist in this debate may be Catharine A. MacKinnon, *Feminism Unmodified: Discourses on Life and Law* (Cambridge, Mass.: Harvard University Press, 1987). For a liberal view, see Rosemarie Tong, *Feminist Thought: A Comprehensive Introduction* (Boulder, Colo.: Westview Press, 1989).

17. Sandra Lee Bartky, *Femininity and Domination: Studies in the Phenomenology of Oppression* (New York: Routledge, 1990).

18. See, for example, *All the Women Are White, All the Blacks Are Men, But Some of Us Are Brave: Black Women's Studies*, ed. Gloria T. Hull, Patricia Bell Scott, and Barbara Smith (Old Westbury, N.Y.: Feminist Press, 1982).

19. hooks, *Yearning*, 36.

20. Terry Eagleton, *Ideology: An Introduction* (London: Verso, 1991), 198.

21. Stephanie Riger, "Epistemological Debates, Feminist Voices: Science, Social Values, and the Study of Women, *American Psychologist* (June 1992): 737.

22. Judith Butler, "Gender Trouble, Feminist Theory, and Psychoanalytic Discourse," in *Feminism/Postmodernism*, ed. Linda J. Nicholson (New York: Routledge, 1990), 327. Also see her reformulation in *Feminists Theorize the Political* that "the constituted character of the subject is the very precondition of its agency," 12.

23. Joan W. Scott, review of *Heroes of Their Own Lives*, by Linda Gordon; Linda Gordon, review of *Gender and the Politics of History*, by Joan Wallach Scott; and responses, *Signs* 15, no. 4 (Summer 1990): 848–59.

24. Nancy K. Miller to the author, 1992, commenting, at my request, on her substitution of "agency" for "identity" in revisions of two of her essays,

"Arachnologies: The Woman, The Text, and the Critic," published originally in *The Poetics of Gender,* ed. Nancy K. Miller (New York: Columbia University Press, 1986), 270–95, reprinted in Nancy K. Miller, *Subject to Change: Reading Feminist Writing* (New York: Columbia University Press, 1988), 77–101; and "Changing the Subject: Authorship, Writing and the Reader," published originally in *Feminist Studies/Critical Studies,* ed. Teresa de Lauretis (Bloomington: Indiana University Press, 1986), 102–20, reprinted in *Subject to Change,* 102–21.

25. Quoted by Guida West, "Conflict and Cooperation among Women in the Welfare Rights Movement," in *Bridges of Power: Women's Multicultural Alliances,"* ed. Lisa Albrecht and Rose M. Brewer (Philadelphia: New Society Publishers, 1990), 166.

26. Ellen Carol DuBois, Gail Paradise Kelly, Elizabeth Lapovsky Kennedy, Carolyn W. Korsmeyer, Lillian S. Robinson, *Feminist Scholarship: Kindling in the Groves of Academe* (Urbana: University of Illinois Press, 1987), 40.

27. Martha Nussbaum, "Justice for Women," *New York Review of Books,* 8 Oct. 1992, 47.

28. Catharine A. MacKinnon, "Feminism, Marxism, Method, and the State: An Agenda for Theory," *Signs* 7, no. 3 (1982): 515.

PART ONE

Agents for Change

ONE

Acting Otherwise

ELLEN MESSER-DAVIDOW

> Our feelings will lead us to our theory, our theory to our
> action, our feelings about that action to new theory and
> then to new action.
>
> —Kathie (Amatniek) Sarachild

Why agency now?

Think about these instances of conservative politics: three presidential administrations that were antifeminist, homophobic, and racist; a Supreme Court dominated by conservative justices who have eroded female reproductive choice, affirmative action, and First Amendment rights; a U.S. Department of Education that attempted to prohibit financial aid targeted to minority students in higher education; a former chairman of the National Endowment for the Humanities (NEH) who opposed feminism, Marxism, deconstruction, and multiculturalism and nominated only political conservatives to the national advisory council; a former acting chairman of the National Endowment for the Arts (NEA) who overturned peer-panel recommendations to award grants to art with erotic content; a National Association of Scholars (NAS), funded by right-wing foundations, that claims academic Leftists are terrorizing their conservative colleagues; dozens of books alleging that "tenured radicals" are on a rampage against Western civilization; a corps of conservative journalists writing for mainstream media who manufacture stories about progressive academics' "political correctness" and "New McCarthyism"; a right-wing public-relations industry that invented the slogans "quota queen" and "pope of political correctness" to slander recent nominees for positions in the Justice Department and the National Endowment for the Humanities.

These instances tell us a thing or two about conservative activism and its agents—agents who, we must recognize, are not merely the leaders of the movement but the organizations that constitute and empower it. Between 1960 and 1980, the Right became a political force by building national organizations, interest groups, PACs, religious networks, corporate councils, and the dominant faction of the Republican party.[1] During the 1980s, conservatives enlarged this infrastructure so that it could become a cultural force as well: they founded scores of think tanks, training programs, foundations, grassroots organizations, and legal centers. As the instances show, the Right uses government and its own organizations to leverage changes that impact cumulatively on the political, social, and cultural structuring of our society.[2]

The Right no longer considers culture a sideline to the central business of politics and economics. Rather, as Paul Weyrich, president of the right-wing Free Congress Foundation (FCF), announced in the mid-1980s, it is the central business now. In a book on "cultural conservatism," the FCF observes that "America has been suffering from cultural drift . . . the gradual emptying of a nation's values of their content."[3] To blame for this drift are the "cultural radicals" (e.g., feminists, environmentalists, gays, welfare recipients), who have attacked the "nation's collective mind, its sense of right and wrong, the way it perceives reality, and its definition of self."[4] According to William S. Lind, an adviser to Weyrich, cultural conservatives must "seek to conserve traditional Western culture" because it "is necessary if our society is to be successful, in terms of what it provides its citizens."[5] The agenda outlined by the FCF asks cultural conservatives to act; they must raise debate, lobby federal and state governments, and reform those institutions—families, schools, churches, professional associations, unions, media—that produce culture. "The politics that carry us into the twenty-first century," the FCF predicts, "will be based not on economics, but on culture."[6]

Seen in light of the infrastructure and goals, the instances show how the politics of cultural conservatives get played out by exploiting points of institutional interaction to make change. First, conservatives make changes in a number of national institutions (e.g., shifts in federal agency personnel and policies, in equal-opportunity laws, in media coverage) that render them more useful in leveraging change on other institutions. Then they bring these institutions (federal agencies, laws, media) to bear on a single target—for instance, on higher education through criticism, regulation, and redistribution of its funding. Finally, the changes made have repercussions beyond their obvious effects. A change in student aid, for example, does not merely de-fund certain kinds of students; it also requires new practices on the part of federal agencies, universities, faculty, and students. When these new practices are routinized, they re-form the structuring of higher education—its demographics, finances, pedagogy, and intellectual products.

The subject of agency is immanent in our national politics and to our well being. Academic feminists cannot afford to treat it merely as a problematic of academic discourse to be teased apart and better understood. Rather, we must recognize that agentic practices are at the heart of the profound changes now sweeping our society and, if we are not attentive, sweeping progressive democracy away. As a feminist scholar and activist who is appalled by conservatism's vision of society and alarmed by its successes, I believe that agentic practices are what feminists most need to perform now. Thus, for me, agency must be translated from an interesting academic problem to an urgent practical one: (how) can feminists act as agents of progressive democracy?

DEFINING AGENCY

Conventionally defined as the capacity to determine and act, agency is attached to an entity—an individual, a collective, or a social structure. As such, it is rather like a chameleon, taking on the coloration of the entity to which it happens to be attached. What are the implications of this attachment for our understanding of agency?

In individualist models, when agency is attached to a "self" and conceived as an element of psychological being, it is said to be an individual's capacity for self-determination realized through decision and action. Or when attached to "persons" and conceived as an element of social being, it is said to be their capacity for social influence and intervention.[7] Constructs of "self" and "society" are, as anthropologists have observed, culturally variable.[8] Contrasting three individualist models of "self"—the Eskimo, Maori, and Western—Rom Harré notes that they vary in their emphases on such qualities as boundedness, unity, continuity, and uniqueness: Eskimos have a weaker sense of the self's inner unity than Westerners do, and Maori have a stronger sense of the self's distinctiveness, inviolability, and self-activation than Westerners do.[9] The particular qualities these models assign to "self" refract how agency is conceptualized.

In short, we conceptualize agency by modeling it. The models that I examine next—individualist, social-structural, poststructuralist, and collectivist—can be differentiated by the entities to which they attach agency, the qualities they attribute to these entities, and the elements they include in agency. But the compelling issue in all models is change. To account for change they must provide answers to these questions: Where is determination located? How do actors come to act otherwise? What kinds of change may occur, and why?

Models of Agency

Individualist models, which attach agency to a "self," vary not only in terms of the qualities that constitute the "self," such as bound-edness and unity, but also in terms of the elements included in its agency—for instance, power and action in the Islamic model, or volition, decision, and action in the Western one. According to the Islamic model, God determines and reveals the path of action; agents do not need to choose a path, but they do need power to go down the determined one. Islamic agency, then, is exercised as the personal power by which individuals go down the path to a greater or lesser extent. By contrast, according to the Western model, agents choose a path of action. Choice, Harré notes, implies the "realizability of more than one path. Decision is called for because possibilities of action seem to branch. Agency, then, is exercised in a choice between branches, and the focus of morality is on those choice-points and the reasons and motives for choosing one or the other." Harré contrasts the elements of Islamic agency to those of Western agency: "The doctrine of human responsibility is formulated in terms of power, not of freedom; of capability to do, not freedom to choose; of the capacity to do what is required, not the freedom to decide for oneself what is desirable or proper. God determines in advance the proper path; man may fail to move along it."[10]

Determinist models of agency, such as the Islamic or social-structural, raise an important question about the possibility of change: (how) can actors act otherwise than it has been determined they act? In the Islamic model, acting otherwise is seen as moral failure: the individual lacked the power to fulfill what is divinely determined. In the Western model, acting otherwise may sometimes be seen as moral triumph: the individual chose to act, with integrity and at cost to herself, against (im)moral conventions or advice. While both models make the individual their operative unit, they assume different limits to individual determination. The Islamic agent does not determine the course of his action, and the Western agent does not determine all the consequences of her action, which is why the Western model allows for unintended consequences. By contrast, in

social-structural models, "subjects" are not individually determinative; rather, the social formation determines them, precluding their
capacity to decide and act otherwise. Such models situate determination in the social formation—as did structural Marxists who argued that the economic base produces individuals as "subjects" who
function as the agents of production. Later theorists tried to attenuate economism and determinism by building on Louis Althusser's
concepts of interpellation and overdetermination.

To reproduce the conditions of production, Althusser had argued,
a social formation must supply both the materials needed for production and the skills and wages needed by the agents of production
(workers, managers), but it must also ensure that individuals will be
agents of production by producing their subjection to the ruling ideology and their mastery of its practices. Ideological state apparatuses
(religious, educational, familial, legal, political, cultural institutions)
"steep" them in an ideology that both represents and addresses them.
It represents their "imaginary relationship . . . to the real conditions
of existence" (i.e., represents them as free agents) and hails (or inter-
pellates) them. In recognizing that it addresses them, individuals are
constituted as "subjects" that occupy the places and participate in the
practices designated by the ideology.[11] Thus produced by and for the
social formation, "subjects" act, even if they believe they are self-
determining, as determined by it. Although Althusser's model atten-
uates economism by setting up a reciprocity between base and super-
structure, it appears to preclude the possibility that "subjects," as an
effect of social structure, can act otherwise.

Critics have focused on the problem of how "subjects" might act
otherwise. Determinism was problematical for such humanist-
Marxists as E. P. Thompson, Steven B. Smith explains, because it
denied "the role of human agency in history" and consequently
expelled "from the Marxian canon the humanist thesis that 'we
make our own history.'" To retain this thesis, Thompson attached
"conscious human choice" to actors who could form themselves
into classes that act to make history.[12] Doing so, he also retained a
feature of individualism. According to individualism, what makes
us distinctively human is the very ensemble of qualities (volition-
decision-action) that allows us to be more or less determinative. As
seen through the individualist lens, the Althusserian model is extremely problematical: to be determined by a social formation is to
be dehumanized, and to be dehumanized is to be unable to assume
the status of "self," "person," or "class," the operative units in individualist and humanist-Marxist models. Or, as Smith remarks, for

Thompson the Althusserian model casts actors not as human agents who make history but merely as "the bearers or supports of the relations of production."[13]

However, in Althusser's model, all economic, social, and cultural entities are both determined and determining. Any particular entity is, to use the term he borrowed from Freud, "overdetermined" by all of the other entities that together function as causes and outcomes, practices and their contexts.[14] Thus each individual, as Stephen Resnick and Richard Wolff put it, "is the site of the different effectivities of all other social entities . . . for example, of the effects of class, parents, jobs, religions, politics, literature, biology, etc."[15] Amplifying this explanation of how "subjects" might act otherwise, Paul Smith draws on poststructuralism. "Subjects," he argues, are interpellated by a welter of discourses that require them to take up diverse subject-positions. Since they are "incapable of colligating [or binding together] these positions without contradiction" even when interpellated as an allegedly unified "self," the contradictions release them "from perfect self-identity, homogeneity, and fixity." Because "subjects" cannot subsist in a state of contradiction, they are enjoined "to construct, recognize, and exploit difference" and thus produced as agents who can act otherwise.[16]

In contrast to individualist, social-structural, and poststructuralist models, collectivist models attach agency to groups and conceive of it as collective forms of organization and process. The models of agency put forward by the civil rights, New Left, and women's liberation movements of the 1960s expanded the humanist-Marxist notion of working-class agency in history. These movements believed that they, too, could act as the agents of history by making change but that they needed to make it in, as well as through, organizational forms and processes.[17] Aiming to transform the hierarchy, bureaucracy, and violence of the dominant social order, the New Left believed that its own order must prefigure and perform the desired transformation. Participatory democracy, in which ordinary people shared in the decision making that affected their lives, was both the means by which the New Left attempted to operate and the end it sought for society. To accommodate participation, it needed organizational forms that were horizontal rather than hierarchical and processes that were more like those of a community than a bureaucracy.[18] Consequently, during its brief existence the New Left was arguably more successful in establishing alternative institutions, such as free schools, underground newspapers, and food co-ops, than it was in changing national institutions.[19] In the New Left model, acting otherwise is conceived as counterforming some structures to transform others.

The women's liberation movement, as well as writers who have studied it, conceptualized agency as the capacity to make change in three registers: individual consciousnesses, personal lives, and society. Typically, they demarcate the changes women made in their consciousnesses—learning to conceptualize "women as an oppressed group," to view personal experiences as political data, and to analyze the oppressive mechanisms of patriarchy—from those they made in their personal lives and through social activism. Joan Cassell notes that "for some women the consciousness-raising group seems to act as a matrix for wide-ranging personal changes. For others, however, the group appears to function as a safety valve, allowing hostility and resentment to be vented without threatening the participant's life outside the group. The group, then, helps some women change, while helping others not to change."[20] Florence Howe underscores the demarcation, referring to it as "the leap from consciousness to action."[21] Indeed, Anita Shreve's retrospective study shows that while most participants in CR (consciousness-raising) groups became feminists and made changes in their personal lives, they did not become activists.[22] The problematics of acting otherwise are thus more complicated in the feminist model. A woman may act otherwise in the first register but fail to do so in the second and/or third registers.

The models of agency I have surveyed demarcate actor/structure and subjective/objective, whether framed as volition/decision/action (individualist), subjectivity/social formation (social-structural and poststructuralist), or group consciousness/mobilization (collectivist). Having made the demarcation, they then locate the *possibility* of acting otherwise primarily in one register: the individual's decision, the class's power, the contradictions of subjectivity, the form(ing) of counterinstitutions. They do not address the *practices* performed in all registers. Rejecting the antecedence of these demarcations, I will redefine agency as articulatory practices that coproduce actors and social structures and will examine these practices as they were performed in CR groups of the women's liberation movement during the 1970s.

Agency and/as Articulatory Practices

Agency, according to Anthony Giddens, is coproduced. Actors act. Their actions, regularized, are practices; practices, distanced in space and time, become structural properties of a social system. In acting, however, actors do not "create social systems: they reproduce or transform them, remaking what is already made in the continuity of *praxis*."[23] When they act conventionally, they maintain a given state of affairs; when they act otherwise, they "intervene in the world, or . . . refrain from such intervention, with the effect of influencing a . . . state of affairs."[24] Although actors are always agents of history, they do not necessarily make a history of their choosing because they act in and through structure, which should be "understood as the rules and resources implicated in the 'form' of a social system."[25] Acting by means of structure, they remake structure, which in turn remakes them. This coproduction of action and structure is what Giddens calls "the recursive [or self-reproducing] nature of social life"—the fact that "the structured properties of social activity . . . are constantly recreated out of the very resources which constitute them."[26] Taking recursivity into account, I redefine agency as both the regularized practices of actors and the structured processes of their social system. Agency, then, is neither a capacity of the individual nor a function of the social formation, but the co-(re)constitution of individual practices and social processes.

But what exactly do actors do when they act as agents? Giddens claims that they may act linguistically or nonlinguistically, a distinction he maintains because he believes that poststructuralist accounts of agency assimilate all practices into linguistic ones. Some actions, he argues, are carried out "knowledgeably, but without necessarily being available to the discursive awareness of the actor," and even when these actions are imbricated with language, their meanings "do not originate solely in the differences created . . . by language" but "derive in a more basic way from the 'procedures' which agents use" in monitoring and interpreting a course of practical action in which they and others participate.[27] Thus actors act, understand, and act anew by means of language and also a "capacity to understand what they do while they do it."[28] This capacity, practical consciousness, is "grounded in the continuous monitoring of action which human beings display" and "operates only partly on a discursive level." The knowledge it produces is what "actors know tacitly about how to 'go on' in the contexts of social life without being able to give them direct discursive expression."[29]

Giddens's model of agency, formulated to resolve the actor/structure dualism, is an important frame for analyzing how actors' practices and social processes are coproduced, but it has its own problematic discontinuity and continuity. First, Giddens equates discourse with language and then radically demarcates linguistic activity from the practical activity of monitoring and understanding action. Although he acknowledges that linguistic and practical knowing may take place together in the same context, he does not view both of them as discursive modes. Moreover, he tends to explain linkages among actions in terms of continuity—e.g., the time-space distanciation of actions appears as a "*continuous flow of conduct*" and the even more "deeply sedimented" practices that, for him, are institutions[30]—thus making it difficult to account for breaks, reversals, and transformations in practice. To supplement Giddens's account of agency, I turn to Ernesto Laclau and Chantal Mouffe's explanation of articulatory practice.

Laclau and Mouffe consider both linguistic and nonlinguistic activity to be elements of discourse. They provide this example: "Let us suppose that I am building a wall with another bricklayer. At a certain moment I ask my workmate to pass me a brick and then I add it to the wall. The first act—asking for the brick—is linguistic; the second—adding the brick to the wall—is extralinguistic." Having made the distinction, they point out that the two acts "are both part of a total operation which is the building of the wall. . . . This totality which includes within itself the linguistic and the non-linguistic, is what we call *discourse*."[31] Discourse, on their definition, is a systematic though unstable set of relations that makes acts meaningful, and different discourses make a particular act differently meaningful. For instance, kicking a ball down the street and kicking it in a football game may be similar actions, but their meanings differ because the actions are integrated within different systems of relations.

Since a discourse is always changing in itself and as it comes up against other discourses, the meanings of its elements must be stabilized through articulation. "*The practice of articulation*," Laclau and Mouffe write, "*consists in the construction of nodal points which partially fix meaning; and the partial character of this fixation proceeds from the openness of the social*," which can never be completely stabilized.[32] For them, articulation is the practice of binding the elements of discourse together in order to partially fix meaning. Stuart Hall adds that "the form of the connection that *can* make a unity of two different elements" is not the same in every instance; rather, it is contingent upon the social conditions in which the elements become articulated.[33] Since the forms of linkage are contingent, the practices of making them may also be contingent and thus variable. This discursive model of agency refines Giddens's model by suggesting that the making of linkages is not a

continuous flow of action, nor is it an identical practice in all circumstances. Indeed, the instances of activism previously cited show
that linkages can be made both horizontally among actions (the New
Left's participatory democracy) and vertically between actions and
structure (the Right's institutional leveraging).[34] But this discursive
model still does not explain what exactly actors do when they make
linkages and how they may have learned to make them.

To supplement this model, I turn to the research of Daniel N.
Stern and others on the constitution of subjectivity in preverbal
infancy. Newborns, who already have the motor and perceptual capacities to perform and monitor daily social interactions, actively
participate in constructing meaning and their own subjectivities. By
interacting, according to Stern, they develop certain "senses of self":
they sense themselves as cohering physically, authoring their actions, maintaining regularity while changing, experiencing patterns
of feeling, creating organization (concerning the body and later the
subjectivity), achieving intersubjectivity with another, and transmit-
ting meaning.[35] Although Stern's discourses are empiricist psychology and psychoanalysis, his insights can be applied to the discursive
model of agency. His senses of "self" might be seen as conditions
of individualist, social-structural, poststructuralist, and collectivist
agency. Without the reflexive apprehension of activities and relations to others, an individual cannot decide to act, a subject cannot
notice the contradictions of heterogeneous interpellation, and a
group cannot achieve consciousness.

Stern conceives of "self" as a construct-in-process organized by
procedures that infants use in their interactions with others. These
procedures are intra- and intersubjective (though not always linguistic) articulations that produce what Stern calls an infant's sense of
an "emergent self," a "core self," a "subjective self," and a "verbal
self." The procedures that organize the infant's sense of an "emergent self" include transferring patterned information across perceptual modes (linking haptic and visual perceptions of a nipple); experiencing vitality-affects (surging, fading away), accompanied or not
by particular emotions (a rush of anger); and associating affects with
perceptual qualities. "The sense of an emergent self thus includes
two components, the products of forming relations between isolat-
ed experiences and the process" of doing so itself.[36] The procedures
that organize the infant's sense of a "core self," which is necessary
in order to experience another in merger or separation, are reflexive: an infant apprehends its authorship of actions, its physicality
as a locus for those actions, its patterns of feeling, and its regulari-

ty in change.[37] The sense of a "subjective self," organized through sharing affect states, intentions, and foci of attention, is the product of psychic intimacy with others.[38] To participate in forming these self-constructs, infants must be able to link cross-modally what Stern calls invariants: "that which does not change in the face of all the things that do change," whether those invariants "belong" to the infant, to the other, or to aspects of the relationship between them.[39] Thus to share an affect state (which Stern calls affect-attunement), an infant and its mother must already be able to experience vitality-affects, associate them with perceptual qualities, and recognize patterns—in short, to link invariants cross-modally.

Let us consider the practice of affect-attunement, which participates in forming the sense of a "subjective self." This practice consists of two activities: achieving affect resonance, and recasting the affect into another form of expression.[40] Here are two examples of the many videotaped by Stern and his colleagues:

> An eight-and-one-half-month-old boy reaches for a toy just beyond reach. Silently he stretches toward it, leaning and extending arms and fingers out fully. Still short of the toy, he tenses his body to squeeze out the extra inch he needs to reach it. At that moment, his mother says, "uuuuuh . . . uuuuuh!" with a crescendo of vocal effort, the expiration of air pushing against her tensed torso. The mother's accelerating vocal-respiratory effort matches the infant's accelerating physical effort.[41]

> A 9-month-old boy is sitting facing his mother. He has a rattle in his hand and is shaking it up and down with a display of interest and mild amusement. As mother watches she begins to nod her head up and down keeping tight beat with her son's arm motions.[42]

Here, the infants' affect, expressed through motor activity, is matched by and expressed through the mothers' oral and motor activity. The matching occurs in several dimensions: intensity, contour of intensity (arm/voice or arm/nod extension), timing (arm/voice or arm/nod beat, rhythm, duration), and shape (arm/voice or arm/nod up-and-down motion). Affect-attunement is an intersubjective, not imitative, practice. "What is being matched," Stern explains, "is not the other person's behavior *per se*, but rather some aspect of the behavior that reflects the person's feeling state." The performance, when an infant shakes his rattle and a mother nods, expresses "the quality of feeling of a shared affect state without imitating the exact behavioral expression of the inner state."[43]

Instances of affect-attunement support two important claims.

First, while some matches involve vocalization on the mother's part (first example), others (second example) occur through nonvocal procedures, such as nodding, facial scrunching, and shoulder shimmying. But in both vocal and nonvocal matches, infants engage in meaning-making activity. The meaning for the infant is probably multiply derived from its awareness of its own affect, the mother's match, further affect elicited by the match, and eventually the attunement procedures themselves. These matches with and without vocalization support Giddens's claim that not all of the meanings of action derive from linguistic practice and that some derive from performing and monitoring nonlinguistic action. But they also support Laclau and Mouffe's claim that both linguistic and nonlinguistic actions may be meaningful. Such research suggests that attunement is an activity preliminary to, in the sense that it occurs earlier than and contributes to, the formation of a "verbal self."

Second, a great deal of research shows that infants are not passive; they actively initiate and break contact with their mothers, thereby regulating both their own affect states and their mothers' attunement to them.[44] But what exactly is it that preverbal infants do? Affect-attunement is a form of articulatory practice: the infant cross-modally binds its own affects, perceptions, and actions, and it cross-modally binds them to those of another, thus constructing what Laclau and Mouffe call the nodal points for fixing meaning, or what Stern describes more fixedly as invariants. I would describe them as contingent invariants because, although the infant may experience a particular affect (e.g., "elation"), the meaning affixed to it is contingent upon the particular ensemble of actions and affects in which it is experienced.

I use this model of agency, derived from Giddens, Laclau and Mouffe, and Stern, to argue next that some of the women who participated in the CR groups of the women's liberation movement were able to reconstitute themselves as feminists by means of articulatory practices. Traditional accounts of CR groups have emphasized the participants' conceptualization of "women as an oppressed class under patriarchy" as potentially stimulating them to make change in three registers—consciousness, personal lives, and social activism. I, by contrast, assume that the most pertinent distinctions are the kinds of articulatory practice that allowed feminists to act otherwise in all three registers. Thus I emphasize not what women thought but what they *did* to change what they felt, thought, and did. Finally, I argue that both the successes and the failures of feminism are attributable to the kinds of practices feminists performed. The successes occurred because they performed horizontal articulatory practices to bind women in "sisterhood" for the women's liberation movement. The failures occurred because they did not subsequently perform vertical articulatory practices to make social-structural change.

THE PRODUCTION OF AGENCY
IN CONSCIOUSNESS-RAISING GROUPS

At present, most of the American public is aware that women as a group are disproportionately employed in lower-paying service jobs, or victimized by sexual violence, or omitted from studies of heart disease. In the early 1960s, these ideas were unthinkable because "women as a group," let alone experiences common (in both senses of the word) to the group, had not been conceptualized. Writing retrospectively, Mary Fainsod Katzenstein attributes the success of the women's movement, in large part, to the diffusion of a feminist consciousness. Because the movement

> targets "the private realm" along with the "public sphere," it must place a particular reliance on consciousness as a tool of social change. . . . The reshaping of friendship, of family, of love (in their abstract formulation), and of the decision structure around the relationships of sex, child care, and household financing (in its more concrete expression) . . . are matters that can be reached only in part by legislation, public policy, and judicial action. They are, therefore, necessarily the business of consciousness change.[45]

Consciousness change allowed the conceptualization of women as a group, discontent with women's circumstances, and the belief that gender disparities are illegitimate. In short, it produced new affects and values, as well as cognitions, about the current state of affairs.

In the early days of the women's liberation movement, a feminist consciousness was to be attained through consciousness-raising. As practiced by a few radical feminist groups in the late 1960s and eventually by the thousands of localized groups that made up the massive but decentralized women's movement in the United States during the 1970s, CR was a small-group process designed from the start to be the matrix of feminist transformation. The object was to raise women's consciousness about their oppression so that they might become agents of change in their lives and society.

Several precedents for CR are widely cited by the early feminists themselves. Juliet Mitchell wrote that it was a reinterpretation made by middle-class women in the United States and Britain of the Chinese peasants' revolutionary practice of "speaking bitterness." "The first symptom of oppression is the repression of words. . . . 'Speaking bitterness' is the bringing to consciousness of the virtually unconscious oppression; one person's realization of an injustice brings to mind other injustices for the whole group."[46] Carol Hanisch mentions the Guatemalan guerrillas' strategy of talking to villagers about their own lives and, in turn, encouraging them to talk about theirs. As a result, the villagers "who thought that their deepest problems and frustrations were their individual problems discover that their problems and longings are all the same." From this "discovery of their common humanity comes the decision that men must unite together in the struggle to destroy the conditions of their common oppression."[47] However, Sarachild and Hanisch also credit the civil rights movement. Sarachild reports that members of New York Radical Women (NYRW) "were applying to women and to ourselves as women's liberation organizers the practice a number of us had learned as organizers in the civil rights movement in the South in the early 1960s."[48]

The basic format of CR was simple. Four to fifteen women met weekly, often in one another's homes, to share their experiences and feelings on a designated topic. Each woman spoke as long as she liked; the others refrained from interrupting her but occasionally made supportive comments. According to one format, the group had two processes. The "women were encouraged to speak personally, specifically, and only from their own experiences. Generalizations, theories, and abstractions were discouraged. The idea was not to try to say what you thought was happening to women as a whole, but only what was happening, or had happened, to yourself personally."[49] During the summing-up process at the end of the meeting, they connected their experiences and drew conclusions. According to another format, the group had four overlapping processes. In "opening up," the women spoke about their feelings in order to overcome isolation and build trust. Through "sharing," they aggregated their specific experiences and came to realize the categorical nature of women's oppression. By "analyzing," the women understood "not only the why's and how's of [women's] oppression but ways of fighting that oppression." In "abstracting," they used their new concepts of oppression to build theory.[50] Sometimes they also used critical methods in order to understand women's oppression and determine the action necessary to remedy it.[51]

Probably first practiced in 1968, CR spread rapidly. During 1969, groups started up in some 40 cities, including Boston, New Haven,

New York, Chicago, Cleveland, Minneapolis, Iowa City, San Francisco, New Orleans, and Durham.[52] By the end of 1970, Anita Shreve writes, "every major city in the country" had CR groups: "New York City alone had hundreds of such groups."[53] San Francisco had 35 groups, and Cleveland had a dozen, with another 31 elsewhere in Ohio.[54] By 1972, according to one estimate, "every block in Manhattan had at least one active consciousness-raising group,"[55] and across the country chapters of the National Organization for Women (NOW) were offering courses in CR.[56] "In the year 1973 alone, some 100,000 women belonged to CR groups nationwide—making it one of the largest-ever educational and support movements of its kind for women in the history of this country," but "by the mid-1970s, most CR groups had disbanded."[57] Feminism continued to proliferate through other organizations—women's studies programs, rape-crisis centers, bookstores, music festivals, national political-action organizations—but since CR groups were the matrix of early feminism, I examine what happened in them.

The educational purpose of CR groups was to show women that their personal problems had social causes and therefore political solutions. The organizational purpose was to separate them from Left political movements and bourgeois male-centered households in order to integrate them as an independent women's movement. Necessarily emphasizing women's commonalities—the categorical oppression they suffered and their collective interest in opposing it—the CR process was supposed to bind them in "sisterhood," thereby reconstituting those subjected to patriarchy as feminist agents who would oppose it. Opposition was a familiar concept from the civil rights and New Left movements; "sisterhood" was indigenous to this one. It was not friendship, according to June Arnold, but "the common bond you feel with another woman because you understand that she has been oppressed and because you know you can work with her as a woman for all women."[58] "To be 'sisterly,'" Florence Howe wrote, "was not only personal but political. . . . One did not simply 'make friends' with women; one became political 'sisters' in a growing women's movement."[59] The "common bond" functioned to promote relationships among women and the growth of a political movement: "sisterhood" was affective bonding in the service of an activist purpose.

Articulatory Practices in Consciousness-Raising Groups

In 1970, Sarachild stressed the importance of affectivity: "In our groups, let's share our feelings and pool them. . . . Our feelings will lead us to ideas and then to actions. Our feelings will lead us to our theory, our theory to our action, our feelings about that action to new theory and then to new action."[60] Critics of CR argued that the emphasis on feelings turned these groups into therapy sessions and that, in any case, feelings were not a legitimate object of political analysis.[61] Advocates answered by differentiating therapy from CR: "Therapy," Hanisch asserted, "assumes that someone is sick and that there is a cure, e.g., a personal solution. . . . Women are messed over, not messed up!"[62] The sharing and analyzing of feelings, which in therapy was a means to achieving a cure, in CR was a means to achieving action. In retrospect, we know that CR did not necessarily have this effect: some participants who became feminists did not become activists.[63] To assess the importance of affectivity, I explore what these feelings may have been, how they functioned within CR groups and in organizing the movement, and where this functioning failed.

Catherine, a member of the CR group studied by Shreve, recalls hearing two women talking at the first meeting about their weight and their breast size. At first, she didn't understand why such attractive women were complaining. *"But then, I began to notice, as the women talked, that it didn't matter how they actually looked— each of them thought there was something wrong with her. It was exactly how I'd felt, how I was feeling then. . . . It was incredible. There were all these women, all so very, very different, and yet we all had these same feelings."*[64] The usual understanding of what is happening here—construction of the category "women"—results from too gross an analysis; my model of agency allows a finer one. Catherine does apprehend a commonality among different women (each thinks something is wrong with her), but she reaches that apprehension by binding herself to them affectively (*"It was exactly how I'd felt"*). The nodal point that binds her to them is not a feeling they name (e.g., a sense of worthlessness), but an affect-attunement, a match between her and their affect, which she recognizes through the texture of their complaints.

Sandi, a member of the same group, recalls a similar experience. She *"was most impressed by the commonality of all the women's problems. . . . She began to see that the other women had been carrying around the same burden as she had—the burden of depression. 'And I thought to myself* [about two women very different from herself] *. . . so how is it that we three are sitting here in this same room and the words that are coming out of their mouths are exactly what I feel?'" "You cannot imagine how wonderful that felt!,"* she exclaims later.[65] Sandi binds herself to the women affectively and names the feeling—depression. As a pressing down of affect, it has an intensity and shape that contrasts with the elation ("wonderful," "incredible") she and Catherine feel in experiencing a match. My point is not merely that these women experienced a match or even that it moved them from depression to elation, but that such attunements, through repetition, were an articulatory practice that could lead to the reconstitution of subjectivity. Just so, Sandi comments retrospectively, "*It was absolutely my rebirth as a human being.*"[66]

The reconstitution of subjectivity required conceptualization of the category "women," but more fundamentally it required an ambiance of psychic intimacy where women could safely perform the intersubjective practices that bound them in "sisterhood." Cassell emphasizes this point: "The women in the case study learned to be intimate with other women in the consciousness-raising group. I believe that teaching women to *bond* is the single most important function of such a group. . . . Central to this raising of consciousness is the experience of intimacy and trust between women in the small group."[67] The women's interpersonal practices of sharing and supporting, without personal criticisms that would disconfirm their feelings and experiences, created the ambiance of psychic intimacy where women could perform such intersubjective practices as affect-attunement that fostered their reconstitution of their subjectivities.

For Betty N., whose subjectivity had been repeatedly disconfirmed by her husband, affect-attunement was galvanic. She recalls another woman in her CR group complaining that her husband never heard what she said and later would deny that she had said it:

> I remember that I brought my hands to my face, and I might have said something like, "Oh, my God." I'd been living for months in a state of constant confusion and bewilderment because my husband always did the same thing to me. I'd sometimes thought seriously that I was losing my mind, that he was right, that I *hadn't* actually said the thing to him. But here was this other woman, with the very same experience. And once that opened up, everything opened up. It changed my life. . . . When I realized how it all worked, it was like this huge, heavy burden was lifting off my shoulders. I literally felt lighter. I'd thought I was depressed, that there was something wrong with me. And then I realized none of this was my fault at all. There were things that had been done to me, been done to all of us, and we could get free if we wanted to.[68]

The repeated disconfirmation of her experience had produced Betty's self-alienation ("I was losing my mind") and depression, whereas her attunement with the other woman restored her vitality (a burden lifted, she felt lighter). With this change in affect came the realization that what had been done to her had been done to other women. Her passage through attunement, change in affect, conceptualization of the category "women," and recognition that women could get free is a concrete instance of Sarachild's abstract statement: "let's share our feelings and pool them.... Our feelings will lead us to ideas and then to actions."

Although affective articulation was a galvanic moment in the constitution of feminist agency, there is no question that conceptual articulation was a necessary step on the road to acting otherwise. Feminists have said that women took this step because they shared jarring experiences in their everyday lives. Hester Eisenstein describes how conceptual articulation occurred. When women shared such experiences as illegal abortion, rape, incest, and physical abuse, they could see "all of these intimate and 'shameful' facts about the lives of individual women, by means of the process of consciousness-raising . . . in a different light." They were not individual mishaps but "symptoms of a society-wide structure of power and powerlessness, in which the victimization of women by the men holding the power of official authority, whether husband or public official, was hidden from public view by the mechanism of privatization."[69] Conceptual articulation was the practice of aggregating and analyzing "privatized" experiences that allowed women to read symptomatically the map of patriarchy. But how does it occur? According to Shreve,

> The heart of the matter . . . was "the click"—the light bulb going off, the eye-popping realization, the knockout punch. It was the sudden comprehension in one powerful instant, of what sexism exactly meant, how it had colored one's own life, the way all women were in this together. It was that awe-inspiring moment of vision and of commonality, when a woman was instantly and irrevocably transformed from naïve to knowing, from innocent to experienced, from apolitical to feminist. It is a moment that women recall with utter clarity. . . .[70]

The power of "the click" quite obviously derives from the intensity of affect, as well as of insight.

June Arnold describes the intensity of a "click" that occurred in 1970. Four women recounted experiences of trivialization to their CR group:

> "The counterman . . . always tells me that I don't mind waiting while he serves the men first, do I? because they have to get back to work. He's been saying that for years and today I knew I did mind. (If

I'd been a male novelist my writing would have been considered work too)."

"My husband asked if he could wash the dishes for me and I suddenly exploded: what do you mean for *me?* They're not *my* dishes."

"Coming out of the subway, I saw a cop coming in an exit door just as a woman was going out. She was almost as big as he was and she pushed back. He pushed and she pushed back again. Of course he succeeded but I felt that she had won. I said, 'Good work, sister.' I couldn't have said anything a week ago."

"When I told Joe that I was going to come to these meetings once a week, he said, 'Boy, this takes up more and more in your life! Are you going to become one of those women who're always flitting around?'"[71]

The women discover that these men had dismissed their "lives, however divergent on the surface . . . as composed of 'trivial' details. 'Trivial' we had picked up from men as a word to put ourselves down with."[72] Conceptual binding occurs around the nodal point of "triviality." But so too does affective binding: devitalization in being trivialized followed by revitalization through attunement. The "click" is a complex articulation that overloads "triviality" with meaning: their similar experiences and feelings about them, their attunement, their change in affect and insight—revealed the pervasiveness of women's denigration and allowed a symptomatic reading of patriarchy.

While the four anecdotes have in common a man's denigration of a woman, the third one differs. Here a woman is elated by another woman's resistance to male intimidation, overcomes her reticence, and speak words of support. For her, the binding through elation leads to a binding in "sisterhood": "Good work, *sister.*" For the group members, articulation was more complex, but unquestionably it galvanized what they did next. During the following week, they acted in their personal lives. One woman insisted that her son share the housework with his sisters; another told her husband she was joining women's liberation; a third refused to do extra typing for a male coworker and was threatened with being fired; and a fourth found herself attacked by acquaintances for declaring that women were oppressed.

Arnold comments, "Our anger came out; as if we had each been simmering for years like a back-stage volcano, we erupted all over the place—at home, at work, in the streets, in restaurants, subways, at parties, in bed. . . . We were too new to know what to do with our anger; for the present we were exhilarated just to let it out. We came together the next week high on our own energy."[73] This account confirms what was foreshadowed in Betty N.'s story: affective and conceptual articulation excited the women to action. But it also reveals a limitation: they scarcely knew how to handle the hostile responses to their actions. That handling, I believe, requires other practices—those of negotiating ways through patriarchy.

Articulatory Practices and Movement Structure

Through consciousness-raising practices, some women bound themselves in "sisterhood," constructed the category "women," and changed their personal lives. These practices were sufficient to structure the movement but not to build it and make social-structural change. "People," Ethel Klein observes, "need to see themselves as objects of collective discrimination or as victims of inadequate social institutions before they can become politically active." The linking of "the self to social institutions allows problems that were once thought to be personal to be seen to have a social cause and probably a political solution."[74] In other words, a woman must make vertical linkages between herself and institutions in order to see and change the social-structural causes of seemingly personal problems. To explore the limitations of CR practices, I return to Howe's and Arnold's explanation of the function of "sisterhood."

Consciousness-raising traded on "sisterhood" to structure the movement. "One did not simply 'make friends' with women," Howe observed; "one became political 'sisters' in a growing women's movement." Sarachild and others expected CR-group participants to become "sisters" who organized new groups, which in turn would produce more feminists and groups.[75] Binding in "sisterhood" and organizing new groups were the practices that produced the movement's structure as a horizontal network among individuals and among groups. In producing both feminist activists and movement structure, CR-group practice was what Giddens terms reflexive and recursive. That is, it consisted of linguistic and nonlinguistic activities that coproduced actors/structure.

Jo Freeman, a member of women's liberation groups in Chicago, characterized movement structure "as a network—decentralized, segmentary, and reticulate"—whose basic unit was the small group. "The thousands of . . . [groups] around the country are virtually independent of one another, linked only by numerous publications, personal correspondence, and cross-country travelers. They form and dissolve at such a rate that no one can keep track of them."[76] Local groups were said to proliferate by "fission," splitting when they became too large to sustain a participatory culture or when their members disagreed over ideology or practice. They were connected by "fusion": individuals' memberships in several groups, coalitions of groups, and events where group representatives came together.

Through their organizing practices, movement "sisters" were both produced by and productive of CR groups. These organizers were the nodal points of the movement's reticulation, and the CR groups were the matrix for constituting actors and structure. In this view, "sisterhood" may be seen as the name for two kinds of articulation: the binding of feminists affectively and conceptually for a political purpose, and the linking of the movement's units.

AGENCY AS SOCIAL-STRUCTURAL CHANGE

Consciousness-raising practices functioned well enough, as we have seen, to make changes in some registers: women's consciousness, personal lives, movement structure. But how well have they functioned over time in other registers, such as movement growth and social-structural change? Put another way, what can we now say are the successes and failures of the women's movement? "One indicator of 'success,'" Carol McClurg Mueller remarks, is "the degree of diffusion of the collective consciousness"; another is "the transformation of culture, and the appropriation of the apparatus of socialization."[77] Is there, for the women's movement today, a gap between the two?

Successes, Failures, . . .

Mueller argues that the movement only *seems* to have limited success because the literature on social movements employs resource-mobilization theory. While this theory calls "attention to professional leadership, organizational resources, technological innovations, and political constraints, the neglect of consciousness has proved a major liability in understanding social movements based on a massive shift in collective consciousness." Only the successful diffusion of consciousness, she adds, can explain why "the Equal Rights Amendment (ERA) became the unifying focus of the movement; why a woman's control of her body is considered more valuable than the life of a fetus; why an army of women are [sic] laboring in women's studies to redefine the canons of art, art history, and literature; why women at the highest levels of electoral office are beginning to talk about feminizing the nature of political leadership."[78]

But Klein argues that feminists' success in diffusing consciousness is limited by our failure to build a movement that includes

women of diverse races, classes, ages, religions, and political affili-
ations. Indeed, from the start, participants in the women's liberation
movement and women's rights organizations (e.g., NOW) were overwhelmingly white, middle- or upper-middle-class, young (twenties
and thirties), urban or suburban, college-educated women.[79] For this
reason, feminism today "lacks an organizational base that penetrates
these various communities of women and is therefore currently
incapable of aggregating and consolidating policy preferences across
these groups."[80] Since American politics is now reorganized around
interest groups, the failure to build an inclusive movement makes
coalitions among these groups and feminist policy advocacy more
difficult.[81]

Clearly, the remedy today cannot be the one that might have
worked twenty years ago. However feminists might have articulated a more inclusive category "women" during the first decade, we
cannot do so now, for criticisms have invalidated the category
"women" as specifically constituted by the movement and in general. No longer viable in the old sense of women's commonalities,
this category has been superseded by a more complex understanding of identities and oppressions that multiply differences. Since the
articulations practiced in CR groups foregrounded only some wom-
en's commonalities, what kinds of practice can feminists use now
to build a more inclusive movement? The obvious answer of coalition building does not tell us how to articulate across subjective,
intellectual, and social differences. Put plainly, how does anyone
come to feel and see how it is for others, whose feelings, ideas, and
experiences she does not and may never share?

The failures highlighted by Klein's analysis are also owing, I think,
to the fact that feminists have mainly practiced the horizontal articulations required for diffusion of consciousness and movement
reticulation to the neglect of the vertical articulations required for
social-structural change. Although coalition building may bring
groups together across their differences and lead to organizational
successes, they are not sufficient to make social-structural change.

. . . And Lessons

The failure of feminists to make social-structural change is underscored by contrasting conservative and feminist agency during the
past twenty years. Conservatives, like feminists, built a reticulated
movement. But they organized through institutions coordinated by
umbrella organizations (e.g., Christian Roundtable, Business Roundtable) and events (e.g., annual meetings of the Heritage Foundation

Resource Bank and the Philadelphia Society). Thus, from the start, conservatism's reticulation was more enduringly institutionalized than was feminism's. Also, by putting conservatives in public office, conservatives appropriated national institutions and used them to leverage change on the local ones that produce subjects and culture. Feminists, by contrast, have not controlled national institutions and, in principle, disapprove of using them instrumentally. It might therefore be useful to point out that conservative "instrumentality" consists of another set of articulatory practices—vertical ones that can produce social-structural change. These practices involve constructing institutional nodal points to leverage changes in national and local institutions, and then using local institutions to (re)constitute individuals as subjects of a conservative society. Failing to practice vertical articulation, feminists will always be stymied by a gap between localized and social-structural change.

Reviewing the Economic Research and Action Project (ERAP), in which New Left activists attempted to organize poor communities in northern cities, Wini Breines highlights the nature of this gap. Some local groups did win "concessions . . . from the city, state or federal government in areas such as education, housing, sanitation and discrimination, but once some demands were met . . . the situation reverted to its former state" because "the conditions which produced their grievances in the first place were not changed." "The gap," she adds, "between forcing a landlord to make repairs, tutoring a ghetto child, getting a traffic light installed, or helping someone receive welfare payments, and fundamental social change was enormous. . . . there seemed no way they could achieve social and structural change by providing a service role to the community and by sticking to local issues."[82] Local organizing does not necessarily produce and may even retard the making of social-structural change.

While the New Left example suggests that actors cannot get from local organizing to social-structural change, the conservative example suggests that they can get from a locally reticulated movement to social-structural change *by way of* appropriating institutions. However, to diffuse change throughout society, conservatives now realize that they have to do more local organizing. In an interview, Edwin J. Feulner, Jr., president of the Heritage Foundation, emphasized the development of a nationwide membership base. The think tank communicates its ideas to its 175,000 members; maintains the Resource Bank, which includes 1,600 conservative scholars and 400 organizations; and supports 55 state-level think tanks, established to influence state and local policy.[83] Feulner believes that "conservatives need much better grass-roots organizations" to reach the media, universities, and "Hispanics, blacks, Asians, and other minorities who have had only liberals to speak for them."[84]

To strengthen its grassroots organizations, conservatives have deployed two new technologies that complement their long-standing use of direct-mail. Town Hall, a nationwide interactive computer network launched jointly by Heritage and the *National Review* magazine, is intended to "strengthen communication among members of the conservative movement by offering a venue for the exchange of information, grassroots activism and discussion." Using such on-line services as publications, daily newswires of Washington politics, electronic mail, and instant polls of members' views, grass-roots subscribers share local plans for legislation and activism. Commenting on Town Hall, William F. Buckley, Jr., calls it "the technology conservatives can use to capture tomorrow."[85] The second technology is exemplified by National Empowerment Television, a nationwide interactive television network sponsored by Coalitions for America, an arm of the Free Congress Foundation. "Kingston Live," one of its monthly talk shows, features government officials and legislators discussing issues and proposed legislation. The viewers, "businessmen, taxpayer activists, service group heads," are invited to phone in their comments on a toll-free line and "follow up . . . with your own strategy session on how best to attack problems in your state and community." A program brochure states, "unlike other meetings that are all talk and theory, Kingston Live is about action,"[86] and, unlike CR groups, it produces immediate action on policy issues. According to a network officer, viewer phone-ins have influenced guests on "Kingston Live" to make changes in proposed legislation that conservatives oppose.[87]

These contrasting cases, a movement that stopped short of vertical articulation and another that articulated vertically and is now articulating horizontally throughout the grass roots, teach us a lesson. Agency, misconstrued as individual (self-)determination or social-structural (over)determination, is practices and processes that coproduce actors and structures. Actors wishing to transform or reproduce the social order must, in the first instance, create a matrix in which to perform articulations in all registers of change— subjective, interpersonal, and social-structural. Even so, articulatory practices are only potentially reconstitutive ones. To transform or reproduce a social order, actors must act through the instrumentalized mediation of institutionalized practices.

NOTES

The statement by Kathie (Amatniek) Sarachild that forms the epigraph for this chapter comes from her essay "A Program for Feminist 'Consciousness Raising,'" in *Notes from the Second Year: Women's Liberation,* ed. Shulamith Firestone (New York: n.p., 1970), 78. I am grateful to Andrew Elfenbein, Judith Kegan Gardiner, Diana Saco, and Larry T. Shillock for their helpful comments on drafts of my article, and to Roslyn Seligman for directing my attention to affectivity in the first place. An expanded version of this essay will appear in my forthcoming book, *Disciplining Feminism: Episodes in the Discursive Production of Social Change.*

1. For background on the conservative movement, see Jerome L. Himmelstein, *To the Right: The Transformation of American Conservatism* (Berkeley: University of California Press, 1990); Sidney Blumenthal, *The Rise of the Counter-Establishment: From Conservative Ideology to Political Power* (New York: Times Books, 1986); and Paul Gottfried, *The Conservative Movement,* rev. ed. (Boston: Twayne, 1993).

2. For a detailed analysis of the Right's apparatus, see Ellen Messer-Davidow, "Manufacturing the Attack on Liberalized Higher Education," *Social Text* (Nov. 1993): 40–80.

3. *Cultural Conservatism: Toward a New National Agenda* (Washington, D.C.: Institute for Cultural Conservatism/Free Congress Research and Education Foundation, 1987), 5.

4. *Cultural Conservatism,* 2, 4.

5. William S. Lind, "What Is Cultural Conservatism?," *Essays in Our Times* 2, no. 1 (Mar. 1986): 2–3.

6. *Cultural Conservatism,* 1.

7. Rom Harré, *Personal Being: A Theory for Individual Psychology* (Cambridge, Mass.: Harvard University Press, 1984), 26–27.

8. See Harré, *Personal Being,* 26; Clifford Geertz, "'From the Native's Point of View': On the Nature of Anthropological Understanding," in *Culture Theory: Essays on Mind, Self, and Emotion,* ed. Richard A. Shweder and Robert A. LeVine (Cambridge: Cambridge University Press, 1984), 123–36; and Richard A. Shweder and Edmund J. Bourne, "Does the Concept of the Person Vary Cross-Culturally?," in *Culture Theory,* ed. Shweder and LeVine, 158–99.

9. Harré, *Personal Being,* 86–92.

10. Ibid., 243.

11. Louis Althusser, "Ideology and Ideological State Apparatuses (Notes towards an Investigation)," in Althusser, *Lenin and Philosophy and Other Essays,* trans. Ben Brewster (New York: Monthly Review Press, 1971), 127–33, 162–75.

12. Steven B. Smith, *Reading Althusser: An Essay on Structural Marxism* (Ithaca: Cornell University Press, 1984), 22.

13. Ibid., 23.

14. See Louis Althusser, "Contradiction and Overdetermination: Notes for an Investigation," in Althusser, *For Marx*, trans. Ben Brewster (London: Verso, 1990), 100–103, 111.

15. Stephen Resnick and Richard Wolff, "Althusser's Liberation of Marxian Theory," in *The Althusserian Legacy*, ed. E. Ann Kaplan and Michael Sprinker (London: Verso, 1993), 63.

16. Paul Smith, *Discerning the Subject* (Minneapolis: University of Minnesota Press, 1988), 150; see also 16–18, 37.

17. See Wini Breines, *Community and Organization in the New Left, 1962–1968: The Great Refusal*, new ed. (New Brunswick, N.J.: Rutgers University Press, 1989), esp. 96–122; and Richard Flacks, "Making History vs. Making Life: Dilemmas of an American Left," in *Toward a History of the New Left: Essays from Within the Movement*, ed. R. David Myers (Brooklyn: Carlson, 1989), 125–52.

18. See Breines, *Community and Organization*, 46–66. Rich Rothstein argues that Students for a Democratic Society (SDS) failed in its attempt to create this form of organization ("Representative Democracy in SDS," in *Toward a History of the New Left*, ed. Myers, 49–62).

19. See, for instance, John Case and Rosemary C. R. Taylor, eds., *Co-ops, Communes and Collectives: Experiments in Social Change in the 1960s and 1970s* (New York: Pantheon, 1979).

20. Joan Cassell, *A Group Called Women: Sisterhood and Symbolism in the Feminist Movement* (Prospect Heights, Ill.: Waveland, 1977), 51.

21. Florence Howe, "Women and the Power to Change," in *Women and the Power to Change*, ed. Florence Howe (New York: McGraw-Hill, 1975), 138.

22. Anita Shreve, *Women Together, Women Alone: The Legacy of the Consciousness-Raising Movement* (New York: Viking, 1989), 30, 33, 206–7.

23. Anthony Giddens, *The Constitution of Society* (Berkeley: University of California Press, 1984), 171.

24. Ibid., 14.

25. Anthony Giddens, *Social Theory and Modern Sociology* (Cambridge: Polity; Oxford: Blackwell, 1988), 220.

26. Giddens, *The Constitution of Society*, xxiii. For a summary explanation, see Giddens, *Central Problems in Social Theory: Action, Structure and Contradiction in Social Analysis* (Berkeley: University of California Press, 1990), 55–73.

27. Giddens, *Social Theory*, 63.

28. Giddens, *The Constitution of Society*, xxii.

29. Ibid., 63 (first quotation), 3 (second quotation), xxiii (third quotation).

30. Giddens, *Central Problems in Social Theory*, 55, 80.

31. Ernesto Laclau and Chantal Mouffe, "Post-Marxism without Apologies," *New Left Review* 166 (Nov./Dec. 1987): 82.

32. Ernesto Laclau and Chantal Mouffe, *Hegemony and Socialist Strategy: Towards a Radical Democratic Politics* (London: Verso, 1985), 113. Laclau and Mouffe's italics.

33. Lawrence Grossberg, "On Postmodernism and Articulation: An Interview with Stuart Hall," *Journal of Communication Inquiry* 10, no. 2 (Summer 1986): 53.

34. I am grateful to Diana Saco for the terms "horizontal articulation" and "vertical articulation" to distinguish linkages made among subjects and groups from those made upward or downward among institutions or between institutions and subjects.

35. See Daniel Stern, *The Interpersonal World of the Infant: A View from Psychoanalysis and Developmental Psychology* (New York: Basic, 1985), especially 5–8, 70–71.

36. Stern, *Interpersonal World*, 47. For detailed discussion, see 47–67.

37. Ibid., 70–94.

38. Ibid., 129–30.

39. Ibid., 71–72.

40. Ibid., 146–47.

41. Ibid., 140.

42. Daniel N. Stern, Lynne Hofer, Wendy Haft, and John Dore, "Affect Attunement: The Sharing of Feeling States Between Mother and Infant by Means of Intermodal Fluency," in *Social Perception in Infants*, ed. Tiffany M. Field and Nathan A. Fox (Norwood, N.J.: Ablex, 1985), 250.

43. Stern, *Interpersonal World*, 142.

44. See, for instance, Daniel N. Stern, "A Micro-Analysis of Mother-Infant Interaction," *Journal of the American Academy of Child Psychiatry* 10, no. 3 (July 1971): 501–17; and Lynne Murray and Colwyn Trevarthen, "Emotional Regulation of Interactions Between Two-Month-Olds and Their Mothers," in *Social Perception in Infants*, ed. Field and Fox, 177–97.

45. Mary Fainsod Katzenstein, "Comparing the Feminist Movements of the United States and Western Europe: An Overview," in *The Women's Movements of the United States and Western Europe: Consciousness, Political Opportunity, and Public Policy*, ed. Mary Fainsod Katzenstein and Carol McClurg Mueller (Philadelphia: Temple University Press, 1987), 7–8.

46. Juliet Mitchell, *Woman's Estate* (New York: Pantheon, 1971), 62. Mao Tse-tung's "On Practice" (1937) and William Hinton's *Fanshen* (1966), two sources for this practice, were widely read by movement activists in the late 1960s. See Kathie (Amatniek) Sarachild, "Consciousness-Raising: A Radical Weapon," in *Feminist Revolution*, ed. Redstockings, rev. ed. (New York: Random House, 1978), 146, 149.

47. Carol Hanisch, "An Experience with Worker Consciousness-Raising," in *Feminist Revolution*, ed. Redstockings, 184. Hanisch's source for the Guatemalan strategy is Greg Calvert, Students for a Democratic Society (SDS), 1967.

48. Sarachild, "Consciousness-Raising: A Radical Weapon," 145.

49. Shreve, *Women Together*, 44.

50. Pamela Allen, "Free Space," in *Radical Feminism*, ed. Anne Koedt, Ellen Levine, and Anita Rapone (New York: Quadrangle, 1973), 271–79.

51. See Sarachild, "Consciousness-Raising: A Radical Weapon," 148–49.

52. See Kathie (Amatniek) Sarachild, "A Program for Feminist 'Consciousness Raising,'" in *Notes from the Second Year: Women's Liberation,* ed. Shulamith Firestone (New York: N.p., 1970), 78–80; Judith Hole and Ellen Levine, *Rebirth of Feminism* (New York: Quadrangle, 1971), 130–33; Maren Lockwood Carden, *The New Feminist Movement* (New York: Russell Sage Foundation, 1974), 64; and Ann Hunter Popkin, "Bread and Roses: An Early Moment in the Development of Socialist-Feminism" (Ph.D. diss., Brandeis University, 1978).

53. Shreve, *Women Together,* 11.

54. Carden, *The New Feminist Movement,* 64–65.

55. Cassell, *A Group Called Women,* 34.

56. Jo Freeman, *The Politics of Women's Liberation* (New York: David McKay, 1975), 86.

57. Shreve, *Women Together,* 6, 30.

58. June Arnold, "Consciousness-Raising," in *Women's Liberation: Blueprint for the Future,* ed. Sookie Stambler (New York: Ace, 1970), 161.

59. Howe, "Women and the Power to Change," 137.

60. Sarachild, "A Program for Feminist 'Consciousness Raising,'" 78.

61. For summaries of the controversy, see Hole and Levine, *Rebirth of Feminism,* 132, 137–42; and Alice Echols, *Daring to Be Bad: Radical Feminism in America, 1967–1975* (Minneapolis: University of Minnesota Press, 1989), 83–91.

62. Carol Hanisch, "The Personal Is Political," in *Notes from the Second Year,* ed. Firestone, 76.

63. See, for instance, Diane Kravetz, "Consciousness-Raising Groups in the 1970s," *Psychology of Women Quarterly* 3, no. 2 (Winter 1978): 168–86.

64. Shreve, *Women Together,* 39–40. Shreve's italics.

65. Ibid., 59. Shreve's italics.

66. Ibid. Shreve's italics.

67. Cassell, *A Group Called Women,* 50–51.

68. Shreve, *Women Together,* 54–55.

69. Hester Eisenstein, *Contemporary Feminist Thought* (Boston: G. K. Hall, 1983), 37–38.

70. Shreve, *Women Together,* 53. For examples of the "click," see the letters that readers sent to *Ms.* magazine throughout 1973.

71. Arnold, "Consciousness-Raising," 157.

72. Ibid.

73. Ibid., 157–58.

74. Ethel Klein, "The Diffusion of Consciousness in the United States and Western Europe," in *The Women's Movement of the United States and Western Europe,* ed. Katzenstein and Mueller, 24.

75. Sarachild, "A Program for Feminist 'Consciousness Raising,'" 80.

76. Freeman, *The Politics of Women's Liberation,* 103–4.

77. Carol McClurg Mueller, "Collective Consciousness, Identity Transformation, and the Rise of Women in Public Office in the United States,"

in *The Women's Movements of the United States and Western Europe*, ed. Katzenstein and Mueller, 94.

78. Mueller, "Collective Consciousness," 94.

79. Carden, *The New Feminist Movement*, 20–22, 28–30.

80. Klein, "The Diffusion of Consciousness," 32.

81. Ibid., 33.

82. Breines, *Community and Organization in the New Left*, 146–47.

83. See Adam Meyerson's interview with Edwin J. Feulner, Jr., "Building the New Establishment: Edwin J. Feulner, Jr., on Heritage and the Conservative Movement," *Policy Review* 58 (Fall 1991): 6, 8–9; and "Burgeoning Conservative Think Tanks," a special issue of *Responsive Philanthropy* (Fall 1991).

84. Meyerson, "Building the New Establishment," 9, 11.

85. Information about Town Hall from "Heritage Foundation and National Review Announce Joint Venture: First Nationwide Conservative Computer Network," press release of the Heritage Foundation and the *National Review*, Washington, D.C., 20 Feb. 1992.

86. "The Coalitions for America Broadcasting Network: Kingston Live" (Washington, D.C.: Coalitions for America, n.d.).

87. Michael Schwartz (Senior Vice President of Coalitions for America), presentation on a panel titled "Tomorrow's Town Hall: Technology as Empowerment," at "Ideas Have Consequences: A Conservative Battleplan for the 1990s," Heritage Foundation Fifteenth Annual Resource Bank Meeting, Chicago, 23–24 Apr. 1992.

TWO

Consciousness and Action: Historical Agency in the Chicago Women's Liberation Union

MARGARET STROBEL

The women's liberation movement of the late 1960s and 1970s is a particularly striking example of women acting as historical agents for both individual transformation and social change.[1] In chapter 1, Ellen Messer-Davidow identifies consciousness-raising groups as a major articulating practice in the development of the second wave of feminism from the late 1960s on. She argues that the key process in CR groups was not merely the recognition of "woman" as a category with common experiences but the "affect-attunement" that accompanied this recognition—the shared affect among women in the group. Messer-Davidow's analysis points out two accomplishments of consciousness-raising: the arrival at consciousness of oppression and the development of a sense of sisterhood. Some women moved on to change their personal lives; others, to change structures of processes outside their individual lives as well.

An examination of the activity of members of the Chicago Women's Liberation Union (CWLU) identifies other articulating practices, particularly those that were intended to move individuals beyond a raised consciousness into action to transform themselves and society.[2] The CWLU, which existed from 1969 to 1977, served as a model and inspiration for several other socialist feminist women's unions around the country. CWLU activists were committed to intervention, indeed, to massive transformation in people and in institutions. True to their New Left roots, the group's founders emphasized action over consciousness-raising, even while they incorporated small groups and CR into its structure. The recollections of former CWLU members that form the basis for this chapter reveal the importance of the affective attunement to which Messer-Davidow refers: these women developed intense emotional connections to one another.[3] Beyond this important feature of their experience, however, they report expectations on the part of their sisters in the organization that they could and should act to transform themselves and society. Moreover, CWLU leaders built mechanisms for bringing about such transformations. Thus, the shift from the individual to society as an arena for activism and change emerged not only from consciousness-raising but also from CWLU members' ideology, expectations about themselves, and organizational structure.

THE CHICAGO WOMEN'S LIBERATION UNION

The several dozen women who attended the founding conference in the fall of 1969 came from various small women's liberation groups in the Chicago area. Like others around the country in the late 1960s, these women met to discuss their growing sense of their oppression as women and to engage in actions to expunge that oppression. Those who exercised particular leadership in directing the new organization included women who had served in community organizing and other organizing projects.[4] Their evolving ideology embraced antisexist, antiracist, and anticapitalist sentiments and affirmed lesbian rights. Thus, CWLU activists envisioned societal, not only personal, transformation.

From the start, the CWLU leadership was committed to action, not just consciousness-raising, following the collectivist New Left model to which Messer-Davidow refers.[5] Naomi Weisstein, speaking in particular of the "Westside Group," the handful of women some of whom later called the founding conference of the CWLU, saw a tension between the power from and need to do consciousness-raising and a commitment to action. She recalled, "We harried ourselves constantly over the fact that we weren't doing action. After all, the New Left *was* action, no more study groups. No more sitting around and talking about strategy vs. tactics, [rather,] *action.* . . . There we were, talking about orgasm, and the contempt and hostility that we felt from the males in the New Left, and our inability to speak in public. This was not action. God! Did we feel guilty."[6]

By the early 1970s, the CWLU had a core of two hundred to three hundred active, highly committed members, a level it maintained until the conflicts that led to its demise in 1977. The forty-six members I have interviewed are representative of the CWLU membership. They were born between 1915 and 1954, with the median year being 1945. Except for one Asian American, all were European American; they included a substantial Jewish contingent. (The CWLU had a few African American members, but it was overwhelmingly white.) Although the women I interviewed tended to be single and childless, a large minority were married or were parents. A substantial portion were lesbian or bisexual. Most grew up in suburban areas, although a substantial minority reported their family as below middle class. The vast majority were getting or had received college degrees while in the CWLU. Their parents were relatively liberal, but not radical. Despite periodic efforts to recruit beyond a homogeneous base, CWLU members remained concentrated in the Lakeview and Hyde Park neighborhoods that were home to many progressives.

As an umbrella organization, the CWLU included chapters (affinity-based groups that discussed personal and/or political issues) and work- or project-based groups. Over its eight-year existence it developed a remarkable list of projects. Its members organized high school and college students, initiated a Liberation School, ran an underground abortion group and raised other health issues, attacked park district discrimination against women's sports, helped female janitors at city hall successfully sue the city, supported prisoners, ran a legal clinic, published newspapers directed at the feminist and lesbian communities, began a graphics collective, and played in the Chicago Women's Liberation Rock Band. Indeed, compared with the nearly two dozen socialist feminist women's unions that existed across the country during the seventies, the CWLU's strength lay in its practice.[7]

At a time when the women's movement was emphasizing the evils of hierarchy and leadership, CWLU activists took a somewhat different position. They shared the suspicion of hierarchy but rejected the option of "leaderlessness." Instead, acting on the New Left belief in the importance of establishing organizational forms that prefigure the desired future society, CWLU founders sought to establish leadership positions accountable to the membership and also to develop democratically the capacity of many women to become leaders and acquire other skills.[8] Their vision derived from a profound sense of the capacity of individuals to change themselves and society.

PERSONAL TRANSFORMATION

Stories told by CWLU participants reveal various patterns in explaining why some women moved from consciousness to action in terms of their personal lives *and* the wider society. Some members, particularly the earliest, transferred action as a response to other people's issues and other social problems to action on behalf of all women and themselves. They were already "acting otherwise" with regard to blacks, or workers, or the Vietnamese, for example.[9] For them, feminist consciousness, sometimes but not always derived through consciousness-raising, meant expanding that critical sense to include themselves as individuals and women as a group.

The antiwar movement spurred Vivian Rothstein's interest in the condition of women. Rothstein, a CWLU founder, was a key figure in both mentoring individuals and establishing the structure of the group. "Before we formed the CWLU, I worked in JOIN [SDS's community organizing project in a white working-class part of Chicago]. Before [JOIN], I worked in the South, in Mississippi with CORE during the summer of '65, and before that I had been a student at Berkeley and gotten involved in civil rights demonstrations and mass arrests in San Francisco." In 1969, at age twenty-one, she attended a peace conference in Czechoslovakia and visited North Vietnam. "[At the conference and in Hanoi] there were efforts on the part of the Vietnamese women to meet with the women in our delegation separately. . . . They felt that there were issues that we had to discuss that were very special issues for us. They wanted to talk about the special ways that women had suffered as a result of the war. They talked about Vietnamese women being used as prostitutes; they talked about people being separated from their children. They talked about particularly courageous women who had left their families and engaged in some sort of struggle in the North or in the South, and taken leadership. . . . I learned an enormous amount from them." Thus her feminism derived from lessons taught by Vietnamese women. "I didn't come [to feminism] out of . . . feminist anger. I came . . . [to] it much more from sort of an affirmation that women have a special sensitivity about war and peace, and have a special contribution to make."

Rothstein's political commitment to ending the war moved her to overcome her hesitancy about speaking. She recalls, "I had never done much public speaking. It wasn't real easy for me, but it was something I felt a responsibility to do. [It] thrust me into some kind of leadership position." As she spoke, Rothstein's sense of agency clashed with her audience's assumption of female passivity. "When I came back and I would speak, first of all I would speak to big [mixed-sex] groups. They would always be shocked that a woman who was young could convey information. They would come up and say that to me as a compliment. 'Gee, we never thought you could've had this experience; this was really remarkable.' And it was really their sexism and their prejudice against me, their assumption [that] I couldn't do anything."

For some women, including those with extensive political and organizing experience, belonging to a consciousness-raising group was critical to translating political understanding to a personal and domestic level. Around 1970, Vicky Starr was recruited by a CWLU activist into a CR group specifically designed to bring together older working-class women. (Such a group is evidence of the CWLU's commitment to heterogeneity, even if it was atypical.) Starr, who appears as Stella Nowicki in the film *Union Maids*, was in her mid-fifties at the time. She already held feminist sentiments, drawn from her experience as a meat cutter and as a Communist Party (CP) activist. But the CR group introduced new dimensions to her feminist understanding, particularly in the areas of domestic life and sexuality. The group created a supportive atmosphere in which the women could come to understand their situations, and it offered concrete support for those who chose to extricate themselves from their current domestic arrangements:

> I was in a very strained [marital] relationship [and had four young children]. . . . If it weren't for the CR group, I don't think I could have had the courage to break up our relationship. . . . When I was ready to break up with my husband, [a woman from the CWLU] offered financial aid for me to help move—a thousand dollars. . . . One of the people in the group had a husband who was physically abusive. This woman separated from her husband. Moved out. She had six children. . . . This group gave us the courage and support to be able to do this. . . . We were able to see ourselves in a different role, not just as the housewife, not just going along, tradition, the way we were brought up.

The CWLU also offered activities outside consciousness-raising groups in which women could participate. When the CWLU's Liberation School offered a "Bodies" class, using *Our Bodies, Ourselves* as a text, at the YWCA in the middle of an Eastern European, Catholic, working-class neighborhood, Starr enrolled in it with her daughter. She credits the course with enabling her to talk with her daughter about sex and "the whole question of the double standard in our society." In addition, the "Bodies" course and interactions with lesbians in the CWLU provided her with a sympathetic understanding of homosexuality, which became invaluable as she came to understand that one of her sons was gay. In her case, the understanding derived from consciousness-raising led logically to action, in part because as a union and Communist Party activist, she was schooled in action. But the CWLU fostered activity beyond CR as well, in this case by offering a second step in the form of a Liberation School class.

Sandra Lee Bartky, a contributor to this volume, participated in the civil rights movement in the late 1950s and, moved to action by her "revulsion to the Vietnam War," joined her campus New University Conference (NUC) chapter. NUC's effect on her life was profound, intellectually and philosophically; she credits it with moving her from existentialism to Marxism. NUC disintegrated, and its female members, spurred by the rise of women's liberation nationally, read various feminist articles circulating at the time. In the early 1970s, Bartky and Judith Kegan Gardiner, the editor of this volume, formed Circle Women's Liberation and the Women's Studies Program with other women at what is now the University of Illinois at Chicago. Both units embodied feminist principles, and Circle Women's Liberation functioned as a workgroup/project of the CWLU. Bartky notes that "the act of organizing a political group and having responsibility for it [was] incredibly empowering. . . . The really finally transforming experience for me was in that small, face-to-face collective, Circle Women's [Liberation]. I think I got a whole new sense of myself." Although she acknowledges the power of the small group, whose activity involved consciousness-raising, Bartky sees the *act* of forming the group as critical in itself, a point echoed by Rothstein regarding the formation of the CWLU.

Another woman brought substantial experience of "acting otherwise" to the founding of the CWLU. Heather Booth grew up in a middle- to upper-class Jewish family "believing that all people should be equal. It didn't really occur to me that there were different rules for women." After she returned from a summer's civil rights work in Mississippi, two important events took place. First, a friend of Booth's "was pregnant and totally hysterical—nearly suicidal—and I helped her find a contact for an abortion. That led to thinking about this as a woman's right. A friend of mine was raped on campus at knifepoint in her bed and was given a lecture on promiscuity by the Student Health Service."

In 1965 Booth attended her first SDS conference in Urbana-Champaign, at which a group of women got together to talk. The meeting began as a mixed-sex session. Booth recalls:

> The men kept asking certain questions . . . they challenge[d] whether certain things were true. . . . You would say, "Women find it hard to talk in a group." No woman would doubt it, and the men would say, "Well, is that really true? If it's true, why do you talk all the time?" [So a number of the women met separately to continue the conversations.] We just had so much in common, just talking about the positives and strengths we found: What it meant to be part of a movement for finding yourself and finding new freedom, and what at the same time it meant to be in a position where it was difficult to function and where you weren't given full respect and support.

As a founder of the CWLU, Booth clearly transferred her understanding of the oppression of blacks and the urban poor to women as a group. In addition, she had ideas about structure, organization, and action into which she channeled her emerging sense of women's situation. After she found an illegal abortion for her friend who had been raped and received other calls for help, she organized an abortion referral service out of her University of Chicago dorm room. The service became the basis for Jane, the underground referral service that has now become famous in pro-choice circles.[10] Booth's response to a problem—whether her own or a friend's—was to create an institution, not to find an individual solution.

DEVELOPING ACTIVISTS

An important force in propelling many individuals in the CWLU to action was the organizational expectation that one would act in some way, even that one could act in ways once thought inconceivable. Penny Pixler recalls, "[The CWLU] changed my life, literally changed my life. From the time I walked into the Belmont office and I looked at the wall, there was a great big sign that said, 'Learn, Change, Grow.'" CWLU leaders combined this expectation with intensive mentoring and coaching and with a structure that provided a wide range of possible activity from which to choose.[11] The following examples illuminate the power of such an expectation and the importance of the diversity of experiences that the CWLU opened for its members.

Margaret Schmid became cochair of the CWLU in 1973. The

CWLU blended her concerns about women's issues with those about other aspects of social, political, and economic equality and justice, and she drew upon skills developed in high school and college organizations. She had grown up in a white, upper-middle-class, suburban Wisconsin Republican family. "Everybody always said how smart I was, but no one ever talked about what kind of career I'd have." Despite spending her childhood surrounded by McCarthyism, during college she moved closer to Democratic party politics. She ended up in the CWLU through serendipity. A friend put Schmid, recently divorced with a two-year-old daughter, in touch with a North Side "rap" (discussion) group, which turned out to be one of the groups involved a year later in founding the CWLU. Schmid found the support offered in a consciousness-raising group to be "wonderful, . . . totally eye-opening." She did volunteer work in the CWLU office but "didn't myself have any real political view much one way or another. . . . I ended up [three years later] being cochair for a year: I ended up being sort of a leader." She went on to head a university professors' union in Illinois and then to other work as a union organizer and lobbyist. Schmid's story reflects the combination of forces that led to feminist activism and, in her case, leadership: a background of organizational activism, a growing concern about social justice and opposition to the war in Indochina, and a CR experience that channeled her into the CWLU and beyond.

Jenny Rohrer, a paid CWLU staff member in 1970–71 and cochair in 1973 (with Schmid) and 1975, brought to the CWLU a background of high school experience in the Young Democrats and in religious organizations. Her moment of transformation to feminism came by way of the written word. Coming from a farm family in northwestern Minnesota with a "strong mother," Rohrer attended DePauw University for a few years and then moved to Chicago in late 1969 to work in the antiwar and women's movements. She reports: "[I had] jumped into superconformity in my freshman year. But the turnaround happened very quickly, because by the beginning of my sophomore year [1968] I was in a picket line outside the Miss De-Pauw pageant, protesting it as a form of women's oppression." Essential to her activism had been reading, with friends, a copy of a key women's liberation article from the 1960s, "The Myth of the Vaginal Orgasm."[12] "I deactivated [left] my sorority. . . . The sororities in the United States started in DePauw. . . . So the tradition was very strong, and they hadn't seen a deactivation in sixteen years, so it was handled by the Dean of Women. By the time she was through trying to talk me out of it, I took two of my sisters with me." Rohr-er lived initially in a house with Catholic draft resisters, and then moved in with a former DePauw friend who was in the CWLU.

Her experience highlights the role of the CWLU in fostering action and leadership in people. When the CWLU solicited applications for a paid staff position, she applied and was selected as one of two. "When they selected me . . . I thought they were nuts. . . . I felt very much like I was a greenhorn from the farm and had no idea what I was doing. . . . For a number of years [I] felt like I was catching up, catching up, catching up. . . . People kept giving me more responsibility, often more than I thought I could handle. . . . I remember, around the Indochina Women's Conference, Vivian [Rothstein] making me make speeches and do things. . . . I was terrified and felt it was way beyond my abilities."

By the 1970s, the CWLU was recruiting members who did not have prior experience in activism on behalf of some other group. For such women, a central insight lay in achieving individual transformation through collective action. Recruited to the CWLU through the sports organizing project around 1973, Cady Hurst recalls, "I hadn't really thought about feminism. I thought about my life and the kinds of struggles that I was in all the time from very young, growing up and being in isolation. . . . The women I met on the softball team, they were involved in making changes in their life and dealing with problems from a collective point of view. . . . [The CWLU softball team members] didn't particularly talk about individual, personal struggles. . . . The people were involved in different issues and I was able to listen to women talk to other women about these problems."

From a Chicago working-class family, Hurst "started out slow. I started out being on the softball team." Then the leaders of the sport organizing group urged her on: "Jenny and Rinda and Susan . . . said, 'Bring [*Secret Storm*, the sports organizing newspaper] out there and talk to people.' . . . I loved it. I thought that if people just knew, that they would change, they would join us, make things different." In her conversations, she drew upon the CWLU's resources for referrals to deal with problems of the women she met. After five months she became a member of the paid staff.

Another CWLU member recalled that other members expected much of her. "I felt [that] once I got into Secret Storm [the sports organizing project], I'd have to know how to do all these things, how to organize. In fact, when we'd be giving the workshops . . . to our new recruits, we wouldn't volunteer; you were chosen—whatever your talents were. . . . [When the Liberation School was offering a course on auto mechanics, I knew] how to open the engine and put oil in, so I gave the workshop in car repair!"

While they were expected to act in new ways, CWLU members received careful mentoring. Ingrid Christiansen recalls being trained by Vivian Rothstein in how to deal effectively with the media. "I was afraid to call news reporters. Vivian [would walk me through it]. 'Now why not make the call? What's the worst thing that could happen?' We would work through my fears. Then it would turn out I'd make the calls and be *good* at them. There was quite a lot of talking through, staring down whatever the problem was, and figuring out the attack." Initially she felt she didn't have the skills to represent Ms. O'Leary, her chapter, on the CWLU steering committee. The other members replied "'Of course you do.' They told me how to do it, which I did. Somebody would talk with me before . . . , saying, 'These are the issues that are likely to come up. Let's think them through.'" Christiansen took responsibility for part of the CWLU's move to a new location: "[We said,] 'We can find a lease for this place; we can fix it up; we can take care of the plumbing problems,' saying, as an organization, we can make a commitment and follow through. That seemed miraculous to me. . . . We were confident we could raise the money. I was timid, and it was good to see this."

For Christine Riddiough, the Liberation School was important in providing an entré into the CWLU as a whole. "In 1970 I was a graduate student at Northwestern, and Ellen DuBois . . . was trying to get women from that group involved in the Women's Union. . . . I have a recollection of [Vivian Rothstein] calling me up and asking me to join [the Liberation School]. It was exciting to be called."

In establishing the Liberation School in 1971, CWLU organizers created a structure that provided several ways to enable women to see themselves as agents. Basic classes promoted a different consciousness of oneself and other women. Others taught concrete skills women needed to be effective organizers, for example, public speaking or graphic production. Still other courses provided women with the knowledge of their own and other social movements' histories so that they might develop better strategies for social change. The act of taking control of one's own learning was enabling in itself. As Riddiough notes, "Here was Vivian, one of the leaders of the Union asking me to join and to be a part of this whole new idea of taking the educational process into our own hands, figuring out what it was we wanted and needed to know. I had never been involved in anything like this. When I was at college I was in teach-ins on the anti–Vietnam War movement, but certainly nothing this sustained in terms of alternative education."

Moreover, for Riddiough and others the CWLU and its Liberation School were mechanisms for discovering themselves as lesbians. "[I was in the process of] trying to put together the idea of being a lesbian in the women's movement, trying in little baby steps to come out. . . . [At meetings] it was breathtaking in a lot of ways, to hear people talking about this openly and not being afraid to talk about being gay. . . . Just the fact that there were things to read about lesbianism, and then people would sit around and talk about them, was both scary and at the same time exciting."

About six or seven months later, when the Liberation School offered a course called "Women's Liberation Is a Lesbian Plot," Riddiough signed up. "I think I got nudged into taking it by people who sort of saw in me more than, at that point, I saw in myself, in terms of being a lesbian activist."

The various aspects of empowerment in Riddiough's story are intertwined: the CWLU-sponsored meeting and the course offered a place for her to explore a new self-definition, a new vision of herself and other women. At the same time, she was being asked, by CWLU leaders who saw leadership potential in her, to *be* more than she thought she could be. Indeed, Riddiough served in a leadership capacity in the CWLU and later in democratic socialist feminist organizations, the New American Movement and Democratic Socialists of America; she became a lesbian and socialist feminist activist in Chicago and later in Washington, D.C.

In addition to expecting women to be capable of acting and mentoring them to do so, CWLU members structured its work in ways that promoted agency and learning. Projects typically developed when a group of women perceived a need or recognized shared interests. "One of the first steps in building people who are going to be politically active is to build the ownership over [a project]," notes Judy Sayad, reflecting the CWLU's somewhat voluntarist approach. This voluntarism resulted in a high level of commitment and energy on the part of members, who felt they had an impact, both on and through their project.

Beyond voluntarism, however, the CWLU's emphasis on evaluating its program and on political education promoted a collective discussion of people's efforts. "Everything was broken down into the smallest part, and we had to take it apart and figure out how the decisions were made," recalls Susan Nussbaum. "And people were criticized." Thus, action was seen not just as an individual expression, but as a collective expression, even while an individual received significant emotional rewards. Difficulties arose, however, because the various projects had to be evaluated by criteria developed over time by the whole CWLU, not only by the criteria held by the project initiators, who might have a tenuous relationship to the larger organization. Thus, the individual and collective impulses coexisted in tension.[13]

Not only was activity balanced in terms of the individual and the collective, it was balanced in other ways as well. CWLU members devised a schema for analyzing their work at annual conferences, assessing a particular project along the axes of education (consciousness-raising or more academic learning), service (meeting needs of women), and direct action (challenging power structures). Where a particular activity was not capable of embodying all three aspects, the range of CWLU projects filled out the triad. These evaluative criteria enabled members to plan a strategy more effectively in order to accomplish broad societal change, rather than fixing on momentous but narrower individual transformation.

The CWLU's expectation that these women could act, its provision of a variety of arenas in which to act, and its training in necessary skills were critical to their development as individuals and as activists. A detailed look at one particular project of the CWLU, the speakers bureau, complements the foregoing focus on individual stories and transformation. The evolution of the bureau parallels the CWLU members' position on, and ambivalence about, leadership that was noted earlier.

SPEAKERS BUREAU

It is hardly surprising that the speakers bureau came up most often in my interviews as an example of personal empowerment. Feminist scholarship records the importance of women's voices, of naming, of breaking silences. The speakers bureau represented, at the collective level, an alternative way of structuring responsibility; at the personal level, it offered a profoundly transforming experience. Many CWLU members noted their apprehension about speaking in public. Coral Norris recalls, "I was very shy and timid, and it was very difficult for me to go and speak. [The speakers bureau] made me do that. It gave people a sense that they could do things. I was not the only one, I know, [who] was transformed by that experience."

Vivian Rothstein and Naomi Weisstein identified the establishment in 1970 of a "democratic speakers bureau" as a singularly important event in the early history of the CWLU, a critical example of how a group could "*structure out* elitism" rather than see structure only as contributing to oppression.[14] The speakers bureau responded to an avalanche of requests for speakers, averaging twenty-three per month in the early 1970s, as "women's lib" hit the popular consciousness. The requests that arrived from schools, churches, and other groups were initially filled by volunteers from the CWLU. This resulted in the group's equivalent of "stars"—anathema to women's liberation—since only the women who already had confidence did the speaking.

So the CWLU introduced training sessions—including role playing, videotaping, and evaluation—to combat media-created stars. Weisstein, who organized the first sessions, found them "dismaying," not just in terms of speaking itself but in terms of the shallowness of people's understanding of the ideas, "the blindness to the underlying principles, the unthought-out-ness of the position." But she was, in her words, "an absolute egalitarian democratic feminist, believing that if the social context changed so that women were valued, any woman could learn to speak." Her dismay did not dampen her enthusiasm for the project. "This is good," she remembers saying to herself despite her dismay. "This gives us all a chance to really work out some of these issues." Since there were few books to learn from, each woman had to think creatively.[15]

To augment the training, the CWLU compiled sample talks for particular audiences, and speakers wrote down evaluations of their experiences and strategies. Thus speeches became not the private experience and property of an individual, but rather the shared experience of the group. One anonymous speaker who had appeared before a mixed-sex group of progressive, middle-aged Jews reported that she would not have tried this three years earlier, but that she had received lots of support from her friends: "Love and gratitude to [various named women] (and to my husband for providing me with a constant source of material)!" Other sample talks were directed toward audiences of high school students and religious groups.[16]

In the early days of the bureau, the engagements were handed out among chapters in rotation, without regard to expertise. Chapters were responsible for providing a speaker. (It is not clear whether chapters also rotated the responsibility among members, but this was the intention.)[17] Two women were to attend each event, one to give support and feedback to the one who spoke.[18] The University of Chicago chapter drew lots to choose the speaker for the Women's

Strike Day rally on 26 August 1970. The woman selected was new to the movement and had little experience, but chapter members worked together to prepare the speech, which went well.[19]

There were periodic reviews of and debates about the speakers bureau policy. In one instance, Weisstein wrote "In Defense of the Absolutist Position on Speaker's and Media Policy," arguing that people can grow and develop and that no single person is best for all audiences.[20] Three other members, in "Reconsidering the Speakers Policy," stated that since the CWLU did not rotate all jobs, to insist upon rotating speaking was to accept "competitive society's view that public recognition is the chief measure of importance or self-worth." They found it "coercive" to insist that everyone, irrespective of talents and backgrounds, speak. Furthermore, they held that the existing policy put the goal of developing the members ahead of the goal of having an impact on the audience: "ALL WOMEN HAVE A RIGHT TO BE TURNED ON [TO] THE MOVEMENT." Finally, they believed that elitism should not be confused with leadership, and elitism should be overcome by political education and training, not by penalizing skilled people.[21]

At the core of the policy debates were some assumptions shared by many feminists. First, they believed that behaviors could be modified by force of will. Indeed, a basis for this belief lay all around them in the actions of women who were changing—finding the strength to challenge husbands or lovers, to be assertive, to speak, to theorize, to take themselves seriously. Second, following the notion of "the personal is political," they held personal feelings of inadequacy subject to collective scrutiny. Thus, a reluctance to speak, indeed fear of speaking, was not taken as a valid reason for not speaking.

The speakers bureau represented activity in the areas of service (providing information to audiences and building the skills of the speakers) and education (since preparation for speeches involved considerable learning and creativity). Through lectures given by speakers, CWLU recruited women into other activities of the union.

Any number of examples from the CWLU's rich array of activities would show that individual enterprise was intertwined with collective action. At times the individual and the collective existed in tension, as exhibited in the debate above over the speakers bureau. But overwhelmingly, individuals in the CWLU felt enriched by being part of a wider effort. In the words of one member, "I came to understand the lack of personal solutions [in the absence of] a base in an organization or movement."[22]

CONCLUSION

The Chicago Women's Liberation Union saw itself as an agent of historical change, a concept that CWLU officers acted upon when they began sending documents to the Chicago Historical Society, well before the demise of the union, so that a record of its role could be preserved. Individual women felt drawn to action and challenged by their experiences in the CWLU. They felt, in today's parlance, empowered. They grew to see themselves as capable of agency in part because other people expected them to be agents, encouraged them to try untried things, and structured personal and organizational development into CWLU activities. Their ideology stressed societal, not just individual, transformation. Individuals also grew and changed because they believed in the importance of the larger changes they hoped to effect; their commitment enabled them to take the personal risks to try to be and do what they had not attempted before.

NOTES

Many former CWLU members have made useful comments on drafts of my CWLU material. For their criticisms of this article I wish to thank Bill Barclay, Judy Gardiner, Stephanie Riger, and Lynn Weiner.

1. Basic sources on the women's movement include Jo Freeman, *The Politics of Women's Liberation* (New York: Longman, 1975); Maren Lockwood Carden, *The New Feminist Movement* (New York: Russell Sage Foundation, 1974); Sara Evans, *Personal Politics: The Roots of Women's Liberation in the Civil Rights Movement and the New Left* (1979; New York: Vintage, 1980); Myra Marx Ferree and Beth B. Hess, *Controversy and Coalition: The New Feminist Movement* (Boston: G. K. Hall/Twayne, 1985); Alice Echols, *Daring to Be Bad: Radical Feminism in America, 1967–1975* (Minneapolis: University of Minnesota Press, 1989); Barbara E. Ryan, *Feminism and the Women's Movement: Dynamics of Change in Social Movement Ideology and Activism* (New York: Routledge, Chapman and Hall, 1992).

2. Case studies of particular cities or organizations (not other women's unions as such) include Ann Bookman and Sandra Morgen, eds., *Women and the Politics of Empowerment* (Philadelphia: Temple University Press, 1988); Lisa Albrecht and Rose M. Brewer, eds., *Bridges of Power: Women's Multicultural Alliances* (Philadelphia: New Society Publishers, 1990); Judith Sealander and Dorothy Smith, "The Rise and Fall of Feminist Organizations in the 1970s: Dayton as a Case Study," *Feminist Studies* 12, no. 2 (Summer 1986): 321–41; Margaret Blanchard, "Speaking the Plural: The Exam-

ple of *Women: A Journal of Liberation,*" *NWSA Journal* 4, no. 1 (Spring 1992): 84–97; Robin Leidner, "Constituency, Accountability, and Deliberation: Reshaping Democracy in the National Women's Studies Association," *NWSA Journal* 5, no. 1 (Spring 1993): 4–27; Sandra Morgen, "The Dream of Diversity, the Dilemma of Difference: Race and Class Contradictions in a Feminist Health Clinic," in *Anthropology for the Nineties,* ed. Johnetta Cole (New York: Free Press, 1988), 370–80; Sandra Morgen, "Contradictions in Feminist Practice: Individualism and Collectivism in a Feminist Health Center," in *Transcendence in Society: Case Studies,* ed. T. M. S. Evens and James L. Peacock, vol. 1 of *Comparative Social Research: A Research Annual* (Greenwich, Conn.: JAI Press, 1990), 9–59; Susan B. Murray, "The Unhappy Marriage of Theory and Practice: An Analysis of a Battered Women's Shelter," *NWSA Journal* 1, no. 1 (Autumn 1988): 75–92.

3. This research draws upon extensive interviews with forty-six former members of the CWLU conducted between 1986 and 1993, as well as upon archival materials. Quotations, unless otherwise cited, come from these interviews. The research was assisted by an NEH fellowship, a University of Illinois at Chicago Institute for the Humanities fellowship, and funds from the Campus Research Board of the University of Illinois at Chicago. Transcripts of my interviews are deposited at the Chicago Historical Society, which houses the CWLU archives. References to these archives are provided as follows: CHS/box x/folder y. I researched these archives *before* the CHS organized them in their present form. With the help of Vickie Kukulski, I have done my best to confirm the box and folder numbers indicated in these notes.

4. For example, Heather Booth, Amy Kesselman, and Vivian Rothstein. This community organizing experience had important implications; the founders applied the negative and positive lessons learned to develop in the CWLU accountable and democratic leadership structures. See Jennifer Frost and Margaret Strobel, "JOIN and the CWLU: Women's Organizing in Chicago, 1964–1977," paper presented at conference "Toward a History of the 1960s," 29 Apr.–1 May 1993, Madison, Wisconsin.

5. See chapter 1.

6. Weisstein, tape-recorded self-interview; see also Naomi Weisstein, "The Early Years of the Women's Liberation Movement in Chicago," *Phoebe: An Interdisciplinary Journal of Feminist Scholarship, Theory and Aesthetics* 1, no. 1 (Feb. 1989): 3–20.

7. This can be compared, for example, to the more theoretical orientation of the Berkeley-Oakland Women's Union (BOWU). I have interviewed women from BOWU, the Twin Cities Women's Union, the Los Angeles Women's Liberation Union, the Buffalo Women's Liberation Union, the Women's Union of Baltimore, and the San Francisco Women's Union. For women's unions in general, see Margaret Strobel, "Women's Liberation Unions," in *Encyclopedia of the American Left,* ed. Mari Jo Buhle, Paul Buhle, and Dan Georgakas (New York: Garland, 1990; Urbana: University of Illinois Press, 1992), 841–42, and Karen V. Hansen, "The Women's Unions

and the Search for a Political Identity," *Socialist Review* 16, no. 2 (Mar.–Apr. 1986): 67–95.

8. See Margaret Strobel, "Organizational Learning in the Chicago Women's Liberation Union," in *Feminist Organizations: Harvest of the New Women's Movement,* ed. Myra Marx Ferree and Patricia Yancey Martin (Philadelphia: Temple University Press, 1994).

9. See Evans, *Personal Politics.*

10. Pauline Bart, "Seizing the Means of Reproduction: An Illegal Feminist Abortion Collective—How and Why It Worked," *Qualitative Sociology* 10, no. 4 (Winter 1987): 339–57.

11. Suzanne Staggenborg sees the wide range of CWLU activity as a shortcoming. She argues that the CWLU was flawed in its inability to prioritize, compared with Chicago NOW, and thus was limited in its effectiveness; "Stability and Innovation in the Women's Movement: A Comparison of Two Movement Organizations," *Social Problems* 36, no. 1 (1989): 75–92.

12. Anne Koedt, "The Myth of the Vaginal Orgasm," in *Radical Feminism,* ed. Anne Koedt, Ellen Levine, Anita Rapone (1970; New York: Quadrangle, 1983), 198–207.

13. Schweikart's essay in this volume (chapter 12) discusses this tension.

14. Vivian Rothstein and Naomi Weisstein, "Chicago Women's Liberation Union," *Women: A Journal of Liberation* 2, no. 4 (1972): 4–5.

15. This idea derives from an interview with Amy Kesselman, 24 Apr. 1986.

16. CHS/18/3–9.

17. 1972 conference packet, speakers bureau report, CHS/8/1–2.

18. Steering committee minutes, 20 and 27 Aug. 1970, CHS/4/10.

19. University of Chicago chapter report, *CWLU Newsletter,* Sept. 1970.

20. Undated, CHS/18/3. Having become a powerful orator, Weisstein experienced considerable pain over the anti-stardom position, when she was forbidden by the CWLU to accept public speaking engagements in light of the interest of the women's movement in avoiding the creation of stars. She totally agreed with the policy—indeed she was a key architect of it—and did not speak publicly for a number of years. But when she went to important events where an inexperienced speaker was doing a poor job, she had to suppress the urge to grab the microphone and belt out the message. Self-interview and personal communication, 26 Aug. 1993.

21. E.A., P.M., and J.P., undated, CHS/18/3.

22. Jeri R., application for staff position, *CWLU Newsletter,* 5 Jan. 1973.

THREE

Mothers of Invention: Women's Agency in the Kenyan State

PATRICIA STAMP

What kinds of questions can a text on female agency ask about African women? They must certainly be new questions, ones that aim to elicit what women are doing as active agents of resistance and change in the maelstrom of contemporary African affairs. Chandra Mohanty takes Western feminists to task for having asked the wrong questions, thereby producing "the 'third world woman' as a singular monolithic subject," oppressed by a singular, universal patriarchy.[1] This chapter intends to dismantle the "singular monolithic subject," using the example of Kenyan women's agency to demonstrate the "constitutive complexities which characterize the lives of women in [African] countries."[2] The concepts of agency and subjectivity are particularly useful tools for elucidating the cultural and historical specificity of African women's experience. Conversely, a comparative analysis presenting concrete realities greatly different from North American ones sheds light on the utility of these concepts for feminist theorizing.[3]

Here as elsewhere in the volume, agency is understood to comprise both action and representation. Concretely, this definition requires the investigation of both the strategies and the subject position of Kenyan women as agents in the contemporary Kenyan state. I argue that women's agency resides in their communal endeavors and is constantly reinvented in the context of political and social change. Precolonial political practices provide the material from which women shape their discourses; the elements of precolonial subject positions that survive in the postcolonial era are vital constituents of contemporary female subjectivity. While precolonial Kenyan societies were not free of patriarchal ideology, counterbalancing discourses and practices established a relatively advantageous political, social, and economic position for women, especially in horticultural societies.[4]

The chapter explores the colonial and neocolonial distortions of earlier practices that have created the more pervasively patriarchal terrain upon which women must struggle.[5] The language of custom and tradition is pressed into service by both progressive and conservative forces; motherhood is a powerful conceptual weapon used by both in the battle to define women's political and social place. An analysis of the self-help strategies among women of a major ethnic group, the Kikuyu, illuminates the link between contemporary collective agency and precolonial gender relations and female subjectivity. An account follows of the influential actions of elite women during several recent dramas in the life of the nation, showing how such actions complement the struggles of peasant women in their village associations.

Two of the dramas starred individual charismatic women who personify the progressive patriotism that confronts the authoritarian and sectarian tendencies of the Kenyan state. First, the widow Wambui Otieno engaged in a sensational battle with her late husband's clan for custody of his body. Losing the five-month court contest in 1987, Wambui nevertheless made a moving contribution to feminist discourse in Kenya and throughout Africa. The second one-woman drama was the 1990 crusade by Kenya's leading environmentalist, Wangari Maathai, to protect the capital city's park from a corrupt government development project.

The final sections of the chapter discuss the women's movement and national politics. In 1991 and 1992, Kenya's formerly quiescent women's movement found its voice, first, in a soul-searching response to a national tragedy, the July 1991 massacre of nineteen schoolgirls and rape of seventy-nine more by schoolboys at the coeducational St. Kizito Secondary School, and later as a vital part of resurgent democratic politics, as Kenya returned to a multiparty system after twenty years of one-party rule. The awakened commitment to action against sexual violence among leading Kenyan women led to a new militancy in politics generally. Courageous women, Wambui Otieno and Wangari Maathai among them, staged dramatic protests in 1992 against the repressive tactics of President Daniel arap Moi's regime and sought a central place among the political forces organizing for a democratic change of government.[6] The analysis of Kenyan women in the locality and on the national political stage reveals women's agency to be a central dynamic in Kenyan politics.

ORIENTATIONS

What is thought about African women today? Facile but compelling Western popular imagery reduces the African woman to the anguished, helpless mother holding a famished child. In the last twenty-five years, a group of feminist anthropologists and historians, both African and Western, has worked hard in the face of the stereotype to explore and explain the subtleties of women's actions and positions in African societies. These scholars have contributed valuable ideas—for example, about women's central economic role; about complex interlocking rights and responsibilities regarding use of resources; about women's political power.[7] At least as important as these ideas, however, is the wealth of empirical detail in the studies about African societies and women's lives. A corrective to sexist social science, this empirical material provides a sharp reminder that we must not generalize from Western cultural experience of gender relations, female subjectivity, and societal order in general.

One achievement of this literature has been a challenge to Western concepts of the individual. In the African context, Western concepts of the individual and rational choice are problematic for an understanding of female agency, because identity—male and female—is grounded in a profoundly different relation of the self to the social group. A sense of privacy and a strong individualism are absent, but this does not mean a lack of self-esteem or of awareness of one's effectivity. Most women live communally (even the urban elite family usually includes extended kin). With a sexual division of labor that places much food production and all childcare and cooking in the female domain (and by extension, for the elite, financing of education and household expenses in many cases), it is unlikely that a woman will feel helpless or that she will perceive a need to "find herself" as an individual.

In this context, "rights" does not mean the right of an individual to exercise untrammeled personal liberty, but the inalienable right of each individual to contribute autonomously and authoritatively to the collective good. Control of material resources is necessarily a vital dimension of this right. We learn much about female subjectivity and its relation to African social relations and life course regimes from the reflections of the widow Wangeci, one of a Kikuyu group of eight life history narrators:

> Which of my roles in life is most important to me? Now, the most important is cultivating my farm and doing the work of the homestead, because those are needed before all else. Then I would say be-

ing a member of the Mother's Union and Uritu wa Gatwe ["Power of Gatwe"—a self-help group], because the women's groups help me a lot, as I've said. Being a mother or grandmother is next most important. Then the one of being a wife to my husband, because the role of being a daughter was a long time ago. . . . My strongest character is that I like people and I'm hospitable to all—even when calling you to come and eat my food, it is with a clean and happy heart that I do it. I can't think of anything I'd like to change—I feel satisfied with myself. Being a woman means being able to keep things to myself, to go ahead and do them but not talk about them.[8]

Wangeci and the other narrators stress the importance of using one's intelligence: being a mature, responsible adult is graphically described in terms of having "more brains."

Why make a point about African women's reflections on intellect and self-esteem? Unfortunately, the research that demonstrates women's active agency in African societies has not had much impact on development studies, the dominant paradigm for understanding Third World women. Key articles are too scattered in feminist readers and journals, and books are ghettoized under "women's studies" keywords that banish them from bibliographical searches on economy, politics, and the state. Further, the advances in scholarship described above have been piecemeal and have not yielded a theory of African gender relations to counter the hegemonic views produced in the West, including the generalizations of mainstream Western feminism.

Women in Development (WID), the branch of development studies that investigates women's roles, pays little attention to the empirical and conceptual findings that confirm the "constitutive complexities" of African women's lives.[9] The development enterprise, ranging from academic writing to the design, implementation, and monitoring of aid projects by public and private agencies, reaffirms a view of African women as passive, problematic targets of benevolent interventions. Because women's active, intelligent—and collective— agency is unimaginable within this paradigm, the myriad and sophisticated ways in which women cope daily with problems of "development" are lost to view. It is a truism that women do two-thirds of the world's work and grow half the world's food. Yet women's choices are seen as reactions rather than actions. A peculiar inertia is seen to grip them all: they must be "taught," "shown," reached through "extension programs," and disabused of their "beliefs," which can never be construed as thought-out positions, decisions based on long experience and deep knowledge or strategies of resistance.

The paradox is that women have never been more on development planners' minds. Agencies have "gender sensitivity" criteria attached to project approval; endless verbiage promotes women's inclusion in the "development process." WID efforts to convince the wielders of international power of women's importance succeeded at an unfortunate moment. From the mid-1980s the International Monetary Fund (IMF) has imposed punitive loan conditions (euphemistically known as Structural Adjustment Programs) upon Third World nations. The consequence has been a massive, coerced dismantling of state services. Women, revealed by WID reports to be an untapped resource, are expected to shoulder the burden of the health care, social services, and economic support thereby lost to their communities. Phalanxes of nongovernmental organizations from all the Western countries ("as many as can find their way there" says Wanjiku Mwagiru)[10] provide a vast array of advice on health, agriculture, family planning, nutrition, and every other aspect of community life. All this uncoordinated activity fills the vacuum left by decaying state apparatuses. Out of the best intentions, development workers are coopting local initiatives, subverting indigenous habits of self-reliance, and undermining the bases of local knowledge.

I suspect that both the sinister and goodwill efforts to coopt women's energy and initiative cannot contain what is going on in Africa, however. Both in the locality, the so-called site of development where women collaborate to sustain their communities, and at the national level where new political discourses are constantly shaped, women's agency can be seen as constitutive of a new political order in the African state.

SELF-HELP

Ngwatio is the Kikuyu word for the cooperative work by which each woman's farm is cultivated in turn. My research spanning eleven years with Rebecca Njeri Chege on Mitero village in the Kenyan highlands revealed the centrality of women's collaborative endeavors for the life of rural communities. The practice of cooperation and the discourse of communality surviving from precolonial times animates the women's contemporary self-help groups. Nothing to do with aid projects, the Mitero self-help groups flourish as a means for women to cope creatively with the sweeping postindependence economic and social change and with the exigencies of a neocolonial political economy.[11] *Ngwatio* and another term, *matega*, referring to women's mutual help during childbirth, have taken on new meanings expressing collective economic and social strategies to cope with their double domination, as peasants in an exploitative petty commodity production system, and as women, a subordinated category within the peasantry.

The Kikuyu are a patrilineal Bantu-speaking ethnic group of over three million people that has dominated the Kenyan political economy for much of the postindependence period. They have practiced horticulture in a fertile hilly region of central Kenya since the fifteenth century. The Kikuyu were "kin-corporate," to use Karen Sacks's term for such societies.[12] Lineages and clans, the local and wider kinship groups, formed the basis of all political, economic, and social relations and collectively owned the means of production. Women were affiliated with their husband's patrilineage through bridewealth, which legitimized the marriage, secured their use-rights in lineage land, and established lineage membership for their offspring. The very constraints and obligations of the bridewealth gender system—to bear children for their husband's lineage, to produce food and offer hospitality, to act as the linchpin in a wide network of affinal kin relations—provided women the opportunity to exercise political power and the authority to make decisions.[13]

Lineage wife was not a Kikuyu woman's only subject position. Women retained membership in their natal lineage, were expected to participate with brothers in lineage decisions, and could exercise rights in lineage resources if necessary. As sisters in their own lineage, women thus held higher status than as wives in their husband's lineage (see Johnson, chapter 7 in this volume). Sister authority remained a potential rather than an actuality for many Kikuyu women, who lived out most of their lives as wives. However, the fact that women possessed an alternative subject position that could be activated at any time ensured that the position of wife was not as subservient as lineage ideology dictated. First, a woman acceding to the orders of her marital lineage could at the same time be exercising her sister authority in decisions regarding the wives, children, and resources of her natal lineage. Second, the subject position of sister acted as a constraint upon bad treatment of wives by husbands, in that every wife was somebody's valued lineage sister. Third, there was a discourse of decision-making "sisterhood" that extended to all women, providing a collective subjectivity for the wives in a patrilineal village.

Kin corporate societies were characterized by an egalitarian authority structure where there was, in Leacock's words, "a wide dispersal of decision making among mature and elder women and men who essentially made decisions—either singly, in small groups, or collectively—about those activities which it was their socially defined responsibility to carry out. Taken together, these constituted the 'public' life of the group."[14] The Kikuyu are among those African societies where age-grade organizations formally structured elders' power. Age grades cross-cut the political structure of the patrilineal descent group and provided both women and men with a counterbalancing source of authority and power.

Women's age-grade associations were the means by which coresident lineage wives exercised joint authority, marshalled material resources, and counteracted the patriarchal tendencies of lineage ideology.[15] The age-grade structure divided women into elders (*nyakinyua*), younger, childbearing women (*kang'ei*), and apprentice adolescents (*mumo*).[16] Women elders interviewed in our study on Mitero village in 1974 gave detailed accounts of ongoing organizations known as *ndundu* (often translated as "council") which had operated since before the time of their grandmothers and which combined economic, social, and juridical functions. A central purpose of the *ndundu* was cooperative cultivation, but they provided women with organizational and affiliative bases for nonagricultural pursuits as well. *Kang'ei* women operated under the authority of *nyakinyua* and were required to perform services for the latter in order to progress through the organization's ranks. Thus, the control of younger lineage wives by their female elders represented a legitimate authority counterbalancing patrilineal control of women and also put considerable human labor at the disposition of women elders as a group.

Kikuyu society was transformed by colonialism and capitalism. In the postcolonial state, precapitalist elements are retained in a dominated and distorted form among the peasantry. There are distorted remnants of kinship structures and relations of production, age-based organizations, gender relations, and traditional ideologies. Reciprocity between elders and juniors has been undermined: patron-client relations between individual elders and juniors have replaced collective decision making for the community by senior age grades. In gender relations, the patriarchal tendencies have been reinforced at the expense of those elements that provided women with autonomy and counterbalancing power. The carving up of communally owned land into plots under individual male title created an onerous obligation for women to generate surplus for their husbands, while undermining their formerly inalienable use rights in land. The transformed gender system serves to subsidize an under-developed form of capitalism based on peasant production of cash crops for export. From colonial times to the austere International Monetary Fund–regulated present, male elders have been recruited to substitute cash crop for subsistence production. Not only is food thus lost to the family, but women also lose the economic autonomy and social power that flow from control of subsistence production. To the international aid community, it is axiomatic that this reordering of the indigenous political economy constitutes good development; the transition to underdeveloped capitalism is thus fostered intentionally by aid schemes.

Women cling to the remnants of their age-based organizations, patterns of authority, and practices of autonomy in order to resist the negative impact of these changes or to convert innovations to their advantage. Their self-help groups are the contemporary form of the precolonial *ndundu*. Women prefer to grow vegetable crops for cash sale in the market or to engage in wage work on neighboring coffee plantations. While work on their own coffee bushes yields good returns, it represents cash for their husbands and loss of control over their own labor. By contrast the earnings from casual labor, though meager, can be channeled directly into group funds. This economic strategy has two purposes. First, by channeling cash from vegetables and casual labor into their groups, women prevent the appropriation of their labor by their husbands. Second, the accumulation of collectively owned capital (sometimes invested in small business and commercial real estate) is an attempt to protect and enhance their fragile incomes and compensate for lost subsistence production. Women's economic strategies lead to conflict in the village. The Mitero women indicated that there was a considerable struggle over women's labor and earnings. A number of informants pointed out that men often disapprove of women's business activity and seek to undermine it. This is evident in accounts of husbands who beat their wives for participating in the groups. "Men fear women when they are in a group." Overt hostility between men and women points to the dramatic sharpening of gender contradictions in the contemporary era.

Women's ideological defense of their activities is subtle. They champion their groups under the banner of *harambee* ("pull together"), the government-devised slogan to encourage local development initiatives. Participating in groups is patriotic, they say. Women also have made self-help a literal motherhood issue. Maxine Molyneux, in her analysis of the ways in which women became "political subjects" in the Nicaraguan revolution, advances the concept of "combative motherhood."[17] This concept usefully characterizes African women's appropriation of a discourse of motherhood for their contemporary struggles. The Kenyan peasant women take the sexual division of labor, and their socioeconomic responsibilities within their marital lineages, as the very basis of their struggle to retain and expand the autonomy and authority that the system formerly provided them.

Thus, while men protest in the name of "traditional" family values, women cautiously argue for the maintenance of their position and for the improvement of their economic lot in terms of those same family values. They say that women's independent economic activity serves children and the home, and progress in this sphere in the modern nation requires new tactics for the fulfillment of their time-honored tasks. It is possible for men and women to draw contradictory messages from "tradition" because the ideals of men's dominance over women and of women's primacy in their own realm of authority were held simultaneously. The idea of male dominance is reinforced by Christian and capitalist values, but precapitalist African values regarding women's power in the political economy of the village remain a forceful weapon in the discourse.

It is important not to view African women's discourse of combative motherhood through the lens of North American gender politics, where motherhood and family responsibility have been the rallying cry of patriarchal political forces. Rather, we should apply to them, in the words of Barbara Marshall, "a perspective on gendered subjectivity which emphasizes its historically specific, multiple and often contradictory nature, and which sets the stage whereby *actively interpreted identities* may become political points of departure."[18] In this light, women's use of a discourse of family solidarity and welfare and their assertion of their authority and responsibility as mothers, wives, and mainstays of their community is revealed as an astute and tactically sound ideological strategy on the part of Kenyan women.

Women's choices in disposing of their labor time and channeling their earnings into self-help groups may be seen as resistance to the appropriation of their product by the international commodity market through the agency of their husbands. As such it is a resistance to dual exploitation by the gender system on the one hand and by underdeveloped capitalist processes on the other. Their strategies fuse precapitalist gender elements—economic, political, and ideological—with contemporary practices aimed at fostering self-sufficiency. As such, their actions can more truly be called "development" than most projects thrust upon African women by aid donors.

HEGEMONY AND RESISTANCE

Women's collective actions and self-representations must be seen as more than pragmatic responses to exploitation and the challenges of change, however. We must view them as a powerful political agency woven into the very fabric of the colonial and neocolonial state. Colonialism imposed capitalist states upon indigenous societies: for the enterprise to succeed, the populace had to be brought under social, economic, and political control. In Africa, colonial authorities collaborated with local power structures—specifically, the male lineage leadership—to establish hegemony. For example, the colonial populace of Tanganyika was organized and controlled by a discourse and administrative practice that established the "countryside" as the "private" sphere, appropriately the domain of women and unemployed men, while the "city" became the "public" sphere, justifiably restricted to employable men. The outcome was a docile, manageable, and cheap workforce, produced and subsidized by a cordoned peasantry, staffed by women, and controlled by male heads of households.[19]

Women's resistance to colonial rule has only recently begun to be recognized and analyzed as such. Refusing the chief's order to plant the colonizer's cash crops was construed as laziness by colonial authorities and ignored by social scientists. Only recently has women's disobedience of agricultural directives—in the past or present—been viewed as a systematic economic strategy with political ends.[20]

The "collaborative hegemony"[21] by which the male-dominated kin group was given patriarchal power in the service of the state has continued to the present. The two sites of women's resistance in Kenya are the locality, as shown above, and the national political discourse. Today, the struggle over the definition of the state and over the entrenchment of patriarchy continues, not only among village women but also in national dramas involving celebrities. The struggle by a few elite women for the public imagination—waged in the courts, newspapers, streets, and homes of the nation—represent some of the most profound challenges to the Kenyan state since its inception. The tie between elite and peasant women's actions is closer than it seems in that the national dramas affect the climate in which women at the level of the locality can succeed. Moreover, the political warriors, educated, worldly, and economically privileged, draw on the same subject positions as their peasant country-women, often using them in a very sophisticated way, and working on a more overtly ideological terrain. Presenting themselves as mothers, wives, providers, responsible social agents, and loyal citizens, they engage with the patriarchal laws and repressive politics of the state.

The most compelling drama was the battle between a Kikuyu widow and her Luo husband's clan, fought out in the courts and the media for five months in 1987 (the Luo are Kenya's third largest ethnic group).[22] S. M. Otieno, a prominent criminal lawyer, died intestate in December 1986, and a sensational contest over his remains ensued. Wambui Waiyaki Otieno, a noted activist and an organizer of the 1985 international women's conference in Nairobi, became the eye of a storm about customary law, women's rights, and intertribal marriages when the Umira Kager clan took her to court to block her burial plans. According to Wambui and her witnesses, Otieno had asked to be buried near the Nairobi home where he had lived out his married and professional life and raised fifteen children and foster children. A series of court cases, involving twelve separate court actions and concluding in May 1987 with a Court of Appeals ruling, awarded the custody of Otieno's remains to his clansmen for burial in his birthplace in Western Kenya according to Luo custom.

Wambui's lawyers argued that Otieno had, through his choice of partner, Christian beliefs, lifestyle, and residence, forsaken "tribal" custom for a modern life as a Kenyan citizen, and that customary Luo burial law therefore had no jurisdiction in his case; rather, Kenya's common law applied. Otieno's clan asserted that, on the contrary, Otieno's birth and upbringing as a Luo was paramount. Kenyan legal statutes do not spell out clearly which legal system takes precedence in a clash between common and customary law; the courts—with the tacit approval of the government (some say at Moi's urging)—chose to come down on the side of "custom" as defined by the clansmen. Their decisions set back women's rights and the development of a national, progressive jurisprudence in Kenya. They also fanned the country's ethnic tensions and threatened the idea of a supraethnic national identity, fostered during forty years of Kenyan colonial and postcolonial history. The funeral in the clan's district was treated as a triumphant homecoming and a vindication of

Luo culture and values. Wambui refused to attend the ceremony as custom required of widows; Otieno was thus, ironically, buried as a single man. Wambui called a press conference after the final appeal court ruling to announce that she would have no more to do with the clan and henceforth would be known by her father's name, thus reclaiming her sister status in the eminent Waiyaki family.

The burial saga revealed some important things about the nature of state and society in Kenya. It showed that "custom" and "tradition," far from being timeless essences called from the precolonial past, are potent inventions of the present, constructed to serve the interests of protagonists on the modern political stage. Scholarly research on precolonial Luo gender relations reveals that they were more akin to the Kikuyu system described above than to the hidebound "traditions" presented by the professors and elderly Luo men who were the clan's expert witnesses.[23] Moreover, contemporary Luos rarely practice the romantic, simplified version of their social customs that was presented to the court.

The case also revealed that the contemporary African state and subnational structures such as clans and lineages have an economic and political interest in the cooptation of gender relations and the control of women. Gramsci's concept of the relation between "civil society" and "political society" is useful here. Political society is the realm of the governing regime and the formal institutions of power. Civil society is the realm of culture, religion, and kinship. According to Gramsci, civil and political society must collaborate in political rule; civil society's acquiescence, even advocacy, is essential to the hegemony of the state.[24] The hegemony of the Kenyan state, both during colonialism and following independence, has been founded on this collaboration.

Although Wambui lost custody of her husband's body and was vilified by national politicians, the press, and the judges, she showed Kenyan women the possibility of defiance. During the high court trial, Wambui emerged as an almost mythical figure in the popular imagination. She did not plead her case from overt feminist arguments—even though she was no stranger to feminist polemics. Rather, she claimed the authority of a founder of the nation—"I fought for independence and this judiciary"—and spoke eloquently about Christian duty, Otieno's standing as a cosmopolitan Kenyan, and her rights as a widow. Both in and out of court, she demonstrated a shrewd understanding of the currents and vehicles of political discourse in Kenya. She initiated a stream of legal actions, protests, commentaries, and press conferences throughout the five month saga, and her refusal to be silent outraged the male protagonists, authorities, and public. She also projected a powerful physical presence, with flamboyant displays of grief and anger.[25]

Wambui triumphed in another way. While the clan was bathed in symbolic glory, the lineage was denied by her actions, S. M. Otieno's prestige, children, wife, and estate—the human and material furnishings of a lineage's well-being. The court outcome can thus be seen as a Pyrrhic victory for both clan and state, partners in the collaborative hegemony that sought through the case to tighten control of gender relations and the realm of civil society. Not many would wish to be defamed as she was, but she proved that women could resist the control of their marital lineage and use the courts to do so. Wambui thus opened the political space for future feminist struggle against the coercive power of social institutions and the state.

The other dramatic figure who personifies women's resistance to state coercion in the public imagination is Wangari Maathai, a world-renowned environmentalist. Formerly a professor of veterinary anatomy, she founded the Greenbelt Movement, an internationally acclaimed organization promoting tree-planting and environmental awareness throughout the country, with an emphasis on women's involvement. Using her authority as a scientist and environmentalist, she mounted a solitary challenge to the self-aggrandizing actions of President Moi's regime. In 1989, the government announced plans for a massive media complex to be built in Nairobi's Uhuru Park and owned by the single national party, the Kenya African National Union (KANU). The sixty-story office tower and two flanking ten-story wings were projected by enthusiastic government and party supporters to be "the most magnificent and prestigious building in Africa."[26] A four-story statue of President Moi was to stand in front of the complex.

The Architectural Association of Kenya complained to the government that "200 metre high concrete monoliths, generating a dynamic population of several thousand people . . . will change Uhuru Park beyond recognition and [cause] a complete loss of the greenbelt."[27] Yet no one except Maathai was prepared to mount a full-scale challenge to the grandiose project.[28] Maathai filed suit in the high court in November 1989 seeking a permanent injunction against the buildings' construction. Claiming that KANU and the government's media trust had violated Kenyan law and Nairobi's official development plan, she castigated them for ramming through the project "against the constitution and without the consent of the majority of Kenyans,"[29] in the process ignoring both environmental concerns and the needs of Nairobi's urban poor, for whom the park was the sole means of recreation.

Maathai's appeal struck a chord among Nairobi residents as the flood of letters to newspapers attested. "I beg you, our leaders: you already have a lot of what you want—cars, homes, offices. Please allow us only this," wrote one.[30] The court refused on a technicality to entertain her suit, however, and the president responded contemptuously to her challenge, inciting the party-controlled umbrella organization for women's groups, Maendeleo ya Wanawake, to stage police-led demonstrations against their "wayward colleague," and to call for her expulsion from KANU.[31] Interestingly, the demonstrators burnt their anti-Maathai placards after the demonstrations, suggesting a divergence between the party line and women's actual sentiments toward her. In the ensuing two months, Maathai and her organization suffered constant harassment. The Greenbelt Movement was ordered to quit its headquarters in a government-owned building within twenty-four hours, and several members of parliament called for the deregistration of the organization. Maathai herself was banned by another MP from visiting his constituency.

To all the harassment Maathai responded that "it ought to be possible for an individual to raise any issues on matters of public interest and even in international courts to protect mankind on issues concerning the environment," and that no Kenyan should "entertain the dream of banning another Kenyan from visiting any part of the country."[32] She reiterated her position that Uhuru Park was a national monument of "utmost political, religious and cultural value," and warned that local hostility to Greenbelt employees over the issue was threatening the tree-planting program, which provided a livelihood to a number of poor rural women.

Maathai's crusade, like Wambui's ordeal two years before, was an important moment in Kenya's recent politics of dissent. Not only did she effectively raise the issue of freedom of speech, but she also succeeded in putting the environment on the political agenda, using the same discourse of progressive patriotism and motherly outrage as Wambui. For all their bluster, the regime and the party were sent into retreat on the mega-project. As a result of the furor, aided by Maathai's growing international stature as an environmental hero, Kenya's international aid donors forced the Kenyan government to set the project aside.

THE STRUGGLE FOR A FEMINIST VOICE

Maathai's and Wambui's actions are the most dramatic instances of individual women's political courage in the face of an authoritarian, patriarchal regime. At the level of national politics, however, women have found it difficult to create and sustain an explicitly feminist challenge. Indeed, women's associations have been slapped down or coopted when they appeared too threatening to the collaborative hegemony of state and local kin-based power. Right-wing and sexist forces attack self-proclaimed feminists—whether they are inspired by Western feminists or not—as yet another tool of imperialist domination undermining authentic African culture. This perversion of liberational critique has nevertheless been effective in silencing women who have sought to articulate a more overt feminist agenda.

The dilemmas of Kenyan feminism are exemplified by the contradictions that have faced Kenya's two umbrella women's organizations, Maendeleo ya Wanawake ("Progress of Women") and the National Council of Women of Kenya (NCWK). In the late 1980s, the first was coopted by the Moi regime; the second was discredited and silenced. Maendeleo was founded in 1952 by a British settler to promote the interests of rural women and to organize village groups. The national organization, however, has been the vehicle for the political aspirations of elite women with close ties to the government and seldom acted democratically on behalf of its peasant constituency.[33] Further, it espoused Kenya's conservative development ideology and eschewed feminist rhetoric. Maendeleo officers wrangled continually over the perquisites of office and the disposition of funds, sparking melodramatic scandals in the mid-1980s.

However, the Moi regime recognized the political potential of the female peasantry, whose political consciousness had ironically been activated by the cornucopia of WID aid projects showered on a staunch Western ally in Africa. Taking advantage of the strife among the elite leaders, KANU annexed Maendeleo in 1987. Party control was consolidated in 1989 when male politicians took over the running of Maendeleo's elections, ensuring that their relatives and allies were nominated for leadership positions at local as well as national levels.

The NCWK by contrast did support the causes of rural women and espouse a feminist position. Founded in 1964 as a voluntary coordinating body for women's organizations in Kenya, the organization attracted progressive intellectual and professional women to its leadership. Precisely because of its overt feminist position, the NCWK was branded as Western-influenced and hence elitist—an inauthentic voice for Kenyan women. When it attempted to support Wambui's cause with a signature campaign for a petition to correct statutes that violated women's rights, the campaign was roughly disrupted by the police and excoriated in the media. In Molyneux's terms, Kenyan feminists found it difficult to promulgate "strategic gender issues," the abstract issues familiar to Western women such as political inequality and institutional discrimination (the NCWK's attempted strategy). Rather, they were constrained to advocate the "practical gender issues" related to women's responsibilities within the sexual division of labor, such as family welfare (Maendeleo's historical mandate).[34] Much energy was safely channeled into the practical WID activities of development agencies.

The most anguished moment for the leaders of Kenya's women's movement came with the July 1991 school massacre. Most of St. Kizito's 306 boys went on a planned rampage in revenge for the girls' refusal to join a strike against the headmaster (allegedly over a number of boys' being barred from attending a sports meet the day before because they had not paid their activity fees). A day-long Saturday protest turned into a berserk assault on 271 girls barricaded in their locked dormitory. "We were attacked as if by a pack of hungry hyenas," said one of the injured survivors.[35] Shockingly, no one came to their aid, and the police waited two hours before responding to the report of a fleeing teacher.[36] The massacre triggered a wave of soul searching and self-criticism among male leaders in Kenya. Sexism became a serious media topic for the first time. The women's movement for its part was shocked into action: the disparate groups buried their differences to present a forceful position paper on women's equality to the presidential commission formed to investigate the school disturbances.[37]

Reflecting on the massacre, women leaders understood the penalty women were paying for the movement's quietism. In steering clear of strategic gender interests in order not to incur accusations of disloyalty and collusion with selfish Western feminists, the women's movement also had steered clear of the issue of sexual violence. "By our silence it has come to this. . . . We failed to tell [the St. Kizito girls] that they are not sexual objects," said Njoki Wainaina the coordinator of an African women's network, FEMNET.[38] Maria Nzomo, a political science professor and rising feminist leader, courageously indicted women leaders for their ineffectiveness and self-interest. She also sharply criticized the government for its tactics of divide and rule and favoritism vis-à-vis women's organizations. "The male-dominated political system has succeeded in coopting the conservative leaders within the women's organisation, while marginalising the radical ones."[39] Out of the reevaluation following the massacre came a more militant agenda and a more assertive stance toward sexism in Kenyan society.

The most powerful product of the new activism was a group of professional women calling itself Mothers in Action, formed to support the surviving victims. Each girl received a letter of consolation and advice addressed "Dear Daughter." The girls wrote back to the "dear mums" gratefully. "Thank you for remembering the girls who survived the tragedy. . . . I was crushed under a bed for three hours. I wait for more encouragement from you."[40] The group immediately began a campaign against sexual violence, publishing a pamphlet entitled "Women! Girls! You Can Defend Yourselves," planning a women's shelter, and starting a commemorative quilt honoring the murdered girls.[41] In December, they held an intensive counseling session for the victims, 40 percent of whom had revealed suicidal feelings. Almost all of the counseled girls felt that their "old selves were restored and figured they had a cause for living."[42] From practical support for the victims, the Mothers—as they came to be known in press headlines—went on to establish their presence as a national pressure group advocating the rights of women and children. Spurred by an unspeakable tragedy, Kenyan women leaders had at last generated a collective political will and a determination to voice strategic gender issues.

WOMEN AND DEMOCRATIC POLITICS

Though virtually absent from national party politics, women were never quiescent in local politics, exercising their voting rights and debating political issues as vigorously as men. Logoli politics are probably typical of most ethnic groups in Kenya: women discussed politics "at every opportunity: in yards, on the fringes of men's groups, at markets and at church. . . . Men did not acknowledge women's contributions to political discussion. [However] men made use of the information women provided. . . . Women assure their continuing power through a cultural posture of ideological and institutional acceptance of male elder rule while at the same time making decisions from the back door."[43]

In 1992, women started to knock at the front door, seeing in the return to political pluralism their first opportunity to influence the course of party politics. Following the December 1991 repeal of the 1982 constitutional amendment that had made KANU the sole legal party, women threw themselves wholeheartedly into the movement to restore democracy and remove the repressive Moi regime from power. They held seminars to develop a political platform, asserting that "gender differences are 'socially constructed,' and can, therefore, be changed by society."[44]

The Mothers in Action group was at the center of these events, moving from immediate concerns with sexual violence and the massacre's aftermath to asserting their presence on the national stage. They issued a manifesto supporting the democratization process but warning that the time had come to recognize women's political power. "Since women constitute at least half of the voters in Kenya, it is not conceivable that they should be considered a 'wing' of any party. . . . We contend that they must be seen, heard and recognised as the soul and body of any respectable and credible party, organisation or government. . . . We do not accept tokenism and patronage of any kind."[45] The manifesto laid out the classic strategic gender issues, such as equal rights, equal opportunity, affirmative action, and legislative reform of property and family law. Mothers in Action also launched a campaign to educate women on democratic participation and strategized for the election of large numbers of women to local authorities and to the national parliament. With these actions Kenyan feminism, explicitly expressed in the discourse of combative motherhood, became a formal political player for the first time.

There has never been a more exciting time of debate and political experimentation in Kenya's independent history. The movement chiefly responsible for the return to a multiparty system was the Forum for the Restoration of Democracy in Kenya (FORD). When FORD constituted itself as a political party following the December repeal, a number of prominent women, Wambui and Maathai among them, took up leadership positions, seeking to inscribe feminist principles in the new party's political agenda.

In March 1992 women once again captured the public imagination with a dramatic and defiant act, one that has joined Maathai's and Wambui's sagas as a crucial moment in the popular narrative of Kenyan politics. The mothers of fifty-two political prisoners began a hunger strike in Uhuru Park to force their release and draw attention to human rights violations. After several days riot police set upon the strikers and their supporters, destroying their camp, dubbed Freedom Corner, and viciously beating a number of them—

including Wangari Maathai, who was hospitalized with serious injuries. Some of the women used African women's confrontational tactic of last resort: they exposed private parts of their bodies to the police, who were deeply dismayed thereby. A reversal of the strict code of modesty, such exposure is the ultimate curse women elders can levy against the targets of their defiance. Across Africa, women have resorted to the tactic when threatened by violence from repressive regimes. Spurred by the women's example of defiance and solidarity, FORD called a national two-day general strike for the release of the political prisoners. The strike did not paralyze the nation but nevertheless represented a successful mobilization of popular opposition to the regime.

As of late summer 1993, the outcome of Kenya's push for democratic renewal hung in the balance. Moi was returned to power in the December 1992 elections, due to the fragmentation of the opposition into three parties and to alleged corruption at the ballot box. State-inspired ethnic violence raged in the center of the country, while elected opposition members were harassed both in the parliament and in the local councils. A hard-won social consensus was threatened by the gravest economic crisis in the country's history. Nevertheless, women succeeded in climbing upon the national political stage. Men and women alike were talking about Maathai for president in the next elections, as the environmentalist spoke out courageously on behalf of the citizenry's democratic ideals and against ethnic factionalism, thus provoking the regime into further acts of repression against her. According to Nzomo, the women's movement was gaining cultural and political legitimacy.[46]

The collective and individual acts of women described above do not stand as ephemeral moments in the flow of Kenyan history but remain vividly present in the nation's political imagination. The currency of the past characterizes political discourse in societies that formerly were created and reproduced through oral narrative. Through these acts, women exercised their moral authority as "mothers of the nation" to promote the conception of a more enlightened Kenyan state: the Kenya that was forged in the progressive early days of independence—a democratic, socially liberal pan-ethnic society.

CONCLUSION

Kenyan women's subjectivity was shaped by the gender relations in precolonial kin-corporate society and tempered in their resistance to the state's encroachment upon their autonomy and power through a hundred years of colonial and neocolonial rule. The collective and multiple nature of their subjectivity is the bedrock of their agency in the Kenyan state today. The subject positions of sister, wife, and, above all, mother, are played imaginatively in the discourses they create to promulgate their ends, whether at the level of the village or on the national stage. The legacy of rhetorical skills, essential in preliterate societies, ably serves today's literate women as much as it does the peasant women in the village; they know well the political consequences of the language and the media they choose as vehicles for their causes. They have created what Judith Butler would call a "strategic essentialism—a performative discourse seeking to constitute a political effect and a political community."[47] Butler shares Laclau and Mouffe's desire to safeguard in theory "an open future for the constitution of subject positions."[48] The example of Kenyan women's actions and representations suggests that African women, far from being the passive, unresisting objects of patriarchal politics and exploitative economics portrayed in much of the WID and Western feminist literature, are dynamic inventors of their own agency in the African state.

NOTES

1. Chandra Mohanty, "Under Western Eyes: Feminist Scholarship and Colonial Discourses," in *Third World Women and the Politics of Feminism,* ed. Chandra Mohanty, Ann Russo, and Lourdes Torres (Bloomington: Indiana University Press, 1991), 51.

2. Ibid., 54.

3. It is important as well to avoid creating a monolith of African women. With appropriate caveats regarding the specificity of Kenyan experience, however, it is possible to justify the use of Kenya as a representative society on the grounds that its political formation is typical of anglophone African countries in many important respects. Further, Kenyan gender relations are rooted in the patrilineal kinship system and horticultural or pastoral peasant economy that characterizes much of sub-Saharan Africa. Finally, Kenya is fertile ground for gendered political analysis, due to its unbroken record of civilian rule and its tradition of vigorous political debate since independence, in contrast to those countries that have suffered outright dictatorship or military rule. The tension between repressive and democratic tendencies in the country has raised the stakes of political contest and renders the gender issues that have been part of this contest all the more fascinating.

4. See Patricia Stamp, "Kikuyu Women's Self-Help Groups: Towards an Understanding of the Relation Between Sex-Gender System and Mode of Production in Africa," in *Women and Class in Africa*, ed. Claire Robertson and Iris Berger (New York: Holmes and Meier, 1986), 27–46.

5. See Judith Carney and Michael Watts, "Disciplining Women? Rice, Mechanization, and the Evolution of Mandinka Gender Relations in Senegambia," *Signs* 16, no. 4 (Summer 1991): 651–81; Nakanyike Musisi, "Women, 'Elite Polygyny,' and Buganda State Formation," ibid., 757–86; and other articles in this special issue of *Signs* on "Women, Family, State, and Economy in Africa." See also Fiona Mackenzie, "Gender and Land Rights in Murang'a District, Kenya," *Journal of Peasant Studies* 17, no. 4 (1990): 609–43.

6. The analysis of Kenyan gender relations and politics in this essay is based on twenty-three years' research on Kenya, during which almost four years were spent in the country. For an analysis of the contemporary political process in Kenya see Patricia Stamp, "The Politics of Dissent in Kenya," *Current History* 90, no. 556 (May 1991): 205–8, 227–29.

7. Women's autonomy and political power through much of sub-Saharan Africa in the precolonial era, and their subsequent declining position, have been well documented by these scholars. See Patricia Stamp, "Burying Otieno: The Politics of Gender and Ethnicity in Kenya," *Signs* 16, no. 4 (Summer 1991): 811, n. 4, for reference to some of the contributors to the consensus on this position. Margaret Strobel's review essay, "African Women," in *Signs* 8, no. 1 (Autumn 1982): 109–31, documents the emergence of a coherent scholarly approach on African gender relations. More recently, the "life histories movement" has proven a useful new interdisciplinary tool for investigating women's agency in pre- and postcolonial Africa. As the Personal Narratives Group asserts, personal narratives "are essential primary documents for feminist research" into gender relations and "the construction of a gendered self-identity." (Personal Narratives Group, ed., *Interpreting Women's Lives: Feminist Theory and Personal Narratives* [Bloomington: Indiana University Press, 1989], 4, 5). See especially Marjorie Mbilinyi, "'I'd Have Been a Man': Politics and the Labor Process in Producing Personal Narratives," 204–27 in that volume.

8. Jean Davison with the Women of Mutira, *Voices From Mutira: Lives of Rural Gikuyu Women* (Boulder: Lynne Rienner Publishers, 1989), 138–39. Wangeci is a pseudonym.

9. See Patricia Stamp, *Technology, Gender, and Power in Africa* (Ottawa: International Development Research Centre, 1989), for a critical overview of WID approaches. See also Mohanty, "Under Western Eyes," 53, 55, and the DAWN manifesto by Gita Sen and Caren Grown, *Development, Crises, and Alternative Visions: Third World Women's Perspectives* (New York: Monthly Review Press, 1987). Eva Rathgeber charts the connection between WID approaches and mainstream developmentalism in "WID, WAD, GAD: Trends in Research and Practice," *Journal of Developing Areas* 24 (July 1990): 489–502.

10. Wanjiku Mwagiru, "Gender Dynamics in Rural Resources Management in Kenya: A Focus on Participation," paper presented at the annual meeting of the African Studies Association, Baltimore, Nov. 1990.

11. The analysis of Kikuyu gender relations and of the self-help groups is drawn from Stamp, "Kikuyu Women's Self-Help Groups." Eight of the ten women's groups in Mitero were studied during field research in 1974, 1981, and 1985. Rebecca Njeri Chege was a social worker with Thika Municipal Council when I invited her to assist the research; she is currently supervisor of family welfare in the Nairobi City Council.

12. Karen Sacks, *Sisters and Wives: the Past and Future of Sexual Inequality* (Westport, Conn.: Greenwood Press, 1979), 115–22, and passim.

13. See Carolyn M. Clark, "Land and Food, Women and Power, in Nineteenth-Century Kikuyu," *Africa* 50, no. 4 (1980): 357–69, esp. 361, and Stamp, "Kikuyu Women's Self-Help Groups," 34–37.

14. Eleanor Leacock, *Myths of Male Dominance* (New York: Monthly Review Press, 1981), 24.

15. It is problematic to designate societies such as the Kikuyu patriarchal, even though they are patrilineal. For a critique of the generic concept of patriarchy, see Stamp, "Burying Otieno," 813.

16. It was the Nyakinyua women of Mitero village who in 1974 informed Rebecca Chege and me that individual women were not the proper objects of our inquiry into Kikuyu women's perceptions of social change. They instructed us to study their collectivities: the self-help groups. Only under the rubric of group membership did they allow us to interview individual women. The lesson in African women's collective agency—and in their right to shape research questions—has informed all our subsequent work on Kenyan women. We described this experience in Patricia Stamp and Rebecca Njeri Chege, "Ngwatio: A Story of Co-operative Research on African Women," *Canadian Woman Studies/les cahiers de la femme* 6, no. 1 (Fall 1984): 5–9. See also Rebecca Njeri Chege, "Communal Food Production: The Mukuru-Kaiyaba Women's Group in Nairobi," *Canadian Woman Studies/ les cahiers de la femme* 7, nos. 1 and 2 (Spring/Summer 1986): 76–77.

17. Maxine Molyneux, "Mobilization without Emancipation? Women's Interests, the State, and Revolution in Nicaragua," *Feminist Studies* 11, no. 2 (Summer 1985): 227–54, esp. 228.

18. Barbara Marshall, "Re-producing the Gendered Subject," *Current Perspectives in Social Theory* 11 (1991): 169–95, esp. 170; emphasis added.

19. Marjorie Mbilinyi, "'City' and 'Countryside' in Colonial Tanganyika," *Economic and Political Weekly* 20, no. 43 (1985): 88–96.

20. See for example Marjorie Mbilinyi, "Agribusiness and Women Peasants in Tanzania," *Development and Change* 19 (1988): 549–83, esp. 571–72, for an account of women tea growers' spearheading a strike against the Tanzanian Tea Authority in 1983.

21. Zakia Pathak and Rajeswari Sunder Rajan use this concept, adapted from Gramsci's ideas on hegemony and civil society, in their case study of an Indian Muslim divorcée's case ("'Shahbano,'" *Signs* 14, no. 3 (1989): 558–

82). They call the male-dominated kin group "that state within a state" (569).

22. This account of the burial saga is drawn from Stamp, "Burying Otieno." Once again, I express my gratitude to Wambui Otieno for her willingness to meet with me and for her commentary on the manuscript. The interpretation of the case is mine alone, however.

23. For an account of Luo gender relations, see Achola Pala Okeyo, "Daughters of the Lakes and Rivers: Colonization and the Land Rights of Luo Women," in *Women and Colonization: Anthropological Perspectives,* ed. Mona Etienne and Eleanor Leacock (New York: Praeger, 1980), 186–213.

24. See Antonio Gramsci, *Selections From the Prison Notebooks* (New York: International Publishers, 1971), 12–13, and passim.

25. Wambui recounted the singing of a funeral song in the chief justice's office, much to his displeasure (personal communication, July 1989).

26. *Weekly Review* (Kenya), 1 Dec. 1989, 9.

27. Ibid., 10.

28. I refer to Maathai by her last name, and Wambui by her first, as this is how they are known in Kenya as public figures. Otieno refers to Wambui's husband in media reports; moreover, she has publicly rejected her marital lineage affiliation. (In 1989 she informed me that she was founding a new clan, named S. M., and that several grandchildren were already named S. M.).

29. *Weekly Review* (Kenya), 1 Dec. 1989, 9.

30. *Globe and Mail* (Toronto), 27 Dec. 1989, 1.

31. *Weekly Review* (Kenya), 22 Dec. 1989, 9.

32. Ibid., 12 Jan. 1990, 17.

33. See Audrey Wipper, "The Maendeleo Ya Wanawake Organization: The Cooptation of Leadership," *African Studies Review* 18, no. 3 (Dec. 1985): 99–120.

34. See Molyneux, "Mobilization without Emancipation?" 220–33.

35. *Weekly Review* (Kenya), 19 July 1991, 8.

36. The St. Kizito massacre was only the worst of a spate of devastating schoolboy riots across the country, all for flimsy reasons. Twenty were reported and many more went unreported in the space of the previous two months (ibid., 12). An analysis of the breakdown of social control behind the children's pathological behavior is beyond the scope of this article.

37. *Weekly Review* (Kenya), 9 Aug. 1991.

38. Quoted in Michele Landsberg, "School Attack Inspires Action by Women of Kenya," *Toronto Star,* 12 Oct. 1991, F13. I am grateful to Landsberg for sharing materials given to her by members of the Mothers in Action group.

39. In an August 1991 seminar paper for the influential Association of African Women for Research and Development, which was much cited in the Kenyan press (*Weekly Review,* 13 Sept. 1991, 17).

40. The letters arrived during the meeting of Mothers in Action with Landsberg, and were read aloud (ibid.). On a point of semantics, it is impor-

tant to note that in most African societies that the category of "mother" refers more broadly than to only the birth mother. A child has as many additional mothers as her mother has sisters. For the St. Kizito girls, therefore, there would be deep significance in the acquisition of a group of supportive new "mums." As with the concept "sister," the concept "mother" also expands to include a collectivity of women. Another layer of meaning was thus activated in the relationship between Mothers in Action and the victims: the *Nyakinyua-Mumo* relationship of patronage and support, whereby women elders supported and instructed teenage girls and inducted them into adult social responsibilities.

41. *Weekly Review* (Kenya), 13 Sept. 1991, 17.

42. Sophie Njoroge and Grace Kahuria, "Fight against Violence: Site Selection Meru, St. Kizito Girls in Kaaga Highschool," Mothers In Action Project Report, Nairobi, n.d. [1991], 10 pp.

43. Judith Abwunza, "Logoli Women of Western Kenya Speak: Needs and Means," Ph.D. diss., University of Toronto, 1991, 193.

44. *Weekly Review* (Kenya), "The Power of the Female Vote," 24 Jan. 1992, 14.

45. Njoki Wainaina, Mothers in Action Manifesto, printed in the *Daily Nation* (Kenya), 8 Jan. 1992.

46. Personal communication, Nairobi, 3 Mar. 1993.

47. Judith Butler, "Anti-Essentialism and Performative Discourse: Recent Directions in Feminist and Radical Democratic Theory," Cultural Studies Seminar, York University, Toronto, Jan. 1991.

48. Ibid. See also Ernesto Laclau and Chantal Mouffe, *Hegemony and Socialist Strategy: Towards a Radical Democratic Politics* (London: Verso, 1985), 114–22.

FOUR

Local and Global: AIDS Activism and Feminist Theory

KATIE KING

> The juncture ... is comprised of the differential form of op-positional consciousness which postmodern cultural con-ditions are making available to all of its citizenry in *a his-torically unique democratization of oppression* which crosses class, race, and gender identifications.
>
> —Chéla Sandoval

> AIDS activists know that silence equals death, but we also know that this cannot be *said*, it must be *performed* in an anarchistic politics that sometimes coincides with and supports the political action of our allies working within the unitary power system, but sometimes contradicts it, or seems simply mad in the traditional public realm.
>
> —Cindy Patton

> Feminism is focusing increasingly on the *identity-effects* produced by ... contradictory social realities and "identi-ty" has emerged—as the semantically surfeited term it is—to occupy large areas within feminist work: multiple iden-tities, strategic identities, identity politics.
>
> —Elizabeth Weed

With Chéla Sandoval I wonder at the meanings and possibilities of what she calls "postmodern cultural conditions," although I tend to think instead in terms of "transnational culture/s." I prefer to focus on the debates about subjectivity and the limits of agency within the contexts of what we see happening in Cindy Patton's "in-ternational agitprop activism," which is contemporary AIDS activ-ism. I call this arguing from the activism *up;* I say this believing that we don't need to tease theory into action since theory is always al-ready action, even if its scope and sphere worry at us, seem too limited, or claim too much; and activism is always mired in theory, whether it deploys theory self-consciously or not. What actions are meaningful produce change, create new political groupings, mobilize and/or restrain various "powers"; I take it that these issues are what matter when discussing the politics of "agency" and, for that matter, the meanings of "theory" in feminism.

I display two major interests in this essay. First, I'm concerned with what I call global gay formations and local homosexualities, a single example of many interconnected and complex current historical shifts. I'm interested in these, on the one hand, as a theoretical apparatus in production, and on the other hand, as a means of naming the historical circumstances this apparatus describes and even shapes. Second, I connect this apparatus with an interest in the construction of political identities. I'm concerned with both the political identities that cluster around the term "gay" and those mobilized by feminist theorists as they construct an apparatus that locates them theoretically and politically. A guide through this essay is an emphasis on these historical conditions, called both postmodern and transnational. I use the work of Chéla Sandoval especially to make some of these links, but implicitly refer to the epigraphs by Cindy Patton and Elizabeth Weed as well. Feminists as theoretical agents are both accountable to and shaped by these shifts that are radically altering transnational locations of power. An attention to AIDS activism and its international art activism requires feminist theorists to swim in this rich sea of reconfiguring alliances, descriptions of reality, and political interests.

I make a case here about the complex interactions *between* global gay formations and local homosexualities; and I try especially to unpack the meanings of "global gay formations" in the substantial illustrations I give. The relation between "global" and "local" is not the relation of "universal" to "particular" (although it plays with this relation to some extent). My point here is to highlight the historical specificity of these abstract relations; to suggest indeed that they may determine the horizon of our abilities to conceptualize gay theory at this time. This is the reason for returning to meanings of the term "postmodern." My *method* enacts the shifts of political meanings and alliances as it describes them (indeed, I doubt they can be adequately described any other way). Although one might call the political purposes here generally "historical," I try not to reproduce unitary histories since I criticize them. Instead I want to emphasize movement and change: how political objects look like one thing at one time and turn out to be something quite different later on. This insight informs my ideas about the feminist debates on agency and how they enact theoretical agencies: how they make certain kinds of political change inside feminist theory.

Rather than mobilizing the term "poststructuralist" in considering these debates—a term that names a set of powerful theoretical tools honed by divergent theorists in more and less politically engaged variants, in Euro-centers and peripheries, in self-consciously Third World appropriations, and in U.S. theoretical geographies—like Sandoval I prefer to consider a set of historical conditions. Indebted to the theoretical stew that Elizabeth Weed says shifts a focus from psychic identity to subject positioning, to what she calls "identity-effects produced by those contradictory social realities," the historical conditions I'm most interested in right now are global gay formations and local homosexualities. I take one visual emblem of these conditions from the objects produced in AIDS art-theoretical activism: the ACT-UP appropriation of Barbara Kruger's appropriation art, a hand grasping the words "I am out therefore I am." I'll return to this visual emblem after some preliminary remarks.

AIDS activism domestically and internationally draws upon Foucauldian histories and anthropologies of sexuality—particularly drawing on the periodizations and inventions of sexualities—literalizing, refiguring, imploding such theory in interventions into forms of global gay formations and local homosexualities.[1] Such activism has three direct consequences for feminist theory. First, there is a new appreciation for "cultural feminism," which I claim is the proper name for our apparatus for the production of feminist culture: a sometimes essentialist and sometimes anti-essentialist synthesis of identity politics and sex-radical productions of feminist and gay culture.[2]

Second, in AIDS activism we see an altered terrain of what counts as the "gay and lesbian community" in the United States; for example, there are new coalitions among feminists—lesbian and other. Who and what these "others" are is under contention as "heterosexual" destabilizes as a category. We see lesbian interests in AIDS activism producing new community with gay men, and lesbian interests in safe sex redefining lesbian sex *practices* and meanings. At the same time a backlash, or troubled sense of priorities, incites some lesbians to challenge involvement in AIDS work or policy priorities for AIDS, while other lesbians and heterosexual women, women of color, prostitutes, drug users—these overlapping groupings of women—make new coalitions to describe AIDS as a

Adam Rolston, *I Am Out Therefore I Am*,
1989, crack-and-peel sticker, offset lithogra-
phy, 3 7/8" x 3 7/8". Used with permission.

"women's disease." Lesbian sex radicals call for a return to, but at
the same time a revision of, the consciousness-raising group as a site
for the production of theory about sex, while antiessentialist, anti-
autobiographical individual and collective feminist writing and film
projects re-structure and re-vision bodies and body parts. These coalitions and alliances I situate inside "international art-theoretical
activism," that is, cultural analysis, critique, even theory in agitprop
and other art activist forms, which are sex-radical productions of gay
culture.[3]

The third consequence for feminist theory comes from the new
visibilities created by such activism, visibilities that suggest directions for gay/lesbian/feminist/gender studies in global gay formations and local homosexualities. The cultural and historical appropriations that create homosexual continuities across time and space
are in material tension with the imperatives of transnational influences and realities that create some kinds of gay organization globally. The flows of capital that appear to be linked to the possibilities of gay urban formations, intervening into family forms of
organization, intersect with flows of sexual repressions and license.
International feminists begin to understand that lesbianisms in specific cultural locations are subject to multinational receptions.[4] Such

contemporary material circumstances offer us new insight into the "global" formations of historical continuities and the "local" understandings of historical specificity.

Let me clarify my evocation of Sandoval's use of "postmodern cultural conditions." Sandoval's use of the term "postmodern" diverges from Fredric Jameson's precisely as Sandoval emphasizes utopian possibilities of the present moment rather than dystopian analysis of the lost project of modernism. Jameson's coinage retains a Frankfurt school pessimism about the homogenization of "world culture."[5] Sandoval's stunning shift instead describes as "differential consciousness" the results of "a historically unique democratization of oppression." This utopianism ironically builds itself upon and counters dystopian analysis. I'm less comfortable with such assertive utopianism than Sandoval is, and I tend to emphasize a range of complex contradictions, as if they could be shorn of either celebration or denunciation. But I know they can't be. I'm not as single-hearted as Sandoval, although I find courage and power in her reframings. I'd like to claim, for example, that my use of "global gay formations and local homosexualities" is only descriptive, but I don't believe that it is possible simply to describe conditions without being politically implicated in the powers identified, framed, and reconstructed in such naming. I do claim that agency is a heady mixture of historical, group, and individual movement, that intention plays a smaller role than the fiction of heroic actors would suggest, that political people can often only respond to social conditions that are too complex to be fully understood rationally as they try to make the most of circumstances they cannot control. It is the assertive belief (I might call it hope) that one can do all this that Sandoval's utopianism energizes.

It is to illustrate these concerns that I take another visual emblem—one of the complexities of power in its transnational forms, its problems and pleasures—a work of international art activism by the Japanese artist Masami Teraoka: his painting from the AIDS series *Black Ships and Geisha*.[6] I wouldn't press to describe Teraoka's painting specifically as resistance art, unlike ACT-UP's art-theoretical objects. Rather I would stress how, as a kind of postmodern art, it ambivalently and carefully depicts uniquely postmodern interests that are *not yet* decidedly politically progressive or recuperative, interests that despite and because of such uncertainty require our recognition and intervention. The painting's humor depends upon and empowers uncertainty. Its ambicultural, multilinguistic locations are not reciprocal but aligned along paths of commodification, the production of cultural identities in the United States, and along points of political, artistic, and commercial reception. Teraoka's work effectively places its own cultural production inside the transnational systems that I mean to resound with my term "global gay formations," where I attempt to make more complex (less utopian?) the celebratory resonances of the word "gay," but without denying their appropriate traces. Global gay formations—among other multinational systems—are depicted, parodied, and politicized in Teraoka's work. Teraoka uses watercolors to simulate ukiyo-e woodblocks, linking them with U.S. pop art and commerce. Throughout the AIDS series, Teraoka uses Kabuki imagery. *Black Ships and Geisha* is set up as a theatrical scene; written across the top, as if the entire scene were a Kabuki illustration, is a description of four aspects of the action.[7] The inclusion of two women samisen players decorating the narrative suggests its genre: a Kabuki chant. The chant names the cast and then describes the four acts. In the first act, Surgeon General Koop arrives in the black ship for a special symposium between the United States and Japan. In the second scene described in the chant, trade friction is depicted in a condom-trading agreement negotiated between Japan and the United States, while the stock market crash is also treated. In the third, dinosaurs sink the To-Shi-Ba boat, which is engaging in secret trading; the text describes the sound the boat makes as it sinks. In the final act, an international conference on condoms is being held, in which women train to use a super-giant version.

Presiding over the scene is the head courtesan, who is a Kabuki female impersonator, identified by the orange cloth over her head. She holds a long scroll on which is written: "New educational material for sex—your spirit must be prepared for the use of condoms." On the condom packages—their brand name is "Safe"—is written "giant size, bargain price." In Teraoka's work, multinational commerce is the site of new engagements of people and everyday life—cultural imperialisms wryly shown to be eagerly embraced—of links between old and new sexualized pleasures and new sources of exploitation and power. Teraoka presents sexuality as various and not centered in dichotomous homosexuality/heterosexuality. I first discovered a catalog of Teraoka's work in a gay men's bookstore in Toronto, a bookstore specializing in international gay travel. The catalog, as an object, is itself embedded in global gay formations moving along the lines of tourism and multinational capital.

Now I return to the emblem from ACT-UP,[8] reflecting again on Elizabeth Weed's point that "'identity' has emerged . . . to occupy large areas within feminist work: multiple identities, strategic identities, identity politics."[9] Some of the objects produced in ACT-UP's strategic activism comment on the limits of art activism, the implications of the New York art world's position in the national willful ignorance of AIDS. They facilitate direct action, draw upon gay and lesbian resources, and model citizen health research and citizen intervention into health institutions and regulatory mechanisms. Such activism literalizes radical theoretical insights into the social construction of disease; for example, it insists on explicitly politicizing such construction and engaging in political struggle to participate in such construction, thus affecting and changing the systems that produce diseases as social objects and produce drugs to manage diseases. In the coalitions formed by AIDS activism, sexual identities are becoming politically subordinated to the permutating meanings and reconfigurations of specific sex practices, just as sex practices must be prioritized over earlier euphemized "risk groups" (defined by race, sex, and class) in education on HIV transmission.[10]

Consider, for example, the benefit performance for the Santa Cruz, California, AIDS Project, called "Feeling the Heat: An Evening of Erotic Entertainment, for Women Only." This sex-radical, safe-sex performance participates in redefinitions of lesbian sex practices and meanings, producing forms of what one might call "public lesbian sex."[11] Not only do such events support and elaborate lesbian sex (and safe-sex) practices, but such reframings along the lines in which gay men's sex practices are usually stigmatized (as "public," in which lesbians are somehow seen as private, or innocent) reflect some new meanings of "sex radical." Such deliberately constructed similarities drawn between lesbians and gay men reflect some lesbians' refusal to collude with the stigmatizing of gay men's sexual practices. The emphasis on women's pleasure *and* safety publicly displayed is mirrored in the homemade lesbian safe-sex posters plastered around my neighborhood in Washington, D.C. Although they were immediately defaced, they originally graphically depicted women's genitals being touched through dental dams, with the slogan "Dam It Janet!" My neighborhood gay bookstore sells dental dams along with condoms, but interestingly enough, dental dams are not sold at the feminist bookstore a few blocks away. Feminists and lesbians are still in contention over sex-radical politics. All of these examples reflect political realignments affected by AIDS activism and by the new emphasis on sexual practice. Earlier versions of such political realignments emphasizing shared interests between gay men and lesbians and challenging sexual stigma occurred in the feminist debates about lesbian s/m.

In such activist engagement and political realliances, overlapping AIDS activisms challenge the simple binaries and the misleading charges of essentialism that academics use to process, categorize, and taxonomize political identities, struggles, and literatures and to manage political alliances in U.S. feminism. The political alliances emerging from AIDS art-theoretical activism exceed management within this framework. Indeed, we need such theoretical-activisms to overflow in these messy ways, in order to avoid what Eve Sedgwick analyzes as the genocidal "Western project or fantasy of eradicating [individual gay] identity."[12] I am especially interested in the analogies between the social construction of political identities—as revealed by AIDS activism—and the social construction of disease, or more broadly, of scientific objects of knowledge. As we know and have been talking about for a long time, identities are produced; I would emphasize here the *nodes* of their dynamic political production—processes, positions, moments, chronologies, epistemologies—an apparatus for description that I'm developing here. "I am out therefore I am"; the political struggles within which identities are produced, their production over time, the kind of playing with, parodying, literalizing that takes place in AIDS art-theoretical activism—each of these elements in the nodes of dynamic political production makes more visible that "essentialism" is often but one epistemological moment in the production of identities, not itself the essence of identity formation.[13] Such "moments" of essentialism consolidate political unities, sometimes only "momentarily," sometimes maintaining them "stably" at great cost.

Education about HIV infection and AIDS internationally has underscored the real global influence of historically white Euro-American consolidations of sexual identity, that mutual social construction through which "heterosexuality" has defined itself against "homosexuality" in the last century, mostly in the United States and Europe, and there in several dominant discourses. (As the *Oxford English Dictionary* points out, the terms "heterosexual" and "homosexual" were invented in nineteenth-century sexology discourses—"heterosexual" is the more recent term. Notice how the word "invented" requires us to separate counterintuitively names and practices that are not coterminous for all communities of people even in the United States.) AIDS activists point out how educational efforts such as those of the World Health Organization have often seriously misrepresented the sexual practices and behaviors currently understood to transmit HIV because they are fascinated with reconstructing a heterosexuality innocent of, and mutually dichotomous with, homosexuality. In doing so, they ignore or appropriate local sexual practice.

Earlier I suggested the insufficiency of the term "heterosexual," also in feminist alliances, that "heterosexual" is no longer a sufficiently stable or enveloping category to include those not named by the term "lesbian." Heterosexuality is politically granulating as feminist struggles over bisexuality—that sometimes third reification, sometimes overflow category, sometimes liminal impurity—are conflated with loss of control over the naming of sexual identity. The coming-out story as a technology to reconstruct sexual identity doesn't work when feminist life histories—not only from Euro-American centers but spoken and written transnationally—increasingly cannot be captured in the names "heterosexual" or "lesbian" or "bisexual." The debates around essentialism as they have functioned in gay studies work as strategies to name collectivities. Other new social formations loosely allied under the rubric of "Queer Nation" include the "transpersons" mentioned by the National Coalition of Black Lesbians and Gays; the "queers" of Queer Nation, Queer theory, Queer writing; the "bisexuals" of LABIA (Lesbians and Bisexuals in Action); and "transgender"-ed people mentioned in *Anything That Moves*, the magazine of the Bay Area Bisexual Network.[14]

What does it mean to privilege the historical conditions named by the terms "global gay formations" and "local homosexualities"? In what contexts are the terms meaningful? What does this examination add to feminist debates about agency? I want next to give two extended examples to illustrate my use of these terms, and to show these vibrant examples as a rich sea of shifting and refiguring political interests.

One genre of AIDS discourse describes the realities of what work against AIDS means in specific cultures. "Silences: 'Hispanics,' AIDS, and Sexual Practices" by Ana Maria Alonso and Maria Teresa Koreck, published in the U.S. feminist journal *Differences*, belongs to this written genre.[15] Alonso and Koreck place their analysis historically in terms of the multinational production and consumption of "Hispanics." I would also place it within the historical location of "transnational cultural studies," a term I borrow from the editors of the journal *Public Culture,* Arjun Appadurai and Carol Breckenridge, who contend that "the state is increasingly dominated by elites who are transnational cultural producers and consumers." However, Appadurai and Breckenridge also stress the "multiplicity of world-systems" that "now emerge from many centers and reach out to many peripheries":

Furthermore, the dialogue between elites and masses, or from another point of view, between cultural producers and consumers, grows ever more complex. National elites raid each other's cultural repertoires for useful representations of themselves, while the masses, who are their audiences, themselves as tourists, television-watchers, immigrants and *gastarbeiter*, constitute a partially deterritorialized and occasionally counter-cosmopolitan audience whose tastes and knowledge are ever-changing. Thus the foundations of the sort of critical theory that emerged from the Frankfurt school need fundamental rethinking before they can be brought to bear on the emergent global forms of public culture.[16]

Alonso and Koreck describe the "attractive packaging" of the "Hispanic" by U.S. media, corporations, and the state. The category "Hispanic" mystifies the significant differences among various Latino populations. They question the dominant assumption that disproportionate numbers of "Hispanics" and "blacks" are HIV positive because of greater IV drug use rather than because of sexual practices. This analysis refutes stereotypes about both drug use and sexual practices among the many groups reductively named by these two terms. For example, Alonso and Koreck cite studies that differentiate modes of HIV transmission among persons in the U.S. who are of Puerto Rican origin from those of Mexican and Cuban origin.

Alonso and Koreck's analysis deconstructs the terms "heterosexual," "homosexual," and "bisexual" as mainstream Anglos use them. Drawing upon ethnographic research on sexuality in Mexico and focusing on receptive anal intercourse as "high-risk" for HIV transmission, they locate two categories of male behavior: (1) men who exclusively engage in insertive anal intercourse with men and anal and vaginal intercourse with women, and (2) men who engage, primarily or exclusively, in receptive anal intercourse with other men. Members of the first group are not socially stigmatized, indeed their honor, power, and virility is enhanced by their sexual behavior. Reporting on a study by Mexican researchers in Guadalajara, Alonso and Koreck contrast both these local sexual behaviors with those by men who engage both in insertive *and* receptive anal intercourse with other men:

> Significantly, males playing both roles are called "internationals," a term which indexes the "foreignness" of practices which are much more like those of American gays than the ones discussed here. Carrier suggests that "internationals" tend to be middle-class and that their divergence from the type of *macho-joto* relationship discussed here is a result of influences from the U.S. and the impact of the gay

liberation movement in Mexico. In the areas where we carried out our preliminary study, where the population is largely composed of agriculturalists and rural workers, there were no "internationals."[17]

Here the designation "international" indexes one edge to global gay formations, which are a complex mixture of transnational influences in their *layered* representations: (1) here as "foreign" within an indigenous set of sexual practices; (2) as etic (outside, not local) analytic categories deconstructed but also used by ethnographers both Mexican and U.S. North American; (3) as material impositions operating as explanatory indexes both for U.S. cultural comparison and for U.S. cultural defamiliarization; and finally (4) as shadows of international political alliances, powerful and not innocent of domination. I offer this set of issues as one example of the meaningfulness of "global gay formations and local homosexualities."

In their essay, Alonso and Koreck have difficulties in shifting the ground in which anal sex and homosexuality come to define each other; at times they seem eager to uncover a "real" homosexuality in disguise. Their work is directly connected to education about modes of HIV transmission, and they stress anal intercourse as risky sex requiring protective practices. Strangely, they unproblematically accept the absence of lesbianism reported by informants; this absence is unquestioned rather than being the object of a similarly nuanced investigation considering practices not coextensive with identities. The AIDS education imperative may have appeared less urgent and motivated here. The difficulty lies in the overwhelming power of the ideologies of sexual identity that seemingly specify sexual practices.

Before I briefly discuss the second ethnography I mentioned, I would like to reflect on my use of several terms. I have said before that global gay formations are a complex mixture of transnational influences in their *layered* representations. I think of layerings of instance, of political meanings constrained in particularity, inseparable and mutually constructing, yet distinct; I think of differing patterns of abstraction, *dynamically* shifting ground and foreground, interacting and correcting and deconstructing each other. Precisely this complexity of interaction marks these material systems as "postmodern" or "transnational." The terms "global" and "local" have begun functioning for me as layers of abstraction with differing patterns. Saying this, I mean explicitly *not* to posit a binary between the abstract and the concrete, but instead to posit that relation as mobile. I want to look at abstractions layered next to each other in the *relation* abstract to concrete, or as map to territory.

Of course, this alters the common-sense meaning of the word "abstraction," since such layerings become both maps and territories. In a materialist discourse, one must now ask the question, What counts as the material? The mobility of what counts as the material, I also claim, is an aspect of what is meant by the term "postmodern."[18] When I now talk about "global gay formations and local homosexualities" I'm talking about layerings of maps and territories that also interact, correct and deconstruct each other, which describe distinct and important *systems* of *material* circumstances.[19] Using the term "global gay formations" suggests how analytic models are sometimes material systems, as the term also refers to the models of sexual identity that gay liberation has dispersed through the world and made powerful in new political locations. The term "local homosexualities" also ironically displays its own generic use of the sexological term (homosexual); while pointing to local form(s), it still keeps in view the sexological term's currency and power. The fluidity of sexual desire itself is what is currently stigmatized as *bisexual*—for example, in public policy discourses labeling "human vectors" of AIDS, or in politically recuperative feminist concerns about the stability of the category "lesbian."

Given this use of layerings, global and local, I want to turn to a second ethnography. Earlier I said that international feminists begin to understand that lesbianisms in specific cultural locations are subject to multinational receptions.[20] For example, the theoretical apparatus of Jennifer Robertson, a U.S. anthropologist and Japanologist, depends upon tensions between global gay formations and local homosexualities in her study of the Tekarazuka Revue, an all-female Japanese theater founded in 1914. Her essay "Gender-Bending in Paradise: Doing 'Female' and 'Male' in Japan" is an ethnography of an international art practice.[21] "Paradise" is the name of the theater in which the gender-specialists of the Tekarazuka Revue perform. Its theatrical locations resonate with Teraoka's investments in the Kabuki theater. Robertson's essay may be seen as part of a newly proliferating genre of lesbian writing that stabilizes and destabilizes constructions of "the lesbian," but where, and for whom?

Paradoxically, according to Robertson, a genre of literature that was most associated with a lesbian author inspired the Tekarazuka theater, yet the theater's purpose was to valorize *hetero*sexuality. Nonetheless, its teenage and working-woman fans appropriated the theater as their model for a lesbian subculture, "namely, 'butch/

femme,'" says Robertson. The actors of the Tekarazuka and their fans use the kinship terms "older brother" and "younger sister" for female couples or lesbian sex. Robertson distinguishes these terms from several other "expressions used in reference to female couples," for example, a generic term meaning "same-sex love," and several slang terms, such as "Class S," which Robertson says conjures up the picture of crushed-out schoolgirls, a typical moment in the Japanese female life cycle. Another term, "take out lunch box," alludes to the gender-saturated meanings associated with rice.

The term that corresponds to "lesbian," Robertson says, "was not used to name a politicized female identity . . . until the 1970's." The Tekarazuka expressions highlight not the same-sex of the couple, as do the other Japanese terms, but rather "the differential gender roles." The configurations of the Tekarazuka terms overlay two differentiated systems: *kinship*—both the "older brother"/"younger sister" distinction; and ambiguously *gender transitivity/intransitivity*—"the asymmetrical but interdependent relationship" between the "male and female gender specialists" in the theater; specializations which complement but don't duplicate the all-men gender specialists of the Kabuki theater, which offer ideal representations of maleness and femaleness. Robertson says that "the division of sexual labor here recalls American butch/femme bar culture in the 1950s," and she suggests that while the same-sex terms represented socially innocuous couplings occupying a moment in a woman's life cycle, the oppositional Tekarazuka couples confounded heterosexuality. In pre–World War II Japan, as nativism was increasingly valorized, outraged critics of the subculture saw "butch" sexuality in particular as Euro-American and un-Japanese. The oppositional possibilities of the Tekarazuka Revue have shifted across historical moments. Note that this "international art practice" thus is not *necessarily* a politically resistant one, at least not over all the historical moments within which it has refigured.

I would locate Robertson's use of butch/femme distinctions as the "global gay formation" utilized here, not in a universalization of U.S. bar culture of the fifties, but as a key theoretical concept etically (here, not Japanese) used to distinguish among the varieties of local homosexualities in their more and less resistant forms and to code in Robertson's theoretical apparatus, which assumes a unified analysis of gender and kinship. It functions in the political shadows I've already described as "global gay formations." At the same time, global gay formations also structure some *consumptions* of these representations of Japanese lesbianisms.

In the last few years materials have become available in the United States that point out and sometimes play out U.S. consumption of the global maps that include local and cosmopolitan lesbianisms. For example, I would pair two evocative collections, one edited by Ines Reider and Patricia Ruppelt, *AIDS: The Women* (1988)—which connects materials from the United States, Brazil, Denmark, Germany, Austria, the Philippines, Zimbabwe, Nicaragua, Haiti, and the Netherlands—and another edited by Reider alone, the "urban stories by women," *Cosmopolis* (1990)—which draws upon a similar though different range of locations and implicitly constructs local and cosmopolitan "lesbianisms." Reider is one of the founders of *Connexions*, a magazine that translates into English materials in a variety of languages from international feminist movements and publications. Compare Reider's sex-radical materials to *Finding the Lesbians: Personal Accounts from Around the World*, edited by Julia Penelope and Sarah Valentine in 1990, which is from a different political location.[22] Who are these books for? What are the relations that permit them to exist in the United States, in English, for the consumption of U.S. lesbians and feminists and overlapping cohorts? How are they similar to and different from the series of anthologies that proliferated new lesbianisms in the 1980s? How do they reflect or create alliances among feminist movements? How do they stabilize and destabilize constructions of "the lesbian," and, again, *where* and *for whom?* U.S. feminists must work to locate the United States and U.S. feminism in transnational systems of power and to examine U.S. feminism in its constitutive appropriations of globally intertwining activisms and inside the history of decolonization.[23] These politicized systems map feminist conversations through which theory moves.

Thinking in terms of layerings requires locating oneself in the material systems dynamically modeled. In my work, I describe the reconfigurations of power and the new formations of identities in order to value which differences make a difference, which changes make change. Feminist debates about agency regularly polarize over how well our theoretical apparatus can adequately come to grips both with elaborating the varieties of power in subjection and the qualitatively different abilities of individuals and groups to make effective change in opposition to or in deployment of such powers. For example, when Linda Gordon and Joan Scott stage themselves in debate in *Signs* as for and against poststructuralist theory, as against humanism or against determinism, *both* are struggling to claim and articulate the most dynamic and complex model of women's agency they can produce.[24] I consider the connections that translate *across* feminist uses of poststructuralism and social and political theory especially significant in both Gordon's and Scott's theoretical practice, in contrast to the ritualized oppositions they produce in their staged debate, oppositions that obscure their actual practice and the theoretical reception of their work. Chéla Sandoval's elaboration of "oppositional consciousness" similarly translates *across* feminist uses of poststructuralism and social and political theory, appropriating and dramatically transforming the work of Jameson and Foucault, and predating but participating in current feminist uses of "positionality." Positionality is a term with poststructuralist resonances, which functions effectively to connect a poststructuralism—U.S., Euro-centered, and Third World—that is profoundly produced and affected by feminism in its colonial, decolonized, and internally colonized manifestations, to a U.S. identity politics that is increasingly influenced by U.S. women of color—as they understand and produce relations between, with, and about women in the Third World. This is an identity politics also mapping across lesbianisms, mapping coalitions across classes, sexualities, religions, nationalities, and ethnicities.

In examining global gay formations and local homosexualities I draw upon work by Sandoval and by the science studies theorist Bruno Latour.[25] I am interested in the ways they hint complexly at the dynamic quality of the production of political and historical subject-positions, suggesting that such production occurs unstably over time and through several epistemological moments, each with new forms of agency/constraint, stability/instability, historical determination/universal use, and so on.[26] For example, Sandoval describes the making of the category "women of color" within political struggles in a specific and historically powerful location: the 1981 National Women's Studies Association conference in Storrs, Connecticut.[27]

Thinking in layers means placing feminist theorists within the historical meanings of postmodernism; thinking of feminist theorists as theoretical agents; thinking of the political struggles within which identities are produced, within which theoretical agents play roles as "subject-effects." In other words, such thinking means noting that, for example, not only are the meanings of lesbian and gay community consolidated "stably" in the costly epistemological moments of essentialization, but so are the theoretical identities of "poststructuralist feminist theorist" and "socialist feminist historian" (Scott and Gordon's polarized locations in their staged debate). When I say that theoretical agents play roles as "subject-effects," I deliberately conflate two partially overlapping, partially exclusive systems of analytic tools—which could be represented in the theoretical identities of "poststructuralist feminist theorist" and "socialist feminist historian"—thereby creating simultaneous compartmentalizations and messy overflows. An emblematic example in the debates on agency is the meaning of the word "subject." To disentangle a bit of this wonderfully felted-together term, consider the following distinctions. On the one hand stands the dichotomy "subject/object"—an analytic tool with a long feminist history, a history to which Linda Gordon appeals in her critique of Joan Scott and of poststructuralism, claiming in the *Signs* debate that to describe agency as a "discursive effect" drains the word of any meaning. On the other hand stands the very duplicity of the terms "subject" and "to subject" (noun and verb)—an analytic tool that precisely balances upon the undecidability of agency: can agency be assumed prior to knowing what actions are meaningful, produce change, create new political groupings, mobilize and/or restrain various "powers"? To what extent does trying to locate "agency" make it impossible to see how power is shifting and moving? Is it the right unit of analysis?

I presented a version of my work on global gay formations and local homosexualities at an international feminist theory conference in Glasgow, Scotland, in 1991. I was impressed there by the deep desire of international lesbians to produce an intellectually and materially autonomous lesbian studies innocent of, not dependent upon, not a supplement to, or in any way indebted to anything from "gay studies." To me, charting the courses of power in the formations we produce and work within seems necessary to any intellectual work on lesbianism. To know lesbianism "subject" (in some ways) to "global gay formations" doesn't destroy the active meanings of the political struggles of the differing groupings of lesbians found in either the International Lesbian and Gay Association (once called the International Gay Association, and, after being politically called to account, required to change its name and its politics by these lesbians) or the International Lesbian Information Service (a lesbian-only offshoot of the ILGA, separating from gay men in their own protest), however progressive or recuperative these struggles might be.[28]

Is agency a reflective, retrospective category, shot through with complicity, misunderstanding, contingency? Sandoval insists that we know agency exists: we (oppressed peoples, a very *new* category of historical location) have already used it to make change; we use it, know it daily, intimately. What does it mean that Sandoval challenges an emphasis on *women's* agency, describing instead a so-called "democratization of oppression"? What units of analysis are shifting here, and for what historically significant reasons? Notice that Sandoval's "democratization of oppression" suggests world historical changes that substantively alter current feminist classifications of privilege and oppression. This "we," drawn together by new political interests, is made up of some of those who once (during a past Sandoval claims is rapidly receding) were among the "privileged." This ironic—even bitter—but strangely hopeful "democratization of oppression" simultaneously names new extensions of oppressions on a world scale; yet it also names "a new arena for unity among peoples" as power realigns on a scale yet to be understood or assessed.

Notice how the terms in which Sandoval names this ironic "democratization" reframe those now-canonical objections to postmodern politics. For example, its putative relativism I would say is a misunderstanding by its critics of the very meanings of "tactical," "mobile"; its apparent lack of political commitment, of radical politics, rather precisely names critical misperception of the meanings of "differential consciousness";[29] its so-called inability to discuss power is instead a misreading of those new skills that actually read the webs of power; furthermore, the perception and concern by critics that, just as women are becoming subjects, men are destabilizing subjectivity, should be understood rather as a misleading effect of white women's privileged male/female (unraced, unclassed) dichotomy out of which that "democratization of oppression" as a historically spreading transnational experience is invisible.[30]

Within shifting feminist theoretical agencies (those named in new theoretical apparatuses, and those enacted by feminist theorists as historical conditions shift and as theorists shape and are shaped by these conditions), the Gordon-Scott debate can best be understood emblematically. In this debate a putative dichotomy is resynthesized (in theoretical practice), as current reformulations in feminist theory that destabilize the political identity "socialist feminist" are reconfigured in a formulation profoundly influenced by new coalitions among academic feminisms. This reshaped theoretical agency (reshaped for good and ill; it is not yet decidable) might be named "materialist feminist"—in which the meanings of "materialism" are transformed, in feminism, as they must now be transnationally. Will we (theoretical agents recasting materialist feminism) work out the uses of "what counts as the material?"—an understanding provisional, historically shifting? Will we refigure our claims of what is given priority, immediacy, of what is immediately important in some "strategic materialism"? This book is an example of such new provoking agencies.

NOTES

The statement by Chéla Sandoval that forms the first epigraph to this chapter appeared in her article "U.S. Third World Feminism: The Theory and Method of Oppositional Consciousness in the Postmodern World," *Gender* 10 (Spring 1991): 22, n. 50. The second epigraph is from Cindy Patton's book *Inventing AIDS* (New York: Routledge, 1990), 131. The third epigraph is from Elizabeth Weed's "Introduction: Terms of Reference," in *Coming to Terms* (New York: Routledge, 1989), xx. In each epigraph, the italics are mine.

1. Foucault's most influential text is this area is *The History of Sexuality*, vol. 1: *An Introduction*, trans. Robert Hurley (New York: Pantheon, 1978). Eve Kosofsky Sedgwick wonderfully describes some of the ironies of defamiliarization when gay theorists deploy Foucauldian periodization: how periods move, how homosexuality today becomes transparent; see Sedgwick, *Epistemology of the Closet* (Berkeley: University of California Press, 1990), 44–48.

2. I mean here to disentangle a premature reduction of cultural feminism from the much-needed critique of the antipornography movement. For more argument on this point, see my "Producing Sex, Theory and Culture: Gay/Straight ReMappings in Contemporary Feminism," in *Conflicts in Feminism*, ed. Marianne Hirsch and Evelyn Fox Keller (New York: Routledge, 1990).

3. Several examples of AIDS art activism are pertinent. Regarding ACT-UP, see *October* 43 (1987), "Issue on AIDS: Cultural Analysis/Cultural Activism"; on The NAMES Project, see Cindy Ruskin, Matt Herron, and Deborah Zemke, *The Quilt: Stories from the NAMES Project* (New York: Pocket, 1988). On priorities and women's coalitions: Jackie Winnow, "Lesbians Working on AIDS," *Outlook* 5 (1989): 10–18; "PWA Coalition Portfolio," *October* 43 (1987): 147–68; Suki Ports, "Needed (For Women and Children)," *October* 43 (1987): 169–76; Carol Leigh, "Further Violations of Our Rights," *October* 43 (1987): 177–82. On revisioned bodies: Amber Hollibaugh and Cherrie Moraga, "What We're Rollin Around in Bed With—Sexual Silences in Feminism: A Conversation toward Ending Them," *Heresies* 12 (1981): 58–62; Frigga Haug et al., *Female Sexualization*, trans. Erica Carter (London: Verso, 1987); Trinh T. Minh-ha, *Woman, Native, Other* (Bloomington: Indiana University Press, 1989); and three films directed by Trinh T. Minh-ha: *Reassemblage* (Idera, 1982), *Naked Spaces—Living Is Round* (Idera, 1985), *Surname Viet Given Name Nam* (Idera, 1989).

4. See Lourdes Arguelles and B. Ruby Rich, "Homosexuality, Homophobia, and Revolution: Notes toward an Understanding of the Cuban Lesbian and Gay Male Experience," pt. 1, *Signs* 9 (1984): 683–99, pt. 2, *Signs* 11 (1985): 120–36. For the term "multinational reception" I am indebted to Lata Mani, "Multiple Mediations: Feminist Scholarship in the Age of Multinational Reception," *Feminist Review* 35 (Summer 1990): 24–41.

5. Fredric Jameson, "Postmodernism, or the Cultural Logic of Late Capitalism," *New Left Review* 146 (July–Aug. 1984). See Sandoval, "U.S. Third World Feminism," 22 n. 50, for her reading of the essay.

6. Masami Teraoka, *AIDS Series/Black Ships and Geisha*, 1987, watercolor study on paper, Space Gallery, Los Angeles; reproduced in Howard A. Link, *Waves and Plagues: The Art of Masami Teraoka* (Honolulu: The Contemporary Museum; San Francisco: Chronicle Books, 1988), 69, cat. no. 27.

7. This description is a paraphrase of Link's commentary in *Waves and Plagues*.

8. This artwork (which also was used on a T-shirt) and others are discussed in Douglas Crimp and Adam Rolston, *AIDS/DEMO/GRAPHICS* (Seattle: Bay Press, 1990), 103.

9. Weed, "Introduction," xx.

10. Cindy Patton made some choice remarks about this reemphasis in Sue O'Sullivan's interview with her; see "Mapping: Lesbianism, AIDS, and Sexuality," *Feminist Review* 34 (Spring 1990): 120–33.

11. Program from benefit performance, Kuumbwa Jazz Center, Santa Cruz, California, 27 Feb. 1988.

12. Sedgwick, *Epistemology*, 41, 43.

13. I'm indebted to Diana Fuss's *Essentially Speaking* (New York: Routledge, 1989) for helping me think through the idea that "essentialism" is not itself the essence of identity formation.

14. See, for example, the premier issue, Winter 1991.

15. Ana Maria Alonso and Maria Teresa Koreck, "Silences: 'Hispanics,' AIDS, and Sexual Practices," *Differences* 1 (Winter 1989): 101–24.

16. Arjun Appadurai and Carol Breckenridge, "Editor's Comments," *Public Culture* 1 (Fall 1988): 2–3.

17. Alonso and Koreck, "Silences," 114.

18. I'm deliberately confounding entailed dichotomies such as Hartsock's interlocking concrete/abstract entailing materialist/idealist and entailed by female/male (although I find the formulation "abstract masculinity" very useful). See Nancy Hartsock, *Money, Sex, and Power* (New York: Longman, 1983), esp. 231–51.

19. My understanding of these issues is most indebted to the manifestos and ruminations of the editors of and contributors to the journal *Public Culture*, which engages in transnational cultural studies, whose historical reframings contain the dynamism that shifts *who* gets to count as a center, *where*, why, and how, which I see in examining international art activism.

20. See King, "Producing Sex."

21. Jennifer Robertson, "Gender-Bending in Paradise: Doing 'Female' and 'Male' in Japan," *Genders* 5 (Summer 1989): 50–69. All subsequent quotations from Robertson are from this article.

22. Ines Reider and Patricia Ruppelt, *AIDS: The Women* (San Francisco: Cleis, 1988); Ines Reider, *Cosmopolis* (San Francisco: Cleis, 1990); Julia Penelope and Sara Valentine, eds., *Finding the Lesbians: Personal Accounts from Around the World* (Freedom, Calif.: Crossing, 1990).

23. In my work on "feminism and writing technologies" I attempt to anchor some discussion of politicized systems of language, technology, publication, and multinational capital. For one description of this large research project, see my "Bibliography and a Feminist Apparatus of Literary Production," *TEXT 5: Transactions of the Society for Textual Scholarship* (1991): 91–103.

24. For the exchange between Gordon and Scott, see their reviews of each other's books and their responses in *Signs* (Summer 1990): 848–60.

25. See Bruno Latour and Steve Woolgar, *Laboratory Life* (Beverly Hills, Calif.: Sage, 1979).

26. For example, also consider the similar intellectual feminist genealogies producing "woman/women."

27. "Women Respond to Racism: A Report on the National Women's Studies Association Conference, Storrs, Connecticut" (Oakland: Center for Third World Organizing, n.d. [1982]). A revised version is reprinted in Gloria Anzaldúa, *Making Face, Making Soul: Haciendo Caras, Creative and Critical Perspectives by Women of Color* (San Francisco: Aunt Lute 1990), 55–71.

28. See Shelley Anderson, *Out in the World: International Lesbian Organizing* (Ithaca, N.Y.: Firebrand, 1991); International Lesbian and Gay Association, *Second ILGA Pink Book* (Utrecht: Interfacultaire Werkgroep Homostudies, 1988).

29. Sandoval writes, "U.S. feminists of color, insofar as they involved themselves with the 1970s white women's liberation movement, were also enacting one or more of the ideological positionings just outlined, but rarely for long, and rarely adopting the kind of fervid belief systems and identity politics that tend to accompany their construction under hegemonic understanding. This unusual affiliation with the movement was variously interpreted as disloyalty, betrayal, absence, or lack: 'When they *were* there, they were rarely there for long' went the usual complaint, or 'they seemed to shift from one type of women's group to another.' They were the mobile (yet ever present in their 'absence') members of this particular liberation movement. It is precisely the significance of this mobility which most inventories of oppositional ideology cannot register" ("U.S. Third World Feminism," 14).

30. This is my paraphrase of the kinds of repetitive critiques of postmodern politics I hear repeatedly. Some of these are also drawn explicitly and implicitly from the Gordon-Scott debate.

PART TWO

Reproductive Agendas

Reproductive Technologies and the Negotiation of Public Meanings: The Case of Baby M

VALERIE HARTOUNI

By the time Bergen County Judge Harvey Sorkow handed down his ruling upholding the surrogate agreement in the so-called "Baby M" case, much of the drama that had suffused the seven-week trial had been spent. For weeks, major newspapers had featured pictures of Baby Stern/Whitehead being passed from birth mother to biological father with state troopers near at hand to ensure an orderly transfer. Often accompanying these pictures were character sketches and lengthy life histories of the principle players to the dispute. The viewing public had been invited "to contemplate with anguish the constant pressures and conflicts the baby would confront throughout her growing years"[1] and to consider which of the two families seemed best able to provide for this child, who, experts claimed, would eventually suffer some kind of psychological trauma no matter how the dispute was resolved. Was it in the best interest of "Baby M" to be placed with a family of stable, mutually supportive, educationally motivated professionals, living "private, quiet, unremarkable lives"; or could the full range of her anticipated needs be met by high school dropouts, the one a sanitation engineer, alcoholic, and subordinate male, the other, a former stripper with dyed hair and suicidal tendencies?

By the time Judge Sorkow issued his landmark decision giving sole custody of the child to the unremarkable Sterns, the commercial practice of "surrogate motherhood" was under close and critical scrutiny in a variety of arenas. Hearings had been scheduled in state legislatures across the land to assess the status and commercial aspects of such agreements and to begin consideration of other, similarly "novel" forms of reproductive technology which, like surrogacy, existed in "legal limbo." Juvenile-rights attorneys had begun to assess the implications of "biomedical advances" for laws on adoption, custody, and parental rights, and public policy analysts to call for stricter guidelines and tighter regulation of what, upon closer inspection, looked like "bucks for babies" deals. Journalists had reviewed the "disturbing" challenges such advances posed for American society, while psychiatrists pondered, scholars wrestled, and women's rights activists marched—some specifically on behalf of Mary Beth Whitehead's natural, "maternal" claims, others to draw attention to the continued degradation and oppression of women, reflected in the twisted character of the proceedings, and the specious testimony of "expert" witnesses regarding Whitehead's alleged personality disorders.[2] The issues were many and confused, the conventional understandings and assumptions, destabilized. If the proliferation and deployment of new reproductive technologies had "brought society to the brink of something almost like the atomic bomb," as the former president of the British Medical Association, Sir John Peel, put it, "Baby M" seemed clearly to indicate the first sign of serious fallout.[3]

It had not been entirely unexpected. In a case that preceded the Baby M trial and concerned the brokering of surrogate agreements, the Kentucky Supreme Court had cautioned that surrogacy and other "novel" solutions to infertility offered by advances in biomedical science were ushering in a confusing "new era of genetics." Earlier in the decade, Doris J. Freed, head of the American Bar Association's family law section, had likewise warned that the deployment of these new technologies would provoke a "moral, social and legal nightmare."[4] Judge Harvey Sorkow, then, seemed merely to be echoing these widely held sentiments when he observed in his ruling that reproductive science and technique, while presenting "awesome opportunities," were rapidly outpacing society's ability to cope with them in a coherent, effective fashion. Indeed, so technically exceptional was the phenomenon of "surrogate mothering," Judge Sorkow maintained, and so distinctive were the family forms beginning to emerge from it, that no existing law pertaining to adoption, custody, or the termination of parental rights could be considered applicable or relevant to resolving the dispute. What lay before the judge, as he apparently saw it, was unsettled legal frontier. Upon this frontier, his would be one of the first flags raised, and raise it he did in the name of the father: "[B]ut for him there would be no child," wrote Sorkow. "The biological father pays the surrogate for her willingness to be impregnated and carry his child to term. At birth, the father does not purchase the child. . . . He cannot purchase what is already his."[5]

Sorkow's efforts to settle the legal bush were undone within a year when the New Jersey Supreme Court reversed many of his findings upon appeal. While acknowledging surrogacy's novelty as a reproductive arrangement, the court moved to resituate the practice within the framework of existing state law and public policy, arguing that its principle objective was "to achieve adoption through private placement." Read in the idiom of adoption, surrogate arrangements entailing payment appeared to the court to be a form of baby-selling—"illegal, perhaps criminal, and potentially degrading to women."[6] Also recast with this shift was the surrogate contract or "prebirth agreement" delimiting the terms of collaboration between a "surrogate" and "commissioning couple" and providing specifically for the termination of a surrogate's parental rights and claims. Such agreements, the court maintained, were coercive and unenforceable. In private-placement adoption as well as adoption through an approved agency "the formal agreement to surrender occurs only *after* birth . . . , and then, by regulation, only after the birth mother has been counseled."[7] Invoking what it took to be settled interpretation of New Jersey law, the court contended that surrender of custody and consent to present one's issue for adoption were only rarely irrevocable: indeed, when rescinded early enough, such agreements were generally considered irrelevant. Finally, and perhaps most significant, the court maintained that surrender of custody and consent to adoption were binding only when both were made "knowingly, voluntarily, and deliberately," or in a manner, it argued, that neither could be in the case of surrogacy, given the terms and circumstances likely to accompany any prebirth agreement.[8] "Under the contract, the natural mother is irrevocably committed before she knows the strength of her bond with her child. She never makes a totally voluntary, informed decision, for quite clearly any decision prior to the baby's birth is, in the most important sense uninformed, and any decision after that, compelled by a pre-existing contractual commitment, the threat of a lawsuit, and the inducement of a $10,000 payment, is less than totally voluntary."[9]

Whereas Judge Sorkow had sought to stabilize destabilized practices, relationships, and identities through an act of founding—offering, as we will see in more detail shortly, an account of origins resonant of the story that the ancient Greek playwright Aeschylus tells in the *Oresteia* of the "original" founding—the New Jersey

Supreme Court looked instead to conventional legal categories, cultural values, and public standards. In contrast to Sorkow, who, in their words, "had assumed [he] was writing on a clean slate," the higher court seemed to assume that it could merely read from one, already given and inscribed;[10] and yet, such matters are hardly so simple. Just as there are no clean slates upon which a court might simply write—no empty cultural spaces, no unclaimed, uncontested, or uncontestable fields of meaning—there are no plain slates from which a court might plainly read. Paraphrasing James Boyd White, legal texts are never "simply" read, they are always only read in the context of their making.[11] To "read" such a text is simultaneously to make it and, through it, a world; to read is to (re)configure social reality and relations or, in the case of surrogacy and the higher court's ruling specifically, to suture precisely those categories, identities, and relations rent by the practice.

If we situate the two rulings in the Baby M case side by side, we can see some striking similarities in the world that each produces even while the set of stories each ruling tells in the process of producing that world appears on the surface to be dramatically different. The world Judge Sorkow "founds" beyond the present boundaries of law—a world organized and naturalized in terms of male prerogative—is the world which the New Jersey Supreme Court, positioned within these boundaries, "recovers" in the name of natural motherhood and maternal yearning. Sorkow ruled in the name of the father and the supreme court on behalf of the mother, but natural motherhood, traditionally at least, has presupposed a world of male prerogative or one in which paternal rights, while not absolute, are certainly primary.

The higher court, then, did not so much turn back Sorkow's findings as reframe them—and the difference is significant. Indeed, what I want to insist is that both rulings are equally constitutive, both are sites for the production of cultural meaning, both (re)consolidate cultural meaning even as they also simultaneously produce it. When Sorkow declares himself to be on uncharted legal terrain, the constitutive quality of his ruling is somewhat more apparent than when the supreme court finds for the "natural mother" and roots this finding in settled interpretation of New Jersey law. In fact, it is precisely because Sorkow's ruling is so obviously constitutive of a world without women that it must be turned back at least ostensibly.[12] Following Foucault's insight, power operates effectively only to the extent that it can hide its own operation, and this is what Sorkow fails to do in rendering Baby M a "technobaby" of purely paternal origins.[13] And yet, in finding on behalf of the "natural mother," the supreme court's ruling is no less constitutive than Sorkow's; through a series of rhetorical moves, it stabilizes the notion of motherhood as natural and the biological discourse that grounds it as well as male prerogative. The ruling also simultaneously (re)constructs this notion of motherhood or circumscribes and naturalizes the social practices and relations that constitute what is called "mother" even while it appears only to be recovering it. Conventional understandings of what constitutes "motherhood" are, after all, precisely what new reproductive practices and surrogacy specifically, partial as well as gestational, have denaturalized, demystified, and thus thoroughly destabilized. Recovering the "natural mother" entails, *inter alia*, re-covering—reconstituting as natural precisely what these new practices have revealed to be historically contingent and conditioned by relations of power.

"In every opinion," writes James Boyd White, "a court not only resolves a particular dispute one way or another, it validates or authorizes one form of life . . . or another."[14] The reading that I proffer in this essay of the original ruling in the Baby M case as well as the subsequent ruling that overturned it shares in this sense that the making of law is also the making of life—that law is not a neutral, disinterested, or discrete area of activity set apart from social practices and relations, but a politics or site of struggle, the means by which "one form of life" is authorized and codified against other forms and through both is constructed. Each ruling in the case of Baby M marks a particularly revealing instance of authorization and construction. A close scrutiny of both cases allows us to see not only how law simultaneously repairs and mystifies the relations of power that constitute "mother," "father," and "family" in the wake of their rupture while also constructing these contested relations. It also allows us to see the ways in which the move to contain the proliferation of interpretive possibility is most centrally about containing the political possibility such proliferation necessarily forces open.

When Mary Beth Whitehead enrolled as a potential surrogate at the Infertility Center of New York in 1982, she assumed at least initially that she would function only as a host for someone else's genetic material.[15] When Bill Stern contacted the center some two years later in pursuit of biological offspring, he too assumed that the reproductive collaboration he was about to engage in would entail intricate biomedical maneuverings rather than sophisticated legal ones.[16] However, the procreative alternative that produced Baby M—"traditional surrogacy" as it is now called[17]—required no real medical expertise and nothing more sophisticated, remarkable, or technologically exceptional than masturbation and the use of a syringe. Whitehead contributed an egg to Bill Stern's reproductive effort and was artificially inseminated with his sperm—but only after she had signed a maternity contract that suspended her parental claims to any child who might be produced as a result of the insemination and which held that this suspension was in the child's best interest. The truly novel feature of their procreative collaboration had little to do with the much-valorized efforts of medical science to negotiate the "reproductive imperative." The procedure that produced Baby M was legal rather than medical and designed to remedy issues of legitimacy and infidelity or potential malfunctions in the social body rather than perceived malfunctions in the physical one.

This important and obvious point was, if not lost on New Jersey Superior Court Judge Harvey Sorkow, certainly buried by him in the opening pages of his decision. In these pages, Judge Sorkow inscribes as a matter of fact a set of popular fictions that were iterated throughout the 1980s regarding infertility and part of the decade's deeply conservative pronatalist and racist agenda with respect to reproduction.[18] Insofar as the construction of facts and the construction of law are mutually constitutive enterprises,[19] the judge's preamble not only frames the case of Baby M but tells us something about the terms in which it will be settled. Thus he begins, for reasons having largely to do with lifestyle, "large segments of our potential childbearing population" are now unable to fulfill "their intense drive to procreate naturally."[20] This, together with "a dearth of adoptable children," has forced ever-increasing numbers of individuals to seek the assistance of medical science with its ever-expanding arsenal of new conceptive techniques.[21] According to the judge, these new techniques—and he includes "surrogate mothering" among them—provide the infertile with what may be the only truly viable means now available for obtaining a family, even while this form of "family" may itself be distinctly new and undefined. As Sorkow presents it, the rapid advance of reproductive science and technique has given society opportunities that are both "awesome" and as yet only partially realized. Whether these opportunities fully evolve ultimately depends, in his view, upon the judiciary's willingness to define and direct the world they force open.[22]

Judge Sorkow's preamble presents the phenomenon of infertility as a seamless and self-evident reality. However, when infertility is read against a somewhat different social text, the "constitutive" quality of this reality becomes clear. Consider the court's observation that infertility is affecting an ever-broader segment of society and the claim that gives this observation prescriptive force, that procreation is a biological necessity—a "drive that exists within the soul of all men and women"—and that those unable to realize it are both dysfunctional and desperate. Presented in this way, "infertility" establishes the need for the new conceptive technologies and legitimates their use; indeed, their necessity and legitimacy are placed beyond question. But there are other angles from which to view the phenomenon, and, seen from these angles, infertility assumes a considerably different profile. It is the case, for example, that the actual rate of infertility in the United States has remained relatively constant over the last two decades.[23] What has changed, particularly in the last ten years, is the expansion of possibilities for treatment, and much about the sudden appearance of an epidemic of infertility seems clearly related to the aggressive marketing of these treatments, themselves still experimental and of disputed effectiveness. It is also the case that incidences of infertility are one and a half times higher among poorer, nonwhite populations than in middle-class white ones, or higher in precisely those "segments of our society" in whom medical science appears to have the least interest and who, in any event, have the least access to its assistance. Contrary to the court's inference, moreover, infertility is attributable not only or even primarily to delayed childbearing, but to a diverse combination of social and iatrogenic factors: environmental pollution, exposure to hazardous toxins in the workplace, and unsafe working conditions, in addition to inadequate health care provisions and sterilization abuse. Finally, the "dearth" of adoptable children, which the court links to widespread abortion and contraception use, speaks only to the availability of "healthy" white infants.

What these "details" allow us to see is the way in which "infertility" is itself a contestable composition of specific and even predictable interests. The judge proffers an account that establishes the need for the new conceptive technologies, including surrogacy—they are "medical treatments" for a "medical condition"—while also featuring the novelty of these technologies. Surrogacy is about new science; new science is about a new world—not yet Huxley's *Brave New World*, in the judge's view, but new forms of life, relationship, and identity, the meanings of which have yet to be determined.[24] In other words, through his account of infertility and the rapid advances of science to treat it, Judge Sorkow has positioned himself and the case before him at the border of extant law and a new frontier. Arguing that the former is inadequate to the task of settling the latter—that law cannot inhabit a world its makers could not imagine and for which it was not intended—the judge crosses this border, thereby placing himself beyond the bounds of charted legal terrain: "It is submitted that at the time that even the most current adoption laws were adopted, no thought or consideration was given to the law's effect or relevance to surrogacy. . . . To make a new concept fit into an old statute makes tortured law with equally tortured results."[25]

Thus, Judge Sorkow is Columbus at Guanahani, the Pilgrims at Plymouth, Perry at the Pole. He will bring definition and order to the frontier that is reproductive technology and, like those before him, his first gesture is an act of extended nomination. He issues a deed of possession; he claims this new land in the name of the father. Listen again to the judge's declaration: "[B]ut for him there would be no child," he writes. "The biological father pays the surrogate for her willingness to be impregnated and carry his child to term. At birth, the father does not purchase the child. . . . He cannot purchase what is already his."[26] Arguing in effect that the technobaby that is Baby M is born of the father's blood and scientific ingenuity, and only incidentally of a surrogate's/mother's/woman's body, Judge Sorkow (re)invents paternity. This should not especially surprise us given that paternity has traditionally been regarded as the cornerstone of culture; and culture, new forms of relationship and identity, are precisely what the judge understands himself to be founding in the wake of reproductive science and technique.[27] Still, the irony of this founding moment is considerable, particularly if we situate Judge Sorkow's declaration against the story that the ancient Greek playwright Aeschylus tells in the *Oresteia* of the "original" founding, the founding of the law court of the Areopagus and thus of a new civilized and civilizing community of men, the founding, indeed, of Western culture.

In the *Eumenides*, the third play of the trilogy that makes up the *Oresteia*, Aeschylus celebrates the creation of a new civic order and vividly stages as part of that creation a dream that the classicists Jean-Pierre Vernant and Pierre Videl-Naquet argue never ceased to haunt the Greek imagination. This is the dream of a purely paternal heredity, of a world if not without women then one in which women are both controlled and contained.[28] The drama opens at the temple of Delphi where the chief protagonist of the play, Orestes, has fled in hopes of enlisting the help of the god Apollo. Orestes has slain his mother, Clytemnestra, to avenge the death of his father, King Agamemnon. Although Orestes has acted by divine decree, he is nevertheless pursued by the Furies or Eumenides, female goddesses of an older age who champion the claims of blood-ties, in this case Clytemnestra's claims, and who demand retribution for the matricide that Orestes has committed. The Furies surround him at Delphi, but with the aid of both Apollo and Hermes, Orestes is able to steal away and journeys to Athens where he appeals to Athena for absolution. Arguing that the case is too difficult for a single person to judge, Athena establishes a court of law and seats jurors to hear the dispute. The Eumenides contend that Orestes must give back blood for the mother-blood he has spilled. Orestes's defender, Apollo, dismisses their claims, arguing that the maternal blood bond is insignificant: "since the active regenerating function is exclusively male . . . maternal blood can never run in the veins of the son."[29] "The mother is no parent of that which is called her child, but only nurse of the new-planted seed that grows. The parent is he who mounts. A stranger she preserves a stranger's seed, if no god interfere."

Having asserted the procreative primacy of the father, Apollo moves to establish the truth of his assertion by reminding his audience of the parentage of Athena, the goddess who was born not of woman but of the head of Zeus: "I will show you proof of what I have explained. There can be a father without a mother. There she stands, the living witness, daughter of Olympian Zeus, she who was never fostered in the dark of the womb yet such a child as no goddess could bring to birth." Sperm was thought by the ancients to originate in the brain or head of men and, thus, to be a substance of mind, pure logos or reason.[30] Generated solely of mind, Athena herself represents its uncorrupted embodiment—she personifies reason and stands, by her own account, "always for the male." When the jurors' votes tie, she casts her ballot in favor of Orestes, thereby absolving him of the matricide.[31]

In founding order on the new frontier that is reproductive science, Judge Sorkow simply restages the apollonic fantasy of reproduction with Baby M herself the living witness that "there can be a father without a mother." The technobaby that is Baby M is born of surrogacy or, as we have seen, what the judge (mis)identified in the opening pages of his ruling as a new reproductive technique. She is the "brain-child" of late twentieth-century ingenuity, the personification of reason, the embodiment of rational choice, all of which are commonly regarded as the hallmark of reproductive science. Like

Athena, who was born from the head of Zeus, Baby M springs from the head of the man-god scientist and thus is also "a child as no [woman] could bring forth." The judge's findings suggest, indeed, that for all practical purposes no woman did bring this technobaby forth—for at birth, the court contended, Baby M had neither mother nor family.[32]

The yearning that produced Baby M—according to Judge Sorkow, the procreative drive—was Bill Stern's, not Mary Beth Whitehead's; male procreative desire is, after all, precisely what traditional surrogacy is deployed to facilitate, even while it is presented in popular discourse as something women do for other women. "But for him there would be no child," which is to say, sperm and sperm alone is the active or creative force and as such ensures right of access and ultimately of ownership—women themselves cannot hire a surrogate.[33] While Whitehead may have been related genetically to Baby M, her relationship, as the judge construed it, was from the beginning provisional and revocable by virtue of the contract she had signed. By virtue of this contract, her relationship could be neither meaningful nor maternal in any traditionally rendered sense of the word, given that "mothers"—or rather, "fit" mothers—do not sell their children or sell their bodies for breeding purposes. Whitehead was a surrogate or instrument of science, "a stranger [who] preserve[d] a stranger's seed," a "viable vehicle" for the fulfillment of what Judge Sorkow argued in the end was Stern's constitutionally protected right to procreate.[34] Indeed, in the end, "[Whitehead's] rights could be terminated because, as she had never really been the baby's mother, they had never existed."[35] She was someone who had made a deal—and broken it.

Positioned on the new frontier of reproductive science and beyond the bounds of charted legal terrain, Judge Sorkow's task as he understood it was to found new forms of life, relationship, and identity. What the judge did at this moment of founding was suture precisely that form of life and precisely those relationships and identities rent by surrogacy's deconstruction of the biological discourses grounding and legitimating conventional understandings of motherhood and family. In response to the discursive and material disorder produced by the radical transformation of reproductive practices and processes, Judge Sorkow (re)invented paternity or paternal law; through the warm, sensitive, humane, and victimized figure of Bill Stern, he naturalized and sentimentalized what is a form of life or a set of social relations and practices rather than simply or even primarily a physiological relationship. At this founding moment,

Judge Sorkow also (re)composed a corresponding form of family, organized around male prerogative and presupposed by it. Out of a novel reproductive arrangement he constructed an utterly conventional one—a good, "old-fashioned," two-parent, economically self-sufficient, "American" family, with Bill Stern, the kindly paternal provider, and Betsy Stern, the legally "naturalized" mother, a pediatrician who would curtail her career to meet the infant's special needs and whose earnings, according to the court, would "supplement the family economy."[36] The techno–Baby M would live a privileged life in a suburban home. She would grow up with the "opportunity for music lessons and athletics. . . , attend college . . . , [receive] professional counseling as required" and live, along with her parents, "a quiet, private, unremarkable life."[37] Such was the "new" world Judge Sorkow found on the frontier of reproductive science and technique—and the world that the New Jersey Supreme Court reconsolidated and reinscribed while ostensibly reversing Sorkow's findings upon appeal.

The Supreme Court of New Jersey invalidated the surrogacy contract between Bill Stern and Mary Beth Whitehead, arguing that when surrogacy for payment was situated within the framework of existing state law and public policy, the practice constituted a form of baby-selling. Stern had paid for a product rather than a process— he had "purchased a child, or at the very least, a mother's right to her child."[38] The record with respect to such transactions or the commodification of labor, love, and life—a record the court presented as historical and legal as well as moral—was, in its view, absolutely clear; yet, as I suggested earlier, in "reading" the record, the court was also simultaneously engaged in producing it. Like Sorkow, the higher court moved to restabilize the social relations and practices surrogacy disturbs and to found order in the wake of its disruption. In a manner reminiscent also of Sorkow, it did both through the telling of an ideologically familiar but no less constitutive tale of origins—a tale that sutures the biological and social or finds in natural bonds the basis for social ones. "In a civilized society," the court began,

> [t]here are some things . . . that money cannot buy. . . . In America, we decided long ago that merely because conduct purchased by money was "voluntary" did not mean that it was good or beyond regulation and prohibition. . . . Employers can no longer buy labor at the lowest price they can bargain for, even though that labor is "voluntary" . . . , or buy women's labor for less money than is paid to men for the same

job . . . , or purchase the agreement of children to perform oppressive labor . . . , or purchase the agreement of workers to subject themselves to unsafe or unhealthful working conditions. . . . There are, in short, values that society deems more important than granting to wealth whatever it can buy, be it labor, love, or life.[39]

This passage provides a rich account of ongoing social and political struggle reconfigured, however, by the court as "history" and condensed into a tale of collective moral restraint and mastery over the drives and desires of capital. In a "civilized" society or what is called "America," meaning and value are stable; they are also stabilizing forces governing capital and restraining it from whence it would otherwise boldly go: babies are not commodities for sale nor women merely sites for their production as commercial surrogacy would render each. But also contained in this passage is another kind of origins story, submerged but related to the dominant tale the court tells, having to do with natural motherhood and maternal yearning. For in the works of classical liberal theorists and critics alike, what tames and contains capital and makes possible a civil and civilizing community is the bond between mother and child.[40] This bond has traditionally been regarded as the original site of community— the prepolitical basis of collective life as well as the natural or constitutive basis for all social and moral relations. Characterized by the New Jersey Supreme Court in a subsequent section of its ruling as a force whose strength is second only to that of survival, it is, in the end, what permits us to become persons capable of treating other persons as ends rather than instruments.

In its ode to the birth of a civilized nation, the supreme court (re)establishes social order not only by (re)grounding that order in nature or the maternal bond, but by reinscribing, through that grounding, a thoroughly gendered division between public and private spheres, activities, and identities. Indeed, what the court founds is a world that is organized around and to sustain male prerogative and paternal right—a world in which there is a public sphere of contract and market relations, of labor, exchange, calculation, distribution, and exploitation, conventionally defined as the world of equal and autonomous men, and a so-called private sphere of the family.[41] Traditionally regarded as the natural foundation of social life, the private sphere is, of course, where women, as guardians of order and morality, have been situated in the service of things concrete, particular, and bodily, as well as the family's male head. It is where women have engaged in their "distinctive" and "legitimate" life-giving and preserving work, the unpaid work of childbearing and rearing that they are said to be fitted by nature to perform and whose performance has traditionally rendered them economically disadvantaged and dependent, subordinate, and, at least within classical liberal discourse, unfit for public life.

The court's founding tale recovers both the maternal bond or a conception of motherhood as something instinctual, natural, and ahistorical as well as the world this bond presupposes and produces, "an institutional arrangement that is widely held to be one, if not the, linchpin of women's subordination."[42] It also reinvents the conception it recovers insofar as the process of recovery is simultaneously and necessarily one of construction. In recuperating "natural motherhood," the court rebiologizes motherhood or naturalizes what surrogacy in particular and new reproductive practices more generally reveal as a thoroughly social and historically specific set of relations, constructed and conditioned by power. It (re)assembles and thus stabilizes conventional meanings of "motherhood" that surrogate practices dissemble by forcing deliberation with respect to whether the "real" mother is the contractual mother, the genetic mother, or the gestational mother. As Teresa de Lauretis argues with respect to gender—its construction "goes on as busily today as it did in earlier times"—so too obviously with "motherhood."[43] In recuperating "natural motherhood," the court authorizes and codifies as well as constructs against other possible meanings, practices, or formations who and what will count as "mother": Elizabeth Stern is the naturalized mother, but Mary Beth Whitehead is the authentic or natural one.

Having recovered "natural motherhood" in the process of determining the status of commercial surrogacy, the court moved next in its judgment to instantiate it in the figure of Mary Beth Whitehead. Arguing that she had been harshly appraised by Sorkow as well as by some of the experts called upon to evaluate her mental and emotional stability, the higher court ruled that Whitehead's claims to the child she had borne—her genetic and gestational contribution—were equal in every respect to Stern's as the natural father. Although she had lied on numerous occasions and broken the law on numerous counts, breached a contract, and reneged on "a very important promise," she had acted, in the court's estimation, as any "natural" mother would have acted if forced to surrender her newborn. "[W]e think it is expecting something well beyond normal human capabilities to suggest that this mother should have parted with her newly born infant without a struggle. Other than survival, what stronger force is there? We do not know of, and cannot conceive of, any other case where a perfectly fit mother was expected to surrender her newly born infant, perhaps forever, and was then told she was a bad mother because she did not."[44]

Determining that Baby M's "parents were, and were to remain, her two biological parents,"[45] the court reconfigured the dispute between Stern and Whitehead as one regarding custody. It settled that dispute by awarding primary custody of the child to Stern. Although Whitehead was the "real" mother, Stern was the "real" and preferred parent. This judgment was perfectly consistent with the logic of the ruling's subtext regarding natural motherhood and so too was its basis. While willing to grant her visitation rights, the court refused Whitehead's bid for custody, citing precisely the same "evidence" or "expert opinion" that Sorkow had deployed in the process of erasing maternity and which the higher court had rejected as harsh when restoring it. Sorkow had characterized Whitehead as manipulative, impulsive, irrational, irresponsible, narcissistic, domineering, and uneducated and concluded that such a woman "could not be an impressive mother in general, or in particular, a good mother to Baby M."[46] While the higher court argued that Whitehead had been if not a "good" mother, certainly a fit one—she had yearned for her newly born infant and struggled when forced to part with it— they nevertheless joined Sorkow in the conclusion that her personality would impede the child's growth. "[W]hile love and affection there would be, Baby M's life with the Whiteheads promise[s] to be too closely controlled by Mrs. Whitehead. The prospects for wholesome, independent psychological growth and development w[ill] be at serious risk. . . . [T]he evidence and expert opinion based on it reveal personality characteristics that might threaten the child's best development."[47] In the view of the court, the kind of life that would best meet the full range of Baby M's many and special needs would be provided by her "natural" father and his wife, or as they were described by the court, the loving, giving, nurturing, rational, open-minded, and financially secure Sterns. It was the Sterns who appeared to the court to approximate most closely what is called "family" and the Sterns who were once again constituted as such.[48]

Both rulings in the case of Baby M represent moments of instability and invention in the production of cultural meaning. Indeed, as we have seen, both rulings create and contain the social relations and practices that constitute what is called mother, father, and family in the wake of their rupture. Both contest for a world forced open, discursively as well as politically, by the radical transformation of reproductive practices and processes. Finally, both rulings stage the possibility—even as they also seek to foreclose it—of naming and figuring new forms of life, relationship, and identity. If the Superior and Supreme Courts of New Jersey produce the seemingly always already made—and much of this essay has been devoted to mapping the process of this production—then clearly what is made can and must be made differently. As Jana Sawicki observes, "although the new reproductive technologies . . . threaten to reproduce and enhance existing power relations, they also introduce new possibilities for disruption and resistance";[49] they represent new forms and practices of life that weaken the alibi of other forms and practices and place their terms at issue.

To exploit these possibilities positively, we must proceed on several fronts, mapping the unarticulated theoretical underpinnings and shifting complexities of contemporary reproductive contests and controversies. We must also generate concrete strategies of address that work to cultivate and expand the shifting field of political openings that produce and are produced by these contests. As the new and, in the case of surrogacy, ostensibly new reproductive technologies are further developed and deployed, an already high-stakes struggle between opposing social forces over the reorganization of the processes and practices of contemporary life will only intensify. There are no guarantees that efforts to interrupt or transform this reorganization will not be cannibalized by the dominant structures that shape them—no guarantees and no definitive programs or settlements that might function as such. Nevertheless, these efforts mark the nascent figurings of alternative worlds—a possible elsewhere—that are contained within but are counter to the world presently being (re)produced in and through rulings like the ones handed down in the case of Baby M.

NOTES

I offer this essay in memory of Jaye Miller, a committed teacher, activist, and knowing friend who died in August 1991 of an AIDS-related illness. Jaye walks in the world now through the steps of others, but I miss him still.

1. *New York Times*, 18 February 1988, 1.
2. "In re Baby M," N.J. Superior Court, Bergen County, 31 Mar. 1987, 58–62.
3. *Time*, 10 Sept. 1984, 55.
4. Ibid., 54.

5. "In re Baby M," 103, 71.

6. "Baby M," N.J. Supreme Court, 537 A.2D 1227 and 1234.

7. Ibid., 537 A.2D and 1240.

8. Ibid., 537 A.2D and 1246.

9. Ibid., 537 A.2D and 1248.

10. Ibid., 537 A.2D and 1238.

11. James Boyd White, *Justice as Translation: An Essay in Cultural and Legal Criticism* (Chicago: University of Chicago Press, 1990), 135.

12. I am not suggesting that the world Sorkow's ruling produces is one in which there are literally no women; it is rather a world in which women do not count in any substantive sense. Within the logic of paternity, women function only as a natural medium for life, as soil for the seed. For a provocative discussion of these issues see Carol Delaney, "The Meaning of Paternity and the Virgin Birth Debate," *Man* 21 (1986): 494–513.

13. Michel Foucault, *History of Sexuality Vol. 1* (New York: Vintage, 1980), 86. Foucault also writes: "We must make allowance for the complex and unstable process whereby discourse can be both an instrument and an effect of power, but also a hindrance, stumbling-block, a point of resistance and a starting point for an opposing strategy. Discourse transmits and produces power; it reinforces it, but also undermines and exposes it, renders it fragile and makes it possible to thwart it" (101).

14. White, *Justice as Translation*, 101.

15. Mary Beth Whitehead with Loretta Schwartz-Nobel, *A Mother's Story* (New York: St. Martin's, 1989), 7.

16. "In re Baby M," 28.

17. With traditional surrogacy, a surrogate "donates" an egg to the reproductive efforts of a commissioning couple and is genetically related to the child she gestates. With gestational surrogacy, a surrogate is hired to gestate an embryo that has been fertilized in vitro and surgically implanted. She bears no genetic relationship to the child that she produces.

18. I develop this reading at greater length in "Containing Women: Reproductive Discourse in the 1980's," in *Technoculture*, ed. Andrew Ross and Constance Penley (Minneapolis: University of Minnesota Press, 1991), 27–56.

19. Kim Lane Scheppele, "Facing Facts in Legal Interpretation," *Representations* 30 (Spring 1990): 60.

20. "In re Baby M," 13–15.

21. Ibid., 13, 14.

22. Ibid., 16.

23. Hartouni, "Containing Women," 46–47.

24. "In re Baby M," 15.

25. Ibid., 71, 108; and elsewhere in the ruling, "Use of laws not intended for their intended purpose creates forced and confusing results" (74).

26. Ibid., 103, 71.

27. For ruminations on "paternity," see Thomas W. Laqueur, "The Facts of Fatherhood," in *Conflicts in Feminism*, ed. Marianne Hirsch and Evelyn Fox Keller (New York: Routledge, 1990), 205–21.

28. Jean-Pierre Vernant, *Myth and Thought among the Greeks* (London: Routledge, 1983), 134. See also Pierre Videl-Naquet, "Aeschylus, the Past and the Present," in *Myth and Tragedy in Ancient Greece*, ed. Jean-Pierre Vernant and Pierre Videl-Naquet (New York: Zone Books, 1988), 266, and Froma Zeitlin, "The Dynamics of Misogyny: Myth and Mythmaking in the Oresteia," *Arethusa* 11 (1978): 149–77.

29. Vernant, *Myth and Thought*, 134.

30. G. E. R. Lloyd, ed., *Hippocratic Writings*, trans. J. Chadwick and W. N. Mann (New York: Penguin, 1978), 317–20. Also, Aristotle, *Generation of Animals*, trans. A. L. Peck (Cambridge, Mass.: Harvard University Press, 1979), 103–13; and Plato, *Timaeus*, trans. Desmond Lee (New York: Penguin, 1977), 122–24. Zeitlin elaborates, "The major component of semen is *pneuma*, a foamlike airy substance which contains the seed of the divine. Originating in the brain, semen is responsible for endowing offspring with the essential human capacity for reason, for logos. Seed of generation, of intellectual ability, and of the divine element in the human species, semen confirms the innate superiority of male over female." "Dynamics of Misogyny," 169.

31. Aeschylus, *Oresteia*, trans. Richard Lattimore (Chicago: University of Chicago Press, 1953), lines 658–61, 662–66, 736–40.

32. "When Melissa was born on March 27, 1986, there was not attendant to the circumstance of her birth the family gatherings, the family celebrations or the family worship services that usually accompany such a happy family event. . . . In reality, the fact of family was undefined if nonexistent [*sic*]. The mother and father are known but they are not family. The interposition of their spouses will not serve to create family without further court intervention." "In re Baby M," 111.

33. In the view of Judge Sorkow the terms of the surrogacy contract are fixed with conception—in other words, sperm seals the deal: "This court holds . . . , that although the surrogacy contract is signed, the surrogate may nevertheless renounce and terminate the contract until the time of conception. . . . [O]nce conception has occurred the parties are fixed, the terms of the contract are firm and performance will be anticipated with the joy that only a newborn can bring." "In re Baby M," 75.

34. Ibid., 91.

35. Janet L. Dolgin, "Status and Contract in Surrogate Motherhood: An Illumination of the Surrogacy Debate," *Buffalo Law Review* 38, no. 2 (Spring 1990): 538–39.

36. "In re Baby M," 45–46. Janice Doane and Devon Hodges offer a somewhat more thorough discussion of the family form fashioned by Sorkow in "Risky Business: Familial Ideology and the Case of Baby M," *differences* 1, no. 1 (Winter 1989): 67–81.

37. "In re Baby M," 46.

38. "Baby M," 537 A.2D and 1248.

39. Ibid., 537 A.2D and 1249.

40. I am thinking in particular of the arguments proffered by John Stu-

art Mill in *The Subjection of Women*, ed. Sue Mansfield (Arlington Heights, Ill: AHM Publishing, 1980); Mary Wollstonecraft, *A Vindication of the Rights of Women*, ed. Carol H. Poston (New York: Norton, 1975); and Jean-Jacques Rousseau, *Emile*, ed. Allan Bloom (New York: Basic Books, 1979). For a general discussion of gender as text and subtext in liberal discourse, see Carole Pateman, *The Disorder of Women: Democracy, Feminism, and Political Theory* (Stanford: Stanford University Press, 1989); Pateman, *The Sexual Contract* (Stanford: Stanford University Press, 1988); and Jane Rendall, "Virtue and Commerce: Women in the Making of Adam Smith's Political Economy," in *Women in Western Political Philosophy*, ed. Ellen Kennedy and Susan Mendus (Brighton, Eng.: Wheatsheaf, 1987), 44–77.

41. On this division and the ways in which it serves as an elaborate institutional mechanism to both constitute and sustain male prerogative and paternal right, see, in addition to Pateman (previous note), Nancy Fraser, "What's Critical About Critical Theory? The Case of Habermas and Gender," in *Unruly Practices: Power, Discourse and Gender in Contemporary Social Theory* (Minneapolis: University of Minnesota Press, 1989), esp. 127–37; Mary O'Brien, *The Politics of Reproduction* (London: Routledge, 1981); Genevieve Lloyd, *The Man of Reason: "Male" and "Female" in Western Philosophy* (Minneapolis: University of Minnesota Press, 1984); and Anne Phillips, *Engendering Democracy* (Cambridge: Polity Press, 1991).

42. Fraser, "What's Critical About Critical Theory?," 122.

43. Teresa de Lauretis, "The Technology of Gender," in *Technologies of Gender* (Bloomington: Indiana University Press, 1987), 3.

44. "Baby M," 537 A.2D and 1259.

45. Dolgin, "Status and Contract," 540.

46. Ibid., 537.

47. "Baby M," 537 A.2D and 1258, 1260.

48. Lest it seem this argument is overly exercised with respect to the court's findings, see Katharine T. Bartlett, "Re-expressing Parenthood," *Yale Law Journal* 98, no. 2 (1988): "[T]he best interest of the child is a highly contingent social construction. Although we often pretend otherwise, it seems clear that our judgments about what is best for children are as much the result of political and social judgments about what kind of society we prefer as they are conclusions based upon neutral or scientific data about what is 'best' for children. The resolution of conflicts over children ultimately is less a matter of objective fact-finding than it is a matter of deciding what kind of children and families—what kind of relationships—we want to have" (295).

49. Jana Sawicki, *Disciplining Foucault* (New York: Routledge, 1981), 88.

SIX

Cyborgean Motherhood and Abortion

PATRICIA S. MANN

The increasingly global reach of reproductive technologies is undermining a heretofore unquestioned organic identification of women with motherhood. Both contraception and abortion are important components of family planning practices that have become common not simply in the West but throughout the world over the last twenty-five years.[1] As women's reliance upon abortion has grown, however, political opposition and moral reaction have grown apace. Recent abortion controversies in Poland, China, Ireland, Brazil, Germany, and the United States are a multicultural symptom of gender ferment just under the skin of the global body.[2]

The abortion controversy puts the changing quality of women's agency on the line.[3] If there was one social role with which women were universally identified, it was the role of motherhood. It was a sex-specific site of significant social behavior corresponding with diverse sites of significant male behavior. While male public-sphere agency has been associated with notions of rational individual motivation and reward, however, the maternal role of women has been characterized primarily in terms of its onerous obligations and duties. An individual woman might be enthusiastic about becoming a mother, or she might not be. Her generic, womanly desires were inferred from her birth as a woman; her actual individual desires were simply not relevant. She might reap great rewards as a consequence of her performance as a mother, or she might not. Hopes of recognition or reward were not a socially acceptable basis for choosing to mother, as they were a self-evidently necessary basis for male public-sphere activities.

We might be tempted to say that women were denied the most important aspects of agency insofar as their individual desires were not taken into account under traditional patriarchal kinship arrangements.[4] Women were denied independent identities under patriarchy. They typically lived out their lives as subsumed nurturers, unobtrusively supporting the public identities of their husbands and male children. Women and their actions were taken for granted, regardless of the significance of their contribution to the public achievements of the master or husband. Yet women were allowed a sense of participation in the lives of their husbands and families. Socially recognized as bearing the children who would carry on the family name, women were not merely human instruments but were seen by others and by themselves as significant parts of the family whole. In this sense, women exercised maternal and other forms of agency under patriarchy. But the agency of women was not characterized by the individuated choices and rewards accorded to liberal men. It was their individual responsibilities as subsumed nurturers that provided women with a sense of their own importance, and in this specific sense, of their agency.

INTERPERSONAL AGENCY: RETHINKING OUR PARADIGMS OF ACTION

With the social enfranchisement of women, the scope of women's agency changes dramatically, most obviously as they enter the liberal public sphere as economic and political agents alongside men.[5] But the quality of their domestic agency is altered, as well. It is misleading to think of women today as simply augmenting their traditional female role with what was formerly the male role. Neither of the traditional gender roles of subsumed nurturer or patriarchal benefactor survives for very long in the wake of the social enfranchisement of women. Men and women may continue to go through many of the same domestic motions, and so retain the appearances of their former relationship identities. But it is when we evaluate the changing qualities of their still gendered forms of agency that we can mark the magnitude of the transformations taking place.

I believe it is helpful to specify three different dimensions of agency: individual motivations and desires, individual notions of responsibility, and individual expectations of recognition or reward. We attribute agency to an individual if we ascertain that at least one of these dimensions is important in evaluating his or her actions. But not all dimensions are equal in their ability to confer a social identity upon an individual. The oppression of women under Western forms of patriarchy, as well as its current decline, may be tracked quite effectively by taking note of the changing dimensions of agency ascribed to women and men. Under liberal forms of patriarchy, men were understood as the sort of beings capable of choosing their individual destiny, expressing basic material and social desires in individuated ways, and properly seeking particular sorts of social recognition and reward. Women were recognized only for fulfilling subordinate roles in the context of families headed by men; they were not deemed capable of making individuated choices about their own particular destiny or that of their family.

With social enfranchisement, we begin to attribute to women the capacity to make the same sorts of individuated, rational choices about their economic and political destiny as men. Since such choices frequently conflict with traditional maternal obligations, we gradually begin to assume that women will make individuated choices about whether or not to take on the familial responsibilities they were expected to accept unthinkingly under patriarchy. That is, we become interested for the first time in women's particular motivations for becoming wives and mothers. We acknowledge that there may be reasons why a particular woman might choose not to fulfill maternal or domestic responsibilities. We also become interested for the first time in articulating the particular quality of the rewards and forms of recognition attendant upon assuming the maternal role. A more complete notion of maternal agency begins to come into play.[6]

Despite the fact that we now assume the need to understand individual motivations in taking on family obligations, it is not obvious *how* to characterize women's new modalities of agency in relation to the family, or men's for that matter. There is a long tradition of feminist thinkers who have attempted to portray the distinctive quality of women's traditional practices and values within the home.[7] But what we are concerned with here are the practices and values of women and men within the home in a new, nontraditional context of individual familial choice. The controversy over abortion arises in this radically nontraditional context of maternal agency.

Both the inevitability and the inadequacy of analogies with public-sphere motivations and choices are evident in current ways of referring to decisions about whether or not to take on maternal responsibilities. We frequently explain an abortion decision by saying that a pregnancy was "unplanned" or "unwanted," suggesting that children produced under such circumstances would suffer from being "unwanted." Of course, many pregnancies are unwanted, and many children do suffer from lack of attention from their parents. But the phrase summons up thoughts of other wanted and unwanted items in daily life: I want green beans for dinner, and I want it to be sunny tomorrow for the picnic. A child is neither wanted nor unwanted in these terms of immediate daily preference. To speak of a pregnancy or a child as wanted or unwanted is to trivialize the issue a pregnant woman faces when she thinks about whether she has the capacity and the will to devote decades of her life to caring for a child.

Those who oppose abortion believe that women continue to have an unqualified responsibility to become mothers. By contrast, those who believe in the legitimacy of abortion insist that women's maternal responsibilities can now only be articulated in a way that allows for the relevance of women's individual sense of social agency, maternal choice being but one component in such agency. Analogies between the decision of a woman to have an abortion and other sorts of individual choice are typically strained and unconvincing because procreative agency is not very much like the economic and political forms of agency we have most experience in evaluating. We need to begin thinking in terms of a distinctive quality of motivations, obligations, and rewards appropriate to procreative and other familial or communal activities. It may even be appropriate to formulate a specific modality of agency that will conceptualize the common features of the individuated decisions of women and men alike in relation to contemporary kinship and community relationships.

I will thus propose a category of "interpersonal agency," referring to the motivations, responsibilities, and forms of recognition and reward associated with individual efforts to create and maintain affirmative connections with others. I see the advantages of a category of interpersonal agency as two-fold. In the first place, a notion of interpersonal agency will provide the framework for a new paradigm of procreative relationships, enabling us to revise radically our conception of women's maternal agency, and thereby the quality of women's authority to initiate a process like abortion. Secondly, a notion of interpersonal agency asserts a relationship between women's maternal agency and forms of agency exercised more generally by men as well as women in creating and maintaining kinship and community connections.

We can, perhaps, imagine a time not too far off when men and women alike will be able to become pregnant, or alternatively when parturition will take place outside any individual human body. Until that time, pregnancy and the problem of abortion will remain very much women's issues. Decisions about procreation, however, lie on a continuum with decisions about marriage, friendship, parenting, divorce, and a variety of interpersonal connections within workplace and community that have become problematic nodal points in the lives of men and women. A theory of interpersonal agency will help us understand the relationship between procreative decisions and these other issues that are not exclusively attached to women. A notion of interpersonal agency will thus allow us to rethink and revalue an increasingly confusing, gender-, race-, and class-inflected texture of everyday relationships and global practices.[8]

A CYBORGEAN THEORY OF PROCREATIVE AGENCY

In daily life, women increasingly find themselves with both the technical capacity and the social responsibility to decide whether and when and how to have children. As a purely practical matter, they have primary authority for procreative decisions. Yet once a woman becomes pregnant, whether voluntarily or not, religious and naturalistic conceptions of maternal agency imply that she is a participant in an organic process that requires her continued cooperation. She is morally obligated to bring the fetus to term. As a pregnant woman she already has a maternal identity, and her moral authority appears inseparably bound up with her responsibility within a natural process of human reproduction. Insofar as it appears fundamentally unnatural in relation to this process, a pregnant woman's desire to opt out of further maternal participation can easily seem capricious or immoral.

Both women and men who assert that abortion must be an individual woman's right, nonetheless, express moral qualms about abortion. Laurence Tribe assesses the current abortion debate as involving a "clash of absolutes," arguing that most people feel sympathy *both* for the pregnant woman who does not wish to bring a fetus to term and for a fetus that deserves to be protected.[9] Thus women who unexpectedly become pregnant occupy a truly unenviable position: they are destined to choose between the ethically tainted freedom of a rational social agent who has an abortion, and the self-sacrificing goodness of a woman who decides to reconfigure the next eighteen years of her life to accommodate motherhood.

Attempts to justify the abortion decisions of individual women have either emphasized potential conflicts between a woman's political rights over her person and traditional maternal obligations, or they have juxtaposed macroscopic social interests against the traditional maternal obligations of individual women. They have succeeded in making us more sympathetic to the concerns of women who seek abortions, and they have even made some of us self-righteous about believing that women should have abortions in certain circumstances. But they have not provided a sufficient basis for respecting the moral authority and the procreative agency of individual women who choose to abort a fetus. While abortion may be legally defended either in terms of a woman's right to bodily self-defense or in terms of society's interests, it cannot be understood as an act of individual moral agency so long as pregnant women are seen as organically implicated in motherhood.

The problem with both utilitarian and rights-based justifications of abortion is that they attempt to qualify traditional maternal narratives instead of replacing them. Whether a pregnant woman is a willing host or an unwilling hostage, a natural maternal coproducer or an oppressed pregnant laborer, the involuntary quality of her initial participation in maternity is still taken for granted, just as it is in religious narratives that emphasize her absolute maternal responsibility. The problem with justifying a woman's act of abortion today lies with a naturalistic vision of motherhood still implicit in all these narratives.

The philosopher Bernard Williams suggests that the appropriate response to apparently irresolvable moral disagreements is to ask what sorts of "institutions, upbringing, and public discourse" will enable people to feel "ethical confidence" about whatever they choose to do.[10] Williams is perceptive in suggesting that what is needed is a broad-based social reorientation so that women considering abortion can feel confident about whatever decision they finally make. Because naturalistic theories of motherhood are so clearly inadequate for explaining women's current social responsibilities in reproductive matters, we need to reformulate maternal narratives in order to comprehend properly women as procreative agents in a postmodern world. The ethical issue is not about the personhood of the fetus, but about the personhood of women.

I think that a cyborgean analysis of persons will provide the radical shift in perspective we require in order to explain the morality of abortions. Such an analysis will also provide a foundation for the broader effort of rethinking postmodern procreative decisions in such a way as to connect them with other forms of interpersonal agency. Donna Haraway has suggested that we borrow from science fiction the cyborg image of "creatures simultaneously animal and machine, who populate worlds ambiguously natural and crafted," as a means of portraying some of the peculiarities of women's lived experiences in the late twentieth century.[11] One of the most peculiar of these experiences, while also one of the most transformative, as I have tried to show, is women's experience of resorting to various reproductive technologies in order to exercise individual control over the processes of bodily procreation. It may be startling to think of adopting a cyborgean perspective on pregnant women. Yet once we acknowledge the force of Mary O'Brien's argument that the contraceptive revolution makes organic motherhood a thing of the past, we require some radically new conception of maternal agency.[12] I will demonstrate the advantages of a cyborgean analysis of motherhood.

A cyborgean image of persons emphasizes the contemporary breakdown in our once firm sense of the boundaries between our own organic selfhood and the nonorganic machines we increasingly call upon within our everyday activities. Until very recently, we have taken the alien and even alienating qualities of the machinery and technologies we rely upon for granted, their usefulness always bounded by their metallic, clanking lack of ensoulment. The most staunch advocates of the machine age have yet stressed the need vigilantly to maintain human control over whatever artificial intelligences and robotic wonders we may create. In the view of critics, from Luddites and utopian socialists in the nineteenth century to the deep ecologists of today, we must fear for technology's ability to ride roughshod over those aspects of our humanity that we most value.

Yet technology has ceased to be an alien presence in many lives today in the United States. We wake up to the insistent beeping of digital clocks and amiable microwave ovens, slide behind the wheel of a car accompanied by more interactive electronic beeps, and typically maintain intimate aural and physical contact with various technologies throughout a normal day. Moreover, we regularly choose to undergo operations in which our hips, knees, and other organic body parts are removed and replaced with artificial ones. And for most of us who write as a way of life, our personal computer has become our favorite means of accessing our ideas and harnessing our creativity. We describe our relationships to these machines in very peculiar terms, by earlier standards; but these terms express the degree of technological penetration into our personal lives. We gratefully say that artificial hips and knees make us feel "like our old selves again." And after becoming accustomed to writing on a computer, we may express horror at the idea of returning to previous writing practices that may now seem both less effective and less enjoyable.

Are we still in control? Does our dependency upon these machines make us less human? The point of the cyborg image is to suggest that these questions have lost their meaning. These machines make us better able to do the things we most value as individual human beings, and were we forced to give them up we would feel diminished as human beings. This does not deny their quality as machines and technologies. It does imply that we need to rethink our relationship to machines quite radically so as to expunge anti-technological biases that have become hypocritical and misleading, at this point.

The feminist relationship to technology is particularly fraught with confusion. It is important to work out this relationship in the context of the new procreative decisions women and men are called upon to make. Reproductive technologies play an extremely important role in the social enfranchisement of women today. Our relationship with technology is nowhere more intimate or more significant than in our sexual lives. Individually, we may rely upon various sorts of contraceptive technology on a daily basis for decades, abortion providing a safety net for those who find themselves involuntarily plunging toward maternity. We increasingly call upon more esoteric forms of reproductive technology as well, whether as means of enhancing fertility or as means of ensuring the well-being of fetuses prior to birth. Reproductive methods that take place partially or wholly outside the womb or in alternative wombs or womblike structures are developing rapidly.

Our cyborgean dependency upon technology as a normal condition for reproductive decisions has serious implications for how we think about the procreative process. Insofar as the organic conditions for producing a child are interpenetrated with technological and social considerations, children become products of our social decisions in a thoroughgoing sense.[13] In Haraway's political myth, "cyborg replication is uncoupled from organic reproduction." Were this the case for us, it would simplify the analysis. The problems we encounter in this real-life cyborgean moment are often a result of the perplexing entanglement of our old organic relationships with postmodern technological ones. In the case of procreative situations, it seems inappropriate to speak of replication insofar as that implies mechanical multiples of an initial prototype. But the old organic quality of human reproduction is surely dominated today by recent technological procedures and the particular social decisions they make possible and necessary.

If we emphasize the social mediation of both natural and technological processes, I think we have a basis for appropriating Haraway's cyborg mythology for everyday use. One important implication of cyborgean reproduction is that children come to be seen as "social offspring" of many possible procedures and practices in which technology and nature are intermixed inseparably. Unlike Haraway's science-fictional replicants who may do without origin stories altogether, our social offspring are historically specific children, who will surely continue to ask whence they have come. But our answers will refer to the various social decisions that led to a child's birth. It will no longer make sense to think about children in terms of their natural origins. A pregnant mother, for example, will no longer be seen as the natural origin of a child. Even if a particular child is the product of a pregnant mother, she or he will be the social offspring of a decision by this woman, and perhaps others, to produce a child in this fashion. *Mere pregnancy will not be a morally or socially adequate basis for producing a child.* A social offspring must have a properly social point of origin in the conscious decision of one or more persons to raise a child. Mythologies of natural fetal origins remain quite strong today, and antiabortion arguments rely upon them heavily. Such arguments will no longer make sense from a cyborgean perspective. Social offspring are born of acts of interpersonal agency, and only incidentally of women's wombs.

Notice that a cyborgean analysis makes the special parameters of women's reproductive agency quite explicit. So long as the gestation process takes place in a woman's womb, she must have final authority over deciding if and when a gestation will take place. She must be motivated to take on that initial responsibility. An individual woman may choose to give a particular man a role in her decision-making process, of course, particularly if he is willing to commit himself to parental responsibilities after a child is born. Should there come a time when gestation occurs outside a woman's body, the initial interpersonal decision will be shared by those taking responsibility for the development of the child at that point.

FROM FEMINISM TO POSTFEMINISM

I think a cyborgean understanding of reproduction makes a lot of sense today, and I do not see any other way to secure the ethical confidence of women who choose to have abortions than to adopt this postmodern view of procreation. Yet it will not be easy for many people to give up cherished personal visions of natural fetal origins.

I suspect that many feminists may find this cyborgean narrative troubling as well. Feminists have accepted contraceptive technologies quite readily; their potential contribution to the sexual empowerment of women is indisputable. But the organic capacity of women to bear children has provided a sentimental core for an impassioned feminist maternalism.

Twenty-five years ago, a brash young Shulamith Firestone suggested that artificial reproduction was "not inherently dehumanizing" and that it might be part of the solution to women's oppression within the patriarchal family. She pointed out that, "At the very least, development of an option should make possible an honest reexamination of the ancient value of motherhood."[14] Indeed, this was not the sort of examination many second-wave feminists had in mind. A furious outcry arose against Firestone's unsympathetic attitude to motherhood, as well as against earlier feminists such as Simone de Beauvoir who were not overly appreciative of women's capacity to bear children. While the unsubtle romanticization of maternity may have abated recently in feminist theory, there has been no effort to recuperate Firestone. At the point where technology undermines the bodily uniqueness of female procreation, feminism tends to balk.

A skeptical response to various modes of reproductive technology is firmly grounded in feminist political analysis. Within patriarchy, women have been oppressed as mothers; patriarchal institutions of motherhood have transformed a potentially wonderful experience into an unbearable one for many women. In *Of Woman Born*, Adrienne Rich articulates her intense anger in the face of her recognition that she has been alienated from her children and from her own body by patriarchal thinking that has "limited female biology to its own narrow specifications." She emphasizes that women must "repossess their bodies" and struggle for new relationships to their children by destroying patriarchal institutions of motherhood.[15] Reproductive technologies are highly suspect as a recent product of a patriarchal thinking that may defeat this feminist project by extending and strengthening patriarchal control over women's bodies. Barbara Katz Rothman indicts recent medical practices, from sonar womb scanning to surrogacy, for their figurative ability to separate a woman from her body and from the body of her child.[16]

Furthermore, many feminists believe that motherhood has been and continues to be such an important site of female praxis that feminism must extricate it from the patriarchal grasp that has crushed and perverted it, reinstating it as an institution uniquely capable of affirming the social and historical significance of women. In *Maternal Thinking,* Sara Ruddick expresses hope that men will eventually come to participate fully in the "maternal work" of caring for children; and yet she is resolute in her belief that the maternal work of "protecting, nurturing, and training" children should continue to be termed "mothering." Desiring that this historically feminine work may finally transcend gender, Ruddick yet "wants to recognize and honor the fact that even now, and certainly through most of history, women have been the mothers."[17]

Rich, Katz Rothman, and Ruddick provide insightful and provocative responses to the current situation of women; such thinkers represent feminist identity politics at its best. Poststructuralists such as Judith Butler explain very well the dangerous ground such theorists tread in articulating their notions of maternal thinking and motherhood, insofar as such texts are invariably read as imparting universalizable truths (thus falsehoods) about motherhood. Yet the feminist politics of the poet Adrienne Rich and the philosopher Sara Ruddick reflect the experiences of women traumatized by a historically specific institution of motherhood in this country. For much of this century, upper-middle-class women were allowed to pursue the same intellectual preparation as men, yet upon completion of their studies men became poets and philosophers, while women became mothers, with the understanding that as mothers they were disqualified from becoming serious poets or philosophers. Rich and Ruddick, and many other second-wave foremothers of the contemporary era, struggled successfully to demonstrate that patriarchy can no longer dismiss mothers or fail to recognize mother-poets and mother-philosophers. If women in the 1990s decide that it is necessary to develop a politics that conceptualizes the struggle of women somewhat differently, it will be because the experiences of women today, as poets, philosophers, and mothers, are different in significant ways from those of this previous generation of feminists—in large part due to the efforts of these powerful foremothers.

A contemporary feminist strategy needs to adapt itself to an era in which fewer people are willing to become ideologically identified with any political movement, while at the same time many more people are enmeshed in daily gender-based struggles and conflicts. Feminism remains a personal and political origin point for many women today, but with some trepidation I will define abortion as a postfeminist issue.[18] In the first place, abortion politics push us to reach beyond the boundaries of a feminist audience, providing an occasion for us to address a mainstream that is beginning to discover the impact of gendered transformations on its everyday life. A notion of postfeminism signifies a moment when, for better or for worse, feminist concerns have become part of popular culture. I also believe that abortion suggests the need for a theoretical stance that departs significantly from much of classical feminist theory. Cyborgean mothers eschew the sort of maternal identity that has often seemed to lie at the heart of feminist theory. They accept with equanimity the idea that the bodily uniqueness of female procreation may be a historically limited phenomenon, and they locate their sense of maternal agency on a continuum with many other forms of interpersonal agency in which men participate on potentially equal terms. The scope of contemporary reproductive issues leads us beyond solutions articulated in terms of "a female-embodied social subject," to refer to Teresa de Lauretis's recent discussion of the content of any feminist theory.[19]

THE INTERPERSONAL AGENCY OF CYBORGEAN PARENTS

A postfeminist theoretical position attempts to capture the changing quality of our procreative experiences in the context of the more general social process of women's social enfranchisement. Certainly reproductive technologies such as contraception have historically played a contradictory role, at best, in efforts to emancipate women.[20] For so long as we live in a patriarchal society, we will need to remain vigilant against a continuing tendency for medical techniques to be utilized in ways that deprive women of control over their sexual and reproductive lives. Yet there is something very right about Mary O'Brien's bold enunciation of the world-shaking historical force of a contraceptive revolution today. The experiences of women coming of age in the seventies, eighties, and nineties, after contraception and abortion became socially and politically accessible modes of reproductive choice for women, are in some ways radically different from those of women coming of age in the fifties and sixties, when female sexuality and heterosexual love were fraught with the dangers of pregnancy and motherhood. Despite the fact that reproductive choice is not yet distributed equally or fairly among women in our society, the reproductive lives of all women increasingly involve new sorts of responsibilities and decisions.

I would suggest that my own experience of my body and my procreative agency is both peculiarly contemporary, and also rather common among women coming of age in the 1970s or later. I have a cyborgean sense of my personhood, insofar as I have felt sexually empowered for the last twenty years by taking the pill, and can imagine nothing that would make me feel more alienated from my body than to be deprived of this technological means of reproductive security. Were I to become pregnant, I would feel ethically confident in obtaining an abortion because I have the cyborgean belief that children are social offspring and can be morally conceived only by acts of interpersonal agency, wherein one or more individuals consciously commit themselves to a future parenting relationship. Unlike Firestone, I am not recommending a cyborgean attitude toward motherhood as a radical option, to be judiciously evaluated for its possible emancipatory effects on women. I am maintaining that we can hardly avoid a cyborgean sense of our personhood today, reproductive and otherwise.

Attitudes toward abortion and other procreative decisions are only the tip of a postfeminist iceberg, according to this narrative. As interpersonal agents, we are responsible for creating and maintaining, and ending when appropriate, a sometimes terrifying array of relationships and connections within both domestic and public arenas. We may be expected to change jobs, careers, marriages, and geographical venues with the same resignation or optimism as we switch channels. We may be described, without undue exaggeration, as operating within a tangle of motivations, responsibilities, and forms of recognition and reward unmoored from traditional male and female, public and private identities. Given the chaotic state of individual motivations and responsibilities in this scenario, it may be wholly unrealistic to expect anyone to worry very much about establishing firm social identities, feminist, feminine, maternal, or otherwise.

The neediness and dependency of children imply that relationships between parents and children must remain a site of relative stability in this chaotic moment of cultural transformation, however. Insofar as traditional notions of maternal and paternal identity are no longer either available or appropriate as foundations upon which to ground relationships between cyborgean parents and children, we need to rethink parental roles as fundamentally as any others. Moreover, as in the case of other interpersonal renegotiations, this inquiry will typically take place in the context of an ongoing parent-child relationship. Unlike other interpersonal relationships, however, this is a situation in which a basic asymmetry is a dominant factor in the bond between the parties. Because of the dependency of children, neither party can readily put an end to a relationship that goes bad; and because of the intense emotional and cognitive interactiveness of children, parents and children tend to develop psychic connections that endure for a lifetime. The dependency of children places constraints on parental freedom and suggests definite, if now indistinct, parameters of parental responsibility. Parents require new criteria for assessing their actions and the quality of the bond they are creating with their children, often in spite of themselves.

A notion of interpersonal agency provides cyborgean parents with a framework for attempting to achieve ethical confidence as parents. It encourages individuals to attend to their own particular motivations, while attempting to reconcile these with a reasonable sense of obligation toward children. It also suggests the need to evaluate the particular forms of recognition or reward they seek as parents. A concept of interpersonal agency highlights relevant dimensions of women's and men's changing experiences of parenting in the face of women's social enfranchisement and all the consequences it may have for kinship relationships. It can help individuals reformulate parental relationships in the direction of mutually desirable divisions of labor between men and women, as well as between persons within wholly nontraditional parenting communities.

One of the most important functions of a notion of interpersonal agency may lie in its ability decisively to confront and disperse a powerful, but antiquated, aura of moral rectitude that continues to surround motherhood. In many societies in which motherhood is deemed a necessary and natural role of women, a mantle of unqualified goodness descends upon a woman who produces a child. The moral valence of maternity functions like a bribe; it is grounds for a woman to reconcile herself to the burdens of a maternity she cannot refuse in any case. Such a normative privileging of maternity is operative in our society in capricious postmodern forms, with sometimes cruel and frequently inappropriate results. For example, Ann Snitow has diagnosed a "pervasive pronatalism" afflicting various privileged strata of our society.[21] Among couples and single women who have devoted themselves exclusively to careers and worldly possessions, it can suddenly seem necessary to have a child to fulfill a vague sense of unmet desires. Forty-something women who have proven themselves successful at every other aspect of life become prone to feelings of inadequacy for not having fulfilled their maternal potential. Childless women of means resort to extensive and expensive fertility treatments with only the faintest hope of finally bearing a child. Given the maternal obsessions of women who have so many other sources of personal affirmation, we should hardly be surprised when teenage girls from impoverished backgrounds imagine that motherhood will provide them with a sense of personal significance and make their lives more bearable.

The mantle of maternal goodness not only leads people to want children for the wrong reasons; it also puts obstacles in the way of redistributing parental responsibilities. The sex-specific quality of maternal goodness forces men who participate extensively in parenting to operate in drag, as it were. We are likely to be critical if such men admit to motivations, senses of obligation, or feelings of reward that the privileged maternal identity does not sanction. Moreover, many women still jealously guard their claim upon the unqualified goodness of the maternal identity, even when they are drastically overburdened by its responsibilities.

This anachronistic valence of unqualified maternal goodness is diminished by thinking of motherhood as simply one mode of interpersonal agency. It allows us concretely to discuss the motivations, obligations, and rewards appropriate to child-rearing, distinguishing them from the motivations, responsibilities, and rewards possible in other sorts of interpersonal relationships. It helps us to suggest alternative forms of interpersonal agency more appropriate to most teenage girls, for example, or to career-driven women and men. It enables us persuasively to suggest why there is a spectrum of meaningful nonparental personal connections that may better satisfy the psychic yearnings of a particular individual.

On the other hand, by regarding parenting as a subset of interpersonal agency, we also become better prepared to accept and constructively respond to the fact that contemporary parents are likely to exercise qualitatively different forms of parental agency than those associated with traditional mothers of any sort. Women who work outside the home today may have quite different motivations for becoming mothers, different notions of maternal responsibility, and different feelings of reward derived from their parental role than did women fulfilling maternal roles in the past. And we may expect men to begin articulating parental motivations, obligations, and rewards in ways that sound quite novel, or even strange, to a conventional maternal ear. Yet if such reformulations of parent-child bonding make parenting less foreign to men while fulfilling the needs of children, we should encourage them.

CONCLUSION

I have attempted to show that previous notions of maternal identity, whether religious, naturalistic, or humanistic, whether dismissive or celebratory, fail adequately to represent the procreative agency of women today. Inspired by Mary O'Brien's hopeful proclamation of a contraceptive revolution, I have sought to articulate what might come after organic motherhood. Donna Haraway's "blasphemous image of the cyborg" is one of those rare political metaphors with immediate metaphysical resonances. For many of us today, our dependency upon technologies, whether upon computers, or artificial knees, or contraceptives, is such that we would feel "less ourselves" without them. This I take to be a condition of cyborgean personhood, and indeed more particularly a condition of cyborgean motherhood.

Our ubiquitous and intimate dependency upon reproductive technologies means that children may reasonably come to be seen as "social offspring" of various possible practices and procedures in which organic conditions are thoroughly interpenetrated with technological ones. It will no longer make sense to think of a pregnant mother as the natural origin of a child, and pregnancy will not be seen as a sufficient ethical condition for producing a child. Children will be born of acts of interpersonal agency, conscious decisions by one or more persons to take on the social responsibilities involved in raising a child. A cyborgean paradigm of motherhood will provide women with the discursive grounds for ethical confidence in choosing abortion, as well as encouraging both women and men to exercise personal responsibility over whatever procreative technologies become available to them in the future.

NOTES

1. Steven W. Sinding and Sheldon J. Segal, "Birth Rate News," Op-Ed in *New York Times*, 19 Dec. 1991, report that "Third world women are averaging 3.9 children, and more than 50% (55% in Latin America and 70% in Asia) of the women use some form of contraception . . . a stunning change from the 8% who used contraception in 1965 when they were averaging more than six children."

2. Cruel battles over abortion are occurring in Eastern Europe, where abortion was the primary means of contraception and available free of charge under many of the former socialist regimes. In Poland the resurgent political power of the Catholic Church has resulted in an almost unconditional ban on abortion being enacted into law in March 1993, despite the fact that a majority of the public opposes limitations on abortion. See Ann Snitow, "The Church Wins, Women Lose," *The Nation*, 26 Apr. 1993.

3. As a white, heterosexual philosopher in New York City, I can hardly

expect to speak *to*—and certainly not *for*—women the world over. Yet I would hope that my words, particularly on an issue like abortion, will provide insights even to some who do not share my immediate demographic points of reference. A postmodern social philosopher walks a fine line between false hubris and false modesty, generalizing beyond her immediate experiences in order to offer insights to others whose shoes she is not in, yet accepting the danger of false generalization. While the traditional philosopher was in a position to impose "universal truths" on people who had no social or theoretical standing to protest their validity, the power relations between theorist and reader have shifted *somewhat*, insofar as we are more aware of the fallibility of theory. As a theorist who accepts her inability to recognize the particular boundedness of her notions, I leave it to the reader to appropriate whatever she or he finds useful in my alternative narratives.

4. Simone de Beauvoir's analysis of maternity was dominated by the emphasis existentialism placed upon human choice. The involuntariness of the maternal role horrified de Beauvoir, and she described women as being "in bondage to the species," and as experiencing "maternal servitude" because of the *social status* of motherhood as a life project/process to which women could not choose but must submit. *The Second Sex* (New York: Vintage Books, 1974), 25, 29, 39, 41. She has been criticized by many second wave feminist theorists for her failure to appreciate the human meaningfulness of maternal activities. But feminist celebrations of maternity today never fail to emphasize that it must be a voluntary activity. De Beauvoir wrote *The Second Sex* in 1948, at a time when a naturalistic identification of women with motherhood still existed. It is impossible to project ourselves back into such a different historical time, but it seems presumptuous to assume that we would have been any less focused on the involuntariness of maternity than de Beauvoir was in 1948.

5. I use a notion of "the social enfranchisement of women" to designate the dramatic, incomplete process of change in women's status in western, democratic societies over the past twenty-five years. The transformation has been particularly evident with respect to the economic and reproductive rights and responsibilities of women. See Patricia S. Mann, *Micro-Politics: Agency in a Postfeminist Era* (Minneapolis: University of Minnesota Press, 1994).

6. Virginia Held argues that human birth and mothering have always been intrinsically "human" practices, and she is dismissive of thinkers like Hannah Arendt and Simone de Beauvoir who accepted the patriarchal view of them as natural processes. If we think in terms of the different dimensions of agency, we can sympathize with Held's defense of the human meaningfulness of maternal activities historically, while yet understanding why social theorists like Arendt and Beauvoir would designate maternity as a natural activity so long as it remained an involuntary practice required of those human beings born with the biological capacity to give birth, not deemed worthy of the sorts of recognition and reward attached to the social activities of men. See Virginia Held, "Birth and Death," *Ethics* 99 (Jan. 1989): 385.

7. Jane Roland Martin, *Reclaiming a Conversation* (New Haven: Yale University Press, 1985), offers a probing analysis of thinkers such as Mary Wollstonecraft, Catharine Beecher, and Charlotte Perkins Gilman.

8. In chapter 3 of my book *Micro-Politics: Agency in a Postfeminist Era*, from which this essay is excerpted, I analyze the history of abortion theory and politics, and I offer my cyborgean narrative of maternal agency as an alternative to hegemonic patriarchal discourses.

9. Laurence Tribe, *Abortion: The Clash of Absolutes* (New York: Norton, 1990).

10. Bernard Williams, *Ethics and the Limits of Philosophy* (Cambridge, Mass.: Harvard University Press, 1985), 112–17, 170.

11. Donna Haraway, "A Cyborg Manifesto: Science, Technology, and Socialist-Feminism in the Late Twentieth Century," in *Simians, Cyborgs, and Women* (New York: Routledge, 1991), 149.

12. See Mary O'Brien, *The Politics of Reproduction* (Boston: Routledge, 1983), for her seminal arguments for the "world-historical significance of the Contraceptive Revolution."

13. Notice that the cyborgean penetration of technology into our daily lives transcends boundaries of class and culture. Ultrasound scanners, enabling doctors to check the sex of a fetus, have become a popular and profitable form of medical machinery in many of the most rural areas of Asia. In countries such as India and China where there is great pressure to limit families and also great cultural pressure to produce boy children as heirs and economic security for parents in their old age, female fetuses are now regularly aborted. See Nicholas Kristof, "Chinese Turn to Ultrasound, Scorning Baby Girls for Boys," *New York Times*, 21 July 1993.

14. Shulamith Firestone, *The Dialectic of Sex* (New York: Bantam, 1970), 199.

15. Adrienne Rich, *Of Woman Born* (New York: Norton, 1976), 40, 280, 285.

16. Barbara Katz Rothman, *Recreating Motherhood* (New York: Norton, 1989).

17. Sara Ruddick, *Maternal Thinking* (New York: Ballantine, 1989), 40–44. Ruddick maintains that insofar as a person must consciously make a commitment to "protecting, nurturing, and training" a particular child in order to be regarded as its parent once it has been born, "all mothers are adoptive," (49–51), giving mothers a social and voluntary status without questioning the natural origins of children in the labor of pregnant women. Ruddick has found a pragmatic way of addressing the fact that even if women experience pregnancy as a natural process over which they have little control, our society demands that women exert a great deal of individual control over their circumstances as parents. The advantage of a cyborgean account is that it provides women with a moral basis for exerting personal control much earlier, by denying that pregnancy and offspring are at any point natural.

18. Many people associate the term "postfeminism" with a "backlash"

against feminism. Suzanna Danuta Walters, "Premature Postmortems: 'Postfeminism' and Popular Culture," *New Politics* 3, no. 2 (Winter 1991): 103–12, chronicles the angry reaction of feminists to the term. My point is that regardless of how commentators have used a notion of postfeminism, feminists should appropriate it to announce the fact that feminist concerns have entered the mainstream.

19. Teresa de Lauretis, "Upping the Anti (Sic) in Feminist Theory," *Conflicts in Feminism*, ed. Marianne Hirsch and Evelyn Fox Keller (New York: Routledge, 1990), 265.

20. Ellen Chesler, *Woman of Valor: Margaret Sanger and the Birth Control Movement in America* (New York: Simon and Schuster, 1992), shows the social conditions that subverted Sanger's goal of enabling women to control their reproductive lives.

21. Ann Snitow, "Feminism and Motherhood: An American Reading," *Feminist Review* 40 (Spring 1992): 32.

SEVEN

Maternal Agency vs.
the Brotherhood of Males

MIRIAM M. JOHNSON

In this essay, I will explore how maternal agency, and emerging structural changes that support such agency, might transform a liberal society to include women and men in egalitarian relationships. By maternal agency I mean the actions not only of literal mothers but of any and all people who are guided by maternal attitudes of caring for others as people, not as objects to be used. These attitudes are more likely to be found in women, because of their monopoly on childrearing, but they are neither held by all mothers nor held exclusively by females. Achieving equality will require the agency of an active sisterhood and its male supporters with a maternal vision to loosen the grip of the brotherhood of males whose attitudes and actions continue to define women as objects, even while women gain status in the public sphere.

Certainly mothering as a practice, with and without husbands, in this society has heretofore worked against women's equality, but this need not be the case. If we could redefine mothering as an orientation toward caring for self and others in a way that empowers both, it could become a basis for women's solidarity and an orientation potentially to be shared by both sexes and practiced not just in the home. Sisterhood, to the extent that it can be an extension of caring, supportive *maternal* attitudes, may more readily include males as brothers in a nonsexual community. After all, mothers bear and nurture children of both sexes, and men do not acquire the brotherhood of males mentality from their mothers but from other men. Brothers and sisters alike share a maternal origin, but because sisters are female like their mothers, it is they who can together challenge the brotherhood to change their views of women. However, before maternal agency can become a genuinely progressive force, there must be structural changes in the family and the wider society that decrease women's dependence on men and marriage. I will argue that these changes are in fact taking place.

After making a distinction between women as mothers and women as wives, I will trace the recent vicissitudes of women's "mothering" both as it has been organized and contained by the male-headed nuclear family and as a concept within white middle-class feminism. I also examine mothering as it has been differently constructed and more positively interpreted by some African-American feminists. In the second part of the paper I examine the positive possibilities for maternal agency of the so-called "decline" of the nuclear family. I suggest that the new, more diverse and voluntary kin networks that are developing, along with various voluntary associations with maternal goals, are providing a structural basis for a more active sense of sisterhood among women and a community in which men may be included on a new basis. In my view, a maternal emphasis as a focal point for women's agency is not antithetical to the larger aim of feminism to see women and men as both similar and equal. Rather maternal agency provides a way to make that equality a reality.

WIVES VS. MOTHERS

In order to understand my overall argument about maternal agency it is necessary to distinguish between mothers and wives. I have posited elsewhere that it is the wife role, not the mother role, that lies behind women's secondary status vis-à-vis men.[1] This can be argued in many ways but, once pointed out, the claim usually makes intuitive sense, especially to white middle-class women. Although we have come a long way from the legal dictum that "husband and wife are one and that one is the husband," the good wife is still expected *not* to upstage her husband and to let him lead. The good wife knows her place. Consider the country's obsessive concern with Hillary Clinton's lack of wifely humility.

In contrast, motherhood, abstracted from marriage, has traditionally been associated with independent power and agency. We expect mothers to be active, wise, brave, resourceful, caring, and responsible for the growth and development of others. The very fact that real mothers are both idealized as capable of solving everything and blamed for any undesirable outcome attests to the power we impute to them.

But motherhood as organized by marriage has meant performing these functions at the sacrifice of personal autonomy. For example, a recent survey of married and unmarried men and women found that within any given income category and whether or not a parent, nonmarried women see themselves as having significantly higher levels of personal autonomy than do married women, while the same does not hold for nonmarried and married men.[2] The author concludes that "the economic well-being of married women carries a price, paid in personal control." In support of this proposition, Judith Barker finds in a study of a diverse group of single mothers that, despite their poverty, a significant proportion of these mothers report gaining a sense of autonomy and empowerment that they did not feel in marriage.[3] Marriage, then, is the mechanism by which women's symbolic and real power as mothers has been coopted and controlled by men, perhaps especially in the white middle class.

This process of subsuming motherhood under the rubric of wife explains why middle-class women are far more likely to be thought of as weak wives than strong mothers. The dependent, emotional, nonrational stereotype of women is the stereotype of the wife, not the mother. Most significantly, when we do think of women as being nurturing, caring, and nonhierarchical, there is a tendency to assign these maternal virtues to the wife stereotype and consequently to downgrade them as being the result of weakness and timidity. White middle-class feminists themselves fall into this type of thinking when they assume that positive analyses of maternal orientations are regressive and indicate a retreat and a failure of nerve.

Much of what feminists disliked in their own mothers resulted from their mothers' dependence and isolation in the family and also their need to preserve the marriage at all costs in spite of their feeling resentful. Mothers' dependence on husbands can also explain their apparent narrowness of focus as well as why some mothers have not been able to protect their daughters from incestuous fathers.[4]

MIDDLE-CLASS FEMINISM IN THE EARLY YEARS

In the 1960s, one of the central themes emphasized by white middle-class feminists, myself included, was that women were more than mothers and wives—that women were people too, individuals in their own right. Women were not just sex objects and breeding machines, not just housewives and mothers who sacrificed for husband and children. Rather women were competent, educated *people* who had a right to join the real world of meaningful work and sexual freedom. Women wanted to escape the "martyrdom" of their own mothers and participate in the challenges and rewards of the man's world of work and sexuality. Many tended to see marriage and motherhood as inseparable impediments to these goals.

In my view the discrepancies that college-educated women perceived between their training and their treatment by men of their class can go a long way toward explaining the motivational underpinnings of the revival of feminism that arose in the 1960s. Precisely because of class and race privilege, white middle-class women were in a position to feel oppressed *as women* by the standards of middle-class individualism. In this class, male privilege and female dependence have been more marked, and white middle-class women have been defined more narrowly as "wives" than have women in other groups. Trained in college in a manner similar to men and strongly imbued with the individual achievement values of the white middle class, we were incongruously expected to abandon our own aspirations and to make it possible for our husbands to "succeed" by taking care of everything else in their lives. Married professional women and would-be professional women were those to whom Betty Friedan's *Feminine Mystique* (1963) spoke, and their perception that vicarious achievement as privatized wives was not enough fueled the feminist revolt.

A bit later, younger, also largely middle-class women who participated in antiwar and civil rights projects realized that they were not equal citizens. While engaged in political action aimed at racial equality and peace, they were treated by their middle-class male compatriots as sex objects, lackeys, secretaries—as wives or wife-substitutes—and these women resisted.

While class privilege allowed middle-class women to perceive and focus on their unequal treatment *as women*, this same class privilege shared with men has made sisterhood more difficult for middle-class white women to achieve than it has been for less privileged women. The consciousness-raising groups that sprang up and spread among these women did create an awareness of oppression and feelings of victimization and did spawn private and some public actions of resistance. But because middle-class women remained dependent on husbands for status and income there was no structural or material basis for joining together to effect institutional change. Thus it is perhaps not surprising that in spite of consciousness-raising and making the personal political it was difficult to achieve a solidarity sufficient to challenge the brotherhood of males in the workplace.

The two main middle-class feminist tendencies, outside of socialist feminism,[5] were assimilation to the man's world and radical separatism. Assimilationists (usually called liberal feminists) sought inclusion in a male-defined world, and separatists sought escape from that world. But for different reasons, neither group saw maternal values in a positive light. Assimilationists tended to repudiate motherhood and maternal values as an impediment to a serious work commitment and to sexual expression, and separatists, at first at least, saw motherhood as an impediment to sisterhood.

Liberal feminists—which I prefer to call assimilationists, to include many socialist feminists—must be credited with breaking many barriers to women's inclusion and in opening up more and better jobs for women. But joining the labor force in male-dominated jobs put women directly up against the brotherhood of males. Women were presented with the impossible dilemma of either becoming "one of the boys" or being a female as defined by the boys. The latter meant being objects for men or becoming their personal mothers, and sometimes both. In my terminology, we could be "wives," i.e., secondary in any heterosexual context. The assimilationist response to this realization has been to emphasize that women are people and workers and need to be treated as such. But in order to achieve this goal more is needed than formal legal guarantees of equality. The informal power of the brotherhood of males must be transformed through the agency of a sisterhood that can stand together and refuse to play the game.

The perception of male domination went much deeper with radical feminists, especially middle-class lesbians, many of whom became committed to separatism as a political strategy. These women were most acutely aware of the privileges of males (at least those in their class) and the degree to which men took over and controlled virtually all heterosexual situations, be they in the business world, the classroom, or the bedroom. Radical feminists' response was to remove themselves in so far as possible from male influence by establishing women's communities in which they created and lived out a woman-based image of the world. This new image, while often rejecting "mothering" as well as "wifing" as currently practiced, did retain the maternal ideals of mutual caring and support within the group.

Separatism was at the time a logical response to perceptions of the control "the brotherhood" exercised, and it allowed women to construct a life in which they were independent and free of the definitions and needs of males. But neither radical separatism nor liberal assimilation provided women with a base from which they could join together to challenge on any major scale the worldview of the brotherhood of males.

MOVING TOWARD MATERNAL THINKING IN THE WHITE MIDDLE CLASS

By the late 1970s, white middle-class feminists had begun to rehabilitate the idea of mothering and the orientations associated with it. Nancy Chodorow's description of women's relational orientation (obtained from mothering and being mothered) defined women's relational tendencies as at least as desirable, if not more so, than men's tendency to distance themselves from others.[6] Carol Gilligan delineated relational concerns in women's moral thinking and argued that they were an equally valid basis for making moral choices.[7] Sara Ruddick described the concrete orientations that the activity of mothering itself elicited in a way that women who were mothers could appreciate and with which they could identify.[8] As mothering gained ground within middle-class feminism, however, it remained tied to the idealization of the nuclear family. Mothering became something fathers should do too. Shared parenting within the nuclear family became the panacea for gender inequality and gained wide acceptance among feminists and nonfeminists alike.

But shared parenting, desirable as it may be, has been touted more than practiced. Recent studies of sharing work within the family suggest that role differentiation between husband and wife is very difficult to change, and husbands who do not play the traditional husband role are likely to see their nontraditionalism as a gift that requires compensation from their wives.[9]

Beyond this, even if egalitarian marriages and egalitarian child-rearing within the nuclear family could be brought about, these in themselves would not end male dominance so long as the public-private split remains and women as mothers have no power base outside of male control from which they can develop the broader possibilities of maternal agency.

MATERNAL AGENCY OUTSIDE THE WHITE MIDDLE CLASS

Alternative feminist constructions of mothering among African Americans focus beyond the nuclear family and offer a maternal vision of community that includes both males and females as equal "sisters" and "brothers." While this vision has many contradictory aspects—in part because it developed in response to race and class oppression in the United States and may also draw from a West African cultural heritage totally unlike modern industrial culture— it nevertheless deserves to be examined as a stimulus to creative thinking about community and equality.

African-American feminists, for example, have pointed out that sisterhood and female bonding in oppressed groups usually served, rather than opposed, families—and these families included various relatives, not just children and husbands. Both African-American and other minorities saw extended families (not usually in the same household) as a source of strength in the face of class and race oppression. Generally oppressed minorities bitterly rejected radical separatism as insensitive to the oppression of both women and men outside of white middle- and upper-class circles.

The structural base of the African-American vision is matrifocal, a form of organization in which women and men are more nearly equals in the community. Matrifocality is not at all the same as matriarchy but is characterized by women playing culturally valued roles in the larger community, and includes less-differentiated parenting roles between husband and wife along with a lack of centrality of the marriage relationship. Matrifocality does not mean a mother-dominated nuclear family but in African-American communities refers to maternal agents broadened to include "othermothers" and "community othermothers" as well as blood mothers.[10] Moreover this centrality does not mean the absence of husbands and fathers but rather that in child rearing, mothers take on more disciplinary functions and fathers take on more nurturing functions than is usual in the white middle class.[11] It represents a context in which "shared parenting" within the nuclear family could operate without reinforcing male authority or reducing female autonomy.

When I suggest the positive possibilities of matrifocality, I am not referring to impoverished single mothers and unemployed, unmarried, and alienated fathers who "hang out" with each other. The violence against women (and men) associated with this situation is neither descriptive of nor caused by matrifocality per se, since matrifocality has existed throughout the history of African Americans in this country, while the deterioration of the urban black underclass is a separate phenomenon that has greatly worsened since the 1960s.[12]

Now African-American feminists are beginning to suggest that community-based experience might well serve as a guide not only to improving the quality of women's (and men's) lives, but also to realizing a new vision of both individualism and community and the relationship between them. Maternal agency could help redefine the nature of community to make it more human and humane, while contributing to the solidarity of women. As Patricia Hill Collins points out, "Afrocentric models of community stress connections, caring, and personal accountability" (223). Moreover, she asserts that this is not the opposite of individualism, as white male analysts might see it, but is rather "an alternative vision of power based on a humanist vision of self-actualization, self-definition, and self-determination" (224).

Bernice Reagon uses the term "mothering generation" to describe communities working together to nurture and help one another, to sift and transform norms, values, and institutions in order to create a new social order.[13] Reagon is hoping that what began from survival strategies in a hostile world can grow into a basis for multicultural coalitions that can transform the world.

If this vision of community with a maternal base could become a larger part of the thinking of the white middle class, it would mean including the white middle class in a vision not of its own making, but one heavily dependent on the insights and experiences of less-privileged groups and cultures.[14] It is this kind of integration that is important to continued progress, as opposed to the kind of inclusion that involves sacrificing other cultures to the dominant culture.

Obviously, matrifocality as it has existed in oppressed enclaves cannot simply be transferred to the wider society. But examination of matrifocality with its maternal outlook can provide clues as to how to interpret the changes that are already occurring within the white middle and working classes. These changes involve a restructuring that is weakening the radical dichotomy between women and men, private and public, family and nonfamily, and challenging the overweening cultural primacy of the heterosexual couple and the nuclear unit of father, mother, and small children. Ordinarily, the family and voluntary associations are not considered central or primary institutions, but changes in these, by providing new power bases for maternal agency, may prove critical in the next steps toward achieving greater gender equality in the public sphere.

FAMILY BREAKDOWN AND NEW POSSIBILITIES

Whether willed or not, changes in white middle- and working-class families in the direction of matrifocality are already well on their way. These changes increase the possibility of greater solidarity between women from diverse groups based on maternal connections. No-fault divorce and the increasing ease with which the couple relationship can legally be disbanded is part of a trend that loosens the connection between parenting and marriage. We are in a situation where marriage is dissolvable but the parent-child tie usually is not; in fact, it is usually the mother-child tie that remains. This situation is hardly desirable for women or children at present, but as the breakup of an old pattern causes dislocation it may also stimulate new and widening solidarities for women.

As nuclear families break up and new ones are formed through remarriage, the number of kin available to individuals increases and intergenerational ties gain prominence. The individuals who orchestrate these new and old kin possibilities are women—often older adult women with adult children. While divorce has tended to increase women's intergenerational connections, it has decreased men's connection with their own children. Divorced fathers tend not to see their children by a previous spouse and are more likely to connect with the children of their present wife. Moreover, men are more likely to remarry than women, especially after the age of forty. Divorced mothers, by contrast, continue to see their children even when their husbands have custody. As Gunhild Hagestad puts it, "An increasing proportion of men have only precarious vertical ties, both up and down generational lines, while women's intergenerational ties are more varied, complex, and durable than ever before in human history."[15]

Changing adoption practices provide another indication of a trend toward extending familial connections centering around women. Whereas formerly great pains were taken to preserve the anonymity of both parties to an adoption, now "open adoptions" that encourage and facilitate contact between the adopting parent(s) and the birth parent(s) have been increasing rapidly. While the amount of contact they agree to varies, often both parties to the adoption seek to define their relationship to one another as being in some way like kin. This felt kinship rests on the recognition of the emotional tie to the child shared by both the birth mother (birth fathers are most often uninvolved) and the adopting parent(s).[16]

Recent research on contemporary kinship bonds clearly shows that the mother-daughter connection is the key relationship holding together intergenerational ties.[17] Divorced mothers are likely to reestablish or strengthen ties with their own mothers; maternal grandmothers are likely to keep in touch with their divorced son's wife and children as well as their own daughters and their children.[18]

The activation of kin ties outside the nuclear family will provide a wider network of emotional solidarity that can increase the sense of community for both women and children. Adult men can also be integrated into these networks, but such networks would likely remain areas of greater female control.

The new women-controlled families that are being created are more open and fluid and are not based in a single household. These families may include many households, and they may be involved jointly in activities beyond the household. They are also likely to include (or even be built around) categories of women who do not fit well into the nuclear family picture—lesbians, unmarried mothers, widows, and older women in general—who are not "wives" or who do not define themselves as such.[19] It is possible that these women might become united by a vision of mutual mothering that includes men, but not as a mirror image of the way the brotherhood has included women. Men would be included in terms of their relationship to women and children, as family participants, not family heads. Equal parenting by a man and a woman would be guided by maternal standards shared by both.

Whereas in early periods kin groups exerted a conservative pressure on their members, the fact that more women are now working outside the home and have wider contacts with a greater diversity of people enables kinship itself to become a progressive force. As one's kin become more diverse and voluntarily chosen, as more and more "families" contain diverse members, as very different kinds of people find themselves voluntarily "related" to each other, the conservative nature of kinship itself changes. Most important for middle-class women, their dependence on husbands lessens and their affective ties with both men and women outside the nuclear unit become more important and widespread.

Like other guiding social concepts, "mothering" itself is socially constructed and as such can be and is being redefined. In the recent past, mothering has been depicted as demanding great sacrifice on the part of the mother and at the same time as overwhelming and impeding the autonomy of those to whom she ministers. The reality base for both the "martyr" and the "big nurse" images of mothering is the white middle-class nuclear family of the 1950s. But new images of mothering based on new realities are being created. These images see maternal power as empowering for both self and others—not a sacrifice for one and a threat to the other. Moreover, even though mothers are typically older than their children, if one takes the life cycle into account, mother and child roles often reverse with children caring for parents, and, in the middle years, mothers and daughters engage in a kind of mutual support that I see as a proto-type of sisterhood. Because women alone have the ability to bear children, mothering is something that most women, at some level, "understand" and appreciate. Mutual mothering then is a kind of power that can well serve as the basis for a sisterhood that can ap-peal to diverse women. Finally, new definitions of mothering make it possible for men as well as women to "mother."

NON-KIN VOLUNTARY ASSOCIATIONS WITH A MATERNAL OUTLOOK

In addition to the more or less freely chosen kin networks controlled by women, other kinds of voluntary networks are forming that can carry a maternal outlook beyond kin and further widen emotional-ly close kinship and friendship ties. Many contemporary broad so-cial movements have a maternal focus. Examples include the peace movement, which has attracted many women as an extension of "maternal thinking."[20] The women's health movement is a more public extension of mothers' concern with their own and their fam-ily's health and well being. At another level, the environmental movement can be viewed as an extension of caring concern for the total earth and the interdependencies within nature. Beyond this, as Mary Dietz has suggested, a generalized commitment to democrat-ic citizenship and to egalitarian participation and procedures would be a basis for and expression of new kinds of women-based associa-tional membership.[21]

Child care and elder care are themselves major areas in which women have a more direct interest than men and which lend them-selves to creative solutions that operate somewhere between the public and private spheres and which merge issues of race, class, and gender oppression. Informal arrangements for child care in which groups of mothers cooperate have been a pattern among blacks more than whites, and community care for children seems more appro-priate than do more formal impersonal settings. The same is true for elder care, another arena for which women have been made re-sponsible with little support or recognition. In the public sphere, formal and informal unions of domestic, daycare, and senior-care women (and men) are pushing for the recognition of "mothering work" as important and skilled work deserving of real pay.

In the nineteenth century, privileged white women were involved in kin networks and voluntary associations pursuing maternal activities outside the domestic arena, but the context was quite different. In the nineteenth and early twentieth centuries women did not have the vote, had fewer formal rights in general than men, and used their "difference" as mothers to effect change by informal pressure. As women obtained formal rights in the public sphere and as families became smaller and more privatized, women's clubs and other voluntary organizations ceased to be the agents of social action they once were. Now that middle-class white women with children have entered the labor force and are less financially and emotionally dependent on husbands, they are in a position to form social action groups that include men and also to support each other in the political arena and the workplace.

SISTERHOOD ON THE RISE

In the 1990s there has been a striking increase in women's involvement in politics at all levels. While the number of women in public office is still small, the new significance of their presence is that they have the support of a rapidly increasing number of women. Private problems have become public issues on a scale that was impossible in the 1970s, and consciousness-raising has taken place on a broader scale than ever before.

Because of women's increasing emancipation from the narrow confines of wifehood, the "consciousness-raising" familiar in the 1970s has become a more active force based less on feelings of victimization as wives and mothers and more on a sense of agency deriving from a sense of independent personhood. At the same time that women are gaining greater independence from men, they are also gaining a greater sense of common ground with other women. Part of this commonality is a deeper understanding of the solidarity of males, which operates at a level outside of formally egalitarian rules and regulations, and a clearer understanding of the need for a maternal sisterhood to protest these informal understandings between the boys.

A major impediment to real equality in the public sphere is the tendency for the brotherhood of males to sexualize women. Now that women have been included in male-dominated fields, sexual harassment is a ubiquitous problem. It is doubtful that the Anita Hill and Tailhook cases could have received national attention and sympathetic response had it not been for the increasing solidarity that has been developing among women as they become less dependent on male support. These cases have broken the public silence on sexual harassment and rape in work contexts and have made it possible for more women to understand the reality of the brotherhood of males and to conclude that, with the support of other women and men, something *can* be done about it.

While many contemporary women do not call themselves feminists, perhaps in part because it has become (falsely I think) associated with anti-family values, an increasing number of women do seem to be backing each other up against the brotherhood of males. I would argue that the appropriate name for this is "maternal agency," understood as actions motivated by a sense of concern for the welfare and dignity of self and others. Sexual harassment and pornography violate the integrity of the person; they do not take the feelings of "the object" into account. A sisterhood based on maternal agency could include males as equals, not objects, working together with them for the realization of humanistic goals.

CONCLUSION

In this chapter, rather than focusing on concrete acts, I have described the rise of maternal attitudes as a motivational basis for women's agentic action as a sisterhood. I have suggested that a sisterhood would not be a mirror image of the brotherhood of males but would instead ultimately be based on more humanistic maternal values—hence the term, "maternal agency." As women's dependence on men decreases, their solidarity in attacking the brotherhood of males' control of the public sphere increases. Such attacks have also created an increasing public awareness of class and race privilege as well as gender privilege. Indeed many middle-class women's escape from husband dominance through divorce has led them to lose their middle-class privilege. While this has been hard on both mothers and children, it has led to a keener understanding of how class status is tied in with white male privilege.

The process of both articulating and realizing social values that can truly include women and men as equals obviously has far to go. Moreover, the problem is a global one. As women throughout the world begin to seek common ground for attacking the combined evils of gender, race, ethnic, and class privilege, it seems likely that a sisterhood based on maternal agency will assume importance. Because of the universal aspects of women's mothering and maternal attitudes, such orientations may serve as a key factor that can unite women of differing races, classes, and cultures.

NOTES

I would like to thank Bernice Reagon, Lynnea Search, and Sue Wright for their helpful comments on earlier versions of this essay.

1. Miriam M. Johnson, *Strong Mothers, Weak Wives: The Search for Gender Equality* (Berkeley: University of California Press, 1988).

2. Catherine E. Ross, "Marriage and the Sense of Control," *Journal of Marriage and the Family* 53 (Nov. 1991): 831–38.

3. Judith Barker, "Single Mothers, Powerlessness and Empowerment: A Class, Race, and Sexual Orientation Comparison," Ph.D. diss., University of Oregon, 1989. While stigma and poverty are the most frequently cited problems for single mothers, almost all works on their situation mention some cases in which autonomy has been enhanced.

4. I am not arguing for nonmarriage, but for egalitarian marriages that are not anomalous within the society but rather are assumed to be normal within the society. The fact that individual marriages may now be egalitarian or even woman-dominated misses the point. Such marriages exist in an environment that expects male dominance—an expectation to which every couple has in some way to adjust.

5. While socialist feminists have recognized "patriarchy" based on the brotherhood of males, their analyses have tended to make economic changes primary and other institutional arrangements derivative. Suffice it to say that socialist feminists have not made mothering a primary focus and many continue to see such a focus as regressive; see, for example, Lynne Segal, *Is the Future Female? Troubled Thoughts on Contemporary Feminism* (New York: Peter Bedrick, 1987).

6. See Nancy Chodorow, *The Reproduction of Mothering* (Berkeley: University of California Press, 1978). See also her "Gender, Relation, and Difference in Psychoanalytic Perspective" in her *Feminism and Psychoanalytic Theory* (New Haven: Yale University Press, 1989).

7. See Carol Gilligan, *In a Different Voice* (Cambridge, Mass.: Harvard University Press, 1982).

8. See Sara Ruddick, "Maternal Thinking" in *Rethinking the Family: Some Feminist Questions*, ed. Barrie Thorne with Marilyn Yalom (New York: Longman, 1982), 76–94.

9. See, for example, Arlie Hochschild, *The Second Shift* (New York: Avon, 1989).

10. See Patricia Hill Collins, *Black Feminist Thought: Knowledge, Consciousness, and the Politics of Empowerment* (Boston: Unwin Hyman, 1990), esp. 119–23 on matrifocality. Subsequent references to Collins in the text refer to this book.

11. See Diane K. Lewis, "The Black Family: Socialization and Sex Roles" *Phylon* 36 (1975): 221–37. For a general discussion of matrifocality, see Nancy Tanner, "Matrifocality in Indonesia and Africa and among Black

Americans" in *Woman, Culture, and Society*, ed. M. Z. Rosaldo and Louise Lamphere (Stanford: Stanford University Press, 1974), 129–56.

12. See Andrew J. Cherlin, "Black-White Differences," in his *Marriage, Divorce, Remarriage* (Cambridge, Mass.: Harvard University Press, 1981). See also Henry A. Walker, "Black-White Differences in Marriage and Family Patterns," in *Feminism, Children and the New Families*, ed. Sanford M. Dornbusch and Myra H. Strober (New York: Guilford Press, 1988), 87–112.

13. See Bernice Johnson Reagon, "African Diaspora Women: The Making of Cultural Workers" *Feminist Studies* 12, no. 1 (Spring 1986): 77–90.

14. I have focused on African Americans in this paper, but Native American and Hispanic women have also organized from the position of mothering.

15. Gunhild O. Hagestad, "The Aging Society as a Context for Family Life," *Daedalus: Journal of the American Academy of Arts and Sciences* 115 (Winter 1986): 137. For a discussion of men's and women's differing types of social networks after divorce and women's affinity for kin networks, see Naomi Gerstel, "Divorce, Gender and Social Integration" *Gender and Society* 2, no. 3 (Sept. 1988): 343–67.

16. For a review of studies and this latter point, see Harriet E. Gross, "Open Adoption: A Research-Based Literature Review and New Data," *Child Welfare* 72 (May 1993): 269–84.

17. See, for example, Alice S. Rossi and Peter H. Rossi, *Of Human Bonding: Parent Child Relations Across the Life Course* (New York: Aldine de Gruyter, 1990).

18. See Colleen L. Johnson, *Ex Familia: Grandparents, Parents, Children Adjust to Divorce* (New Brunswick, N.J.: Rutgers University Press, 1988).

19. For concrete examples, see Judith Stacey, *Brave New Families: Stories of Domestic Upheaval in Late Twentieth Century America* (New York: Basic Books, 1990).

20. See Sara Ruddick, *Maternal Thinking: Toward a Politics of Peace* (New York: Random House, 1989).

21. Mary G. Dietz, "Context Is All: Feminism and Theories of Citizenship," *Daedalus: Journal of the American Academy of Arts and Sciences* 16 (Fall 1987): 1–24.

PART THREE

Enacting Theories

EIGHT

Women's Agency in
Psychological Contexts

JULIE NELSON-KUNA AND STEPHANIE RIGER

The feminist ideology that emerged in the United States during the 1960s united women on the basis of their status as a subordinate group. This ideology required that women identify themselves as victims in order to share a sense of solidarity with other women. Yet espousing feminism was itself an act of assertion and implicitly a denial of victim status. Although there was little room for agency in a worldview that saw women as a subordinate group, dominated by patriarchy, the assertive acts of women generated the feminist movement of that era. Indeed, women have long acted to solve community and social problems and to bring about social justice in unions, neighborhoods, politics, social service agencies, and many other settings.[1] These actions challenge the idea that women are passive victims of patriarchy.

A similar contradiction confronts the postmodern viewpoints that dominate much of contemporary feminist theory. According to postmodernism, our thought and perceptions are channeled in certain ways by discourses prevalent in our society. The capacity for independent thought and action in the face of hegemonic discourses is problematic. At the same time, many feminists place primacy on giving voice to women and consider that voice to be an authentic reflection of women's experience. This contradiction again centers on the dilemma of conceptualizing agency in the context of women's subordinate status in society.

The concept of agency is central not only in feminist theory but also in mainstream theories of human nature. Much of psychological theory, ignoring the influence of social context and reflecting a belief in individualism that characterizes American society, assumes that individuals are the origins of their actions. Yet accumulated research points to the importance of context as well as individual efficacy in shaping behavior. In the classic formulation of the social psychologist Kurt Lewin, behavior is a function of the interaction of personality and context. Yet many theories of agency have ignored the importance of context in shaping human action. This essay explores research on agency within the traditions of psychology in order to identify some ways out of the apparent contradictions in feminist theory.

Since Freud asserted that a mentally healthy individual was one who could work and love, psychologists have considered agency in contrast to communion. David Bakan was one of the first contemporary psychologists to make this distinction. In his book *The Duality of Human Existence*, Bakan describes agency as an individual acting in self-protection, self-assertion, and self-expansion while communion refers to an individual's sense of being part of a larger whole, at one with others: "Agency manifests itself in the urge to master; communion in contractual cooperation."[2] He further hypothesized that agency and communion are linked to gender. In his view, men's achievement strivings are directed at agentic concerns of self-assertion, attainment of status, and mastery over the environment. In contrast, women strive to achieve communion and are motivated to work cooperatively to attain a sense of harmony with others. However, Bakan does not define the concepts of agency and communion as bipolar opposites, but as separate, independent dimensions capable of coexisting within one person.

While Bakan's formulation of agency and communion is very broad, the sociologist Talcott Parsons's earlier distinction between instrumental and expressive activity is more specific, and thus potentially more useful.[3] In Parsons's formulation, instrumental actions are goal-oriented, while expressive actions are oriented toward relationships. Parsons did not use these terms as personality descriptors. Rather, the concepts of instrumentality and expressiveness refer to the way individuals interact in social systems. Instrumental activity focuses on achievement and accomplishment outside the immediate social group. In contrast, expressive activity involves an orientation toward the relationship interactions that exist within a social system. Hence, expressive actions manifest the principles of Bakan's concept of communion, while instrumental actions manifest those of agency. Like Bakan, Parsons does not view instrumental and expressive behaviors as two ends of the same continuum.

Rather, he stresses the need for both expressive and instrumental actions in individuals and in social groups.

Considerable research in psychology has adhered to the distinction between these two realms of behavior, namely the agentic/instrumental, "doing" realm and the communal, expressive, "feeling" realm. With the advent of feminist theorizing and the growing area of research focusing on the psychology of women, it has become obvious that this simple dichotomy is inadequate. Feminists have pointed out that the two domains are not equally valued in our society. Instrumental action is highly valued and defines what is conventionally considered "success." Expressiveness, associated with dependency, has traditionally had a negative connotation when used to characterize individuals. Jean Baker Miller, in her book *Toward a New Psychology of Women*, pointed out that women are punished for making relationships and connections central in their lives.[4] In a related vein, Carol Gilligan distinguished between autonomy and relatedness, and argued that psychological theories of development give primacy to the former while disregarding the latter.[5] In contrast to proponents of those theories, Gilligan emphasized the importance of relatedness in understanding women's moral actions. Yet this emphasis echoes the traditional concept of "separate spheres" in which woman is defined by her relationship with others,[6] ignoring the variability that exists among women (and men). Linking some behaviors to women and others to men obscures the fact that behavior itself has no gender and can be manifested by either sex.

Grace Baruch, Rosalind Barnett, and Caryl Rivers attempted, in their book *Lifeprints*, to redefine what is "well-being," or healthy behavior for women. They identified two dimensions of well-being, mastery and pleasure. Mastery reflects the instrumental dimension or the "doing" in life, in contrast to pleasure's emphasis on the expressive domain, or "feeling" side of life. According to these authors, women frequently neglect the mastery domain and thus are prone to depression and struggles with a lack of structure in their lives. They argue that "the best preventive medicine for women against depression is fostering their sense of mastery. The confident, autonomous woman is likely to be less vulnerable to depression. If we continue to insist that we will find the answers to a woman's problems . . . only in the realm of her feelings toward others, we will keep on looking in the wrong place."[7]

Although mastery and achievement may be key to women's depression, men's emotional difficulties may lie with expressiveness.

Miriam Johnson and her colleagues tested the separateness of Parsons's concepts of instrumentality and expressiveness by having people rate themselves on adjectives that represented these dimensions.[8] Johnson concluded from her research that the expressiveness dimension is a more basic aspect of gender difference than the instrumental dimension. Her findings suggest that women are able to integrate autonomous qualities with expressiveness in their self-concept, while men appear to deny the expressiveness dimension in their self-image.

These authors challenge the traditional attribution of agency to men and communion to women by maintaining that a balance of both domains is critical for all people. Yet they continue to maintain a false dichotomy. The separation of action and emotion, of instrumental and expressive activity, erects a boundary between "doing" and "feeling" that denies the interpenetration of these domains. Furthermore, considering these concepts as traits located within the person ignores the role of social context in eliciting behavior. Rather than the product of inner traits, gender-related behavior emerges in response to situational demands.[9] As Rhoda Unger forcefully put it, "Gender is created by social processes. When social demands are strong enough, people will behave in sex-characteristic ways whether or not they possess the sex-typed traits supposedly directing their behavior."[10]

A critical factor in women's mental health is the extent to which women's life circumstances permit the opportunity for agency. Abigail J. Stewart and her colleagues examined the levels of stress of women in five life situations: never-married employed women; married employed women without children; married mothers who did not work outside the home; married, employed mothers; and divorced, employed mothers. Although none of the life structures was stress-free, they varied in the risks and opportunities presented. Gaining a sense of agency was problematic for housewives, while single women without children were vulnerable to the opposite extreme: "unmitigated agency." The single working mothers had difficulty experiencing communion, while the working parents found it difficult to coordinate the agentic and communal aspects of their lives. Although not all life structures offer similar opportunities for agency and communion, the critical factor in emotional health appears to be the degree to which the opportunities provided by the life structure fit the needs of the individual's personality.[11]

Rachel Hare-Mustin and Jeanne Maracek view autonomy and relatedness as a function, not of one's gender or personality, but rather of one's position in a social hierarchy.[12] From this perspective, gender is not the sum of personality traits attributed to males and females but rather the product of interactional processes that occur within particular contexts. Those in higher positions tend to advocate rules and rationality, while those lower in the hierarchy emphasize relatedness. The highly valued attributes that our society defines as agentic are those associated with power and status because autonomy and mastery require the freedom to make choices. Frequently, what is considered feminine is the product of powerlessness and low status;[13] those not in a position of autonomy and choice must focus on connection and communal goals to survive. Accordingly, whether individuals act in an autonomous manner or operate in a communal mode reflects their relative position in the social structure.

In our society today, men (particularly white men) are more likely to occupy positions permitting autonomy while many women lack the institutional power, status, and economic independence to act agentically. Those characteristics traditionally viewed as endemic to being female—sensitivity, empathy, and nurturance—may be adaptive mechanisms to women's social position. Jean Baker Miller has claimed that women's subordinate status requires them to be aware of feelings, thoughts, and responses of others. Research by Sara Snodgrass supports the concept of interpersonal sensitivity as a function of social role rather than an innate or socialized gender difference. Snodgrass assessed people's ability to interpret correctly others' thoughts and feelings within interacting pairs of women, men, and mixed sex dyads. Interpersonal sensitivity did not differ by gender, but those in subordinate positions were more sensitive to the feelings of the other dyad member than were the leaders. She concluded that sensitivity is affected by the respective social roles of the participants rather than by their gender.[14]

Snodgrass's research reflects the fact that behavior is, in part, a function of social context. This position challenges the assertion that we are independent human actors, actively controlling our lives. Psychological theories tend to alternate between two paradigms, one that claims that the "person constructs reality" and the other that claims that "reality constructs the person."[15] What is needed instead is a dialectical paradigm that emphasizes the reciprocal, interactive relationship between the person and the social environment.

One such model is proposed by Kay Deaux and Brenda Major in their micro-level model of gender-related social interaction. Using a social psychological perspective, they suggest that three elements produce men's and women's social behavior: a perceiver, who enters an interaction with both a set of beliefs about gender and personal goals for the interaction; a target individual, who enters the interaction with his or her own gender-related self-conceptions and interaction goals; and a situation, which varies in the extent to which gender issues are relevant. This perspective emphasizes the importance of the interaction of situational factors and personal beliefs regarding gender: Gender-related behaviors are context-dependent, highly flexible, and multiply determined.[16]

Beliefs about gender form an important part of Deaux and Major's model. One such gender-related belief is that of self-efficacy, "people's beliefs about their capabilities to exercise control over events that affect their lives."[17] Emphasizing the role of cognition in determining behavior, self-efficacy theory claims that action is influenced by the belief that the activity or behavior can be accomplished, producing a distinction between possessing abilities and being able to enact them successfully. People will avoid situations and make choices in order not to undertake a task that they believe is too difficult. In this way, efficacy beliefs may limit and constrict the choices that one makes in life and may result in a diminished sense of agency.

Efficacy beliefs vary by gender. Among children, girls view themselves as less efficacious than boys on intellectual activities that have been stereotypically linked with males.[18] Compared with males, females tend to have lower estimates of their abilities, performance, and expectations for future success in achievement situations, even when they actually perform as well, if not better than males.[19]

Carol Dweck and her colleagues have identified a possible cause of these gender differences in self-efficacy. Dweck identified differences in the way children respond to task difficulty and experiences of failure. She noted the greater tendency for girls to attribute their failures to low ability rather than lack of motivation or effort. Girls responded to failure (or threat of failure, or even intensified evaluation pressure) with motivational and performance decrements, a phenomenon known as "learned helplessness." Girls consistently underestimate their chance for success while boys overestimate success.[20] The roots of these differences may lie in teachers' differential interactions with girls and boys. In one study, Dweck and her colleagues observed that, while girls received more positive feedback from the teacher than boys, this feedback was more likely to concern nonintellectual issues such as neatness. Almost all of the negative feedback directed to girls concerned the intellectual quality of their work, while only about half of such feedback directed to boys concerned intellectual content of their work and the rest was directed at neatness or form. Overall, the pattern of feedback encouraged boys more than girls to believe that their success reflected academic abilities, while their failures did not.

Self-efficacy beliefs are also influenced by emotions. People's beliefs in their ability to cope with anxiety-provoking situations affect how much depression and stress they experience. Additionally, they will avoid potentially threatening situations because they believe they will be unable to cope with the situation. These beliefs are related to having the coping skills needed to manage a stressful situation. Elizabeth M. Ozer and Albert Bandura created a "mastery modeling" program in which women learned the skills necessary to defend themselves against unarmed assailants. The mastery modeling training enhanced perceived coping and self-efficacy beliefs and decreased perceived vulnerability to attack. Women less often used avoidance as a safety strategy as their feelings of empowerment and self-assurance increased.[21]

In this brief overview, the limits of psychological research on agency are apparent. Much of this work ignores the larger context not only of cultural beliefs and values but also of the distribution of power and other resources that shape not only beliefs about, but also actual efficacy. Agency may have different meanings or take different forms in different contexts, or among different groups of people. Yet this overview suggests some possible directions for feminist theorizing about agency.

First, agency and communion may not be opposite ends of a single continuum; one can be high or low in both agency and communion. Mothering, for example, seems to encompass a high degree of both domains. Second, formulations that distinguish agency from communal or relatedness behavior may oversimplify by dichotomizing the two, creating a false distinction between them. Furthermore, precise definitions of agency are needed that include a cognitive component consisting of agentic beliefs. These beliefs may be a critical link between abilities and action, and they may connect the individual and the environment in a condition of mutual influence. Certainly societal views of women can influence self-efficacy beliefs, but individuals also have the capacity to evaluate their own abilities and to change that evaluation.

The famous dictum of the women's movement in the 1960s and

1970s, "the personal is political," reformulated women's personal problems as socially caused rather than the product of individual deficits. This dictum absolved women of personal responsibility for their low status in society, but it did not remove their responsibility to seek remedies through political action. That is, while social influences may constrain and shape women's agency, they do not remove the ability to act.

Rather than seeing women either as a product of environmental forces or as autonomous determiners of their destiny, it is critical to view women in a reciprocal relationship with their particular situational and structural environment. Agency is possible, but it occurs within a social context that frames it in certain ways. Close examination of women's lives reveals the ways in which subordinate status shapes those opportunities. Feminists are well aware that race, ethnicity, social class, and other factors that mark cleavages in our society limit women's autonomy, yet women respond to these limits in a variety of ways. Theories that incorporate a consideration of specific contexts and that recognize the multiplicity of ways of coping with those contexts will most accurately portray women's experience of agency.

NOTES

1. S. Reinharz, "Women as Competent Community Builders," in *Social and Psychological Problems of Women: Prevention and Crisis Intervention,* ed. A. U. Rickel, M. Gerrard, and I. Iscoe (Washington, D.C.: Hemisphere, 1984).

2. D. Bakan, *The Duality of Human Existence* (Chicago: Rand McNally, 1966).

3. T. Parsons, *The Social System,* (Glencoe, Ill.: Free Press, 1951); T. Parsons and E. Shils, *Toward a General Theory of Action* (Cambridge, Mass.: Harvard University Press, 1952).

4. J. B. Miller, *Toward a New Psychology of Women* (Boston: Beacon, 1976).

5. C. Gilligan, *In a Different Voice,* (Cambridge, Mass.: Harvard University Press, 1982).

6. L. Kerber, "Some Cautionary Words for Historians," *Signs* 11 (1986): 304–10.

7. G. Baruch, R. Barnett, and C. Rivers, *Lifeprints* (New York: McGraw-Hill, 1983), 22.

8. M. Johnson, *Strong Mothers, Weak Wives: The Search for Gender Equality* (Berkeley: University of California Press, 1988).

9. B. Lott, "Dual Natures or Learned Behavior: The Challenge to Feminist Psychology," in *Making a Difference: Psychology and the Construction of Gender*, ed. R. Hare-Mustin and J. Maracek (New Haven: Yale University Press, 1990), 71.

10. R. Unger, "Imperfect Reflections of Reality: Psychology Constructs Gender," in *Making a Difference: Psychology and the Construction of Gender*, ed. R. Hare-Mustin and J. Maracek (New Haven: Yale University Press, 1990), 116.

11. A. Stewart and J. Malley, "Case Studies of Agency and Communion in Women's Lives," in *Representations: Social Constructions of Gender*, ed. R. K. Unger (Amityville, N.Y.: Baywood, 1989), 61–76.

12. R. T. Hare-Mustin and J. Maracek, "Autonomy and Gender: Some Questions for Therapists," *Psychotherapy* 23, (1986): 205–12.

13. Lott, "Dual Natures," 65–101.

14. S. E. Snodgrass, "Women's Intuition: The Effects of Subordinate Role on Interpersonal Sensitivity," *Journal of Personality and Social Psychology* 49 (1985): 146–55.

15. A. R. Buss, "The Structure of Psychological Revolutions," *Journal of the History of the Behavioral Sciences* 14 (1978): 57–64.

16. K. Deaux and B. Major, "Putting Gender into Context: An Interactive Model of Gender-Related Behavior," *Psychological Review* 94 (1987): 369–89.

17. A. Bandura, "Human Agency in Social Cognitive Theory," *American Psychologist* 44 (1989): 1175.

18. J. E. Parsons, D. N. Ruble, K. L. Hodges, and A. W. Small, "Cognitive-Developmental Factors in Emerging Sex Differences in Achievement-Related Expectancies," *Journal of Social Issues* 32 (1976): 47–62.

19. J. L. Meece, J. Eccles-Parsons, C. M. Kaczala, S. B. Goff, and R. Futterman, "Sex Differences in Math Achievement: Toward a Model of Academic Choice," *Psychological Bulletin* 91 (1982): 324–48.

20. C. S. Dweck and T. E. Goetz, "Attributions and Learned Helplessness," in *New Directions in Attribution Theory*, vol. 2, ed. J. H. Harvey, W. Ickes, and R. F. Kidd (Hillsdale, N.J.: Erlbaum, 1978), 157–79.

21. E. M. Ozer and A. Bandura, "Mechanisms Governing Empowerment Effects: A Self-Efficacy Analysis," *Journal of Personality and Social Psychology* 58 (1990): 472–86.

NINE

Agency: What's the Problem?

SANDRA LEE BARTKY

Agency: what's the problem? Bodies of theory that have wide currency at the present time appear to deny that we have it—that's the problem. The various poststructuralisms (and some of the structuralisms) have been taken by many if not most commentators to deny the reality of agency, as we ordinarily understand agency. These bodies of theory proclaim "the death of the subject" and, hence, appear to deny the reality of subjectivity as we ordinarily understand subjectivity.

An "agent" is someone who is contemplating an action, has already acted, or is presently acting. But "action" *tout court* is not incompatible with the agent's being wholly determined by factors outside her control. Hence, the sense of "agency" that appears to be threatened by the poststructuralisms (and some structuralisms) must involve action of a particular sort—action that is self-generated or self-determined, action that arises as a consequence of an agent's (or subject's) having chosen so to act.[1] Agents or subjects that can act freely are called "moral agents" or "moral subjects" by philosophers: a moral agent is someone whose actions can be evaluated according to moral criteria, i.e., whose deeds can be vicious or virtuous, praiseworthy or blameworthy. The moral evaluation of the actions of a subject assumes not only the freedom, hence the responsibility, of the one acting, but, in addition, the rationality and maturity of this subject as well. I have regarded myself as a subject in this sense: Have the reports of my death been exaggerated?

The fashionable poststructuralisms (and some structuralisms) claim, or appear to claim, that I am wholly constructed within the dominant discourses and practices of my society, that I am an "effect" of "regimes" of power/knowledge, that my identity has been constituted within the phony binarisms of Western philosophy, that

I am not someone who produces texts so much as someone produced by them, that I am hopelessly fractured—far too fractured ever to fit the description of the moral agent offered above, having left behind important parts of my "self" when I entered the Symbolic (culture), that I myself have been "interpellated" or "called forth" by the dominant ideology, i.e., that not only are my beliefs forms of ideological mystification, but so is my very sense of myself as a rational and autonomous individual.[2]

The hoary problem of free will versus determinism will not be gainsaid: here it is again. There is more at stake than questions about the freedom and hence the moral accountability of individual subjects; the possibility of radical political transformation appears to be threatened as well. If the least sympathetic critics of poststructuralism are correct, then the political subject who dreams that she is sufficiently free, in concert with other political subjects, to bring into being an even freer subject in a free society is simply deluded. Since it is impossible in a short space to examine all the major poststructuralists, in what follows I will focus on one exemplary poststructuralist: Michel Foucault. I will argue that there is nothing in Foucault's account of the social construction of the subject that threatens the concept of agency or compels us to abandon, in principle, the idea of a subjectivity free enough to build a freer society.

There are two major schools of Foucault interpretation: the one posits a "bad Foucault" who puts forward a theory of the subject that, in effect, denies the possibility of political agency, hence of meaningful political betterment; the other, a "good Foucault" who is himself a rebel against the existing order of domination and whose work is intended merely to warn us of the limits and dangers that are attendant upon projects of social amelioration. Clearly, the "good Foucault" poses no threat in principle to the possibility of moral or political agency. The most effective critics of the "bad Foucault" have argued, on the contrary, that Foucault's conception of the subject is incoherent in that it tacitly assumes in the course of critique what it explicitly denies. Now if Foucault's theory of the subject is incoherent, as these critics claim, and if Foucault's theory of the subject is, in effect, a critique of agency as agency is ordinarily understood, it fails, for an incoherent critique of agency is no critique at all. In the next section, I will examine a version of the "bad Foucault," in the one following, the "good Foucault." In the final section, I will offer some observations of my own that bear on Foucault interpretation and hence on the question of agency.[3]

While Peter Dews's compelling *Logics of Disintegration* takes issue with Foucault's concept of the subject, Dews finds much in Foucault's reading of the nature of modernity that is challenging, provocative, and with which he is clearly in agreement. I have no quarrel with Dews's exposition of Foucault's ideas; hence I will merge my exposition with his and turn to Dews's specific critique of Foucault later in this section.

Foucault claims that from the onset of modern times, the state was committed to forms of administration and the provision of welfare that were unknown in feudal Europe and which led to increasingly more invasive forms of social and psychological control (Dews, 146–47). Hence, the Age of Enlightenment gave birth not only to modern democratic institutions and to the idea of inalienable human rights, but also to multiple projects of control, new and unprecedented disciplines that target the body in order, ultimately, to gain control of the mind.

Power in feudal societies could be exercised in ways that were quite brutal. Nevertheless, this power was haphazard and inefficient; much of civil society lay beyond its reach. The monarch—image and embodiment of power—was a public personage. The king was known, but his subjects were largely unknown; his power was exercised on a largely anonymous body of subjects. Foucault argues that the transition to modern society involved "a reversal of the political axis of individualization."[4] This means that effects of power in modern societies "circulate through progressively finer channels, gaining access to individuals themselves, to their bodies, their gestures, and all their daily actions."[5] As the project of control cannot go forward without the knowledge of how to control, the "human sciences" are thus forms both of knowledge and power, "regimes" of "power/knowledge" enlisted in the service of what Foucault calls the "disciplinary" or "carceral" society. The bureaucratic mode in which power is exercised becomes increasingly faceless and impersonal. Everyman, however, loses *his* anonymity; everyone becomes a case.

Many of the disciplinary practices that Foucault associates with modernity antedate modernity, but they are taken up, refined and expanded, in the peculiarly modern forms of the army, the asylum, the school, the hospital, the prison, the factory, and the family. The new disciplinary practices require that an uninterrupted coercion held in place by constant surveillance be directed to the very processes of bodily activity; a "micro-physics" of power partitions the body's time and its space; it regiments the body's posture, gesture, and motility and requires a minute and precise articulation of the body's relationship to such instruments as the rifle, the school desk, or the machine (DP, 28). "A 'political anatomy' which was also a 'mechanics of power,' was being born; it defined how one may have a hold over others' bodies not only so that they may do what one wishes, but so that they may operate as one wishes, with the techniques, the speed and the efficiency that one determines. Thus, discipline produces subjected and practiced bodies, 'docile' bodies" (DP, 139). Foucault's conception of the practice most indispensable to the creation of "docile bodies"—surveillance—is captured in the image of the Panopticon, Jeremy Bentham's design for a model prison, in which one jailer in a central tower watches many criminals displayed in windowed cells. The arrangement of windows, one facing outward, the other inward, allows an effect of backlighting that makes figures within the cell visible to the supervisor in the tower. "All that is needed, then, is to place a supervisor in a central tower and to shut up in each cell a madman, a patient, a condemned man, a worker or a schoolboy" (DP, 200). "Panopticism" resonates throughout society: it is no surprise then that "prisons resemble factories, schools, barracks, hospitals, which all resemble prisons" (DP, 228).

The effects of surveillance mechanisms directed initially toward the disciplining of the body get a hold on the mind as well; they induce a psychological state of "conscious and permanent visibility" (DP, 201). This perpetual surveillance is internalized, giving rise to that reflective self-awareness which is the hallmark of the individual in bourgeois society. The anonymity of the jailer's gaze from the tower is a metaphor for the impersonality of modern bureaucratic power. The shift from "juridical power" (the power of the monarch, priest, or judge) to the disciplinary power of modern administrative bureaucracies is paralleled by the shift from epic narrative to the modern literature of introspection and to the rise of philosophies of consciousness (Dews, 160).

According to Dews, Foucault is not pointing to the asymmetrical and inegalitarian features of modern society in order to urge upon us democratic reforms that would make possible a true self-determination. "Foucault's argument is that any theory of sovereignty or self-determination must be abandoned, since the 'free subject' upon which such theories rely is in fact intrinsically heteronomous, constituted by power" (Dews, 161). The disciplinary practices of modernity that construct the modern subject do not limit liberty; they are, says Foucault, "the *foundation* of the formal juridical liberties"

(*DP*, 222). Hence, "the man described for us whom we are invited to free"—presumably in both older and newer discourses of liberation—"is already in himself the effect of a subjection much more profound than himself" (*DP*, 30).

Dews maintains that it is Foucault's aim to establish a direct and unequivocal relationship between "subjectification"—the production of subjects—and "subjection" (Dews, 16). This Foucault states explicitly in the first volume of *The History of Sexuality:* "Men's subjection: their constitution as subjects."[6] "Sexuality," says Foucault, "is the set of effects produced in bodies, behaviors and social relations by a certain deployment deriving from a complex political technology . . ." (*HS*, 127). Sexuality has, of course, a biological basis, but as lived by specific historical subjects, it is a system of discourses and practices that "forms part of the intensifying surveillance and control of the individual which is Foucault's central historical theme" (Dews, 165).

The "deployment" of sexuality is not primarily repressive, for power can produce pleasure. "Deployment" constructs subjects both through the incitement to desire and in the fixing of identities. One's identity is now thought to inhere in a core sexual self, a self linked to the ritual of confession. This linkage illustrates nicely Foucault's claim that the constitution of subjectivity itself is an effect of oppressive social practices. Confession, be it religious or psychoanalytic, unfolds within an inegalitarian relationship, for one confesses to another who has authority not only to require the confession but also to determine whether the confession reveals a core self that is virtuous or vicious, mature or immature, normal or abnormal.

Dews is critical of Foucault on a number of grounds. While Foucault appears hostile to the technologies of domination he describes in such detail, the normative standpoint that informs this hostility is obscure. Foucault's rejection of Enlightenment humanism is well known: he cannot reject the carceral society on behalf of a freedom to be won by a potentially free subject, if to be a subject at all is already to have been subjugated. The modern subject is not the autonomous subject of liberal political theory; for Foucault, such a subject is illusory. Remember: "Men's subjection: their constitution as subjects." Dews claims that Foucault is unable to say "how a situation would change if an operation of power were cancelled"; he cannot admit the possibility of such a "counterfactual" because he regards power as omnipresent, not because it would have the privilege of gathering everything under its invincible unity, but because it is produced at every moment, at every point or rather in every relation between points (Dews, 167).

The extraordinary looseness of this conception of power is linked to Foucault's lack of normative clarity. Dews regards this conception of power ("power is everywhere") as a vague metaphysical monism, a night in which all cows are black. There is no longer anything determinate to which a power so conceived could be opposed; moreover, if "effects" of power produce desire, as Foucault argues in the *History of Sexuality*, the link between power and oppression, on the one hand, and desire and liberation, on the other, is severed. Differently put, this diffuse a conception of power removes the teeth from any genuine critique of power.

To his diagnosis of the reasons for Foucault's lack of normative clarity, Dews adds another damaging charge: this involves an alleged incoherence in Foucault's conception of the subject. In spite of the pervasive and suffocating presence of power everywhere in the social totality and in spite of his inability to say precisely what is wrong with modern disciplinary power, Foucault maintains that "where there is power, there is resistance" (*HS*, 95). Resistance, moreover, "is never in a position of exteriority in relation to power. . . . points of resistance are present everywhere in the power network" (*HS*, 95). What precisely are these "points of resistance"? If subjects are constituted within disciplinary regimes of power, *who* is it that resists? Is the "who" that resists not a subject? If not a subject, then what? Why is there resistance at all? Why do some resist and not others? In a word, how is resistance possible?

There are passages in the *History of Sexuality* in which Foucault makes unexplained reference to "the body and its pleasures" as an alternative to the practiced and docile body brought into being by the "deployment" of sexuality. He yearns in one passage for an *ars erotica* in which, unlike the *scientia sexualis*—the regime that now holds sway—pleasure would not be considered "in relation to an absolute law of the permitted and the forbidden, nor by reference to a criterion of utility, but first and foremost in relation to itself" (*HS*, 76). These references to the "body and its pleasures"—to what Dews calls "the libidinal body," a body that could somehow escape the network of power relations and disciplinary practices—appears flatly to contradict the uncompromising theory of the social construction of the subject that Foucault develops in his most celebrated work.

So Foucault appears to be impaled on the horns of a dilemma.

Either he abandons the high ground of an uncompromising social constructionism for some version of naturalism or biological essentialism—a move that would nullify his very premise in the *History of Sexuality*, i.e., the wrongness of sexual liberationist notions of a repressed natural sexuality (the "repressive hypothesis")—or else he is stuck with the incoherent notion of resistance without a resister, a totally untheorized resistance that is knowable only as the absolute Other to power and whose origins and basis lie shrouded in mystery.

I turn now to Jana Sawicki's admirable *Disciplining Foucault*, a feminist retrieval of the "good Foucault," a Foucault whose theory of the subject should hold no terror for female agency or for feminist politics. There are gaps, admits Sawicki, in Foucault's account of the genesis of the modern subject: focusing on the microstructures of power, he is not sufficiently attentive to its macrostructures. Sawicki admits Foucault's lack of normative clarity. Nevertheless, she believes that Foucault's project is compatible with values such as "justice, liberty and human dignity" (11). While Sawicki is aware that Foucault sometimes writes as if the hold of disciplinary power were total, she reminds us too of Foucault's claim that "resistance and struggle are co-present with power and that power is continually transformed in the face of such resistance" (71). Sawicki cites a late interview with Foucault: "I'm not positing a substance of power. I'm simply saying: as soon as there's a relation of power there's a possibility of resistance. We're never trapped by power: its always possible to modify its hold, in determined conditions and following a precise strategy."[7] Foucault's model of the social field is of myriad shifting relations, multiple centers of power confronting multiple centers of resistance. Sawicki understands this to mean that socialization is a theoretical project that is never completely realized in practice. Foucault does not see the relationship between society and the individual as one of univocal determination, but as one of ambiguity and conflict. Nor should we forget that "individuals are the vehicles as well as the targets of power" (64). Hence, Foucault's "social constructionism need not imply social determinism" (41). Nor does his social constructionism pose a principled threat to the reality of human liberty. Again Sawicki supports her reading of Foucault with a citation from another late interview: "Power is exercised only over free subjects and only insofar as they are free."[8] The meaning of Foucault's work for Sawicki is primarily procedural and methodological. His rejection of the atomic, asocial individual of Enlightenment political theory and of theories that posit an authentic human nature can free us for new forms of subjectivity. This is particularly important for feminism, since a strong case can be made that the most influential theories of human nature have been androcentric. While Foucault himself generally neglects gender, his genealogies—i.e., his inquiries into the origin and development of power/knowledge regimes—can, by revealing their contingency, free us from their influence; again, these inherited regimes are androcentric. Foucault's genealogical method is also designed to facilitate an "insurrection of subjugated knowledges"— forms of knowledge that "have been disqualified as inadequate to their task, or insufficiently elaborated: naive knowledges located low down in the hierarchy, beneath the required level of cognition or scientificity."[9] These are the voices of the odd, the mad, the delinquent, the silenced, the different. They are the voices of women, *our* voices. But Sawicki finds in Foucault's conception of a knowledge/ power regime and in its other, subjugated knowledge, a cautionary tale for feminists: the white, middle-class bias of much feminist theory reveals the power of the relatively advantaged to ignore the "subjugated discourse" of the less advantaged. Without any conscious intent to introduce a racism of omission into feminist writing, what was supposed originally to be the articulation of a subjugated discourse can turn out to function as a hegemonic discourse, i.e., as an instrument of domination.

Feminist theory is linked indissolubly with theories of sexuality and in Foucault's theory of the social construction of the sexual subject, Sawicki again finds cautionary tales for feminists. While Foucault does sometimes speak as if the "domain of sexuality were already colonized beyond redemption," he understands sexuality as we must understand it too: neither wholly outside nor yet wholly circumscribed by power, it is an arena for struggle wherein there are no "inherently liberatory or repressive sexual practices"(43). Feminism has produced its own deployment of sexuality: it too has generated normalizing discourses that attach individuals to particular identities, deviation from which bespeaks a low level of consciousness or worse, the scandal that one isn't "really" a feminist. Showing far better political sense than Foucault himself, Sawicki defends "identity politics" in a society that persecutes those it has already attached to stigmatized and despised identities. In the same vein, she quite rightly defends the practice of consciousness-raising as a feminist strategy against Foucault's critique of the confessional.

One methodological feature of Foucault's work that Sawicki especially admires is his nuanced analysis both of the subtle forms of social control that are at work in the "micropolitical" encounters of everyday life and of the "deep regularities and broad and impersonal forces that make us what we are" (99). A knowledge of these anonymous historical processes can give us a certain critical distance on our own sensibilities: such knowledge should not lead to a denial of rational agency but to a more secure understanding of its parameters, its possibilities, and its limits.

Here then are two very different readings of Foucault. Whose Foucault is the real Foucault, the "bad Foucault" whose theory of the social construction of the subject within networks of power denies the possibility of agency, autonomy, and liberation from domination ("Men's subjection: their constitution as subjects") or the "good Foucault" who does not deny the reality of liberty and whose aim it is merely to refine and historicize our understanding of agency ("Power is exercised only over free subjects and only insofar as they are free")? For our purposes, it matters not whose Foucault is the "real" Foucault. If Dews's reading is correct, Foucault's theory of the making of the modern subject is both implausible and incoherent: the implicit critique of agency contained in so flawed an account of the processes of "subjectification" need detain us no longer. If Sawicki's reading is the right reading, then Foucault has added important new theoretical dimensions to our understanding of agency. Either way, agency is saved.

It is difficult to leave this topic without some comparison of two such contradictory interpretations of the same thinker. In some ways, such a comparison is misleading: Dews is far more concerned to attack Foucault than Sawicki is to defend him. She searches out in Foucault's work what feminists, especially, can find useful in it; she raids the master's toolbox.[10] Nor does Sawicki hesitate to take Foucault to task both for his androcentrism and for his political pessimism. Sawicki's project, as I understand it, is to show that Foucault's methodology is compatible with a political framework that continues to privilege the Enlightenment values of "justice, liberty and human dignity." She does, however, offer a general interpretation of Foucault's work that is, on balance, in line with the use she wishes to make of him. Sawicki's Foucault is a philosophical libertarian concerned principally to identify the mechanisms that suppress our liberty.[11]

Part of the problem lies with Foucault himself. Many of his pronouncements in interviews given after the publication of the central texts that established his reputation seem flatly to contradict the tenor and direction of these earlier texts. Furthermore, as I argue below, there are two quite different models of the functioning of power at work in these major texts. What appear to be disparities between the late interviews and the positions Foucault takes in his major texts bespeak, for some, flexibility, a refreshing lack of dogmatism and the courage for constant intellectual innovation. For others, these disparities betray fundamental, indeed fatal, inconsistencies in his thought; when faced with these inconsistencies, it is as if Foucault were saying, "That is not what I meant, not what I meant at all."

Peter Dews's Foucault interpretation relies on the major texts of Foucault's maturity—*Madness and Civilization, The Birth of the Clinic, Discipline and Punish, The History of Sexuality, Vol. 1*—in which the constitution of the modern subject is spelled out in some detail, while a substantial number of Sawicki's citations are to interviews given by Foucault after the appearance of the main body of his work, indeed, after the emergence of the sorts of criticisms of his work that are elaborated in Dews's text. In one of his last interviews, Foucault speaks of liberation, a topic strikingly absent from his central texts: "I do not mean to say that liberation or such and such a form of liberation does not exist. When a colonial people tries to free itself of its colonizer, that is truly an act of liberation, in the strict sense of the word. But as we also know . . . this act of liberation is not sufficient to establish the practices of liberty that later on will be necessary for this people, this society and these individuals to decide upon receivable and acceptable forms of their existence or political society."[12] The phrase "practices of liberty" and the clear implication in this passage that political freedom is not only desirable but possible sounds strange issuing from the great enemy of Enlightenment. The same late interview yields another surprising observation: "I don't believe that there can be a society without relations of power if you understand them as means by which individuals try to conduct, to determine the behavior of others. The problem is not of trying to dissolve them in the utopia of a perfectly transparent communication but to give one's self the rules of law, the techniques of management, and also the ethics, the *ethos*, the practice of self, which would allow these games of power to be played with a minimum of domination."[13] Here, the "relations of power" have been radically demoted: in the great works on which Foucault built his reputation, power does not just "try" to determine the behavior of others, it succeeds in constructing the very subjectivity of the subject—her self-consciousness, her desire, and her identity—the "truth of her being." The self that here gives itself the rule of law seems unlike the docile, practiced, and self-policing subject of *Discipline and Punish* and quite like the Kantian self whom Foucault has been thought to have buried. Nor is there anything in this passage that can explain why a self, or a community of selves capable of giving *themselves* "rules of law," would still have to suffer a "minimum of domination."

Sawicki cites with approval Foucault's claim that "where there is power, there is a resistance." But this seems flatly false: certainly the exercise of power is very often consented to or colluded in. Moreover, neither Sawicki nor Foucault seem able to meet Dews's challenge: If power does indeed create identities and shape desires, *who* is it that resists? Whence comes the desire to resist? What are the origins of this resistance? What are its motives?

I want to argue now that there are *two* quite distinct models of the operation of power at work in Foucault's texts. In addition to the apparent lack of fit between many of Foucault's most influential works and his late interviews, there is a more serious lack of fit between Foucault's differing understandings of the nature and operations of power. Foucault's own conflation of these models gives rise, I believe, to the problem about the nature, identity, indeed, the possibility, of the one who resists the imposition of power.

On the first model, power is the maker of persons. Power is productive and its products are specific forms of historical subjectivity. Since Foucault rejects the claim that there is anything like a human nature that is transhistorical in character, power on this model has in effect a *tabula rasa*—the individual, not yet a subject—on which to inscribe its various constructions. But power so conceived appears to differ very little from socialization. Indeed, Sawicki expressly identifies power as producer of persons with "socialization" (41). But socialization is a largely descriptive, not a normative notion. If the power that is productive of subjects is no more than socialization in disguise, then Foucault's critique of the "carceral society" loses all force. His treatment of modern disciplinary power, however, is thoroughly critical in tone even while the basis of this critique remains obscure, hence his famous lack of "normative clarity." Sawicki can find Enlightenment values in Foucault—"justice, liberty and human dignity"—because these values function as the suppressed, indeed the denigrated premises of his argument.[14]

The second model of the functioning of power is not that of power as person-maker but of power as one player in a social field—really a battlefield—where multiple centers of power confront multiple centers of resistance. Sawicki: "Power circulates in this field and is exercised on and by individuals over others as well as themselves" (25). When asked in an interview who it is that struggles against whom, Foucault answers in a manner worthy of Hobbes: "This is just a hypothesis, but I would say it's all against all. There aren't immediately given subjects of a struggle, one the proletariat, the other the bourgeoisie. Who fights against whom? We all fight against each other. And there is always within each of us something that fights something else."[15] Dews's objection to Foucault's claim that "power is everywhere" is, in my view, vindicated: power conceived in so diffuse a fashion loses its role in an effective political critique. A host of different modes of conflict, some external, some internal, are here distilled into one brew: Dews's "vague metaphysical monism." A bad metaphysics may have crept into the picture, certainly a bad politics. "We all fight against each other": How would this sit with the victims of sexist or racist violence or with the proletariat of Lordstown, Ohio, victims of "crises of profitability" who may well spend the rest of their "immediately given" lives on the dole? Power cannot make us at once the subjected subjects of the carceral society and the antagonists on a Hobbesian "darkling plain" of ceaseless strife.

I end with several cautionary notes of my own. While Sawicki is undoubtedly correct in valuing Foucault's account of "deep regularities" and "broad and impersonal forces" in history, his account is by no means the premier account of such forces. Foucault's attitude toward Marxism is consistently ambiguous: at times he attacks it, at other times patronizes it, and sometimes is at pains to show its continuity with his own work. We should not lose sight of the fact that the various Marxisms have produced detailed and impressive bodies of theory that lay out not only the "deep regularities" and "broad historical forces" in history (regularities and forces to which Foucault pays little attention) but offer accounts as well of the ways in which these forces have structured institutions and generated subjectivities.[16] In my view, we ignore these bodies of theory at our peril.

Foucault is less ambiguous and more openly hostile toward psychoanalysis. While I do not think that a version of psychoanalysis has yet appeared that satisfies fully the requirements of feminist theory, I doubt that without it we will be able to understand unconscious processes, certain kinds of irrational behavior, the genesis and power of many modes of desire, infantile sexuality, or the implantation or perpetuation of gendered identities. Foucault's accounts of "subjectification" are original and compelling, but they need to be supplemented by at least this "human science," whatever its historic entanglement in projects of domination. Once again, we ignore the search for an adequate political psychology at our peril.[17]

Fashions in theory change: Foucault and other poststructuralists such as Derrida and Lacan have recently been in vogue. But we must remember that long before Foucault's writing had found an audience here, indeed, long before Foucault had written many of the works on which his fame chiefly rests, feminists of the Second Wave had already produced an impressive critical analysis of the micropolitics of everyday life, the normalizing practices of masculinity and femininity, the compulsory imposition of identities, and the regimes of knowledge and power that sat like toads on our own emerging but still subjugated discourse. Early on, what many regarded as a subjugated discourse was found to be, by virtue of its unintended racism, a discourse that subjugated others. This discovery was not made by studying the texts of structuralists or poststructuralists but in the context of political struggle, a struggle waged by feminists of color (and some white feminists) against the blindness of a largely white-dominated feminist theory and practice; what was and still is being struggled for is a multiracial, cross-class movement that can bring into being a freer society of freer agents. The discourse that has emerged from this struggle and from struggles around such things as age, class, and sexual preference is feminist discourse too; it is theory linked to practice, which, in turn, is animated by a utopian vision. "Where there is no vision, the people die." Where there is no vision, a political movement may die as well. It is a tribute to Foucault's influence that we find ourselves so often using his terminology to describe what it was we were doing and indeed are doing still. But Foucault's dystopia of skirmish and counterskirmish, of "all fighting each other" into an indefinitely prolonged future, is not our vision. We have powerful and original political and intellectual traditions of our own; flawed though they may be, we ought to honor them.

NOTES

1. For purposes of this essay, I take "agent" and "subject" to be synonymous.

2. The theories alluded to here are, in order, those of Foucault, Derrida, Lacan, and Althusser.

3. Commentators who find a significant degree of incoherence in Foucault's theory of the subject include: Peter Dews, *Logics of Disintegration* (London: Verso, 1987)—hereafter "Dews"; Michael Walzer, "The Politics of Michel Foucault," and Charles Taylor, "Foucault on Freedom and Truth," both in *Foucault, A Critical Reader*, ed. David Hoy (New York: Basil Blackwell, 1986); Nancy Fraser, *Unruly Practices: Power, Discourse and Gender in Contemporary Social Theory* (Minneapolis: University of Minnesota Press, 1989); Fredric Jameson, "Postmodernism, or, the Cultural Logic of Late Capitalism," *New Left Review* 147 (Sept. 1984), 52–92. Feminist critics who find Foucault's theory of the subject incompatible with feminist politics include Susan Bordo, "Feminism, Postmodernism and Gender-Skepticism," and Nancy Hartsock, "Foucault on Power: A Theory for Women?" both in *Feminism/Postmodernism*, ed. Linda Nicholson (New York: Routledge, 1990). See also Linda Alcoff, "Feminism and Foucault: The Limits to a Collaboration," in *Crises in Continental Philosophy*, ed. Arleen Dallery and Charles Scott (New York: State University of New York Press, 1990); and Barbara Christian, "The Race for Theory," in *Gender and Theory: Dialogue on Feminist Criticism*, ed. Linda Kauffman (New York: Basil Blackwell, 1989), 225–37.

Some defenders of the "good Foucault" include Paul Rabinow, Introduction to *The Foucault Reader*, ed. Rabinow (New York: Pantheon Books, 1984); David Hoy, Introduction and "Power, Repression, Progress: Foucault, Lukes and the Frankfurt School," also Richard Rorty, "Foucault and Epistemology," all in *Foucault, A Critical Reader*. Some feminist critics who find Foucault's theoretical framework useful for feminism include Jana Sawicki, *Disciplining Foucault* (New York: Routledge, 1991) (see extended discussion in the text below, where quotations from Sawicki are cited parenthetically); Irene Diamond and Lee Quinby, Introduction and "American Feminism and the Language of Control," in *Feminism and Foucault*, ed. Diamond and Quinby (Boston: Northeastern University Press, 1988). In the same volume see Biddy Martin, "Feminism, Criticism and Foucault," and Mary Lydon, "Foucault and Feminism: A Romance of Many Dimensions."

4. Michel Foucault, *Discipline and Punish* (New York: Vintage, 1979), 44. Hereafter cited as *DP*.

5. Michel Foucault, *Power/Knowledge*, ed. Colin Gordon (Brighton: Harvester, 1980), 151. Cited by Peter Dews, "Power and Subjectivity in Foucault," *New Left Review* 144 (Mar.–Apr. 1984): 17.

6. Foucault, *The History of Sexuality*, vol. 1 (New York: Vintage, 1980), 60. Hereafter cited as *HS*.

7. Michel Foucault, "The History of Sexuality: An Interview," trans. Geoff Bennington, *Oxford Literary Review* 4, no. 2 (1980): 13, cited in Sawicki, 25.

8. Michel Foucault, "The Subject and Power," Afterword in Hubert Dreyfus and Paul Rabinow, *Michel Foucault: Beyond Structuralism and*

Hermeneutics (Chicago: University of Chicago Press, 1982), 221, cited in Sawicki, 25.

9. Michel Foucault, Introduction to *Herculine Barbin: Being the Recently Discovered Memoirs of a Nineteenth Century French Hermaphrodite* (New York: Pantheon, 1980), 126, cited in Sawicki, 26.

10. See, for example, "Foucault, Femininity and the Modernization of Patriarchal Power, in Sandra Bartky, *Femininity and Domination: Studies in the Phenomenology of Oppression* (New York: Routledge, 1990).

11. See esp. her note 18: "The subject presupposed in Foucault's later discourses resembles the creative, nihilating subject found in the writings of French existentialist, Jean-Paul Sartre" (125).

12. "The Ethic of Care for the Self as a Practice of Freedom: An Interview with Michel Foucault on January 20, 1984," in *The Final Foucault*, ed. James Bernauer and David Rasmussen (Cambridge, Mass.: MIT Press, 1988), 12–13.

13. Ibid., 18, cited in Sawicki, 124.

14. The same point is made in a paper by Isaac Balbus, "Disciplining Women: Michel Foucault and the Power of Feminist Discourse," in *After Foucault: Humanistic Knowledge, Postmodern Challenges*, ed. Jonathan Arac (New Brunswick, N.J.: Rutgers University Press, 1988), 138–60.

15. Foucault, *Herculine Barbin*, 208, cited by Sawicki, 25.

16. See, for example, Samuel Bowles and Herbert Gintis, *Schooling in Capitalist America* (New York: Basic Books, 1976); Richard Sennett and Jonathan Cobb, *The Hidden Injuries of Class* (New York: Vintage, 1973); Reimut Reiche, *Sexuality and Class Struggle* (New York: Praeger, 1971); Michael Schneider, *Neurosis and Civilization* (New York: Seabury Press, 1975); Eli Zaretsky, *Capitalism, the Family and Personal Life* (New York, Harper and Row, 1976); Bertell Ollman, *Social and Sexual Revolution* (Boston: South End Press, 1979). Ollman writes very perceptively of the earlier work of Wilhelm Reich, which, while flawed in many ways, attempts to understand character formation in terms of the intersection of the micropolitics of the family with the macrostructures of capitalism. See, for example, Wilhelm Reich, *Sex-Pol: Writings 1929–1934*, ed. Lee Baxandall, with an introduction by Bertell Ollman (New York: Random House, 1972). While their Marxism is very unorthodox, much of the work of the Frankfurt School belongs in this category as well. See for example, Theodor W. Adorno, Else Frenkel-Brunswik, Daniel J. Levinson, R. Nevitt Sanford, *The Authoritarian Personality* (1950; reprint, New York: John Wiley and Sons, 1964). See also Max Horkheimer, "Authoritarianism and the Family," in *The Family: Its Function and Destiny*, ed. Ruth Anshen (New York: Harper, 1949). The remarkable work of Herbert Marcuse should be mentioned in this connection as well: see *Eros and Civilization: A Philosophical Inquiry into Freud* (New York: Vintage, 1962). In *A History of Sexuality*, vol. 1, Foucault consistently underplays his indebtedness to Marcuse and Reich.

17. For an account of what such a psychology would entail, see Dorothy

Leland, "Lacanian Psychoanalysis and French Feminism: Toward an Adequate Political Psychology," in *Revaluing French Feminism: Critical Essays on Difference, Agency and Culture,* ed. Nancy Fraser and Sandra Bartky (Bloomington: Indiana University Press, 1991).

TEN

Subjects and Agents:
The Question for Feminism

SUSAN HEKMAN

It has become a commonplace of contemporary philosophy that the epistemology of modernity is rooted in the epistemology of the knowing subject. Modernity's search for absolute, indubitable knowledge has been defined, at least since Descartes, in terms of the knowing, constituting subject. Descartes's *ego cogito, ergo sum* placed the certainty that is the goal of modern philosophy firmly within "man" himself. The centrality of the subject to modernity, furthermore, has become the focus of the current reassessment of the project of modernity. Critics of modernity, from those who want to reform its project to those who want to discard it altogether, have criticized the definition of the subject that is its hallmark. Even though the subject of modernity is not a unitary one—there are, for example, important differences among the Kantian subject, the Cartesian cogito, and the subject of empiricism—the current critique of the subject encompasses all these varieties. Given the comprehensiveness of this critique it is hardly surprising that the question of the subject has also become central to feminist theory. How feminists should conceptualize the subject and how that subject relates to the now embattled subject of modernity have become crucial to the feminist project in recent decades.

Feminist assessments of the modernist subject, however, predate the current attack on the modernist subject. Considerations of the subject have gone through several stages since the first articulations of feminist thought in the modern era. Early liberal feminist thinkers such as Wollstonecraft and Mill pursued what seemed to be the obvious feminist approach to the question of the constitution of the subject: the appropriation of the modernist subject. For these liberals it seemed apparent that the feminist project must be to attempt to open up the category of the subject to include women. Socialist feminists pursued much the same tactic. Although both liberal and socialist feminism have moved away from an unquestioning reliance on the transcendental subject, this concept has continued to exert a powerful influence. Specifically, the belief in a rational, agentic subject is crucial to the argument for women's equality within both the liberal and socialist camps.

The turning point in feminist assessments of the modernist subject came with the claim by twentieth-century feminists that the subject of modernity, both liberal and socialist, is gendered, that is, that it is defined in exclusively masculine terms. This claim, generated in large part by de Beauvoir's analysis in *The Second Sex*, set the stage for the current controversy over the subject within feminism. There have been four principal responses to the definition of the subject as masculine within feminist thought, approaches that today enjoy various degrees of popularity. First, some feminists have argued that the subject of modernity is only incidentally and not inherently masculine. Thus they have held that this subject can be purged of its masculine elements and that feminists can utilize a neutered, redefined subject. This is the tactic employed by de Beauvoir as well as by a number of contemporary feminists.[1] A second tactic, however, has become more popular in recent years. A growing number of feminists have sought to define an essentially feminine subject in opposition to the masculine subject of modernity. Far from attempting to open up the masculine subject to women, these feminists have instead attempted to define a distinctive feminine subject, a subject that counters the rationality and separateness of the masculine subject. Proponents of this approach, usually classified as radical feminists, see the feminine subject as superior to the masculine subject and all the attendant evils that subject has inflicted on the modern world.[2]

The third response to the claim that the modernist subject is masculine has involved the attempt to explore the social and linguistic constitution of the feminine subject. What have come to be labeled "social constructionist" feminists emphasize the way in which social institutions and discursive forces constitute both the masculine and feminine subject. Social constructionists reject the essentialism of the radical feminists' subject as well as that of the modernist subject. Instead they argue that all subjects are constituted rather than constituting, products of the forces that structure societal institutions.[3]

The introduction of the constituted subject of the social constructionists has had a profound effect on discussions of the subject within feminism. The resulting dichotomy between the constituting subject, whether conceived in terms of a redefined modernist subject or an essentially feminine subject, and the constituted subject structures nearly all contemporary feminist debates over the subject. Social constructionists argue that women have been constructed as passive, irrational, and overly emotional by masculine structures of domination. Liberal, socialist, and radical feminists argue that this conception of the feminine subject is inadequate because it defines women as wholly passive, the dupe of social forces. They argue that unless we retain at least a quasi-essentialist notion of the subject, we will lose what is fundamental to the feminist struggle: agency. Thus the question of agency—what it means and how it can be effected—has come to the forefront of discussions of the subject.

That this dichotomy between the constituted/constituting subject and the attendant problem of the definition of agency is fundamental to an understanding of the contemporary debate over the subject is widely acknowledged. What is not widely acknowledged, however, is that this dichotomy is itself a product of modernist discourse and is, on that account, suspect. The contrast between the constituting, transcendental, essential subject on one hand, and the constituted subject, the "social dupe," on the other is parasitic on the modernist definition of the subject as the source of knowledge and certainty. The insight that this dichotomy itself is the root of the problem of the subject confronting feminist theory and that it ought to be radically deconstructed defines the fourth approach to the subject current in feminist discussions. Although this approach is commonly labeled "postmodern feminism," feminists who employ this approach have developed a perspective that is only related to and not identical with the frequently gender-blind approach of the diverse array of postmodern thinkers. Proponents of this approach argue that the transcendental subject of modernity implies its opposite, the constituted subject of the social constructionists. Further, they argue that, strictly speaking, the constituted subject is, in modernist terms, no subject at all but, rather, an object (hence de Beauvoir's point that woman is not subject, but the Other, the object). It follows that the "dilemma" that informs contemporary feminist discussions of the subject arises out of the rigid dichotomies that characterize modernist, masculinist discourse. Thus the solution to that dilemma is not to be found within that discourse but lies in displacing it. These feminists urge that feminism reject modernist discourse and its problematic in favor of an approach that deconstructs its fundamental dichotomy: masculine/feminine.

Contemporary feminist debate on the subject is wide-ranging; variations on these four responses abound. Many of the discussions within this debate merely reiterate the standard positions. Others, however, move beyond the rigid dichotomies of modernist thought because they attempt to confront the problem of the constituting versus the constituted subject. In the following I will argue for one of those attempts, an approach I will label the "discursive subject." This approach rejects essentialism in all its guises, whether modernist or feminist, but not by turning to the constituted subject of the social constructionists. Rather, it attempts to displace the constituting/constituted dichotomy altogether and thus the problematic that has created the "crisis" of the feminist subject.

At the outset I want to distinguish the approach of the discursive subject from that of another approach to the subject that has become increasingly popular in contemporary feminist theory. Theorists such as Paul Smith, Diana Meyers, Linda Alcoff, and Teresa de Lauretis present what might be called a "dialectical" concept of the subject.[4] At the center of this approach is the attempt to wed some essentialist, constituting elements to a socially constructed subject. On the face of it, proponents of the dialectical subject and advocates of the discursive subject seem to be engaged in the same project: overcoming the dichotomy between the constituted and the constituting subject. But a closer look suggests a different conclusion. Proponents of the dialectical subject are, ultimately, unable to break out of the constraints of modernist discourse. They want to retain elements of the modernist, constituting subject in order to preserve the agency that this subject represents. They thus posit a dialectical relationship between "inner" and "outer" worlds. The approach of the discursive subject is more successful because it involves a more radical critique of the modernist subject. By exploding the constituting/constituted dichotomy it moves the debate onto a different epistemological plane. Most importantly, it provides definitions of agency and creativity that are not bound to the modernist definition of the constituting subject.

What distinguishes what I call the discursive subject is the attempt to displace the modernist subject rather than reconstruct it. The discursive subject shifts the epistemology of the subject onto new ground; it enters what Althusser calls a "new continent of thought." The hallmark of the discursive subject that is emerging in contemporary discussions is the rejection of the binarism that grounds modernist discourse in general and, specifically, discussions of the subject. Oppositions, polarities, and dichotomies have structured modernist thought since its inception. These dichotomies are inherently hierarchical; within the discourse of modernism to declare an opposition is to privilege one element over another. The dichotomy that has structured the philosophy of the subject at least since the time of Descartes is that of subject/object, that is, the opposition between the transcendental, constituting subject and the object of this subject's knowledge. This dichotomy parallels the dichotomy that structures contemporary feminist discussions of the subject, that between the constituted and the constituting subject. Modernist epistemology dictates that the constituted subject is not a subject at all. It is this conviction that has made the constituted subject so controversial in contemporary feminist theory. The current rejection of the constituted subject and the assumption, particularly within feminism, that it is not a "real" subject stems from the long-standing modernist subject/object opposition that defines the true subject as constituting.

The discursive subject displaces this fundamental opposition of modernist discourse. This displacement has several different sources; both postmodernists and feminists have contributed to its articulation. One of the key elements of this displacement is the postmodern attack on binarisms. Postmodern thinkers, and Derrida in particular, have attempted to erase the oppositions of modernist thought, to deconstruct the dichotomies that ground that discourse. Central to this argument is the assertion that the opposition of these dichotomies is only apparent, that opposites "inhabit" each other and thus are not opposites at all. Applied to the modernist discourse of the subject, this has led to the assertion that subjects are not removed from objects of knowledge, but, rather, that they occupy the same discursive space. This has also led to the deconstruction of the constituted/constituting dichotomy. Postmodernists have claimed that there is no neat opposition between these two subjects, but, rather, that subjects are always both constituted and constituting. They thus argue that this opposition does not describe the situation of subjects within discursive spaces.

Another principal theme of the postmodern deconstruction of the subject has been the effort to recontextualize the transcendental subject of modernity. The effect of Foucault's work in particular has been to place the transcendental subject in historical perspective, to reveal this subject as the product of a particular epistemology that arose in the early modern period. The transcendental subject, by definition, lacks a context; what it transcends is historical, social, and discursive influences. Foucault deconstructs this claim by arguing that all subjects—and the Cartesian subject in particular—have a specific context, a discursive space. Foucault further argues that the transcendental subject fails to describe the experience of subjectivity, particularly as we encounter it in the modern world, because subjectivity is always contextual. Feminist thought has also been very influential in contextualizing the subject of modernity. De Beauvoir's work revealed that the subject of modernity does not transcend gender, but, rather, is specifically masculine. Kristeva's work, like that of Foucault, places the constitution of subjects in historical and social contexts but, unlike Foucault, genders the subject as well.[5] The result of these efforts to recontextualize the subject has been to articulate a subject that is historically and socially specific.

The articulation of this recontextualized subject has had a profound effect on feminist discussions of the subject. The dichotomy that informs the subject/object opposition as well as the binarism of Western epistemology itself is rooted in the opposition of masculine/feminine. Like all other binarisms, this opposition is hierarchical: Western epistemology has disprivileged the feminine since its inception. Feminists have decried this disprivileging for centuries but their critique has remained within the epistemology of modernity. Some contemporary feminists, however, are now arguing that modernist epistemology must be radically displaced. Following the postmodern lead they have argued that we must reject the masculine/feminine distinction at the root of that epistemology.[6] Consequently, they have also argued that feminists must displace the gendered dichotomy between the subject and object of knowledge.[7] These feminists claim that the constituting subject of modernity has no relevance to the experience of women. Following Foucault they have asserted that the transcendental subject, the constitutor of knowledge, is particularly inappropriate to the experience of women who have been conceptualized as objects rather than subjects of knowledge.

The advocacy of a discursive subject along postmodern lines has been very controversial in feminist discussions.[8] Many feminist theorists are critical of the emergence of a "postmodern feminism" that they claim is "postfeminist."[9] Three principal issues are problematic. The first is that of identity or essence. If, as those who advocate the discursive subject would have it, the masculine/feminine binarism should be abandoned, does it necessarily follow that the category of "woman," a category that is fundamental to a feminist politics, must also be abandoned? The critics of the discursive (postmodern) subject have asked how feminists can argue for the liberation of women if this subject obviates the category of "woman" altogether. They assert that feminists must seek to define the essentially female apart from the masculine sphere that has been hegemonic for so long.

These are serious questions, but they do not necessarily yield the answers that the essentialists assert. The most telling point to be made against the essentialists is that the definition of the category "woman" has varied historically; it is not a unitary entity. Defining "essential woman," furthermore, has been throughout history a strategy employed by masculine, hegemonic discourses to privilege men over women and a certain class of women over other women who do not fit the preordained category.[10] Feminists have employed many of the insights of postmodern thought in their effort to reveal the historical basis of the category "woman" as well as its repressive power. Foucault's contribution here is significant. His multivolume examination of how the modern self emerged in Western history dethrones the authority of the modernist subject. From a different perspective Charles Taylor also traces the evolution of the modern sense of identity in his *Sources of the Self.*[11] Steven Toulmin presents a similar theme in his work on modernity.[12] Foucault, Taylor, and Toulmin all reject the transcendental self of the Cartesian tradition and seek instead to define the self in historical, relational terms, as a product of the framework (Taylor) or discourse (Foucault) of a historical period.

Despite the value of these accounts, however, their usefulness for feminist discussions is limited by their gender-blindness. None of these accounts emphasizes the gendered nature of the historically evolving concept of self in Western thought. Feminists have filled this gap by stressing the gendered basis of the Cartesian definition of the subject[13] as well as the modernist conception of rationality.[14] The historicizing of the concept of self has freed feminists to explore how identities and selves are constructed and to investigate the power relationships that fuel specific constructions of "woman." The implications of this approach are clearly stated by Donna Haraway: "We need the power of modern critical theories of how meanings and bodies get made, not in order to deny meanings and bodies, but in order to build meanings and bodies that have a chance for life."[15] The perspective of the discursive subject allows feminists to see that the attempt to find the "essential woman" or even to define a unitary concept of "woman" is counterproductive. The aim of feminist theory must be a critical genealogy of gender constructs; universal categories defeat this goal.[16] Universal categories are parasitic on masculinist, hegemonic discourses that disprivilege woman in general and specific groups of women in particular. Deconstructive tools, on the other hand, can be a valuable resource in understanding the discursive construction of conceptions of "woman."[17]

The subject that emerges from this perspective is a heterogeneous subject. It is a subject that is a product of the fluctuating, changing, and often conflictual historical and social influences that impinge on it. This subject is not without an identity, but identity is no longer conceived in even quasi-essentialist terms. Rather, it is an identity that is fluid, heterogeneous, changing. Again, Donna Haraway puts this point very clearly: "Subjectivity is multidimensional. . . . The knowing self is partial in all its guises, never finished, whole, simply there and original; it is always constructed, situated together imperfectly, and *therefore* able to join with another, to see together without claiming to be another."[18] An essentialist conception of identity, whether masculine or feminine, is always unitary and hierarchical. It deals with identity in terms of "difference": the identity of the masculine/feminine is "different from" its opposite. But difference is itself a hierarchical term. Difference presupposes a standard; that which is different from the standard is necessarily inferior to it. Talk of difference also presupposes both a margin and a center. Feminists who argue that we need to overcome the marginalization of women by positing a feminine identity are not eliminating marginality; rather they are positing a new center that will, in turn, create margins of its own.[19] Elizabeth Spelman argues very forcefully in *Inessential Woman* that if we seek to define "essential woman" as a new center this center will not be composed of all women, but, rather, of white, middle-class, heterosexual women; other women will be marginalized. In contrast to this effort to define "woman," the discursive subject posits a subjectivity based on differences, not difference, a heterogeneous, plural, nonhierarchical identity that is not essentialist or constructionist, but entails a displacement of that opposition. This discursive subject does not result in the elimination of the identity of women, but in replacing "woman" with women whose differences are not erased.

A second central issue that confronts the feminist advocacy of the discursive subject is that of agency and the closely related issue of creativity. The dichotomy between the constituted and constituting subject dictates that agency is the sole province of the constituting, transcendental subject. The long-standing philosophical problem of free will versus determinism is a corollary of this dichotomy. The constituting subject is the subject of free will, the subject that determines his place in life, that forges his destiny, that decides to be free. The constituted subject, on the other hand, is determined, a product of social forces rather than their creator, a social dupe. From the modernist perspective, this subject does not deserve the label "subject" at all.

The problems created by this dichotomy are evident in discussions of agency and autonomy in contemporary social and political theory as well as in feminism. But for feminism these problems are particularly acute. Many feminists have argued that if we renounce the Cartesian, constituting subject we are simultaneously renouncing the possibility of agency, particularly the political agency that is central to the project of feminism. Although feminists have been concerned to specify how discursive formations constitute the feminine subject in contemporary discourse, these same feminists have been reluctant to embrace the constituted subject because, they believe, it entails a passivity that is the antithesis of the agentic feminism that they advocate. In the case of the theorists who advocate a dialectical subject, this has resulted in borrowing agency from the constituting subject, that is, the attempt to graft agency onto the constituted subject.

The postmodern attempt to dislodge modernist binarisms suggests another approach. For the constituting subject agency entails reference to an "inner world" untainted by social forces; for the constituted subject, social forces are wholly determining and thus agency is obviated. For the discursive subject, however, agency and construction are not antithetical. Rather, agency is a product of discourse, a capacity that flows from discursive formations. The discursive subject redefines agency in a way that explodes the boundaries imposed by the constituting/constituted dichotomy. It does not entail reference to a prediscursive "I" but, instead, entails that subjects find agency within the discursive spaces open to them in their particular historical period. The perspective offered by the discursive subject suggests that it is not the case that Descartes discovered the "truth" about human subjectivity and its agentic potential, but, rather, that the agency that is the hallmark of the Cartesian subject is created by the discourse of that subject, that is, that it enables those who employ it to speak as agents.

This redefinition of agency has important implications for feminist theory. Unlike the approach I have labeled dialectical, an approach that attempts to graft a Cartesian concept of agency onto the constituted subject, the discursive approach allows feminists to embrace agency without reference to the masculinist Cartesian subject; it allows them to posit an "I" with agency without reference to a presocial entity divorced from discursive forces; and it allows them to describe how the feminine subject is constructed through the multiple discursive formations of a given culture while at the same time asserting that some, although not all, of these discursive formations provide the possibility of agency. Although many of the discourses that construct the feminine within our culture deny women agency, construct them as passive and dependent, others do not. Feminists can look to the enabling discourses for the agency they require, particularly in the political arena. Thus some feminists have employed the discourse of maternity to effect political agency. Others have employed discourses, such as liberalism and socialism, that exclude women, redefined these discourses, and employed the agency implicit in them for feminist ends. Neither of these tactics requires the discovery of the essential "I," the constituting subject within all of us. Rather, it entails using the tools provided us by the discursive mix that constitutes our social existence. Judith Butler puts this point very nicely when she states that "Construction is not opposed to agency; it is the necessary scene of agency, the very terms in which agency is articulated and becomes culturally intelligible."[20]

The question of agency is inseparable from the question of creativity. Agents are subjects that create, that construct unique combinations of elements in expressive ways. Modernist epistemology dictates that creativity, like agency, necessitates a constituting subject, a prediscursive "I." Yet, again, another definition is possible. Central to the definition of the discursive subject is the assumption that, in any given historical era, discursive formations are multiple and heterogeneous. Even though in every era there will be hegemonic discourses, other nonhegemonic discourses will also exist, forming a discursive mix from which subjectivity can be constructed. Foucault calls these nonhegemonic discourses "subjugated knowledges." The redefined understanding of creativity suggested by the discursive subject entails that subjects piece together distinctive combinations, that is, individual subjectivities, from the discursive mix available to them. This does not mean that each subject chooses the elements of that discursive mix that match his/her pregiven subjectivity. Rather, it entails that subjectivities are products of the discourses present to subjects, not removed from or preceding them.

The creativity involved in establishing subjectivity is analogous to the creativity involved in the speaking of a language. Language speakers are bound by their language in their efforts to create unique sentences. Yet they do so in distinct and sometimes awesome ways.[21] The creation of subjectivity is much the same: it is bounded by given discourses, but it can and does result in unique creations. Again Judith Butler puts this point clearly: "There is no self that is prior to the convergence or who maintains 'Integrity' prior to its entrance into this conflictual cultural field. There is only a taking up of the tools where they lie, where the very 'taking up' is enabled by the tools lying there."[22] What results from such taking up of the tools is the creation of a subjectivity that is, as Foucault puts it, a work of art.[23]

The multiplicity of language also informs a third issue that is relevant to the feminist advocacy of the discursive subject: resistance. Once more, the assumptions that inform the constituting/constituted dichotomy define the problem. If the constituting, agentic subject is the subject that resists, then how can resistance be conceptualized apart from this subject? Foucault has been very instrumental in answering this question, and his answer has much relevance for the feminist project. His principal point is that language is not a closed system. The diversity and multiplicity of language creates the possibility of resistance because nonhegemonic discourses can be used to destabilize and subvert hegemonic discourses. Contradictory discourses coexist in social settings; cultural fields are always conflictual. It follows that discourses can be reconfigured and deployed to subvert each other.[24] Foucault's vision of how resistance can occur within discursive formations can be illustrated from the history of feminism. In our culture women have been scripted by discursive formations as passive, emotive, irrational, and unfit for politics. Feminists have subverted these discourses and resisted the subordination of women by employing discourses, such as liberalism and Marxism, that declare universal human equality. Claims for the equality of women that are the centerpiece of contemporary feminism have not come out of nowhere but, rather, have arisen from established discourses that coexist with the repressive discourses.

Another point central to Foucault's argument is that discourses that repress create subjects that resist oppression. For Foucault, subjects resist power by refusing to be the self that power defines for them.[25] They do so by constructing counterdiscourses that disavow power. But these constructions are not independent of social determinations; they do not derive from a "true," asocial self. Rather, they are created out of the resources available to members of the culture, to speakers of the language and the multiplicity of discourses that comprise a language and a culture. It also follows that since discourses are multiple, resistance to discourses will also be multiple, or, as Foucault puts it, local. He argues that those who are the victims of power will devise their resistance "on their own terrain."[26] He refers to "local, popular knowledges" (subjugated knowledges) that have been suppressed that will reappear through local resistance.[27] Resistance, he claims, will be "mobile and transitory," attacking power where it is weakest, attacking at all the multiple points at which power is exercised.[28]

Foucault's argument that resistance, like agency and creativity, comes from within the discursive formations of a society, not from an inner or "true" self, is directly relevant to the feminist project. For feminism it entails that it is not necessary to define a constituting subject, either conceived on the Cartesian model or as "essential woman," to posit a subject that resists. Defining resistance as the employment of existing discourses against hegemonic repression, furthermore, aptly describes how feminists have formulated resistance to masculinist discourses. Finally, Foucault's understanding of resistance as composed of multiple points of resistance has led feminists to the assertion that the discourses that script women as inferior are themselves multiple; they inhabit nearly every aspect of our cultural life. It follows that these discourses can best be resisted heterogeneously. Resistance will form at the points of oppression; it will be diverse because the oppression itself is diverse.

The question of the subject and how feminists should conceptualize subjectivity is central to many of the issues that now confront feminist theory. The issues discussed above, the identity of "woman," the conceptualization of agency and creativity, and the understanding of resistance, are pivotal to the definition of the feminist project. My aim here has been to argue that feminist theory is best served by completely rejecting the modernist philosophy of the subject in all its guises and by embracing what I have defined as the discursive subject. That many feminists have been reluctant to accept this conception of the subject is obvious from contemporary feminist discussions. In the above arguments I have tried to meet the principal objections raised in these discussions. The key to my argument is the assertion that the discursive subject displaces the binarisms that structure the modernist philosophy of the subject. The advocates of the dialectical subject, on the other hand, although they likewise seek to overcome the modernist subject, offer a theory that reinforces the central dichotomies of that subject. The discursive subject represents a more radical critique. One of the strengths of feminist theory has been its success in documenting the exclusion of women from the spheres of knowledge and subjectivity as they have been conceived by modernist thought. The advantage of the discursive subject is that it displaces that epistemology rather than attempting to reform it. This subject offers a viable concept of subjectivity that avoids the masculinist strictures of the modernist subject without sacrificing identity, agency, creativity, or the possibility of resistance.

NOTES

1. See, for example, Margrit Eichler, *The Double Standard: A Feminist Critique of Social Science* (London: Croom Helm, 1980); Barbara Sichterman, *Femininity: The Politics of the Personal*, trans. John Wilton (Minneapolis: University of Minnesota Press, 1986).

2. See, for example, Mary Daly, *Gyn/Ecology: The Metaethics of Radical Feminism* (Boston: Beacon Press, 1978).

3. See, for example, Sherrie Ortner and Harriet Whitehead, eds., *Sexual Meanings: The Cultural Construction of Gender and Sexuality* (New York: Cambridge University Press, 1981). These categories sometimes overlap. Some feminists who identify themselves as radical feminists take a social constructionist position.

4. Paul Smith, *Discerning the Subject* (Minneapolis: University of Minnesota Press, 1988); Diana Meyers, *Self, Society and Personal Choice* (New York: Columbia University Press, 1989); Linda Alcoff, "Cultural Feminism Versus Post-structuralism: The Identity Crisis in Feminist Theory," *Signs* 13, no. 3 (Spring 1988): 405–36; Teresa de Lauretis, *The Technologies of Gender* (Bloomington: Indiana University Press, 1987).

5. Julia Kristeva, *Revolution in Poetic Language*, trans. Margaret Waller (New York: Columbia University Press, 1984).

6. Gayatri Spivak, "Sex and History in *The Prelude* (1805): Books Nine to Thirteen," in Gayatri Spivak, *Other Worlds* (New York: Methuen, 1987), 77.

7. Jane Gallop, *Reading Lacan* (Ithaca: Cornell University Press, 1985), 15.

8. For an extended defense of postmodern feminism see Susan Hekman, *Gender and Knowledge: Elements of a Postmodern Feminism* (Boston: Northeastern University Press, 1990).

9. Nancy Hartsock, "Re-thinking Modernism: Minority vs. Majority Theories," *Cultural Critique* 7:187–206; Rosi Braidotti, *Patterns of Disso-*

nance: A Study of Women in Contemporary Philosophy (Cambridge: Polity Press, 1991).

10. Elizabeth Spelman, *Inessential Woman* (Boston: Beacon Press, 1988).

11. Charles Taylor, *Sources of the Self: The Making of the Modern Identity* (Cambridge, Mass.: Harvard University Press, 1989).

12. Stephen Toulmin, *Cosmopolis: The Hidden Agenda of Modernity* (New York: Free Press, 1990).

13. Susan Bordo, *The Flight to Objectivity* (Albany: State University of New York Press, 1987).

14. Genevieve Lloyd, *The Man of Reason: "Male" and "Female" in Western Philosophy* (Minneapolis: University of Minnesota Press, 1984).

15. Donna Haraway, "Situated Knowledges: The Science Question in Feminism and the Privilege of Partial Perspective," *Feminist Studies* 14 (1988): 580.

16. See Judith Butler, *Gender Trouble: Feminism and the Subversion of Identity* (New York: Routledge, 1990); Irene Diamond and Lee Quinby, eds., *Feminism and Foucault: Reflections on Resistance* (Boston: Northeastern University Press, 1988).

17. See Donna Haraway, "A Manifesto for Cyborgs: Science, Technology and Socialist Feminism in the 1980's," *Socialist Review* 80 (1985): 65–107.

18. Haraway, "Situated Knowledges," 586.

19. Gayatri Spivak, "Explanation and Culture: Marginalia," in Spivak, *Other Worlds*, 104–7.

20. Butler, *Gender Trouble*, 147.

21. M. M. Bakhtin, *Speech Genres and Other Late Essays*, trans. McGee (Austin: University of Texas Press, 1987), 120.

22. Butler, *Gender Trouble*, 145.

23. Michel Foucault, "The Subject and Power," in Hubert Dreyfus and Paul Rabinow, *Michel Foucault: Beyond Structuralism and Hermeneutics* (Chicago: University of Chicago Press, 1982), 287.

24. Butler, *Gender Trouble*, 145.

25. For this interpretation of Foucault, see Michael Shapiro, *The Politics of Representation* (Madison: University of Wisconsin Press, 1988), 216; and Jana Sawicki, *Disciplining Foucault: Feminism, Power and the Body* (New York: Routledge, 1991).

26. Michel Foucault, *Discipline and Punish*, trans. Alan Sheridan (New York: Random House, 1977), 216.

27. Michel Foucault, *Power/Knowledge* (New York: Pantheon Books, 1980), 82.

28. Michel Foucault, *The History of Sexuality*, vol. 1, trans. Robert Hurley (New York: Random House, 1980), 96.

ELEVEN

Feminist Forms of Agency and Oppositional Consciousness: U.S. Third World Feminist Criticism

CHÉLA SANDOVAL

The enigma that is U.S. third world feminist criticism has yet to be confronted fully by analysts of social change. For these late twentieth-century cultural theorists it has remained inconceivable that U.S. third world feminism represents a form of historical consciousness whose very structure lies outside the conditions of possibility that have regulated the oppositional expressions of dominant feminism. In enacting this new form of historical consciousness, U.S. third world feminism provides access to a different way of conceptualizing not only U.S. feminist consciousness but also oppositional activity in general. Indeed, U.S. third world feminism comprises a methodology for theory and action that is capable of aligning U.S. movements for social justice with worldwide movements of decolonization.

Both in spite of and because they represent varying internally colonized communities, U.S. third world feminists generated a common speech, a theoretical structure that remained just outside the purview of the dominant feminist theory emerging during the 1970s. Even though this unimaginable presence arose to reinvigorate and refocus the politics and priorities of dominant feminist theory during the eighties, what remains is an uneasy alliance between what appears on the surface to be two different understandings of domination, subordination, and the nature of effective resistance—a shotgun arrangement at best between what literary critic Gayatri Spivak characterizes as a "hegemonic feminist theory," on the one side, and what I call "U.S. third world feminist theory," on the other.[1] I do not mean to suggest here, however, that the perplexing situation that exists between U.S. third world and hegemonic feminisms should be understood merely in binary terms. On the contrary, what this investigation reveals is the way in which the theory of oppositional consciousness and social movement considered here and enacted under U.S. third world feminism was made deeply invisible, by the manner of its appropriation, in the terms of what became during the 1970s a hegemonic feminist theory and practice.

U.S. third world feminism rose out of the matrix of the very discourses denying, permitting, and producing difference. Out of the imperatives born of necessity came a mobility of identity that generated the activities of a new citizen-subject, a new sense of being and action that insists upon another model for the self-conscious production of political opposition and social movement. In this essay I lay out U.S. third world feminism as the design for oppositional political activity and consciousness in the United States. In mapping this new design, the model reveals a way for social activists to chart the points through which contending liberation ideologies and practices might meet, in spite of their varying trajectories. This knowledge becomes important when one begins to wonder how organized oppositional activity and consciousness can be made possible under the coopting nature of first world "postmodern" cultural conditions.[2]

A BRIEF HISTORY

From the beginning of what has been known as the second wave of the women's movement, U.S. third world feminists have claimed feminisms at odds with those being developed by U.S. white women. Already in 1970 with the publication of *Sisterhood Is Powerful*, black feminist Francis Beal was naming the second wave of U.S. feminism as a *"white* women's movement" because it insisted on organizing along the binary gender division male/female alone.[3] U.S. third world feminists, however, have long understood that especially one's race, but also culture, sexuality, or class often deny comfortable or easy access to either gender category, that the interactions between social categories produce other genders within the social hierarchy. As far back as the middle of the last century, Sojourner Truth found it necessary to remind a convention of white suffragists of her female gender with the rhetorical question, "Ar'n't I a woman?"[4] American Indian Paula Gunn Allen has written of Native women that "the place we live now is an idea, because whiteman took all the rest."[5] In 1971, Toni Morrison wrote of U.S. third world women that "there is something inside us that makes us different from other people. It is not like men and it is not like white women."[6] That same year Chicana Velia Hancock concluded: "Unfortunately, many white women focus on the maleness of our present social system as though, by implication, a female-dominated white America would have taken a more reasonable course" for people of color of either sex.[7]

These signs of a lived experience of difference from white female experience in the United States repeatedly appear throughout U.S. third world feminist writings. Such expressions imply the existence of at least one other category of gender, reflected in the very titles of books written by U.S. feminists of color, such as *All the Women Are White, All the Blacks Are Men, But Some of Us Are Brave* or *This Bridge Called My Back*, titles that imply that women of color somehow exist in the interstices between the legitimized categories of the social order.[8] Moreover, in the title of bell hooks's 1981 book, the question "Ain't I a Woman" is transformed into a defiant statement, while Amy Ling's feminist analysis of Asian-American writings, *Between Worlds*, or the title of the journal for U.S. third world feminist writings, *The Third Woman*, also call for the recognition of a new category for social identity.[9] This in-between space, this third gender category, is also recognized in the early writings of such well-known authors as Maxine Hong Kingston, Gloria Anzaldúa, Audre Lorde, Alice Walker, and Cherrie Moraga, all of whom argue that U.S. third world feminists represent a different kind of "human"—new "mestizas," "Woman Warriors" who live and are gendered "between and among" the lines, "Sister Outsiders" who inhabit a new psychic terrain that Anzaldúa calls "the Borderlands," or "la nueva Frontera," and which is available only through "la conciencia de la mestiza." In 1980, Audre Lorde summarized the U.S. white women's movement by saying that "today, there is a pretense to a homogeneity of experience covered by the word SISTERHOOD in the white women's movement. When white feminists call for 'unity,' they are misnaming a deeper and real need for homogeneity." We began the 1980s, she says, with "white women" agreeing "to focus upon their oppression as women" while continuing "to ignore difference." Chicana sociologist Maxine Baca Zinn rearticulated this position in 1986, saying that "there now exists in women's studies an increased awareness of the variability of womanhood," yet for U.S. feminists of color "such work is often tacked on, its significance for feminist knowledge" and for political practice "still unrecognized and unregarded."[10]

How did 1980s hegemonic feminism respond to this other kind

of feminist theoretical activity? The publication of *This Bridge Called My Back* in 1981 made the presence of U.S. third world feminism impossible to ignore, but soon the writings and theoretical challenges of U.S. third world feminists were marginalized into the category of mere "description" and their essays deferred to "the special force of poetry."[11] Meanwhile the shift in paradigm I refer to as "differential consciousness," represented in the praxis of U.S. third world feminism, was bypassed and ignored. If, during the 1980s, U.S. third world feminism had become a theoretical problem, an inescapable mystery to be solved for hegemonic feminism, then perhaps a theory of difference—but imported from Europe—could subsume if not solve it. I would like to provide an example of how this systematic repression of the theoretical implications of U.S. third world feminism occurs.

FEMINISM'S GREAT HEGEMONIC MODEL

During the eighties, hegemonic feminist scholars produced histories of feminist praxis that have fast become the official stories by which the white women's movement understands itself and its interventions in history. I analyze these narratives as systematic accounts that, once typologized, make clear the structure of a hegemonic feminism. It is U.S. third world feminism, recognized and utilized as a theoretical and methodological apparatus, that enables us to view each category in its relationship to the others as a separate though linked social system of constraints, required repressions, and permissible sublimations. Here, each category is considered a different though connected ideology, a strategy not only of feminist resistance but also of domination and subordination.

Though the overall rationale of this dominant typology of resistance furthers certain feminist political aims, it also denies and makes invisible the expression of another form of feminism, a form capable of transforming the very grounds upon which feminism as an oppositional movement understood itself, the nature of consciousness in resistance, and the possibilities of enacting or "performing" politics. What emerges from this analysis is U.S. third world feminism as theory and method, as the "other" form of consciousness in opposition capable of clarifying the accepted taxonomy of feminist forms and their meanings, while extending their possibilities into a realm of new and more effective oppositional activity under contemporary first world cultural conditions.

In a longer essay I traced the structure of this hegemonic typology, this shared code, through the works of feminist scholars Gayle Greene, Coppélia Kahn, Julia Kristeva, Toril Moi, Gerda Lerner, Cora Kaplan, Alice Jardine, and Judith Kegan Gardiner.[12] For the purposes of this shorter essay, I follow its expression through several key texts of the 1980s: the influential 1985 essay by literary critic and feminist theorist Elaine Showalter, "Toward a Feminist Poetics"; through the introduction to the now-classic set of essays on the "future of difference" in the women's movement published in 1985 and edited by feminist critics Hester Eisenstein and Alice Jardine; and through political scientist Alison Jaggar's massive dictionary of all the possible genera of feminist consciousness and politics, published in 1983.

Elaine Showalter developed what she identifies as a three-phase "taxonomy, if not a poetics, of feminist criticism." What is interesting is that a similar three-stage structure continually emerges across the 1980s text of hegemonic feminist theory and criticism, and this structure is always conceptualized by feminist thinkers as proceeding temporally. For example, in Showalter's version of a first-stage feminism, "Women wrote in an effort to equal the intellectual achievements of the male culture." Meanwhile, feminist thinker Hester Eisenstein apparently agrees, arguing in her book that in a first-phase women's movement, women wanted to "demonstrate that differences between women and men were exaggerated, and that they could be reduced" to a common denominator of sameness. In another place, Alison Jaggar emphasizes that a first stage of what might be considered a feminist history of consciousness, this effort, that is, to find sameness, can be paradigmatically understood as a "liberal" form of feminism.[13]

The second phase of what became a shared feminist typology of the 1980s Showalter describes by saying that women came to "reject the accommodating postures" of the first "feminine" phase, and instead came to "use literature to dramatize wronged womanhood." Eisenstein's typology puts it this way: a second "assumption about difference evolved," she writes, "specifically that women's lives WERE different from men's, and that it was precisely this difference that required illumination." Jaggar's argument is that it was during a second-phase feminism that, historically speaking, women turned to Marxism as a way to undermine first-phase liberalism. Their desire was to restructure the old society so that it becomes incapable of subordinating the differences that the class of women represent.[14]

In the third, "female" and final phase for Showalter, "women reject" both earlier stages as forms of dependency on men and their culture and "turn instead to female experience as the source of an autonomous art." Eisenstein's similar third phase identified "female differences originally seen as a source of oppression" as "a source of enrichment." This is a "woman-centered" phase, she argues, wherein maleness, not femaleness, is the difference that matters—now men, not women, become "the Other"; Jaggar names her similarly conceptualized third phase as either radical or cultural feminist.[15]

Throughout this developing feminist history of consciousness, however, according to Lydia Sargent, "Racism, while part of the discussion, was never successfully integrated into feminist theory and practice."[16] In attempting to remedy this situation, a fourth and utopian category was often added to the previous three. This fourth category always represents the unachieved category of *possibility* wherein differences represented by race and class can be (simply) accounted for; Jaggar names this fourth effort "socialist feminism." In Eisenstein's typology, since it is above all a chronology, the differences represented by U.S. feminists of color become visible only at this last stage. In the eighties, she argues, as the women's movement "grew more diverse," it "became FORCED to confront and debate issues of difference, most notably those of race and class."[17] However, this confrontation with difference (which might have generated a fourth "socialist feminist" category in Eisenstein's typology) disappears from her book, ironically titled *The Future of Difference*, where, she admits, "the very issues of race and ethnicity in relation to feminism" are only superficially "broached."[18] Indeed, the most well-meaning socialist feminist scholars are unable to make socialist feminism account for the differences represented by the political activities of U.S. feminists of color. Alison Jaggar, a leading proponent of socialist feminism, succinctly sums up the situation in 1983. She writes that "a fully adequate theory of women's liberation cannot ignore the experience of any group of women and to the extent that socialist feminism fails to theorize the experience of women of color, it cannot be accepted as complete." Jaggar nevertheless excuses her own book's determined celebration of a fourth-phase socialist feminism by making the following argument: the theoretical contributions of feminists of color (such as Paula Gunn Allen, Audre Lorde, Nellie Wong, Gloria Anzaldúa, Cherríe Moraga, Toni Morrison, Mitsuye Yamada, bell hooks, the third world contributors to *Sisterhood Is Powerful* or *This Bridge*, to name only a few U.S. third world feminist authors published by 1983), operate, she argues, "mainly at the level of description." Those writings that have been theoretical, she continues, have yet to contribute to any "unique or distinctive and comprehensive theory of women's liberation."[19] For this reason, Jaggar explains, it is not that she has "omitted" U.S. third world feminism from her book, but she has rather simply "assimilated" its expressions into one of the "four genera" of hegemonic feminism we have just examined. This unfortunate move limits one's capacities to think or act outside the boundaries of what became for the 1980s women's movement a hegemonic four-phase structure.

This typology of feminist consciousness can be understood as follows: that women are the same as men, that women are a class different from men, that women are superior to men, and that women are a class that is also divided by race was challenged at every level by U.S. third world feminists. Indeed, this kind of conceptual model, this typology for organizing history, identity, criticism, and theory, must be understood as useful for oppositional actors only insofar as it is understood as a mental map of a given time, place, and cultural condition. This symbolic container has its own political aims, both hoped for and achieved, but we must also understand how it has functioned to make the specific presence of U.S. third world feminism, considered as a specific form of political practice, all but invisible.

PERFORMING POLITICS: THE DIFFERENTIAL FORM OF OPPOSITIONAL CONSCIOUSNESS AND SOCIAL MOVEMENT

Let me propose an alternative typology, this one generated from the insights born of oppositional activity beyond the inclusive scope of the 1980s hegemonic women's movement. It is important to remember that the form of U.S. third world feminism it represents and enacts has been influenced not only by struggles against gender domination, but also by the struggles against race, class, cultural, and sexual hierarchies that mark the twentieth century in the United States. It is a mapping of consciousness in opposition to the dominant social order that charts the white and hegemonic feminist histories of consciousness we have just surveyed, while also making visible the different ground from which a specific U.S. third world feminist praxis occurs. It is important to understand that this new typology is not necessarily "feminist" in nature but is rather a history of oppositional consciousness. Let me explain what I mean by this.

Any social order that is hierarchically organized into relations of domination and subordination creates particular subject positions within which the subordinated can legitimately function. These subject positions, once self-consciously recognized by their inhabitants, can become transformed into more effective sites of resistance to the current ordering of power relations. From the perspective of the form of U.S. third world feminism identified here, the histories of consciousness produced by U.S. white feminists are, above all, only further examples of subordinated consciousness in opposition: they are not viewed as particularly *feminist* in nature. In order to make the specific nature of U.S. third world feminist criticism visible within U.S. feminist theory and within the field of cultural studies in general, I suggest in place of the preceding typology a *topography*, a mapping of the ideological spaces wherein oppositional activity in the U.S. takes place (a cognitive mapping, if you will), a mapping that identifies the modes the subordinated of the United States (of any sex, gender, race, or class) enact as political stances in resistance to domination. Unlike the preceding hegemonic feminist version, the topography that follows is not historically organized; no enactment is privileged over any other; and the recognition that each oppositional site is as potentially effective in opposition as any other makes visible another mode of resistance— enacted by feminists of color over the past thirty years—that is particularly effective under late capitalist and postmodern cultural conditions in the United States. The following topography compasses the parameters of an emerging theory and practice of consciousness-in-opposition that gathers up the modes of ideology-praxis represented within previous liberation movements into a fifth, differential, and postmodern paradigm. This paradigm can, among other things, make clear the vital connections, the alliances, that exist between feminist theories in general and other modes of theory and practice also concerned with issues of social hierarchy, race, marginality, and, above all, resistance. U.S. third world feminist criticism, then, considered as an enabling theory and method of differential social movement, brings the following oppositional ideological practices into view as enactments, or performances of politics, of consciousness, and of identity itself:

1. Within the first, what I call "equal rights" enactment of consciousness in opposition, the members of the subordinated group argue that their differences—for which they have been assigned inferior status—lie only in appearance, not reality. Behind what they argue are only *exterior* physical differences from the most legitimated form of the human-in-society, they maintain, is a content, an

essence that is the same as the essence of the human-in-power. These oppositional actors thus argue for civil rights based on the philosophy that all humans are created as equal. Practitioners of this particular ideological tactic will demand that their own humanity be legitimated, recognized as the same under the law, and assimilated into the most favored form of the human-in-power. The expression of this mode of social movement and identity politics can be traced throughout the writings generated from within U.S. liberation movements of the post–World War II era, in all civil rights politics, from the League of United Latin American Citizens (LULAC) to the National Organization for Women (NOW).

2. Under the second and "revolutionary" ideological tactic, members of the subordinated group claim their differences in both form *and* content from those in power, in both physical difference *and* internal being. Practitioners of this mode of resistance thus call for a kind of social transformation that will accommodate and legitimate those differences, by force if necessary. Unlike the previous "equal rights" tactic that insists on the internal similarities between social, racial, sexual, and gender classes across their physical differences, "revolutionary" practitioners have no belief that assimilation is possible within the present categories by which the social order is organized. The enactment of revolutionary ideology seeks instead to affirm subordinated differences through radical societal reformation that will ultimately produce a new culture capable of operating beyond present domination/subordination power axes. Examples of this mode include the Brown Berets, the Black Panthers, and Marxist and socialist feminisms.

3. Under "supremacism," the third form of oppositional consciousness and practice, not only do the oppressed claim their differences, but they also assert that those very differences have provided them access to an evolutionary level superior to that of those in power. Whether one sees one's differences as resulting from biological or social causes is of little final import; what matters is the consequence of those differences: that the group has evolved to a higher stage of cultural and psychological existence than those currently holding power. Moreover, these differences now comprise the essence of what is good in human existence. The mission of these practitioners is to provide the social order with a higher ethical and moral vision and consequently with more effective leadership. We see this in the politics of La Raza Cosmica, cultural feminism, and ethnic nationalisms, for example.

4. "Separatism" is the final tactic of resistance of these most com-

monly mobilized under previous modes of capitalism. As in the previous three forms, practitioners of this form of resistance also recognize that their differences have been branded as inferior with respect to the category of the most human. Under this mode of agency, however, the subordinated do not desire an "equal rights" type of integration with the dominant order, nor do they seek its "revolutionary" transformation or leadership. Rather, this form of political resistance is organized to protect and nurture the differences that define it through complete separation from the dominant social order.

As we saw under the previous hegemonic typology, the maturation of a resistance movement means that these four ideological positions will emerge in response to dominating powers and that these positions will become more and more clearly articulated. Unfortunately, however, as we witnessed in the late 1970s hegemonic women's movement, such ideological positions eventually divide the movement of resistance from within, for each of these sites tends to generate sets of tactics, strategies, and identity politics that historically have appeared to be mutually exclusive. What remains all the more profound, however, is that the differential practice of U.S. third world feminism undermines this appearance of the mutual exclusivity of oppositional practices of consciousness and social movement; moreover, it is U.S. third world feminist praxis that allows their re-cognition on new terms. U.S. feminists of color, insofar as they involved themselves with the 1970s white women's liberation movement, were also enacting one or more of the ideological positionings just outlined, but rarely for long and rarely adopting the kind of fervid belief systems and identity politics that tend to accompany the construction of these ideological positionings under hegemonic understandings. This unusual affiliation with the movement was variously interpreted as disloyalty, betrayal, absence, or lack: "When they *were* there, they were rarely there for long," went the usual complaint, or, "they seemed to shift from one type of women's group to another." They were the mobile (yet ever present in their "absence") members of this particular liberation movement. It is precisely the significance of this mobility that most inventories of oppositional ideology and agency have not been able to register.

Yet it is in the activity of what Anzaldúa calls weaving "between and among" oppositional ideologies that another and fifth mode of oppositional consciousness and activity can be found.[20] I have named this activity of consciousness "differential" insofar as it enables movement "between and among" ideological positionings (the equal

rights, revolutionary, supremacist, and separatist modes of oppositional consciousness) considered as variables, in order to disclose the distinctions among them. In this sense the differential mode of consciousness operates like the clutch of an automobile, the mechanism
that permits the driver to select, engage, and disengage gears in a
system for the transmission of power. This differential represents the
variant; it emerges out of correlation, intensities, junctures, crises. A
differential positioning is thus performative; it is the form of agency
self-consciously constructed to mobilize and enact power. For analytic
purposes I place this mode of differential consciousness in the fifth
position, even though it functions as the medium through which the
"equal rights," "revolutionary," "supremacist," and "separatist"
modes of oppositional consciousness became effectively transformed,
lifted out of their earlier hegemonic activity. Together, when enacted differentially, they become ideological and, above all, *tactical*
weaponry for confronting the shifting currents of power.

The differences between this processual and differential five-lo-
cation topography of consciousness in opposition and the previous
typology of hegemonic feminism have been made available for analysis through the recognition of U.S. third world feminism considered as a theory and method for understanding and enacting oppositional political consciousness and activity. U.S. third world
feminism thus represents a central locus of possibility, an insurgent
movement that works to shatter the construction of any one of the
collective ideologies as the single most correct site where truth can
be represented. Without making this move beyond the hegemonic
typological understanding of resistance outlined earlier, any "liberation" or social movement is destined to repeat the same oppressive
authoritarianism from which it is attempting to free itself and become trapped inside a drive for truth that can only end in producing its own brand of dominations. What U.S. third world feminism
demands is a new subjectivity, a political revision that denies any
one ideology as the final answer, while instead positing a *tactical*,
indeed a performative, subjectivity with the capacity to de- and re-
center depending upon the kinds of oppression to be confronted,
depending upon the history of the moment. This is what is required
in the shift from enacting a hegemonic oppositional theory and practice to engaging in differential social movement, as performed, however unrecognized, over the last thirty years under U.S. third world
feminist praxis.

Chicana theorist Aida Hurtado defines U.S. third world feminism
as a differential and performative mode of social movement and

consciousness in the following manner: "by the time women of color reach adulthood, we have developed informal political skills to deal with State intervention. The political skills required by women of color are neither the political skills of the White power structure that White liberal feminists have adopted nor the free spirited experimentation followed by the radical feminists." Rather, she insists, "women of color are more like urban guerillas trained through everyday battle with the state apparatus." As such, "women of color's fighting capabilities are often neither understood by white middle-class feminists" nor leftist activists in general, and up until now, she asserts, these fighting capabilities have "not been codified anywhere for them to learn."[21] Cherrie Moraga continues by claiming U.S. third world feminist "guerilla warfare" as a way of life: "Our strategy," she writes, "is how we cope" on an everyday basis, "how we measure and weigh what is to be said and when, what is to be done and how, and to whom . . . daily deciding/risking who it is we can call an ally, call a friend (whatever that person's skin, sex, or sexuality)." Feminists of color are "women without a line. We are women who contradict each other."[22]

In 1981, Anzaldúa identified the growing coalition between U.S. feminists of color as one of women who do not have the same culture, language, race, sexual orientation, or ideology; "nor do we derive similar solutions," she insists, to the problems of oppression. For a U.S. third world feminism enacted as a differential theory and method of oppositional consciousness, however, she writes, such "differences do not become opposed to each other."[23] Instead, as Lorde continued the argument in 1979, all ideological differences, all tactical social positionings, must be understood as "a fund of necessary polarities between which our creativities spark like a dialectic. Only within that interdependency," each ideological position "acknowledged and equal, can the power to seek new ways of being in the world generate, as well as the courage and sustenance to act where there are no charters."[24] Such *movement*, however, must be linked to a concurrent desire for ideological location; both are necessary, together, in enacting a differential praxis. Differential social movement creates a space where, in the words of third world feminist philosopher Maria Lugones, "cross-cultural and cross-racial loving" takes place, through the requisite that the self shift its perimeters and identities, to "morph," to multiply its agency in a performative activity self-consciously grounded in the demands of history but organized for the sake of egalitarian social relations, a differential form of social being Lugones calls "world-traveling."[25]

Perhaps we can now better understand the utopian content underlying definitions of U.S. third world feminism written by feminists of color throughout the 1970s and 1980s, as in this statement
made in 1985 by African-American literary critic Barbara Christian,
writing to other U.S. feminists of color: "The struggle is not won.
Our vision is still seen, even by many progressives, as secondary, our
words trivialized as minority issues," our oppositional stances "characterized by others as divisive. But there is a deep philosophical
reordering that is occurring" among us "that is already having its
effects on so many of us whose lives and expressions are an increasing revelation of the INTIMATE face of universal struggle."[26] This
"philosophical reordering," referred to by Christian, the "different
strategy, a different foundation" called for by hooks, must be recognized as, in the words of Audre Lorde, part of "a whole other structure of opposition that touches every aspect of our existence at the
same time that we are resisting." According to Barbara Smith, the
recognition of U.S. third world feminism as a fundamentally different paradigm will "alter life as we know it" for those who act in
resistance to dominant social hierarchy.[27] In 1981, Merle Woo insisted that U.S. third world feminism represents a "new framework."
This framework will not "support repression, hatred, exploitation
and isolation, but will be a human and beautiful framework, created in a community, bonded not by color, sex or class, but by love
and the common goal for the liberation of mind, heart, and spirit."[28]
The praxis of a differential form of oppositional consciousness has
continually called up utopian visions such as these throughout the
1960s, 1970s, and 1980s within the writings of U.S. feminists of
color, and across their boundaries of race, culture, ethnicity, class,
and sexual differences.

U.S. third world feminism must be recognized as that "different
strategy," that "new framework." Indeed, it comprises a theory,
method, and practice of oppositional consciousness in the postmodern world. This theory and method can be understood as apprehend-
ing and organizing consciousness, identity, agency, aesthetics, and
politics around the following five points of resistance to social hierarchy: 1) the integrationist, 2) the revolutionary, 3) the supremacist or nationalist, 4) the separatist, and 5) the differential forms of
U.S. third world feminism. It is the differential mode that allows the
previous four to be understood and utilized as *tactics* for changing
social relations. Under the differential theory and method of U.S.
third world feminist criticism, these five modes of resistance, ideology, and political practice are seen and deployed as *technologies*

of power. When enacted differentially, U.S. third world feminism demands of its practitioners a commitment to the process of meta-morphosis itself: the activity of the trickster who practices subjec-tivity-as-masquerade. This "morphing" is accomplished not simply for survival's sake, as in earlier times. Rather, it is a kind of conver-sion that allows movement through and over dominant systems of resistance, identity, race, gender, sex, and national meanings.

A differential oppositional consciousness views the five technol-ogies of power as consensual illusions, transformable social narra-tives designed to intervene in reality for the sake of social justice. This sleight-of-consciousness creates a new space, a cyberspace where the transcultural, transnational leaps necessary to the gen-eration of new forms of oppositional praxis are made possible. To identify a work as U.S. third world feminist is to find a work born of disruptions and of taking place, of immigrations and crossing borders, of traveling style, politics, poetics, and procedures, of tac-tics, strategies, and movement, all produced with the aim of, as Merle Woo puts it in *This Bridge,* equalizing power on behalf of the third world, the colonized, the class, race, gender, or sexually sub-ordinated. Ironically, given the history of U.S. third world feminism, the so-called "flexibility of identity" demanded for living under colonial and subordinated conditions is currently demanded of ev-ery first world citizen affected by transforming global economies. This condition creates new grounds for coalition across borders in U.S. third world feminist praxis, that is, in an understanding of re-sistance that focuses on the differential deployment of conscious-ness in opposition.

In this chapter I have identified the hegemonic structure that has trapped not only U.S. feminist theory and practice but which has also determined and constricted the politics and forms-of-being possible within all U.S. social movements of the 1950s, 1960s, 1970s, and 1980s. This hegemonic structure of consciousness and agency stands out in relief against the praxis of U.S. third world feminism, which has evolved to center the differences of U.S. third world fem-inists across their varying languages, cultures, ethnicities, races, classes, sexualities, and genders. I have suggested that the "philo-sophical reordering" referred to by Christian is imaginable only through U.S. third world feminism, recognized as a specific and new condition of possibility, another kind of gender, race, sex, and class consciousness that allows us to define the "differential" as a spe-cific form of resistance, agency, and politics. The differential form of oppositional consciousness was utilized by U.S. feminists of color within the 1970s white women's movement, yet it is also a form of consciousness in resistance well utilized among subordinated classes under various conditions of domination and subordination. The recognition and acknowledgment of this consciousness and praxis, this thought and action, carves out the space wherein hegemonic feminisms have the possibility of becoming aligned with other spheres of theoretical and daily practice that are also concerned with issues of marginality.

The form of U.S. third world feminism represented by the differential form of oppositional consciousness is threaded throughout the experience of social marginality. As such it is being woven into the fabric of experience belonging to more and more citizens caught in the crisis of late capitalism and expressed in the cultural angst most often referred to as the postmodern dilemma. The juncture I am proposing, therefore, is extreme. It is a location wherein the praxis of U.S. third world feminism links with the aims of white feminism; with studies of race, ethnicity, sexuality, and marginality; and with postmodern theories of culture, as they crosscut and join together in new relationships through what is becoming a shared comprehension of the dynamics of oppositional consciousness in the postmodern world.

NOTES

An earlier version of this essay appeared in *Genders* 10 (1991), published by the University of Texas Press, as "U.S. Third World Feminism: The Theory and Method of Oppositional Consciousness in the Postmodern World." An updated version will appear in my forthcoming book "Oppositional Consciousness in the Postmodern World: U.S. Third World Feminism, Semiotics, and the Methodology of the Oppressed." Previous versions have appeared in *Sub-Versions*, 1990, Working Paper, University of California, Santa Cruz, and in unpublished but informally circulated manuscripts cited in Donna Haraway's "A Manifesto for Cyborgs: Science, Technology, and Socialist Feminism in the 1980's" (*Socialist Review* 80 [1985]). This essay is a revision of a lecture to the 1987 Modern Language Association panel "Writing from the Margins," chaired by Norma Alarcon. This current essay is dedicated to Rosa Maria Villafane, Antonia Castañeda, Joan Armatrading, Traci Chapman, Queen Latifa, and all new generations of U.S. third world feminists.

1. Gayatri Spivak, "The Rani of Sirmur" in *Europe and its Others*, ed. F. Barker, vol. 1 (Essex: University of Essex, 1985), 147. Here, "U.S. Third

World Feminism" represents the political alliance made during the 1960s and 1970s among a generation of U.S. feminists of color who were separated by culture, race, class, sexuality, or gender identification but united through their similar responses to the experience of race oppression.

The most recent theorization of "U.S. Third World feminism" can be found in *Third World Women and the Politics of Feminism*, ed. Lourdes Torres and Chandra Mohanty (Bloomington: Indiana University Press, 1991). See also Gloria Anzaldúa, ed., *Making Face, Making Soul—Haciendo Caras: Creative and Critical Perspectives by Women of Color* (San Francisco: Aunt Lute Press, 1990). Earlier definitions can be found in Cherríe Moraga's "Between the Lines: On Culture, Class and Homophobia," in *This Bridge Called My Back: A Collection of Writings by Radical Women of Color*, ed. Cherríe Moraga and Gloria Anzaldúa (Watertown, Mass.: Persephone Press 1981), 106. Also see Sandoval, "The Struggle Within: A Report on the 1981 NWSA Conference" (Oakland, Calif.; Center for Third World Organizing, 1982), reprinted by Anzaldúa in *Making Face, Making Soul— Haciendo Caras*, 55–71; idem, "'Comment on Krieger's *The Mirror Dance*,' a U.S. Third World Feminist Perspective," *Signs* 9, no. 4 (Summer 1984): 725; idem, "U.S. Third World Feminism," forthcoming in *Oxford Companion to Women's Writing in the U.S.* (New York: Oxford University Press, 1994).

2. Note the Johnson essay, chapter 7 in the present volume. Also see Fredric Jameson's "Postmodernism, or the Cultural Logic of Late Capitalism," *New Left Review* 146 (July–Aug. 1984): 53–92.

Interesting to certain third world scholars is the coalescing relationship between theories of postmodernism (especially those that celebrate the fragmentations of consciousness that postmodernism demands) and the form of differential oppositional consciousness that has been most clearly articulated by the marginalized and which I outline in this text. The juncture I am analyzing here is that which connects the disoriented first world subject who, like Jameson, is either repulsed by the "de-politicized" aesthetics of postmodernism or longs for the postmodern cultural aesthetic as a key to a new sense of identity and redemption, and the form of differential oppositional consciousness developed by subordinated and marginalized Western or colonized subjects, who have been forced to experience the aesthetics of what is called "postmodernism" as a requisite for survival. It is the members of this constituency who are most familiar with what citizenship in this realm requires and makes possible.

The juncture between all of these interests is comprised of the differential form of oppositional consciousness that postmodern cultural conditions are making available to all of its citizenry in an historically unique democratization of oppression that crosses class, race, sex, and gender identifications. Its practice contains the possibility for the emergence of a new historical moment—a new citizen—and a new arena for unity between peoples.

3. Francis Beal, "Double Jeopardy: To Be Black and Female," in *Sister-*

hood Is Powerful: An Anthology of Writings from the Women's Liberation Movement, ed. Robin Morgan (New York: Random House, 1970), 136. Emphasis mine.

4. Sojourner Truth, "Ain't I a Woman?" in *The Norton Anthology of Literature by Women* (New York: Norton, 1985), 252.

5. Paula Gunn Allen, "Some Like Indians Endure," in *Living the Spirit*, ed. Will Roscoe (New York: St. Martins, 1987), 9.

6. Toni Morrison, quoted by Bettye J. Parker, "Complexity: Toni Morrison's Women—an Interview Essay," in *Sturdy Black Bridges: Visions of Black Women in Literature*, ed. Roseanne Bell, Bettye Parker, and Beverly Guy-Sheftall (New York: Anchor/Doubleday, 1979), 63.

7. Velia Hancock, "La Chicana, Chicano Movement and Women's Liberation," *Chicano Studies Newsletter*, University of California, Berkeley, Feb.–Mar. 1971. The intuition that people of color occupy an "in-between/outsider" status is a frequent theme among third world liberationist writers both within and outside the borders of the United States. See, for example, Desmond Tutu as reported by Richard N. Osting, "Searching for New Worlds," *Time Magazine*, 29 Oct. 1984; Rosa Maria Villafane-Sisolak, from a 1983 journal entry cited in *Making Face, Making Soul—Haciendo Caras*, ed. Gloria Anzaldúa; Alice Walker, "In the Closet of the Soul: A Letter to an African-American Friend," *Ms. Magazine*, Nov. 1986, 32–35; Gloria Anzaldúa, "La Prieta," in *This Bridge Called My Back*, ed. Moraga and Anzaldúa, 198–209.

8. See Gloria Hull, Patricia Bell Scott, Barbara Smith, *All the Women Are White, All the Blacks Are Men, But Some of Us Are Brave: Black Women's Studies* (New York: Feminist Press, 1982); Moraga and Anzaldúa, eds. *This Bridge Called My Back*.

9. bell hooks, *Ain't I a Woman: Black Women and Feminism* (Boston: South End Press, 1981); Amy Ling, *Between Worlds* (New York: Pergamon Press, 1990); Norma Alarcon, ed., *The Third Woman* (Bloomington, Ind.: Third Woman Press, 1981).

10. See Alice Walker, "Letter to an African-American Friend," *Ms. Magazine*, Nov. 1986. See also Gloria Anzaldúa, *Borderlands, La Frontera: The New Mestiza* (San Francisco: Spinsters/Aunt Lute, 1987); Maxine Hong Kingston, *The Woman Warrior* (New York: Vintage Books, 1977); Moraga and Anzaldúa, eds., *This Bridge Called My Back*; Audre Lorde, *Sister Outsider* (New York: Crossing Press, 1984); Maxine Baca Zinn, Lynn Weber Cannon, Elizabeth Higginbotham, and Bonnie Thornton Dill, "The Costs of Exclusionary Practices in Women's Studies," *Signs* 11, no. 2 (Winter 1986): 296.

11. Alison Jaggar, *Feminist Politics and Human Nature* (New York: Rowman and Allenheld, 1983), 11; Hester Eisenstein and Alice Jardine, *The Future of Difference* (New Brunswick, N.J.: Rutgers University Press, 1985), xxi.

12. See Sandoval, "U.S. Third World Feminism: The Theory and Method of Oppositional Consciousness in the Postmodern World," *Genders* 10

(1991), and an extended version forthcoming in my book "Oppositional Consciousness in the Postmodern World."

13. Elaine Showalter, "Toward a Feminist Poetics," in *The New Feminist Criticism: Essays on Women, Literature and Theory* (New York: Pantheon, 1985), 128, 137; Eisenstein, "Difference," in Eisenstein and Jardine, *The Future of Difference*, xvi; Jaggar, *Feminist Politics*, 27.

14. Showalter, "Feminist Poetics," 138; Eisenstein, "Difference," xviii; Jaggar, *Feminist Politics*, 51.

15. Showalter, "Feminist Poetics," 139; Eisenstein, "Difference," xix; Jaggar, *Feminist Politics*, 83.

16. Lydia Sargent, *Women and Revolution: A Discussion of the Unhappy Marriage of Marxism and Feminism* (Boston: South End Press, 1981), xx.

17. Eisenstein, "Difference," xix (emphasis mine).

18. Ibid., xxiii.

19. See Sandoval, "U.S. Third World Feminism," for varying responses by feminist theorists of color to Jaggar's claim.

20. Gloria Anzaldúa writes that she lives "between and among" cultures, in "La Prieta," in *This Bridge Called My Back*, eds. Moraga and Anzaldúa, 209.

21. Aida Hurtado, "Reflections on White Feminism: A Perspective from a Woman of Color," unpublished manuscript (1985). Another version of this quotation appears in Hurtado's essay "Relating to Privilege: Seduction and Rejection in the Subordination of White Women and Women of Color," *Signs* (Summer 1989): 833–55.

22. Moraga and Anzaldúa, eds., *This Bridge Called My Back*, xix.

23. Anzaldúa, "La Prieta," in *This Bridge Called My Back*, ed. Moraga and Anzaldúa, 209.

24. Audre Lorde, "Comments at 'The Personal and the Political Panel,'" Second Sex Conference, New York, Sept. 1979. Published in Moraga and Anzaldúa, eds., *This Bridge Called My Back*, 98. Also see Lorde, "The Uses of the Erotic," in *Sister Outsider*, 58–63, which calls for challenging and undoing authority in order to enter a utopian realm accessible only through a processual form of consciousness that she names the "erotic."

25. Differential consciousness is comprised of seeming contradictions and difference, which then serve as tactical interventions in the other mobility that is power. Entrance into the realm "between and amongst" the others demands a mode of consciousness once relegated to the province of intuition and psychic phenomena, but which now must be recognized as a specific practice. I define differential consciousness as a kind of anarchic activity (but with method), a form of ideological guerilla warfare, and a new kind of ethical activity that is being privileged here as the way in which opposition to oppressive authorities is achieved in a highly technologized and disciplinized society. Inside this realm resides the only possible grounds of unity across differences. Entrance into this new order requires an emotional commitment within which one experiences the violent shattering of the unitary sense of self, as the skill that allows a mobile identity to form

takes hold. As Bernice Reagon has written, "most of the time you feel threatened to the core, and if you don't, you're not really doing no coalescing" ("Coalition Politics: Turning the Century," in *Home Girls: A Black Feminist Anthology,* ed. Barbara Smith [New York: Kitchen Table, Women of Color Press, 1983], 356–68). Citizenship in this political realm is comprised of strategy and risk. Within the realm of differential consciousness there are no ultimate answers, no terminal utopia (though the imagination of utopias can motivate its tactics), no predictable final outcomes. Its practice is not biologically determined, restricted to any class or group, nor must it become static. The fact that it is a process capable of freezing into a repressive order—or of disintegrating into relativism—should not shadow its radical activity.

To name the theory and method made possible by the recognition of differential consciousness, "oppositional" refers only to the ideological effects its activity can have under present cultural conditions. It is a naming that signifies a realm with constantly shifting boundaries which serve to delimit, for differential consciousness participates in its own dissolution even as it is in action. Differential consciousness under postmodern conditions is not possible without the creation of another ethics, a new morality, which will bring about a new subject of history. Movement into this realm is heralded by the claims of U.S. third world feminists, a movement that makes manifest the possibility of ideological warfare in the form of a theory and method, a praxis of oppositional consciousness. But to think of the activities of U.S. third world feminism in this way is only a metaphorical avenue that allows one conceptual access to the threshold of this other realm, a realm accessible to all people. See Maria Lugones, "Playfulness, World-Traveling, and Loving Perception," from *Hypatia: A Journal of Feminist Philosophy* 2, no. 2 (1987): 84–98.

26. Barbara Christian, "Creating a Universal Literature: Afro-American Women Writers," *KPFA Folio,* Special African History Month Edition, February 1983, 1. Reissued in Barbara Christian, *Black Feminist Criticism: Perspectives on Black Women Writers* (New York: Pergamon Press, 1985), 163.

27. bell hooks, *Feminist Theory: From Margin to Center* (Boston: South End Press, 1994), 87; Audre Lorde, "An Interview: Audre Lorde and Adrienne Rich," *Signs* 6, no. 4 (Summer 1981): 168–75; and Smith, ed., *Home Girls,* xxv.

28. Merle Woo, "Letter to Ma," in *This Bridge Called My Back,* ed. Moraga and Anzaldúa, 147.

PART FOUR

Representation in Action

TWELVE

What Are We Doing? What Do We Want? Who Are We? Comprehending the Subject of Feminism

PATROCINIO P. SCHWEICKART

Let me begin by speaking plainly. I am a woman, and I am a feminist. In saying so I voice my discontent with prevailing oppressive social and political conditions, and my desire to change them. However, both my discontent and my desire for change become political *only* to the extent that my concerns become relevant to others, and to the extent that the concern of others become relevant to me. Given the enormous power of the forces and relations sustaining patriarchy and sexism, change necessitates *both* individual *and* concerted action—*both* my personal agency, *and* the collective agency of a political movement. Without other feminists, I am only a discontented woman. The "I" of each feminist is situated in the "we" of feminism.

Today it is commonly said that feminism is plural rather than singular. We differ in our experience and understanding of the prevailing social and historical conditions; we disagree about how these conditions could be changed. Each of us makes her own calculation of what she is in a position to do, the price she is willing to pay, and the risks she is willing to take in relation to the value of certain goals and the probability of their attainment. It would seem, then, that the reference in my title to "the subject of feminism" is wrong; I should have said "the subjects of feminisms."[1]

In response, I would say that in my view the "subject of feminism" is a *collective* noun, and as such, is *both* singular and plural. My title is meant to invoke the problematic ambiguity of collective nouns with regard to the grammatical category of number, and to redress the current one-sided emphasis on plurality.

It might also be objected that "the subject of feminism" implies a transcendental Subject. To this I would say that a collective noun (e.g., the "community") need not imply a transcendental entity. Moreover, on close inspection we see that the transcendental is a cover for collectivity; coded into discussions of "essentialism" or "totalizing theory" is a more specifically political—and for that reason, more unsettling—issue, that of collectivity. The ghost of the "collective subject" haunts feminist discourse no less than it does Marxist discourse. To the extent that the point of feminism is (to borrow Marx's eleventh thesis on Feuerbach) not merely to interpret the world but to change it, the theoretical problem of agency has to be linked to the practical problem of collective will-formation. The full theoretical articulation of feminist politics requires that the issue of agency be addressed in relation to the difficult and hazardous issue of collectivity, for feminist politics—like politics in general—is constituted precisely by the interaction, coordination, and mutual implication of individual and collective interests, needs, desires, and perspectives.

DEFINING FEMINISM

"To be a feminist, one must first become one." This maxim, enunciated by Sandra Bartky in her path-breaking essay "Toward a Phenomenology of Feminist Consciousness,"[2] sets us on an itinerary different from that set by postmodernists who regard "the concept and category of woman as the necessary point of departure for any feminist theory and feminist politics."[3] The latter places the accent on the disjunction between what pertains to a naturally ordained fixed essence and what pertains to social and cultural construction. Since clearly one is not born a feminist, Bartky's maxim unequivocally situates us in the domain of social and cultural processes—where "becoming" is the middle term between two kinds of *social* "being": to be a feminist I must first become one, which is to say, other than what I am. Being a feminist signifies the living out of the project of negating what women (and men) have become and of *realizing* (in the dual sense of "coming to know" and "making real") what they can and ought to be. The "double ontological shock" Bartky describes is one of the moments of this becoming. Bartky repeatedly laments the fact that not all women are feminists. I daresay she would more happily note that, conversely, not all feminists are women. Becoming a feminist is a political process precisely because, among other things, it

involves reflection, deliberation, and a degree of choice and commitment—in short, the exercise of agency.[4]

Shifting the focus from "woman" to "feminism" poses definition
as a different but no less difficult problem. Nothing is more obvious than that feminists are extremely conflicted about whether and
how to address this problem. However, the situation appears in a
new light once we realize that our ambivalence toward definition
is symptomatic of our ambivalence toward the collective dimension
of feminism. We see, on the one hand, that the need for a definition
is motivated not so much by the need to distinguish feminists from
nonfeminists (the usual phrasing of the problem), but by the need
to understand the interrelation among feminists and their various
activities. On the other hand, it becomes clear that "What is feminism?" is an unsettling question for feminists (but not for nonfeminists) because, for each of us, on the heels of any answer comes
Denise Riley's question, "Am I that name?"[5] and a host of corollar-
ies: What does it mean to belong to the group designated by that
name? What sorts of people do I become associated with by virtue
of that name? How am I implicated in what they say and do? What
kinds of ideas, relationships, responsibilities, positions, behavior do
I implicitly take on and what would I be obligated to abjure? How
do these new commitments correspond or interfere with my own
personal interests, needs, and pleasures? In being a feminist do I
surrender myself to a cause? Does being a feminist mean I would
be lumped in with others? Does it mean I would have to accept being
lumped in with other women? Does it mean restraints on my associations with men? Can I be a feminist and remain myself?

The issue of collectivity is implicated in every definition of feminism. "Essence," "the standpoint of women," "common ground,"
"feminist consciousness," "the concept and category of woman," and
even, female or feminine "identity" are actually tropes for feminist
collectivity. The need for a definition that does not gloss over the
heterogeneous meanings of feminism correlates with the need for a
model of collectivity that does not nullify individual autonomy.

THE PROBLEM OF THE SUBJECT

In *Discerning the Subject* Paul Smith notes that the word "subject"
is laden with the etymological sense of "something that is sub-ject-
ed, thrown beneath; . . . a passivity at the behest of forces greater
than it," and simultaneously, via conflation with "individual," with

the sense of being "undivided and whole," free and self-determining, "the source and agent of conscious action or meaning." His title plays on two rarely used English verbs: "to cern," meaning "to accept an inheritance or patrimony," and "to cerne," meaning "to encircle." The "subject" of contemporary theory is a "cerned" subject in the dual sense of being the legacy of the Western philosophical tradition and of being closed to the articulation of agency. He puts forth feminism as the prime example of a discourse engaged in "dis-cerning of the subject." The key move in this process is to break down the "subject" into a "*series* or conglomeration of . . . subject-positions. . . into which a person is called momentarily by the discourses and the world he/she inhabits."[6] Although the subject is necessarily subjected to ideology-in-general, the multiplicity of ideological scripts makes each particular ideology optional. Because one can/must choose a particular position, one can/must resist others. What Smith sees in feminism is the articulation of the possibility of agency on terms that do not reinstate the illusory autonomous, self-contained and self-containing individual consciousness of traditional humanism.

Smith's account fits in with the typical theoretical view of feminism and of Left politics as oppositional projects. However, it is important to keep in mind that, in fact, changing the world also requires the positive work of developing, implementing, defending, and caring for concrete alternatives. A theory of agency that focuses only on resistance has two disadvantages. First, it is able to deliver only an abstract account of agency. Smith, for example, gives us a subject who chooses among several scripts, but he does not indicate how she makes her choice. Is it on the basis of whim, pleasure, duty, desire, rational calculation of self-interest, sense of responsibility to others, abstract allegiance to principle? Assuming, as one must, that all of these factors come into play, how are they actually negotiated to arrive at a concrete decision? Are all choices equally valid and valuable? Is there a fixed collection of scripts? What power does the agent have to revise the script she chooses to play? What power does she have to produce new scripts? How are scripts produced? Are new scripts possible? How do they come about?

A second disadvantage is that a politics of resistance puts the accent on *individual* agency. Even when resistance is massive and focused—as for example, in the Montgomery bus boycott—it is still, to use Sartre's term, *serially* accomplished. The massiveness of the boycott is the cumulative effect of a series of individual (mutually reinforcing) refusals. Each participant has her own reasons: her own grievances, interests, and needs, her own understanding of the situation, her own vision of what she is fighting for, her own way of living out her opposition. Within a politics of resistance, solidarity with others does not require the negotiation of heterogeneous perspectives. We need not inquire into each other's ideals, views, motives, values, or desires; we can leave each to her own—as long as each maintains her opposition to the arrangement in question. The need to address differences becomes more urgent when one is engaged in realizing alternatives. A project such as, say, a feminist child-care center would require the negotiation of different conceptions of the specific goals of the project and the most appropriate means for attaining these goals: of different views regarding the nature of childhood, the needs of children and the needs of those who will be served by the center, the appropriate balance between instilling discipline and promoting freedom and between play and work, the role of adult authority, the cognitive and moral values that should inform the socialization of children, the role of parents, the distribution of power and responsibility among the adults who work at the center, the organization of the process of decision making, the fee scale to be charged, the pay scale of the workers, the ways of addressing the issues of race, gender, class, and sexual orientation, and so on. To the extent that this project is feminist, the participants must consider to what extent it is faithful to feminist ideals, and so, eventually, they must address various conceptions of these ideals and of what the qualifier "feminist" means.

The theoretical counterpart of resistance is critique, and the overvaluation of resistance and critique (a consequence, among other things, of the current dominance of deconstruction and postmodernism) has inhibited the theoretical exploration of the productive moment of feminism as well as of the difficult and hazardous problem of coordinating individual agency into a viable collective enterprise.

COMPREHENDING FEMINISM

Teresa de Lauretis invokes Locke's "The Essence of a Triangle lies in a very little compass. . . . three Lines meeting at three angles . . . make up that Essence" and suggests that we define feminism analogously. "One may prefer one triangle, one definition of woman and/ or feminism, to another and, within her particular conditions and possibilities of existence, to define the triangle as she wants."[7] Unfortunately, de Lauretis's elegant trope places feminism, to use

Locke's words, "in a very little compass." No formula can do for the study of feminism what "three lines meeting at three angles" has done for the study of triangles. What would be edged out of such a definition is precisely what de Lauretis and most of us are most interested in, the comprehension of feminism in its "historical specificity—the particular conditions of its emergence and development, which have shaped its object and field of analysis, its assumptions and forms of address; the constraints that have attended its conceptual and methodological struggles; the erotic component of its political self-awareness; the novelty of its radical challenge to social life itself."[8]

Perhaps the most influential definition of feminism is Alison Jaggar's characterization of four kinds of feminism—liberal, radical, Marxist, and socialist—each grounded in a specific conception of human nature.[9] At first glance, Jaggar's schema appears to be a precise way of "cutting" feminism "at the joints." Notice, however, that her schema breaks down when she tries to define radical feminism.

Liberal feminism speaks in the idiom of liberalism, Marxist feminism in the idiom of Marxism, and socialist feminism is an inflection of the latter. The systematic coherence of the definition of these three positions is a function of the disciplinary (in Foucault's sense) force of the liberal and Marxist "meta-narratives." "Radical" feminism, what Catharine MacKinnon (reacting to Jaggar's taxonomy) called "feminism unmodified," is the "none of the above" category.[10] Its incoherence stems from its *supplemental* and *ex-orbitant* character—from its *novelty*. Following the now familiar pattern of the Derridean argument, the "unruly" practices of radical feminism deconstruct Jaggar's account of the other three varieties of feminism and eventually of the theoretical framework she employs.[11]

The difficulty presented by radical feminism is symptomatic of the problem of defining feminism. Jaggar's definition remains freighted with the trope of essence—she tries to boil down four kinds of feminism to four essential conceptions of human nature, but the heterogeneity and novelty concentrated in radical feminism defeats her project.

Paul Smith shows that a capacity for "discernment" is a precondition for political agency. The title of my essay points to another condition, namely, the capacity for *comprehension*. Here (in the spirit of Smith's game of words) I mean to deploy the verb "to comprehend" in its two senses—that of "to understand," and that of "to include or embrace." To define feminism as a political movement we need a model that accommodates both the capacity to discern among various perspectives, interests, and discourses associated with feminism, and the capacity to comprehend these collectively. To construct this model we must distinguish what we need from what we do not need: we need to account for collectivity, but not for consensus or homogeneity; to represent feminism as a coherent project we must account for the connectedness and interrelatedness of its various constituents, but we can afford to forgo systematicity and logical consistency; we need to indicate the enduring commitments of the movement, but we are not obliged to fix its meaning. The definition of feminism that is called for is one that clarifies and articulates our sense of feminism as a movement whose coherence hinges on the heterogeneity of its constituents, and whose stability and durability depends on its capacity for revision and development.

The trick, of course, is to find a suitable trope. In the following sections I will construct such a trope by means of a process of successive figuration. I will steer clear of the trope of essence.

FEMINISM AS TEXT: FIRST APPROXIMATION

Imagine that we have conducted a survey of feminists that asked them to state what they think "feminism" means. The most frequent responses might be coded as follows:

1. Feminism is dedicated to the achievement of equality between women and men.
2. Feminism is dedicated to the liberation of women.
3. Feminism is dedicated to the abolition of patriarchy.
4. Feminism is dedicated to the abolition of sexism.
5. Feminism is dedicated to the authentic realization of the self-consciousness of women.

These statements codifying the responses to our fictional survey are not to be taken as logical propositions but rather as indications of the recurring themes of the *text* feminism.[12] Note that although these thematic statements are vague ("equality" means different things to different people, and different things in different contexts) they are not altogether meaningless. Whatever "equality" may mean, it stands in opposition to "inequality"; likewise, "liberation" stands opposed to "oppression," "patriarchy" and "sexism" to "matriarchy," "androgyny," and "egalitarianism"; and "authentic self-consciousness" stands against "alienation," "self-deception," and "false consciousness." One term in each opposition signifies the current objectionable state of affairs, the other the future that we are struggling to bring about.

Moreover, these statements ascribe distinguishable and perhaps contradictory goals to feminism. For example, equality in oppression (e.g., the equality of women and men under conditions of racial or class oppression) can hardly be called liberation, and since women are differently positioned with regard to race, class, and other axes of power, they have different experiences of and perspectives on "oppression." The conjunction of the theme of "equality" and the theme of "liberation" raises the question of the relationship of the category of gender with other categories that function as a locus of both difference and domination.

It must also be said that there is nothing sacred about the five themes listed above. The response to our fictitious survey could have been coded so as to highlight different (and a different number of) themes (e.g., "the personal is political," rights versus values, individualistic versus relational subjectivity, gender versus race or class, "humanism" versus poststructuralism), just as the thematic structure of a literary composition can be formulated in various ways. What is important is that as defined above, "feminism" becomes a "literary word," no longer a lexical fixed point (as it would have been had we defined it in the customary way), but the "intersection of textual surfaces."[13] Taken together these themes point to the differences and conflicts within the women's movement. Like the thematic structure of a literary composition, this ensemble of contradictions can serve as the point of departure for many different and possibly conflicting stories, but they do not admit all stories indiscriminately. Note further that this thematic definition is made up of *empty* abstractions (among them, that of the "concept of woman"), and that this is as it should be. Feminism is unfinished business, a text-in-progress. For this reason, any definition must be deficient in meaning so as to remain open to meaning that is yet to be produced.

THE PROJECT: SECOND APPROXIMATION

If the thematic structure cited above is not absolutely binding, is it binding at all? Since there are other possible themes, does it matter which one selects? What governs the selection? I have said that feminism is a process. So far, I have only represented it as a structure. How does a structure become a process?

The choice of structure as a metaphor for feminism conforms to the routine use of nonhuman models for human processes. But such models eventually rob us of the fruits of our ingenuity. An organic metaphor can convey only organic relations, a mechanistic or structural metaphor, only mechanistic or structural relations. Whatever is distinctive to human life exceeds the capacity of such models and so is obscured and mystified. The metaphor of structure used above obscures certain distinctive features of historical processes, namely, human agency and motivation, and personal and social interaction.[14]

As a second approximation to feminism, I invoke Jean-Paul Sartre's idea of *the project*.[15]

> The most rudimentary behavior must be determined both in relation to the real and present factors which condition it and in relation to a certain object, still to come, which it is trying to bring into being. (91)

> The project, as subjective surpassing of objectivity toward objectivity, and stretched between the objective conditions of the environment and the objective structure of the field of possibles, represents *in itself* the moving unity of subjectivity and objectivity, those cardinal determinants of activity. (97)

> Only the project, as a mediation between two moments of objectivity, can account for history, that is, for human *creativity*. (99)

History is usually written as a progression of events such that the earlier events determine the later ones. Such historiography, according to Sartre, is shaped by the "time of Cartesian rationalism," and depends on the principle that causes precede effects. Within this framework, to understand the present we must understand the past: all causes for the present are to be found in the past; the present is no more than the unfolding of a *fait accompli*. To effect any significant social change (say, abolish sexism) we must search the past for the originary causes of the situation in question (private property, the split between public and private, the sexual division of labor) so that we may render them inoperable.

Alternatively, history may be viewed as retrospective rewriting. From within a particular present, submerged in its concerns and reacting to its pressures, the historian narrates a past that explains and ratifies, or at least, leads up to the present. Thus, history is made in the present, for it is always a particular present that endows the past with significance and determines which events, relations, and personages will be central, peripheral, or nonexistent. The present necessarily writes itself into its histories.

For Sartre, neither of these conceptions can adequately portray actual historical processes, for they do not account for the active role of the *future*. Obviously the past and the present determine the future (what will happen depends on what has happened), but Sartre insists that the converse is also true: the future causes the past and the present. We can say, for example, that a child will become a successful teacher, doctor, or business executive because she works hard at her studies; or that he will be a criminal and a drug addict at twenty because he roams the streets instead of doing his schoolwork. But we can also say that a child works hard in school because she is destined to have a successful profession, or that he roams the streets because he is destined (by race, class, poverty, family circumstances) to be a criminal. In the first case, the child behaves so as to fulfill a future that she perceives is awaiting her; in the second case, he behaves as he does because no imaginable future motivates him to do otherwise. Similarly with historical movements. Feminists struggle for the sake of equality, of liberation, of the nonsexist future that they perceive to be in the field of possibles. We judge both the past and the present in light of this future; we write our historical accounts and we carry out our activities so as to fulfill its potentiality. Sartre's goal is to develop a method of historical narration that conveys the reciprocal interactions of past, present, and future.

The idea of the project also stems from the need to locate the motive force of history in human creativity. No doubt history is not "made" by great and powerful heroes. However, Sartre also rejects both the Hegelian theory of a "metaphysical force which by itself engenders the historical process" and the parallel "mechanistic materialism" that credits the action of "material conditions." Through the idea of the project he aims "to restore to the individual his power to go beyond his situation by means of work and action" (99).

The project is the mediation, undertaken by a subject (a human being) in the *present*, between two moments of objectivity, the *past* (and its residues in the present), and the *future* (with its specific anticipations in the present), which the subject wishes to bring about. The individual goes beyond her situation, transforms it, and at the same time, preserves it. The project is the means by which the past and the present are carried into the future; it represents "the practical rationality of a man making History."[16]

Any purposeful activity—say, cooking dinner for my family—is a project. However, Sartre has a particular activity in mind as he articulates the idea of the project, namely the *activity of writing*.

1. The project—a book, an essay—is both the finished text and the

process of writing, the projection of the subject of writing (the writer) onto an object (a text) external to herself. To write is to express—to externalize—my mind, to materialize my thoughts as notations on paper.

2. Writing is a regressive-progressive process. Although I write progressively—one word, one sentence, one unit of discourse follows another—writing necessarily requires regression. I stop occasionally to collect my thoughts, to evaluate and revise what I have written. And beyond this, writing sinks me back into my past—past writings, readings, experiences. But always, the image of what is still to come, the completed work and its future readers, hovers over my work, informing my evaluations and revisions, directing as well as motivating my progress. To write is to project myself out of the past, out of past texts; to liberate a particular text out of what has (always) already been written.

3. Through writing the external and the internal pass into each other. I read (internalize) the world, other texts, my prospective readers, and I externalize my ideas, express my sense of the world, my personality, what I know and what I have read, the "text" that is in me. I am both inside and outside what I write; I am my text, but it is not identical to me; it contains me, and it escapes me.

4. Writing is praxis. Its mental moment is self-evident. However, writing also produces an object that is the product of material production and reproduction—typing, word processing, xeroxing, printing, and so on; texts motivate the production of other texts and other products—paper, ink, copying machines, computers. Furthermore, writing is a profession, a means of making a living. It often brings cash (raises, honoraria, royalties, grants) and generates work for others—typists, editors, typesetters, printers, booksellers, readers, students. As a material practice, writing implicates the writer in other material practices and in the prevailing (i.e., capitalist) mode of production and exchange.

5. Writing is the dialectic of freedom and necessity. For example, one can inquire into the sociohistorical conditions in France during the first half of the nineteenth century, into Flaubert's situation within the bourgeoisie, into the economic conditions of his life, his familial relations, his infancy and childhood, into his education, and the philosophical and literary influences on his work. One can relate all of these factors to the way he lived his life and to the novels he wrote. But even if it were to be done exhaustively, this "regressive" analysis would not account for Flaubert's life or for *Madame Bovary*. It could not comprehend the "progressive" moment of the

project, the specific way he projected himself—lived his life, wrote his novel—out of his situation.

Language and all that has been written and said constitute a realm of necessity, a "practico-inert" for my work.[17] I must write within certain conventions; what I can write depends on what I have read; how I write depends on my anticipation of how I will be read; my work is enabled and constrained by what has been written. But even if, in retrospect, it may appear that I had to write in a particular way, writing was still, for me, the exercise of my freedom. Words and ideas came to me more or less with difficulty, never automatically. In the concrete, writing is experienced as problems, choice, improvisation, invention—as contingency. Furthermore, the boundaries of the historical situation are never evident at the outset. What was necessary can only be inferred from what was accomplished. A writer feels the pressure of constraints, but by exerting counterpressure, she can impose deformations on given structures (e.g., institute the generic pronoun "she," or revise the convention of love sonnets) and, with enough work and luck, prove by her writing that what was thought to be impossible had been possible all along: e.g., female/feminine/feminist poetics, lesbian epistemology, a comprehensive definition of feminism.

6. It is always a human being, not an abstract force, who writes. I am surrounded by other texts, each of which testifies to a human author. What I might feel as a metaphysical, institutional, textual, or linguistic force—the force of ideas, the literary tradition, the "symbolic order," "language"—is actually the effect of the projects of other humans. Everywhere there are only human beings and their projects.

It is not surprising that a writer like Sartre should choose writing as the paradigmatic human activity. However, there are more significant reasons for using this model. First of all, writing produces an *objective* image *par excellence* of human subjectivity. If I cook dinner I produce objects that are mute in themselves. To recover the subjective component of cooking one must articulate it: one must say the dinner is a token of my affection; I cooked because it was my turn to do so; or I simply fulfilled my traditional role. While this articulation could be done through speech, speech has the disadvantage of being ephemeral. But writing yields a durable object that is articulate—a text that presents an image of human subjectivity but is itself external to any subjectivity. While reality is not entirely textual, to be intelligible it must be textualized. Writing serves as the most significant intermediary to the intellection of human experience.

FEMINIST WRITING AND DIALOGISM

While political activity is not reducible to writing, it always involves much writing. We all know texts that have catalyzed revolutions—Paine's *Common Sense*, Lenin's *What Is to Be Done?*, Stowe's *Uncle Tom's Cabin*. The relationship of writing to collective action is fundamental. To write (and to read) is to transcend one's privatized self; to appeal to others (and to respond to another's appeal); to recognize oneself in the other, and the other in oneself—in short, to realize one's social nature. The texts written by a social movement confirm its existence and document its character. They offer an image of its collective agency. The desired transformation of social relations are first realized in the texts of the movement.

Now, what kind of "story" are feminists endeavoring to write? The thematic structure I proposed above, in the section headed "Feminism as Text," indicates its "content." Its "form" has the qualities Bakhtin attributes to the novel. Like the novel, feminist discourse effects a "revolution in the hierarchy of times" that shifts "the time-and-value plane of (artistic/historiograhic) ideation and evaluation" from the "absolute past" to the present. And as the present becomes the "center of the human orientation in time and in the world," the past is "relativized"; it loses its immutability and completedness; no matter how distant it is from us in time, "it is connected to our incomplete, present-day, continuing temporal transitions, it develops a relationship with our unpreparedness." Like Sartre, Bakhtin gives the future an active role. The present "by its very nature demands continuation, ... the more actively and consciously it moves into the future the more tangible and indispensable its inconclusiveness becomes." In the novel, "time and the world become historical: they unfold, albeit at first unclearly and confusedly, as becoming, as an uninterrupted movement into a real future, as a unified, all-embracing, unconcluded process."[18]

Furthermore, feminism and the novel are alike constituted by a polyglot consciousness and linguistic dialogism.

1. Syntagmatic and paradigmatic dialogism is evident in the thematic structure elaborated earlier. In the syntagmatic (horizontal) dimension, each theme involves a pair of oppositions—equality/ inequality, oppression/liberation, and so on. One component of each

pair rests on the historical situation, the other reaches out toward the hoped-for future—each theme dialogizes the two objective contexts of human activity, what Sartre called the "field of instruments" and the "field of possibles." Each theme also commutes and communicates with the other themes along the paradigmatic (vertical) axis:[19] e.g., the theme of "equality" passes into the theme of "liberation"; one interanimates the other—is articulated both in terms of and in opposition to the other.

2. My definition of feminism is addressed to others (especially, but not exclusively, to other feminists), and my relation with these others shapes the relation between my text and the other texts that form its context. The dialogue between subject and addressee is realized in the *intertextuality* between my text and that of others. More specifically, the themes that make up the structure are not my invention (in spite of the fiction of a survey of feminists). They are movement slogans—crystallizations of other feminist texts. The dialogism of the thematic structure is none other than the incorporation into my text of the plurivocal feminist conversation into which I am inserting my own utterance.

3. My text also sets up dialogical links with voices outside the feminist tradition. Smith, Sartre, and Bakhtin (like Bartky, Jaggar, and de Lauretis) appear as "characters" in my "novel." In introducing their language into my text, I create a zone of contact where they can converse with each other and I with them. My definition of feminism, then, proceeds through an interanimation of various languages. In this conversation, which (of course) *I* orchestrate, the "surplus" (unintended and unforeseen) potential in the words of others is put in the service of my (feminist) project.

4. Defining feminism induces in myself a split between the "subject of enunciation" (myself as defining subject) and the "subject of the utterance" (myself as feminist, the subject represented by the definition). "The subject of utterance, in relation to the subject of enunciation, plays the role of addressee with respect to the subject."[20] My definition of feminism is built up from the texts of others. But by defining feminism in a particular way, I am necessarily exerting a force in a particular direction. In defining feminism, I am also defining myself. My agency, my interests, my experience, my reading of other texts is written into my text. The dialogism of my definition is, in this sense, the "trace" of my conversations with myself no less than of my conversations with others.

My definition of feminism as a project whose objective moments have a particular structure is informed, on the one hand, by my comprehension of the collective project, which is to say, the work of others and the interests and needs expressed therein, and on the other, by my own experiences, needs, and interests. My writing commutes/communicates between my discourse with others and my discourse with myself. By means of this dual dialogism I insert my own project (involving my self-definition as a person and a feminist, as a person who is a feminist, as a feminist who is a particular person) into the collective project of feminism, and the collective project into my own. This text is *my* text, *my* definition of feminism. It documents my moral and political agency, and as such it necessarily involves a normative dimension. *I think* this is what feminism *truly is*, which is to say, *this* is how *I want it to be* and how *I think we ought* to define it. Nevertheless, this *ought* is *not* monologic prescription. In the context of the definition I am proposing, normative claims like everything else partake of discursive dialogism and are offered in anticipation of collective discussion and evaluation.

The affinity between feminist and novelistic discourse is no accident: both are set against the unitary voice of "the father." According to Bakhtin, of the many factors at work in the prehistory of the novel, two appear to be decisive—polyglossia and laughter.

> Laughter has the remarkable power of making an object come up close, of drawing it into a zone of crude contact where one can finger it familiarly on all sides, turn it upside down, inside out, peer at it from above and below, break open its external shell, look into its center, doubt it, take it apart, lay it bare and expose it, examine it freely and experiment with it. Laughter demolishes fear and piety before an object, before a world, making of it an object of familiar contact and thus clearing the ground for an absolutely free investigation of it. Laughter is a vital factor in laying down that prerequisite of fearlessness without which it would be impossible to approach the world realistically. (23)

The translation of these remarks to a feminist context is immediate once we substitute for laughter the distinctive emotion in the prehistory of feminist discourse—anger. The conjunction of anger and polyglossia is most palpable in the kind of feminism that has most eluded definition, namely that feminism which is "radical" to the extent that it takes its substance from the "grassroots" of women's experience and culture—or if one prefers, from what has been extraneous, and hence supplemental (in Derrida's sense) to androcentric tradition.

But the appeal of the trope of conversation—the interanimation of various discourses—goes beyond the transgressive (carnivalesque) quality emphasized in the passage quoted above. The work of Carol Gilligan and others indicates that women rely heavily on conversation to accomplish cognitive, moral, and emotional goals and suggests that the trope of conversation has an internal persuasiveness to women because it resonates with their experience and their "common sense."[21] If we remember as well that "consciousness-raising," the process through which many of us were initiated into feminism, is a conversation, then we have good reason to conclude that the trope of conversation has been latent in feminist discourse from the outset.[22]

Sartre's model of a project, our second approximation to a definition of feminism, foregrounds individual initiative and responsibility, "the power to go beyond [one's] situation by means of work and action." The incorporation of Bakhtin's idea of the interanimation of a variety of languages, voices, and styles adds a substantial intersubjective dimension to Sartre's model and enhances our comprehension of feminism as a collective project—which is to say, the interanimation of a variety of constituent projects.

The aversion of feminists to the explicit thematization of collectivity is due in part to distaste for the Marxian model of a party speaking and acting in one voice, and whose unity is enforced by means of strong ideological and disciplinary authority. Paul Smith's claim that feminism is a venue for the reconstitution of "subjectivity," "individuality," and "agency" means that feminism is a venue for the reconstitution of the "self" and "personhood." The process of successive figuration elaborated above, culminating in a model capitalizing on the discursive properties of writing and conversation, is oriented toward a representation of feminism that foregrounds the dialectic between individual and collective agency as the distinctive theoretical and practical problematic of feminism. Implicit in this definition is the recognition that feminism is a venue, not only for the reconstitution of the person, but also for the reconstitution of *sociality*—which is to say, for the articulation of a way of living together, of sharing resources, of negotiating different interests and needs without severing relationships, of working together for the sake of the collective good without doing violence to each other. The particular qualities of feminist sociality are yet to be fully articulated.

As a closing trope, imagine that all of us are in a room, working together on an enormously complicated "novel"—the "story" of feminism. Together we are trying to write ourselves into history. But at the same time, each of us is also engaged in her own personal project of realizing herself as subject—of writing her own personal story. The entire process of production is complicated because: (1) each personal story has to be inserted into the collective text, and the collective text has to be inserted in each personal text; (2) the collective and personal texts are being written concurrently, and since the collective text is the interactive totality of personal texts, it is constantly undergoing revision, and this in turn necessitates the revision of individual projects; and (3) the collective text and the personal texts are reflexive—they include the story of their writing. In other words, the collective and the personal novels are conditioned by intertextuality. At this point, however, we need to remind ourselves that we are speaking figuratively. Writing does not encompass all the activities that constitute either the collective or the personal projects; it is only a model we have adopted for the sake of its heuristic possibilities. Intertextuality, in other words, really indicates intersubjectivity—social interaction and political negotiation.

So, here we are in this room engaged in a collective project that requires considerable interaction; we need to read, comment on, and revise each other's work. We have to share or compete for materials, instruments, and space. We have to coordinate different personal needs, and the collective project with the individual ones. Under these conditions the working relations we establish with each other become crucial. We can trip each other up, we can waste our energies on endless bickering, or we can develop ways of working together and of negotiating differences and conflict so as to facilitate each other's project and each other's contribution to the collective. The progress of the collective project depends on how we interact, and the texts we produce will be marked (or marred) by these interactions.

NOTES

1. For a recent treatment of the differences within feminism see *The Conflicts in Feminism*, ed. Marianne Hirsch and Evelyn Fox Keller (New York: Routledge, 1990).

2. Sandra Bartky, *Femininity and Domination: Studies in the Phenomenology of Oppression* (New York: Routledge, 1990), 11–21.

3. Linda Alcoff, "Cultural Feminism versus Post-Structuralism: The Identity Crisis in Feminist Theory," *Signs* 13, no. 3 (Spring 1988): 405.

4. The situation is the reverse of that described by Alcoff. Feminist con-

sciousness is not founded on a conception of "woman"; rather, "woman" becomes the focus of theoretical and practical concern as a result of feminist consciousness. The thematization of the "concept and category of woman" is the *effect* rather than the point of departure of feminism. Thus, showing that it is neither feasible nor desirable to define "woman" does not foreclose the project of defining feminism. And since "the concept and category of woman" is an effect of feminist discourse, it is clearly a matter for social construction.

5. Denise Riley, *Am I That Name?: Feminism and the Category of "Women"* (Minneapolis: University of Minnesota Press, 1988).

6. Paul Smith, *Discerning the Subject, Theory and History of Literature,* vol. 55 (Minneapolis: University of Minnesota Press, 1988), xxxiii–xxxv.

7. Teresa de Lauretis, "The Essence of the Triangle or, Taking the Risk of Essentialism Seriously: Feminist Theory in Italy, the U. S., and Britain," *Differences* 1 (1989): 6. De Lauretis suggests that the secret subtext of the "essentialism" debate is our (possibly homophobic) anxiety with regard to being identified with and viewed in relation to other women. Something similar may be said regarding our ambivalence toward defining feminism. The popular "I am not a feminist but . . ." has a correlative in the "I am a feminist but . . ." gesture often implicit in feminist discourse.

8. De Lauretis, "Essence of the Triangle," 4.

9. Alison M. Jaggar, *Feminist Politics and Human Nature* (Totowa, N.J.: Rowman and Littlefield, 1983).

10. Catharine A. MacKinnon, *Feminism Unmodified: Discourses on Life and Law* (Cambridge, Mass.: Harvard University Press, 1987).

11. The phrase comes from the title of Nancy Fraser's book *Unruly Practices: Power, Discourse and Gender in Contemporary Social Theory* (Minneapolis: University of Minnesota Press, 1989). In general, radical feminists do not speak of "human nature." They are much more concerned with "separatism," and this, like the associated notion of "sisterhood," is supplemental to "human nature," the point of departure for Jaggar's theoretical analysis. "Separatism" is both radical feminism's distinctive virtue and for many, its distinctive vice—the sign of its "extremism" (see Joan Cocks, *The Oppositional Imagination: Feminism, Critique and Political Theory* [New York: Routledge, 1989]). It is the key contribution of radical feminism to feminist discourse, and is the thread that connects the "radical" feminism of the late sixties and early seventies, and today's "cultural" feminism. Today, the charge of "essentialism" leveled at the epistemological claims of "cultural feminism" is code for the charge of "separatism." De Lauretis suggests that "what motivates the suspicion or the outright construction . . . of a fantom essentialism, may be less the risk of essentialism itself than the further risk of what it entails: the risk of challenging directly the symbolic institution of heterosexuality" ("The Essence of the Triangle," 32).

12. My fictional survey of feminists is comparable to the historical approach advocated by Karen Offen ("Defining Feminism: A Comparative Historical Approach," *Signs* 12 [1988]: 119–57) and others in that both

employ an empirical approach. The recurring themes of feminism are determined inductively from a survey of contemporary opinion in one case and from the historical record in the other. Some might object that my approach is ahistorical since it focuses only on the present. I would refer these objections to the discussion of historical time in the next two sections of this chapter.

13. Julia Kristeva, *Kristeva Reader*, ed. Toril Moi (New York: Columbia University Press, 1986), 36.

14. My use of a thematic structure as a trope for feminism is comparable to Paul Smith's use of "colligated" subject-positions as a trope for subjectivity. In both cases, the structural trope solves the problem of accounting for "negativity" (my thematic structure is really an ensemble of contradictions) and heterogeneity, but is unsuitable for addressing the question of how these themes and subject-positions are produced, evaluated, and negotiated. Donna Haraway's cyborg is another trope for essentially the same phenomenon—that of a subject that is constituted by heterogeneous but colligated fragments. See Haraway, "A Manifesto for Cyborgs," in *Feminism/Postmodernism*, ed. Linda J. Nicholson (New York: Routledge, 1990), 190–233.

15. Jean-Paul Sartre, *Search for a Method*, trans. Hazel Barnes (New York: Knopf, 1963). Subsequent references to this work will be given parenthetically in the text.

16. Sartre, *Critique of Dialectical Reason* vol. 1, trans. Alan Sheridan-Smith, ed. Jonathan Ree (London: NLB, 1976), 33.

17. Sartre defines the practico-inert as the "domain of alienated *praxis* and worked inertia" (*Critique*, 67) formed by the congealed residues of human projects; it functions as a field of necessity enabling as well as undermining individual freedom. The practico-inert is comparable to what poststructuralists call "the always already written."

18. Mikhail Bakhtin, *The Dialogic Imagination*, ed. Michael Holquist (Austin: University of Texas Press, 1981), 30. Subsequent references to this work will be given parenthetically in the text.

19. In mathematics, A and B commute if they can trade places: e.g., $A + B = B + A$. In the vernacular, to commute is to travel regularly back and forth between two destinations—e.g., to travel daily between an urban workplace and a suburban domicile. I mean to play on both senses of the verb "to commute" to portray the dialogical and dialectical interaction, through which one element realizes itself and fosters its development by circulating through the sphere of the other. The play of the commutative interaction described above with linguistic communication is, in my view, the crucial figurative advantage offered by the trope of conversation.

20. Kristeva, *Kristeva Reader*, 36.

21. See Carol Gilligan, *In a Different Voice: Psychological Theory and Women's Development* (Cambridge, Mass.: Harvard University Press, 1982); and Gilligan et al., *Mapping the Moral Domain: A Contribution of Women's Thinking to Psychology and Education* (Cambridge, Mass.: Harvard

University Center for the Study of Gender, Education, and Human Development, 1988).

22. For an example of recent feminist appropriations of Bakhtin's work, see Dale M. Bauer and Susan Jaret McKinstry, eds., *Feminism, Bakhtin, and the Dialogic* (Albany: SUNY Press, 1991). My own interest in the trope of conversation predates my encounter with Bakhtin.

THIRTEEN

Resisting Images:
Rereading Adolescence

MARIANNE HIRSCH

> Family photographs may affect to show us our past, but
> what we do with them—how we use them—is really about
> today, not yesterday.
>
> —Annette Kuhn

For my parents' fiftieth anniversary I make them an album. I make
it for myself as well, to assemble their lives and mine within the
pages of the pretty book I bought for the occasion. I begin with the
few images I could find of them as children (only one of my father,
and he is already about fourteen) and end with a triumphant, slightly
mischievous image, a picture my two boys took of themselves in
their messy room with a self-timer. I make sure to include all the
places my parents have lived in, the people who have been most important to them. I try to find images of their parents, but I don't
know whether the young couple in turn-of-the-century outfits are
indeed my father's parents. I worry, as I assemble and arrange the
images, that looking at them will make my parents sad, will highlight the loss of homes, of friends and relatives, of their own intimacy. Until the last moment I am not sure I will really give it to
them. It is this hesitation, no doubt, that causes me to stress repetitions and continuities in my arrangement of these pictures.

In the album there are several "series":

—Me as a three-month-old held by my parents under the kitch-
en lamp, then me in the same spot held by my grandparents (fig. 1),
and then—in a leap in chronology—each of my children held by one
of my parents, in similar poses though in different domestic settings
(fig. 2);

—My parents and I hiking in the Carpathians (I am about nine),
followed by the three of us hiking in the White Mountains in New

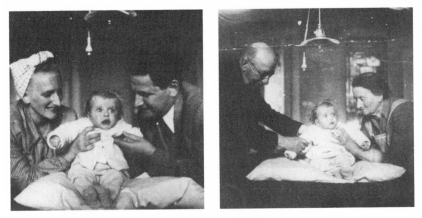

Figure 1. Hirsch family album, Marianne's baby pictures.

Hampshire several years later (fig. 3); the quality of the second photo is better but the pose is the same: we are sitting on a large rock by a brook—it could be the same mountain;

—My father holding me on his shoulders on a Black Sea beach; I am already too old for him to hold me comfortably, but we laugh as we act out an earlier pose. There are two more such images—my father holding each of my two boys on his shoulders. We are now in Florida and he is proving that he can still do it, though in the last picture his face is strained; he is not smiling (fig. 4). It is as though acting out this scenario had become a necessary ritual.

The old pictures especially are small, hard to read, precious. I place them carefully on the page, and I admire the series I create. This is an earnest album—it occurs to me that I could make it funny, that I could juxtapose the pictures to highlight the breaks, the ironies, the discontinuities, that I could come up with witty captions. But that would not be appropriate here. This album erases the ruptures of emigration and exile, of death and loss, of divorce, conflict, dislocation, and alienation. Those realities are submerged between the pages, imperceptible to anyone who looks at it, and, I hope, invisible to my parents at least for the occasion of their anniversary.

This essay is precisely about the discontinuities I banished from my own family album. It is about four texts in which family photographs are used quite differently from the way I used mine. These texts reveal the ruptures and dislocations in the autobiographical and familial narrative so as to find in those gaps spaces for daughterly

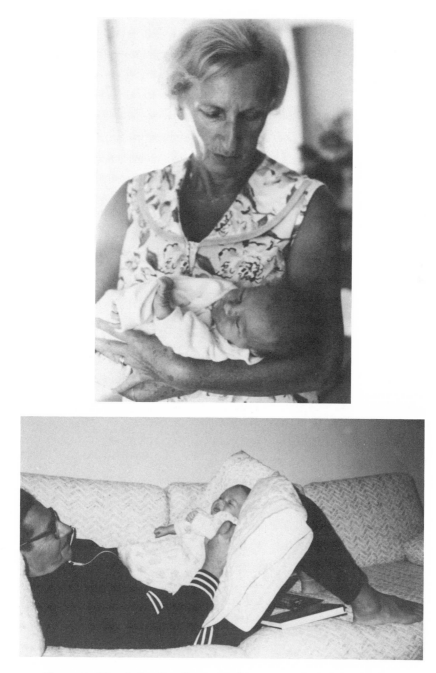

Figure 2. Hirsch family album, "Babies, Parents, Grandparents."

Figure 3. Hirsch family album, "Hiking in the Carpathians" and "Hiking in the White Mountains."

Figure 4. Hirsch family album, "Beach shots."

resistance against familial ideologies—spaces for female agency in the familial and social script. My texts are *Annie John*, Jamaica Kincaid's autobiographical novel (1985); Marguerite Duras's autobiographical novel *The Lover* (1984); two autobiographical essays by the British psychologist Valerie Walkerdine, "Dreams from an Ordinary Childhood" (1985) and "Behind the Painted Smile" (1991); and a photograph by Lorie Novak entitled *Fragments* (1987). In each case, family photos play an important role in the narrator's self-definition as familial daughterly subject, and in each, the photos are manipulated, transformed, mishandled, destroyed, and reinvented, so as to reveal what alternate stories may lie beneath their surfaces or beyond their frames. Changing the photograph becomes a form of intervention, a strategy for the female familial subject to create a space of resistance and agency out of her own submerged and forgotten history.

Although they are all products of the mid-to-late 1980s, these four texts emerge from vastly different cultural contexts with different traditions of visual and verbal representation—the Caribbean, France, England, the United States. Yet three, and maybe also the fourth, are socially marginal, depicting the process of female development as one of cultural displacement. They also use remarkably similar strategies of intervention into their familial and personal stories, strategies that might help us to think about female agency as constituted within the framework of the family and within the space of adolescence.[1]

Annie John is Kincaid's first novel; composed of a number of stories originally published in the *New Yorker*, it tells the story of the narrator Annie's childhood and adolescence on a small Caribbean island (perhaps the author's native Antigua), which, at the end of the novel, she leaves for England.[2] In her later works, especially in *Lucy*, Kincaid writes about her own career as a photographer, a career that eventually leads her to writing.[3] The control of the camera enables Lucy to move from her subordinate position as servant and immigrant to that of self-determining subject who gains consciousness by analyzing the situation in which she finds herself. In contrast to Lucy, Annie John is not a photographer but merely a reader of the conventional family pictures on her nightstand. Yet, her manipulation of the photos endows her with some of the control Lucy gains through taking, developing, and arranging photographs. Whereas Lucy makes pictures, however, Annie erases them to expose the gaps that lie beneath and within.

The Lover, like *Annie John*, is an autobiographical story of individual development and cultural displacement.[4] Just as Annie left her homeland, Duras's protagonist/narrator leaves Indochina and her family for France and her writing at the end of the novel. Family photographs are the pretexts of *The Lover*, which was originally supposed to be entitled "La photographie absolue." The novel—so the story is told—originated with a box of old photographs that Duras's son tried to get published. When the publisher asked that his mother add some captions to the photos, Duras wrote *The Lover* and ended up publishing it with Minuit, but without the pictures.[5] This explanation of the novel's origin accounts for a number of apparent textual incongruities: the characters from the period of the Occupation in Paris who mysteriously appear in the midst of a narrative that takes place exclusively in Indochina many years earlier, and the many seemingly gratuitous reflections on image and photography included in the text. It also explains the text's loose structure: as we read the novel, we can imagine the narrator leafing through a series of photos, returning to linger over some, as she builds a narrative on the basis of images. Yet photographs are ambiguous for Duras; juxtaposed to written narratives they invariably represent the fixity and rigidity that the fluidity of writing aims to challenge: "I believe photographs promote forgetting," Duras says in *Practicalities*. "The fixed, flat, easily available countenance of a dead person or an infant in a photograph is only one image as against the million images that exist in the mind. And the sequence made up by the million images will never alter. It's a confirmation of death."[6] It must be this quality of photography that leads Duras to feature an absent picture, the "photographie absolue." In *The Lover*, the "photograph" that was never taken becomes for the narrator the medium of an alternate set of memories on which the rest of the novel is then based. And this "photograph" "records" the moment of adolescent rupture that alters the course of her subsequent development.

Unlike Kincaid and Duras, Valerie Walkerdine comes to family pictures not as a writer but as a professional reader of images, an analyst of film, photography, and other popular visual media. Her two essays appear in two different collections that feature photographs either as illustration (*Truth, Dare or Promise: Girls Growing Up in the Fifties*) or as subject (*Family Snaps: The Meanings of Domestic Photography*).[7] In the two companion essays, Walkerdine traces both her personal emergence from a small-town working-class British setting in the fifties and her developing insights as a feminist theorist and activist in the late eighties. Photographs of herself permit Walkerdine not only to interpret her childhood and family, but also to engage in a new practice of reading. Her analysis evolves from an early Mulveyan perspective on women as objects of the male gaze to a more complex positioning of women as both objects and subjects, creators and readers of their own images. The pictures Walkerdine creates are the results of a personal psychoanalysis and, at the same time, of her theoretical insights into our gendered relation to the image and the gaze. In confronting radically different images with each other, Walkerdine focuses in depth on a break in her life story—a break located in her girlhood—and she finds in that break the possibility both for active resistance and for insight.

Lorie Novak's photograph *Fragments,* shown in the 1991 Museum of Modern Art exhibition Pleasures and Terrors of Domestic Comfort, also constructs the female subject as both creator and reader of her own self-representations.[8] Novak and Walkerdine engage in a kind of photographic self-creation that begins with the positioning of themselves as camera objects and then manages deliberately to transform that stance in an attempt to gain control through the reframing and manipulation of archival photographic materials. Novak's intervention, even more than the others, describes a female subject who becomes an agent by breaking with a past plenitude to embrace fragmentation, discontinuity, and absence. But what kind of agent is this fragmentary subject? How effectively can she intervene in the ideological script of family and society?

These four texts represent somewhat different examples of a common strategy chosen by feminist writers and artists, at the same moment, but in different cultural contexts: that of reframing images so as to discover fissures and absences that make space for a revision of social roles and positions. These fissures are found to be in specific moments of girlhood and adolescence—different moments in each texts—revealing adolescence as a source of resistance and agency. Why have pictures—conventional and ordinary snapshots, representing, in this case, predictable daughterly roles and positions—served as privileged sites of intervention into familial and social scripts, as useful sites of contestation? Theorists of photography have studied its relationship to agency from the perspective of the photographer's artistic intention and control, a question that has been seen to determine the photograph's status as art.[9] I focus here not on the production but on the reading of photographs and on the ways in which certain forms of reading, rereading, and misreading—particularly of the adolescent moment—can themselves become forms of agency. If the gaze of familiality can be said to construct the girl as a social category, then resisting the image, either at the time or later, in the process of rereading, becomes a way of contesting that construction, of rewriting the present by way of revising the past. For me, this process of rereading is an attempt to intervene in ways that I did not do when I made that album for my parents, to evaluate, through contrast, the familial continuities I chose to stress.

When photos are mentioned in *Annie John*, they represent Annie's confinement within the institution of family—everything that at the end of the novel she rejects for a new life abroad. Thus, her mother's trunk (the trunk she needs to replace as she leaves home) contains, among a series of objects collected since Annie's birth, a "photograph of me on my second birthday wearing my pink dress and my first pair of earrings, a chain around my neck, and a pair of bracelets, all specially made of gold from British Guiana" (20). As a young girl, Annie delighted in rediscovering each of the objects in the trunk and hearing her mother's stories about them; in adolescence she concentrates instead on the rings and chains and bracelets, the images of entrapment in the script of daughterhood and femininity she eventually repudiates. Possibly, the rings and chains made out of gold are also reminders of a slave history Annie can try to leave behind when she goes to England. As she looks around her room in preparation for leaving the island, knowing that she will never return, she sees for a moment only, and without much regret, the "photographs of people I was supposed to love forever no matter what" (131). Annie's remarkable change in the course of the novel revolves around the figures of home and her mother, whom she adores and with whom she feels symbiotically merged as a child, only to despise her, lie to her, torture her, and reject her during adolescence. The transition between a comfortable sense of home and the urgent need to leave that home is certainly a gradual one, told in a series of painful confrontations. A strange encounter with her family photographs is crucial in focusing Annie's shift from compliant daughterly subject to resisting agent.

In the novel's penultimate chapter, Annie suffers from a protracted and inexplicable illness, mirrored globally in the three-month torrential rain that floods the island. Annie spends the rainy months in bed in a retreat to childhood comfort in the constant care of her parents. Her illness follows the most serious fight she ever had with her mother and her consequent request that her father make her a new trunk. The fight is occasioned by Annie's first encounter with boys—a humiliating scene during which Annie runs into a boy she used to play with as a child who subtly mocks her during the chance street meeting. Only later does she remember the last game they had ever played together as small children: the boy had asked Annie to take off all her clothes and wait for him under a tree in a spot that turned out to be a red ants' nest. As she remembers this degrading initiation to sexuality, Annie loses all sense of herself: "I began to feel alternately too big and too small. First, I grew so big that I took up the whole street; then I grew so small that nobody could see me— not even if I cried out" (101). This powerful image of alternate grow-ing and shrinking—an image reminiscent of *Alice in Wonderland*— typifies the daughter's ambivalence about moving from childhood to adolescence; it describes the fractured and disrupted developmen-tal progress of the female subject. Annie's first foray into the world of adult sexuality—punished rather than supported by her mother, who chides her for being a slut because she talked to these boys— sends her literally back to bed in a withdrawal that reads like a clas-sic description of latency.

During this illness, left home alone for a brief period, Annie con-fronts the photographs that surround her bed. The photos suddenly protrude from the background of the room and "loom up big in front of me" (118). Conventional family pictures, each illustrates one of the institutions into which Annie is in the process of being induct-ed as she becomes a social subject. In the first, she is wearing her white school uniform. In the second she is a bridesmaid at an aunt's wedding, again wearing white. The third is simply a picture of her parents: the father wears a white baseball uniform, holds a bat in one hand, and wraps the other hand around the mother's waist. The last photograph is the only one that elicits a memory and a narra-tive: Annie again wears a white dress, her Communion dress, and she wears shoes with a decorative cutout on the side, shoes her mother disapproved of as "not fit for a young lady and not fit for wearing on being received into church" (119). As Annie recalls the argument over the shoes—her wish that her mother were dead and the mother's terrible headache that made Annie fear that she had indeed died—the photos begin to act very strangely:

> The photographs, as they stood on the table, now began to blow them-selves up until they touched the ceiling and then shrink back down, but to a size that I could not easily see. They did this with a special regularity, keeping beat to a music I was not privy to. Up and down they went, up and down. They did this for so long that they began to perspire quite a bit, and when they finally stopped, falling back on the table limp with exhaustion, the smell coming from them was unbear-

able to me. I got out of bed, gathered them up in my arms, took them over to a basin of water on the washstand, and gave them a good bath. I washed them thoroughly with soap and water, digging into all the crevices, trying, with not much success, to straighten out the creases in Aunt Mary's veil, trying, with not much success, to remove the dirt from my father's trousers. When I finished, I dried them thoroughly, dusted them with talcum powder, and then laid them down in a corner covered with a blanket, so that they would be warm when they slept. (119–20)

The result of Annie's feverish manipulation of the photos is that they are completely transformed: "None of the people in the wedding picture, except for me, had any face left. In the picture of my mother and father, I had erased them from the waist down. In the picture of me wearing my confirmation dress, I had erased all of myself except for the shoes" (120).

How are we to interpret Annie's strange intervention? How does the transformation of the pictures relate to her recovery—a symbolic rebirth, a break from her girlhood past, after which she needs new clothes and shoes, speaks with a different accent, develops great contempt for her classmates, and eventually leaves home? I see Annie's intervention as a moment of resistance in which she attempts to extricate herself from the familial gaze, shedding one by one the institutions that have interpellated her as daughter and social subject. The photos enact the process of growing and shrinking, the ambivalent confrontation with adolescent development. Annie reduces them, like herself, back to infancy, so as to have a chance at a different start, one in which bodies, faces, and clothes interact differently and acquire different dimensions. We could say that she acts out her fear of adult sexuality as she tries to remove the photos' bad smell, erase her parents' bodies below the waist, and rub out the stain on her father's pants and the wrinkles in the wedding veil. At the same time, however, she is more deliberate, motivated more by disgust than by fear, as she chooses to resist all the confining white dresses and the institutions they represent.

Yet, we must ask why Annie stages resistance by means of a manipulation of photographs in particular. How does photography further her act of opposition? I would suggest that the family pictures mark Annie's relation to her *past* and therefore to a *future she wants to choose.* For Roland Barthes, the photograph signals the past as what he calls the "ça a été," "the thing that has been there." In Barthes's terms "reference" is "the founding order of photography": "I call 'photographic referent' not the *optionally* real thing to which an image or a sign refers but the *necessarily* real thing which has been placed before the lens, without which there would be no photograph."[10] In washing and changing the pictures and the relationships they depict, Annie can attempt to weaken the "having been there" of the referent. She can attempt to intervene in her past, to rewrite her memories in favor of representations that better fit with the new life she wants to explore. She can assume an adult role in relation to her own childhood poses as she bathes the pictures and powders them as though they were her babies. When she finishes the feverish bath, she has erased the wedding party except for her own face, she has removed her parents' sexuality, and she has preserved the subversive shoes. Her face, her shoes, and her parents' torsos are all that remain, building blocks of new memories and new materials for adult life.

In addition, the photograph, especially a family photograph that depicts the subject embedded in relation and ensconced in institution, reinforces for the subject an imaginary sense of coherence and plenitude. The still picture freezes one moment and enshrines it as a timeless icon with determinative definitional power. Thus, the single still photo can be seen as a form of suture through which the subject closes herself off from the symbolic and the unconscious, from contradiction and lack. The subject gazing at her own image can find this coherence as she bridges the gap between herself as spectator and as object of representation. Annie contests this totalizing and rigidified sense of self—a girlhood self constructed according to social requirements—by washing the pictures and leaving open unmarked spaces within them. Staring at the ruined images the next morning, she can find in them a more tentative, more fluid and permeable subjectivity—one that can include a desired imaginary wholeness even while opposing and rejecting it.

As Annie settles into her berth at the start of her transatlantic escape from a predetermined future, she repeats the erasures she performed on the photos: "I could hear the small waves lap-lapping around the ship. They made an unexpected sound, as if a vessel filled with liquid had been placed on its side and now was slowly emptying out" (148). This image of emptying reinforces Annie's rejection of plenitude. Annie's departure requires not continuity with past experience and the preservation of memory, but empty open spaces on which new narratives can be inscribed. This is the space she makes when she washes the photos.

To describe such a locus of ideological resistance, Teresa de Lauretis borrows a term from film theory, the "space-off," the "space not visible in the frame but inferable from what the frame makes visible."[11] De Lauretis describes a particular movement of resistance staged by "the subject of feminism," a movement I see Annie as charting:

> It is a movement between the (represented) discursive space of the positions made available by hegemonic discourses and the space-off, the elsewhere of those discourses: those other spaces both discursive and social that exist, since feminist practices have (re)constructed them, in the margins (or "between the lines" or "against the grain") of hegemonic discourses and in the interstices of institutions, in counter-practices and new forms of community. These two kinds of spaces . . . coexist concurrently and in contradiction. The movement between them, therefore, is not that of a dialectic, of integration, of a combinatory, or of *différance*, but is the tension of contradiction, multiplicity and heteronomy. (26)

In recasting her family pictures, Annie finds the space-off that was already inscribed in the incongruity between her confirmation dress and the cutout shoes. Bringing the space-off to the surface and into the frame, Annie moves from interpellated subject to agent in her story. She has replaced the space symbolized by the old trunk, colonized by her mother's memories of her and by her mother's memorabilia, with her own tabula rasa—a new trunk to be filled by objects she herself will select. Thus, Annie's agency depends precisely on absence, discontinuity, and incongruity—on the negativity with which she has inscribed her adolescent break, her refusal to consent to a prescribed adult femininity.

Could it be, however, that retrospectively constructing her resistance as a moment of adolescent rupture is for Annie to follow yet another ideological script? From the perspective of Carol Gilligan's reading of girls' development, Annie rewrites her story of childhood connection in favor of what Gilligan calls the "canonical story of human development" in which breaks are mandated and childhood relationships must be devalued in adulthood.[12] Whatever her motivation, Annie inscribes the break in her story as an act of erasure in which photographs play a central function. They stand for the aspect of childhood controlled by the familial gaze, the conventional, institutional side of girlhood leading to a consent to femininity as culturally constructed. And they allow her to forget, or to disavow, the other side of childhood, the world of ecstatic mother/daughter connection, the space of friendship, and the feeling of being at home in the world that she presents in such lush detail throughout the novel's first part.

In *The Lover*, Duras also associates agency with discontinuity. The novel is characterized, in fact, by a perpetual tension between the fixity and rigidity of some of the visual images it describes and the fluidity the narrator wants for her narrative, the breaks and dislocations she insists on. It is as though, throughout the text, the narrator needs to contest the formal family photographs her mother has taken of her children year after year and the ways in which these images force them to see themselves: "We don't look at each other but we do look at the photographs, each of us separately, without a word of comment, we see ourselves. . . . Once they've been looked at the photos are put away with the linens in the closets. My mother has us photographed so that she can see if we're growing normally. She studies us at length as other mothers do other children. She compares the photos, discusses how each of us has grown" (94). Formal portrait photographs of the period equalize their objects, attenuate singular traits in favor of promoting, through similar pose, dress, and expression, what must have been considered a comforting resemblance—a generational and class belonging that erases particularity and self:

> All these photographs of different people, and I've seen many of them, gave practically identical results, the resemblance was stunning. It wasn't just because all old people look alike, but because the portraits themselves were invariably touched up in such a way that any facial particularities, if there were any left, were minimized. All the faces were prepared in the same way to confront eternity, all toned down, all uniformly rejuvenated. . . . they all wore an expression I'd still recognize anywhere. (96–97)

Photographs can well promote this erasure of the particular as they reinforce the plenitude of the imaginary and the external signs of class and institutional allegiance. The touched-up picture her mother had taken before her own death is a good example: "In her photo her hair is done nicely, her clothes just so, butter wouldn't melt in her mouth" (96). Duras contests this death in the very construction of her text: her "photographie absolue" is composed in direct opposition to formal portraiture. Here the process of "touching-up" is reappropriated and taken to an extreme by the subject of the picture.

The Lover begins with the image of the narrator's ravaged old face—the opposite of the touched-up photo of her mother. From a loving description of her old face, the narrative moves on to consider the sudden break, between the ages of seventeen and eighteen, that produced it: something happened to her appearance to give her the face she was to keep and which would then continue to age more gradually. The narrator emphatically *describes* this break between seventeen and eighteen and its ravaging effects, but she never directly *motivates* it in the long narrative that follows. Throughout the novel, we look for hints as to what happened between seventeen and eighteen to make her age so drastically. Duras, however, is more interested in the rupture itself than in an explanatory narrative that might have the undesirable effect of bridging it.

The Lover thrives on such discontinuities: "The story of my life doesn't exist. Does not exist. There's never any center to it. No path, no line" (8). Contrary to images, as Duras constructs them, writing can be made out of emptiness and rupture: "Sometimes I realize that if writing isn't, all things, all contraries confounded, a quest for vanity and void, it's nothing. That if it's not, each time, all things confounded into one through some inexpressible essence, then writing is nothing but advertisement." Image and writing are constructed in opposition in Duras's text, one signaling fixity and cohesion, the other freedom and permeability.[13]

What, in this context, is the function of the "photographie absolue," which is one of the text's multiple foundational images—the photograph that was never taken but could have been? This image of the girl crossing the river at age fifteen and a half is, in both senses of the word, a *cliché* of adolescent rupture and discontinuity: "It might have existed, a photograph might have been taken, just like any other, somewhere else, in other circumstances. But it wasn't. The subject was too slight. . . . It never was detached or removed from all the rest. And it's to this, this failure to have been created, that the image owes its virtue: the virtue of representing, of being the creator of, an absolute" (10).

Why does this particular memory, as significant or insignificant as it may seem in the narrator's autobiographical musings, take the form of a photograph in particular? In what ways does photography enable Duras to construct the specific kind of subjectivity that emerges in *The Lover?* If Kincaid's Annie needs to weaken the "ça a été" of her photos' referent and thereby the fixity of memory and the past, Duras's narrator may need to do the opposite: to strengthen her memory and to solidify the lover's and her own tenuous earlier existence. Since reference is, as Barthes says, the "founding order" of photography, a picture may be the optimal medium for such a process. When we look at a photo, or even when we read a description of one, we do assume that the referent is the "necessarily real thing that was placed before the camera." Even as the narrator tells us that the picture was never taken, we listen to its content and imagine it in great detail. A picture described verbally is the same whether it "exists" or not: the referent of the picture itself seems more solid, but the referent of the description is more or less so according to what the narrator tells us. In this case she tells us that this picture is a construction, and we see it more clearly because the construction is described as a picture, but less so because she tells us that it was never taken.

The details of the picture can begin to suggest the kind of intervention into her life story that the composition of this nonexistent picture constitutes. It is a "picture" of herself at fifteen and a half on a ferry crossing the Mekong River on her way from home to school. As a white girl, she is as incongruous a presence on the boat as the large black car belonging to the Chinese man who is to become her lover. Her description of her appearance begins with the inappropriate silk dress, so old it is already transparent, a dress hardly suitable for a girl on her way to school. Its oddity is increased by the leather belt she wears with it, a belt she probably borrowed from one of her brothers. She is not sure about the shoes—here is where the difference between photography and memory is clearest, for if this had indeed been a photo, the shoes would have been fixed in its image. Her assumption—that she wore gold lamé sandals with high heels—soon becomes fixed in *our* vision, however. But it is the hat that contains the picture's "determining ambiguity." It is a man's felt hat, flat-brimmed, pink, with a broad black ribbon, one such as no one wore at the time. As clearly as she can still remember the hat, as unclear is her memory of its origin. She imagines that she might have tried it on as a joke and then talked her mother into buying it for her because wearing it transforms her appearance drastically: "Beneath the man's hat, the thin awkward shape, the inadequacy of childhood, has turned into something else. Has ceased to be a harsh, inescapable imposition of nature. Has become, on the contrary, a provoking choice of nature, a choice of the mind. Suddenly it's deliberate. Suddenly I see myself as another, as another would be seen" (12–13). This shift from the given to the deliberate in her appearance is in itself an active intervention; the narrator wears the hat in a defiant gesture of self-definition—the self-definition of the adolescent who is breaking away from her family and her childhood. Yet, the incongruities in her appearance are the photo's most important feature—not the hat but the ways in which the hat clashes with the rest of her clothes. In its contradictions, the image can undo the suturing of the act of its construction: with its conflicting effects, the picture acts out the opposing forces that define subjectivity. Contrary to Annie's attempt to move from center to space-off, Duras's narrator creates an image in the space-off that then absorbs the focus as though it were centrally located within the frame. This ambiguity between the construction of memory as photograph (an attempt at solidifying the "ça a été") and the chaotic aspects of the image itself (a reintroduction of fluidity and discontinuity) dramatizes the process of constructing the autobiographical subject out of different positions and within the framework of contradictory impulses and desires. In *The Lover* these positions emerge distinctly as the narrative switches, quite unpredictably and without clear motivation, from first to third person, from the subjective to the objective. The narrator is "I" at first, then she becomes "she" or "the girl"; she acts in the text and, especially in her encounters with the Chinese lover, she watches herself act and being acted upon. The narrator and the girl in the pictures are but two of the different positions Duras assumes in the text.

Paul Smith, in his book *Discerning the Subject*, sees negativity—the space in between different subject positions, the space binding and unbinding them—as central to the subject's construction.[14] Photographs are perhaps best suited to demonstrating the ways in which we want to turn away from negativity and to convince ourselves of our plenitude—the photo is, of course, literally developed from a negative. For Kincaid negativity is nevertheless exposed as she wipes clean certain sections within her photos. Duras describes a more complicated process of negotiating between fullness and emptiness. The absolute she finds in the invented picture is the negativity, the absence around which it takes shape in the narrator's and her readers' imaginations. Resisting the plenitude and fixity contained in conventional family pictures and finding a space of negativity is in itself the intervention of the familial subject as agent—a return to a break between life moments when subjectivity was less fixed, more fluid, more productive of different possible futures. That moment, for the narrator of *The Lover*, is the moment of adolescent rebellion—when she contests bourgeois colonial convention to take a Chinese lover, when she allows him to give her family money, when she identifies with him over her mother or brothers, when, eventually, she leaves for France to become a writer. But, we might ask again our earlier question: in constructing the photo as a break, in highlighting negativity and emptiness, what knowledges, what continuities, might she be denying? Where, in fact, is convention and where resistance, where is agency, in the story of girls' move from childhood to adulthood?

Valerie Walkerdine's first essay, "Dreams from an Ordinary Childhood," defines an agency that transcends negativity, even as it moves from the personal to the political, from the familial to the social. The book in which it was first published, *Truth, Dare or Promise: Girls Growing Up in the Fifties,* is a collection of twelve personal testimonies by British feminists of the postwar generation. Each of the essays locates the author within the institution of the family and in relation to social changes introduced by the Education Act of 1944 and the founding of the welfare state in Britain. The stories the twelve authors tell are stories of upward mobility made possible by the sense of possibility and sense of personal entitlement to which they attest in direct opposition to the myths that define femininity during the fifties. As the editor insists: "There was a general confidence in the air, and the wartime image of women's independence and competence at work lingers on well into the decade in the popular literature and in girls' comics of the day" (6). By going back to their childhood, the authors attempt to trace the sources of feminist consciousness in their family histories and class allegiances, in the courses their lives took in contrast to the lives of their mothers and fathers: "All of these accounts contain an implicit avowal of how we see the world: all as feminists, though perhaps speaking with the voices of different feminisms, and all informed by other commitments—to socialism, anti-racism, or to other recognitions of ways in which the world needs to be changed" (8). The childhoods described in the book are the childhoods of future activists.

Each of the essays is illustrated by a photograph showing the author at a young age, either alone or in the company of a sibling. Some are family snapshots, others more formal photos taken for specific occasions. The picture illustrating Walkerdine's "Dreams from an Ordinary Childhood" is typical of the volume in that it reinforces stereotyped images of girlhood: it is a picture of a little three-year-old dressed as a bluebell fairy (fig. 5). Holding a star, little Valerie smiles tentatively but sweetly at a space that is off-camera, beyond the picture's frame. The picture appeared in the Derby *Evening Telegraph* with the following caption: "Three-year-old Valerie Walkerdine, one of the 'fairies' in the fancy dress parade at Mickleover children's sports and field day last night."

In her analysis of the picture, Walkerdine, a psychologist, focuses on the little girl's off-camera look, on what I have discussed as

Figure 5. Valerie Walkerdine, "Tinkerbell," from the Derby *Evening Telegraph*.

the "space-off": "Whose gaze? In whose vision was I created to look like this, to display the winning charms, so that posing before the judges, they too, like the camera, would be won over? It is my first memory of what winning meant. But towards whom am I looking, who dressed me like this? Like all the fairy fantasies rolled into one? It was somebody's dream, their fantasy, my fantasy, meeting in the mutuality of the returned look; the gentle and uncertain smile created there too" (66–67). The gaze, of course, belongs to her father, who called her Tinky and identified her with the fairy who might repair all his ills—his poverty, his sickness, and the threat of death.

Walkerdine's essay places the bluebell picture in contrast to her subsequent self—the fat, clumsy, frightened child who replaces the sickly and underweight but magical Tinky after she has her tonsils out. This is the break in her life story that the essay interrogates, but it is a break nowhere reflected in the illustration. But even in her new persona, one that fails to correspond to the "pre-adolescent feminist myth" of activity and athletic prowess, Valerie continued to please and to win—in school and in a variety of holiday competitions. Her strategy now is not the magic of Tinky, but the plodding reliability and hard work that girls learn because it gets rewarded in school. This is the price of being allowed to follow the dream of upward mobility: "They held out the knowledge, the position to me, and told me that I could claim it as mine, if I worked for it and had the ability" (75). But claiming the dream now, as she retells the story, is rejecting the good-girl image and asserting a dangerous power and knowledge: "We are beginning to speak of our histories, and as we do it will be to reveal the burden of pain and desire that formed us, and, in so doing expose the terrible fraudulence of our subjugation" (76).

Walkerdine's narrative takes her from the sickly bluebell fairy to the plodding reliable good girl to the rebellious Marxist-feminist who has not only followed the "dream of an ordinary childhood" but has also turned that dream back on itself by exposing its fraudulence and its price. This is not a seamless, linear tale. There is violence at the very center of it—the poison Tinkerbell drinks to save Peter Pan, the surgery Valerie undergoes that removes not only her tonsils but her magic and charm. This is the violence that divides her early life story, a break parallel to Annie John's illness, parallel also to the river crossing and the break between seventeen and eighteen that organizes the Duras text, but found earlier in girlhood for Walkerdine. For Walkerdine, sickliness and charm are replaced by lumpiness and a disgust with her body. In this narrative, femininity is defined either by frailty or by a "lumpen docility": "I find it almost unbearable to look at photographs of myself from that time on" (69). And yet, Walkerdine emerges from the trap created by these two equally unacceptable subject positions as a feminist agent capable of claiming the power that comes with self-knowledge. How?

The gaps that remain in this narrative occasion a second essay, "Behind the Painted Smile." In revising and supplementing her "Dreams from an Ordinary Childhood," Walkerdine takes us beyond the space-off of the Tinkerbell photo and the father's gaze to the space-off of the essay itself where she finds another, a deeply suppressed and transgressive version of herself. In the first essay she described this other self, but here she allows us to *see* it as well; the first essay contained an illustration and an analysis of it, while the second takes us through the work of reframing and reconstructing images: "When I wrote that piece it was as though I had said all there was to say, but I knew at one level then, and I see more clearly now, that there are far more disturbing images to explore, which are hidden and covered over by the erotic allure of the bluebell fairy" (35). To expose those images—and clearly their visual, as opposed to verbal, nature is crucial—Walkerdine first has to tell the story of the first essay's publication:

When I wrote the piece I sent the publishers two photographs: one of the bluebell fairy and another, a school photo of me, aged about seven, looking puffed out, sickly and fat. They wanted to publish the latter. I, having sent it to them in the first place, adamantly refused to let *this* image be the object of public scrutiny. . . . I continued to hide behind a wall of words, academic words, which kept me from exploring the traumatic effectivity of that and other reviled images of myself. (35)

In her subsequent analysis and, even more powerfully, in the essay's illustrations, Walkerdine can expose her own and her generation's subjection as well as her attempt to exonerate herself of any responsibility for it: "On one level, the idea that we are constructed in the male gaze is reassuring. We remain somehow not responsible for our actions, as though we were mere puppets to masculinity. . . . It strikes me as easier to take apart a beautiful image, blame patriarchy, and yet hold on to that image (Yes, yes, I am that really) or to point to a void as its other side than to examine what else may lurk beneath" (36). This—to examine and actually to expose "what may lurk beneath"—is the project of Walkerdine's second essay.

Getting to the space that lies beneath the surface of the image is a complicated and painful, though ultimately powerful, process for Walkerdine—as deliberate an intervention as Annie's act of washing her photos or Duras's construction of a fictional picture. But Walkerdine goes beneath the absence and void central to the other two texts, in favor of the uncomfortable alternative of attempting to find, to touch, and to name what exactly lies outside the frame.

This involves work with images as well as work with words, and here Walkerdine's essay differs from Kincaid's and Duras's. Walkerdine makes slides out of a number of family snapshots, projects them on the wall, draws and colors all over the projected images, shades them in, writes on them, later makes pastel drawings from these new images, and exhibits them in an installation (figs. 6, 7, 8). She describes this as a shocking practice of self-mutilation that results in a series of extremely disturbing self-portraits, a number of which are reproduced with the essay. Two areas of the body are their main focus, the mouth and the abdomen; the rest of Walkerdine's essay provides the analysis that explains their centrality—her obsession with food, her fear of speaking in public, her fear of sexuality. Through her mutilation of the old images, Walkerdine finds what lies beneath their surface—"a terrible rage, depression and anger that have been entirely split off" (40) from the present feminist persona who was the author of "Dreams from an Ordinary Childhood."

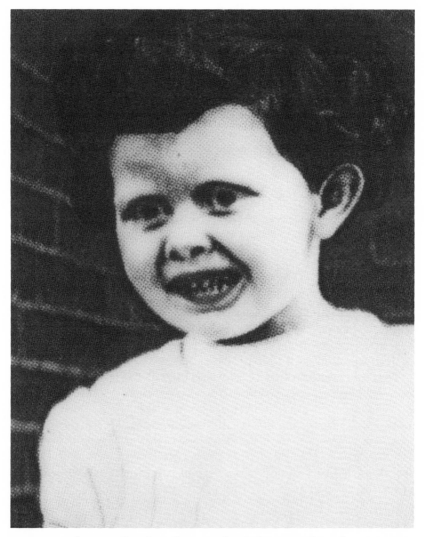

Figure 6. Valerie Walkerdine, from "Behind the Painted Smile." Courtesy of Valerie Walkerdine.

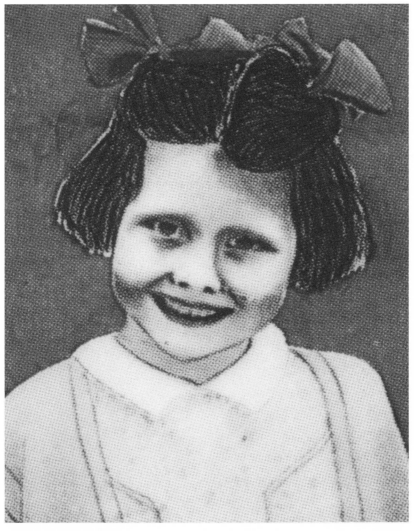

Figure 7. Valerie Walkerdine, from "Behind the Painted Smile." Courtesy of Valerie Walkerdine.

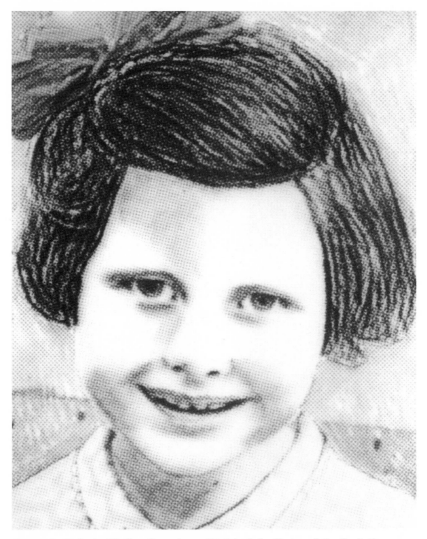

Figure 8. Valerie Walkerdine, from "Behind the Painted Smile." Courtesy of Valerie Walkerdine.

Walter Benjamin finds in photography's methods a route to an "unconscious optics," just as psychoanalysis offers a means to learn about unconscious drives.[15] His notion of "unconscious optics" is contrary to the identification of the photographic image with the subject's wish for an imaginary plenitude. Walkerdine, in "Behind the Painted Smile," concurs: "Like dreams, images are the manifest content which is only the surface cover for what lies latent beneath. Thus, although much radical work on photography has shown us how to read the semiotics of photographs it has not ventured much below the surface" (40). In finding a way to get beyond the surface and in reaching (doubly) outside the frame, and in naming what she finds there, Walkerdine can connect her present active intervention with the active impulses of her earlier self; she can find in the past not only frailty and docility, not only female impersonation and mimicry, but anger and rage, envy and greed.

Identifying anger and rage, envy and greed from the vantage point of the present constitutes a profoundly different definition of agency than they offered her in the suppressed past. During her childhood and even at the moment of the first essay, Walkerdine perceived the break between the frail Tinky (identified with magic) and the docile schoolgirl (identified with compliance and plodding), but she did not perceive its violence. That violence, along with the anger and rage it elicited in her was hidden "behind the painted smile." Both subject positions—the magical fairy and the docile schoolgirl—were dictated from the outside. The space-off in both cases was occupied by the familial and social gaze, the cultural forces that interpellated her into their dreams. The father constructs the fairy, the clapping hands keep Tinkerbell alive because they believe in her, the social institutions reward Valerie's plodding hard work and award her the scholarships that allow her to leave home. Valerie merely fits into the images others design for her. And the only possibilities for her own active interventions are identified with unacceptable emotions and images: her own agency was coextensive with anger and rage, greed and envy, eating too much or saying something inappropriate. "Covered over, I suggest, was the fantasy of the angry child, actively shouting out loud, crying and screaming; the all-consuming, rapacious woman with a large (sexual) appetite" (42). In her direct manipulation of images, Walkerdine can get at feelings she cannot reach through words.

In childhood, the active girl is the angry girl; the desiring girl is the greedy child. In contrast, finding what lies behind the surface of the pictures and in the space-off of her first essay constitutes a different and more constructive form of resistance, the redefined and politically meaningful agency. "I believe that investigating these issues takes us beyond a deconstructive examination of the feminine in representations. It takes us to an exploration of the powerful fantasies and anxieties which keep those representations circulating and provide us with the basis for other narratives of our histories and the claiming of our power" (45). This is the agency of the theorist/autobiographer, the analyst/object of the gaze, the writer/visual artist. In the encounter of these different positions, Walkerdine can claim a power that has emerged through self-mutilation to a self-confrontation that acknowledges and revalues emotions deemed unacceptable, even for feminists. In contrast to Kincaid and Duras, Walkerdine finds these emotions on both sides of the break that constructs her story: leaving childhood or adolescence behind is not in itself a route to liberation. Power and knowledge can rather be found in the process of constructing and reconstructing, of reading and rereading, images both of compliance and of resistance.

Lorie Novak's *Fragments* will serve here as a concluding image, an alternative to my own family album (fig. 9). Novak's photograph is itself a collection of embedded images, the record of a series of superimposed projections: the large black-and-white family picture from the fifties projected onto a corner wall, a picture that itself has a painted portrait at its center, and a color photograph projected over white pieces of board onto the floor, which occupies the bottom half of the work, cutting off the lower portion of the black-and-white photo. There are at least four images of females in the work (two images of the photographer as a child dressed in identical round-collar dresses, one in the embedded painting and the other in the black-and-white image; two adult women, the pregnant mother in the black-and-white photo and presumably the photographer herself barely distinguishable in an inverted image as she lies on the floor on an orange float in a blue bathing suit). There are also at least two images of males (the father in the fifties photo holding the little girl who is sitting on the mantlepiece, and a headless upside-down male torso lying in fragments on the floor next to the woman in the bathing suit). In her construction of *Fragments*, Novak has created a composite image that illustrates the kinds of interventions we have seen in the written texts I discussed above. She has challenged any notion of plenitude that might come from gazing at an image of one's past or present self. She has broken through generational continuities signaled in the resemblance between the mother and daughter.

Figure 9. *Fragments,* © 1987 by Lorie Novak, original in color. Courtesy of Jayne H. Baum Gallery, New York.

She projected that picture onto a corner to make it look three-dimensional even as she has deliberately cut up its frame and cut off its bottom half. The alternate history she proposes lies in fragments on the bottom, and it aggressively protrudes outside even the cut-up frame. Here lies the woman of a new generation, refusing continuity and reflection, finding herself in fragments. As our eyes try to reassemble the fragments we notice hints of irreverence: her closed eyes, which refuse to gaze back at the viewer, or her hand reaching into her male companion's crotch. Her mouth is hidden from view; she doesn't smile as the compliant females in the black-and-white photos do. But the woman of the new generation is not just the collection of pieces of glossy paper on the floor, she is also the photographer who has so subversively assembled herself in them. Conventional family pictures provide Novak with the space of resistance and contestation. As photographer and agent, she can find herself both in the collection of contradictory, incongruous, and discontinuous images, spread across a table and tacked onto a wall, and in the act of reframing and rearranging them to trace a personal (and perhaps also a collective) history against their grain.

What is the relationship between this aesthetic discontinuity and ideological resistance, between negativity and agency? Is agency always located in resistance and contestation? Are Novak's fragmentary aesthetic and the subject-in-pieces she depicts the only manifestations of a feminist agency, or can we also locate agency in my own, equally deliberate, construction of familial and personal continuity? Which one of us is following the more coercive ideological script: the one who insists on continuity and resists the "canonical story" of adolescent rupture, or the one who breaks from the past, revising its pressure to be the good girl who develops into the good woman?

"A person is not simply the *actor* who follows ideological scripts," says Paul Smith, "but is also an *agent* who reads from them in order to insert him/herself into them—or not"(xxxiv–xxxv). With this last choice, of self-inscription "or not," Smith defines agency outside the dichotomy of resistance versus complicity. An agent is one who reads and who, through reading, is able to choose—Kincaid, Duras, Novak, Walkerdine, as well as I. Yet, their texts, unlike Smith's passage, do seem to suggest a necessary link between agency and rupture. It is the consciousness of a break, exposed in the radical and irreverent manipulation of images, that enables intervention, contestation, and change—whether personal or collective. For them, the break occurs in girlhood and adolescence, even if it is not "read" until adulthood. In contrast, my own construction of familial continuity across continents and generations, and across an entire life story, is complicit with familial ideologies that position the daughter as future mother, that present the familial unit as harmonious and free of conflict, that disguise the passions and rivalries, the anxieties and tensions of family relations, and that accept rather than resist the photographic constructions of the familial gaze. Yet in highlighting the break, they support another set of cultural constructions of adolescence as the moment of revolt. In reunifying a fractured personal history, even as deliberately and consciously as I did, I may forgo the possibility of intervention and change, but I resist a discontinuity that has also become coercive. As I contrast my family album with the images in these four texts, however, I begin to perceive the discontinuities within my own story as enabling. Reading these texts against each other and against the images embedded within them is in itself a form of agency, one that has occasioned for me a process of rereading my own adolescence as a space of many possible stories, with many possible interpretations. Making the album and reading it, placing it into this comparative perspective, reveals, moreover, the difficult and elaborate personal work involved in defining feminist agency.

But to what extent can we even see writing, or making pictures, or reading them, as forms of feminist agency? When we intervene in the ideological scripts determining our own lives are we also intervening in the world or are we trapped in the domain of the personal and the aesthetic? Is this work individualistic, self-indulgent, irrelevant to feminist politics? What kind of feminist agent is the maker and reader of images? She can, it seems to me, combine two necessary elements enabling her to intervene and transform hegemonic constructions. She can perceive familial ideologies and see herself both reflected by them and opposed or adjacent to them. She can understand her determinations and interpellations and attempt to confront and resist them. At best, therefore, she can be an empowered actor who can speak and act on behalf of women, for by going from the center of the image into the space-off she can reclaim repressed and censored emotions that can perhaps free her to act. But, by reading and remaking familial images, she can also reveal, through splits and contradictions, through incomplete suturings, the complicated and painful process of identity. She uses available technologies in the practices of her everyday life, reclaiming them from the oppressive spaces to which they have been relegated by cultural critics. She uses these technologies to reread and redefine patriarchal constructions. But she goes beyond this deconstructive process to define a new aesthetic—one that assembles and reconstructs personal and domestic images that are individual yet collective, fragmentary yet continuous, revealing both breaks and interconnections. She can use her anger and her rage as motivating forces in her creation, defining an aesthetics of anger and pointing to its distinctive beauty.

It is thus that I would like to see my work on this essay: as an attempt to theorize agency that is coextensive with its practice, a practice that is both contained in these pages and that lies, unreachable, outside their frame.

NOTES

I am grateful to audiences at the "Alice in Wonderland" conference on Girls and Girlhood in Amsterdam, at Middlebury College, Duke University, and the University of Michigan for their suggestions for this essay. I would also like to thank Brenda Silver for reminding me of the photos in *Annie John* and Judith Kegan Gardiner, Lorie Novak, and Valerie Walkderdine for all their help. A slightly shorter version of this essay appeared in *Girls, Girlhood and Girls' Studies in Transition,* ed. Marion de Ras and Mieke Lunenberg (Amsterdam: Het Spinhuis, 1993).

1. For the purposes of this analysis, I do not focus specifically on the cultural differences between these texts; rather I see them all as representative of certain strategies of self-presentation in pictures and words, strategies relating to the retrospective interpretation of female adolescence. The texts themselves attribute varying importance to other social demarcations inflecting the influence of gender: thus gender is a more prominent social marker than race in *Annie John,* while class is as foregrounded as gender in Walkerdine's work.

2. Jamaica Kincaid, *Annie John* (New York: Penguin, 1984). Page references to this work will be given parenthetically in the text.

3. Jamaica Kincaid, *Lucy* (New York: Farrar, Strauss and Giroux, 1990).

4. Marguerite Duras, *The Lover,* trans. Barbara Bray (New York: Pantheon, 1985). Page references to this work will be given parenthetically in the text.

5. On the novel's photographic origin, see the reviews by Marcine de Martinoir, *Nouvelle Revue Française* 383 (1984): 92–95, and Jean-Marc Turine, "Marguerite Duras fabriquant un livre," *La Nouvelle Revue* 80 (1984): 553–55. See also Madeleine Borgomano, "*L'Amant:* une hypertextualité illimitée," *Revue des sciences humaines* 73, no. 202 (Apr.–June 1986): 67–77, for an analysis of the role of photographs as "hypotexts" structuring the narrative.

6. Marguerite Duras, *Practicalities: Marguerite Duras Speaks to Michel Beaujour,* trans. Barbara Bray (New York: Grove Weidenfeld, 1990), 89.

7. Valerie Walkerdine, "Dreams from an Ordinary Childhood," in *Truth, Dare or Promise: Girls Growing Up in the Fifties,* ed. Liz Heron (London: Virago, 1985); idem, "Behind the Painted Smile," in *Family Snaps: The Meanings of Domestic Photography,* ed. Jo Spence and Patricia Holland (London: Virago, 1991). Page references to these works will be given parenthetically in the text. Both essays have also been included in Valerie Walkerdine, *Schoolgirl Fictions* (London: Verso, 1990).

8. Peter Galassi, ed., *Pleasures and Terrors of Domestic Comfort* (New York: Museum of Modern Art, 1991).

9. See, for example, Umberto Eco, "Le Hasard," *L'Arc* 21, "Photographie" (1990): 74–81.

10. Roland Barthes, *Camera Lucida: Reflections on Photography,* trans. Richard Howard (New York: Hill and Wang, 1981), 76, 77.

11. Teresa de Lauretis, *Technologies of Gender: Essays on Theory, Film and Fiction* (Bloomington: Indiana University Press, 1987), 26.

12. Carol Gilligan, "Women's Psychological Development: Implications for Psychotherapy," in *Women, Girls and Psychotherapy: Reframing Resistance,* ed. Carol Gilligan, Annie G. Rogers, and Deborah L. Tolman (Bing-

hamton, N.Y.: Harrington Park Press, 1991), 5–6. See also Carol Gilligan, Nona P. Lyons, and Rudy Hanmer, eds., *Making Connections: The Relational View of Adolescent Girls at Emma Willard School* (Troy, N.Y.: Emma Willard, 1989), and Carol Gilligan, Carol Janie Victoria Ward, and Jill McLean Taylor, *Mapping the Moral Domain: A Contribution of Women's Thinking to Psychological Theory and Education* (Cambridge, Mass.: Harvard University Press, 1988).

13. For a fuller analysis of how this dichotomy structures Duras's text, see Nina S. Hellerstein, "'Image' and Absence in Marguerite Duras' *L'Amant,"* *Modern Language Studies* 21, no. 2 (Spring 1991): 45–56.

14. Paul Smith, *Discerning the Subject* (Minneapolis: University of Minnesota Press, 1988), 156.

15. Walter Benjamin, "The Work of Art in the Age of Mechanical Reproduction," in *Illuminations,* ed. Hannah Arendt, trans. Harry Zohn (New York: Schocken, 1969), 237.

FOURTEEN

Recuperating Agents: Narrative Contracts, Emancipatory Readers, and *Incidents in the Life of a Slave Girl*

CARLA KAPLAN

> Reader, my story ends with freedom; not in the usual way, with marriage.
>
> —Linda Brent [Harriet Jacobs], *Incidents in the Life of a Slave Girl*

FREEDOM, SLAVERY, AND CONTRACT

In this famous concluding line Harriet Jacobs's narrator, Linda Brent, rejects the marriage contract and, more generally, the conventions regulating women's lives and literature.[1] By opposing freedom and marriage she undermines the nineteenth-century ideology of marriage as woman's "sacred absolute," the means of her personal fulfillment and the proper end of her life.[2] By suggesting, moreover, that freedom does not have the "usual" meaning for black slave women that it has for free white women, she challenges us to think about freedom and agency as specific and contextual, not as abstract and universal, to think about freedom, as she puts it, "not in the usual way."

But what would it mean for us to think about freedom or agency "not in the usual way"? Brent's "freedom" at the end of the narrative is complex and ambiguous. Although "free"—"as free from the power of slaveholders as are the white people of the north"—she is still unfulfilled. "The dream of my life is not yet realized," she writes; "I do not sit with my children in a home of my own. I still long for a hearthstone of my own, however humble" (201). This dream embraces both sides of a double desire.

On the one hand, a home of her own represents a refuge, not only from social conventions, but also from the social relations entailed in her obligation to serve the Northern white woman who has helped obtain her freedom. This dream represents freedom as social escape, counterposing idyllic isolation to the social world that "binds" her and concretizing that line of liberal ideology which understands the individual's freedom as autonomy, as freedom *from* (tyranny, domination, involuntary rule).

Brent's desire for a home of her own also signals that other conception of freedom central to liberal ideology, that which understands the individual's freedom in terms of rights: as freedom *to* (contract, exchange, trade—in short to engage in the whole array of social relations and practices constitutive of civil society). Brent passionately describes the pain of exclusion from this rights-based conception of freedom. "Never should I know peace till my children were emancipated with all due formalities of law" (138). Her efforts are thwarted because, as she is quick to point out, "there was no protecting arm of the law for me to invoke" (138). She is excluded from possessive individualism.[3] "A slave, *being* property, can *hold* no property" (6), she reminds us, including property in one's own person, that supposedly inalienable fulcrum upon which both liberal and patriarchal conceptions of the individual, freedom, and agency rest.[4] As Carole Pateman has argued, ownership makes individuals free and equal. Each individual is both "naturally complete in himself" (55) and the owner of "property in his own person" (55). Therefore, he can engage in contracts with others on a mutual basis. A home of Brent's own, then, might seem to provide just the access to personhood—through possession and possessive individualism—which national law, regional slave codes, the Dred Scott case, the Fugitive Slave Law, and dominant ideology would otherwise deny.[5]

But reading Brent's desire as an endorsement of liberal ideology would be mistaken.[6] With neither the means to escape "the law," nor any protection within it, Brent is caught in a dilemma. How, by whom, and through what mediations can Brent's dilemma be resolved?

By introducing the category of gender into a critique of social contract theory, Pateman's important work on the sexual and social contract illuminates the practical and philosophical conundrum Jacobs's narrator faces. From the seventeenth century on, a rights-based conception of individual freedom and agency (or freedom *as* agency) has taken contract as its basis: "contract is seen as the paradigm of free agreement" (6). Contract offers itself as the point of mediation between the seemingly conflicting ideals of freedom as autonomy and as rights. The possessiveness of free and equal individuals allows for "free agreement" in the form of exchange—"exchange is at the heart of contract" (57)—and conventions function so that the "free and equal" individual can "recognize the others as property owners like himself . . . mutual recognition by property owners is achieved through contract" (56).

Contract, as a balanced, voluntary exchange between individuals, mediates human relationships, derives its meaning from them, and also—importantly—presents itself as having the power to change them. Contract, perhaps not surprisingly then, generally appears as a progressive form of social relations: "Classic social contract theory and the broader argument that, ideally, all social relations should take a contractual form, derive from a revolutionary claim. . . . The assumption that individuals were born free and equal to each other meant that none of the old arguments for subordination could be accepted" (39).

The problem, Pateman argues, is that contract reinforces subordination. Contract perpetuates domination, on Pateman's account, because it is based on two fictions: universal freedom and the equality of individuals. These provide the grounds for the claim—in response to the undeniable fact of social domination—that there must have been a moment, or moments, in which individuals agreed to domination (in exchange for safety or other goods). As free and equal individuals, the argument goes, their domination could only have resulted from their voluntary submission.

Introducing gender and race exposes the circularity of this logic by unmasking the neutral contractarian "individual" as a free, white male, and so-called "universal" freedom, therefore, as a highly contingent state.

And here, traditionally, contracts come in. Where the conditions of universal freedom and equality of individuals do not exist—which is to say, most of the time—it is the task of discrete, individual contracts to provide them. But how is it that contracts produce their own preconditions? How do they override difference, inequality, and domination? When institutionally secured forms of oppression are at play between contracting parties, won't the contract tend to reinforce rather than transcend or transform those inequalities?

Pateman argues that individual contracts fail to provide their own preconditions in freedom and equality and that contract in fact depends upon excluding many people from its equalizing, emancipatory machinery. Hence, her implicit suggestion that the only option available to the excluded is a wholesale rejection of all contracts.

Incidents in the Life of a Slave Girl often seems to join in this suggestion that anyone who is not a free, white male cannot take advantage of a form of mediation within which he or she is categorically disadvantaged at the outset. One of the narrative's most impassioned passages is a powerful rejection of contract. Here, Brent describes her unhappiness upon receiving a letter from her white friend and employer, Mrs. Bruce,

> informing me that my new master was still searching for me, and that she intended to put an end to this persecution by buying my freedom. I felt grateful for the kindness that prompted this offer, but the idea was not so pleasant to me as might have been expected. The more my mind had become enlightened, the more difficult it was for me to consider myself an article of property; and to pay money to those who had so greviously oppressed me seemed like taking from my sufferings the glory of triumph. I wrote to Mrs. Bruce, thanking her, but saying that being sold from one owner to another seemed too much like slavery. (199)

Without her knowledge, Mrs. Bruce successfully pursues Brent's purchase.[7] Brent experiences what might seem to be merely her entry into contract—by becoming "property in her own person"— as a psychological explosion. "'My brain reeled as I read these lines,'" Brent reports: "'The bill of sale!' Those words struck me like a blow. So I was *sold* at last! A human being *sold* in the free city of New York! . . . I well know the value of that bit of paper; but much as I love freedom, I do not like to look upon it" (200).

But while Jacobs demonstrates her categorical exclusion from prevailing ideas of personhood and individuality, she also indicts slavery by exposing its *denial* of contractual human relations. In other words, she rejects contracts to which she cannot be a fully equal and voluntary party, but not the ideals to which such contracts allude. Unlike Pateman who rejects contracts because she rejects the ideology of contract, Brent rejects contracts because, I believe, she endorses and even longs for the ideals and ideologies of individuality embodied by the idea of the social contract.

This position is a precarious one, particularly because writing seems inevitably to entail contracts. In response, Jacobs, I will argue, at once foregrounds narrative contracts and, paradoxically, avoids them.

Incidents in the Life of a Slave Girl has been the subject of an important recent critical recuperation. It has emerged, along with a handful of other texts by marginalized writers, as an exemplar of textual resistance and subversion. But, some of the critical maneuvers of that recuperation have actually occluded Jacobs's modes of resistance and subversion, ultimately reinscribing her within the very contractual mediations she seeks to avoid and expose. Jacobs, as the final section of this discussion will show, attempts a difficult, complex, and often precarious task. Like a number of modern African-American women writers, she seeks to create a new black narrative position, one founded in a rejection of both the attestory position of slave narrators and the seductive one typical of white women's romances. This position aims to avoid being drawn into narrative contracts that cannot either grant her freedom or change her status.

RECUPERATING HARRIET JACOBS

Writing her own story, Brent asserts, is a painful experience, one she undertakes only to aid abolition, specifically to protest the Fugitive Slave Law, enacted in 1850 and in effect as Jacobs writes. Brent describes her earnest "desire to arouse the women of the North" to protest slavery and insists that "I have not written my experiences in order to attract attention to myself; on the contrary, it would have been more pleasant to me to have been silent about my own history" (1–2).

A critical recuperation of Jacobs's text has been necessary to restore its authenticity and recognize the complex sociopolitical conditions of its production. In spite of authorial insistences such as "Reader, be assured this narrative is no fiction" (1), earlier critics, such as John Blassingame, insisted that "the work is not credible."[8] Jean Fagan Yellin's dramatic discovery of Jacobs's letters, in 1981, restored the text's historical authenticity and inaugurated its critical reappraisal.[9]

Jacobs has become, for many readers and critics, proof that human agency can still be affirmed under even the most relentless and repressive conditions. "Jacobs' narrator," Yellin writes, "does not characterize herself conventionally as a passive female victim, but ... was an effective moral agent" ("Introduction," xxx).

The celebration of Jacobs's agency has often rested on valorizing the act of writing itself as a signal achievement of personal power. Certainly the historical conditions slave narrators faced—including the use of (il)literacy as a measure of slaves' (in)humanity—make any published and self-authored account a remarkable achievement.[10]

Literacy is not a transcendent value, however, for Jacobs. It is a social practice deeply inscribed by the forms of power and authority that it mediates and in which it is situated.[11] Taught to read and write by her first mistress, Brent finds that literacy opens her to new forms of assault as well as new avenues of response when Dr. Flint uses clandestine letters to communicate his sexual desires.

Although Brent neither idealizes literacy nor treats it as the measure of her worth, her modern readers have been more sweeping. Minrose Gwin, for example, sees it as a way "to control and dominate, in language, those who controlled and dominated her."[12] Valerie Smith argues that by writing Jacobs "seized authority over her literary restraints in much the same way that she seized power in her life."[13] "By creating Linda Brent, by writing and publishing her life story," Yellin argues, "Jacobs gained her victory."[14]

These readings are part of a broader enterprise of critical recuperation that seeks to rewrite the history of cultural resistance and elaborate our understanding of how literary struggles are both sites and modes of social struggle. This recuperative enterprise has located and resuscitated scores of texts by African-American and women writers; its methods have taught us to read silence, decipher madness, recognize and decode the unofficial documents of our culture.[15]

But the recuperative enterprise has also fostered a sentimentalization of the marginal, the oppositional, and the subversive, not to mention a very particular privileging of writing and narrative as subversive and oppositional practices. *Incidents's* skepticism about the value and status of narrative, as I hope to show, introduces a cautionary note into these abstractions.

Recuperative readings of *Incidents in the Life of a Slave Girl* present a two-sided problem. They define agency too narrowly: as subversive "acts." But they also define it too broadly: attributing it to narration, narrativity, or discourse per se and often, in so doing, tacitly affirming problematic models of individuality and subjectivity. My quarrel here is not so much with particular critics, as with specific critical maneuvers that celebrate literature as a "talking cure" for social ills. This notion often exacerbates the impasses it describes and frequently substitutes the critic's own agency for the textual agency supposedly being restored. Typically, this includes one or more of the following three approaches to recuperating textual agency: locating it in the acts described; locating it in the act of narration itself; and locating it in the relationship between the narrator and the implied reader. In these last two cases particularly, the notions of social and sexual contract that remain at the heart of theories of narration are often the very ones that Jacobs explores and exposes.

EMANCIPATORY READING

Incidents in the Life of a Slave Girl is structured around a series of disappointed expectations of imminent freedom. In the opening chapter Brent relates what she calls the "unusually fortunate circumstances" of her childhood: loving parents, a family home, an extended family, a kind and caring mistress, a father who was allowed to hire out his skills as a carpenter. All this comes to an end when Brent is twelve and her "kind mistress sickened and died." Although promised that this mistress's will would free her, Brent is instead "bequeathed" to the mistress's niece, "a child of five years old." At this point she becomes subject to the child's father, her new master, Dr. Flint.

The rest of Jacobs's account details her attempts to evade Flint's sexual harassment, which begins when she approaches adolescence: "a sad epoch in the life of a slave girl" (27). To avoid Flint's advances Jacobs ultimately takes three actions that she rationalizes, justifies, or explains in terms of relative conceptions of freedom.

First she enters into a sexual liaison and has two children with a white man in the town, Mr. Sands, a decision she describes as a "desperate" "plunge into the abyss" (53). Insisting on her own responsibility for this act, she asserts that "I knew what I did and I did it with deliberate calculation" (54): "It seems less degrading to give one's self, than to submit to compulsion. There is something akin to freedom in having a lover who has no control over you, except that which he gains by kindness and attachment. . . . He was a man of more generosity and feeling than my master, and I thought my freedom could be easily obtained from him. . . . I also felt quite sure that they [her two children] would be made free" (55).

Second, Brent takes refuge in the garret of her grandmother's house, a "dismal hole . . . only nine feet long and seven wide" (113). Insisting again upon her own responsibility, Brent chooses freedom from sexual harassment over the freedom from material discomfort she could obtain by becoming Flint's mistress: "It seemed horrible to sit or lie in a cramped position day after day, without one gleam of light. Yet I would have chosen this, rather than my lot as a slave, though white people considered it an easy one; and it was so compared with the fate of others. . . . On the contrary, I had always been kindly treated, and tenderly cared for, until I came into the hands of Dr. Flint. I had never wished for freedom till then" (115). As she makes clear, her "choice" is paradoxical: true freedom eludes her in either case.

Third, after five years in the garret, Brent writes a series of letters to Dr. Flint, postmarked from New York and Boston to trick him into believing that she is a fugitive in the North. "I resolved," she writes, "to match my cunning against his cunning" (128). Even when Linda's letters fuel Flint's efforts to recapture her, she is optimistic about them: "the letters will do good in the end. I shall get out of this dark hole some time or other" (131). And with Flint convinced that she is in the North, it does prove safer for Brent occasionally to slip downstairs and exercise her atrophying muscles. Since these letters cannot be answered by Flint, they are also an outlet into play, one-way communications that parody the letter-writing exchange they imitate.

These acts form the basis of a surprisingly coherent set of readings of Jacobs's survival strategies as "an act of subversion,"[16] "an indirect assault on her master's domination,"[17] "effective combat,"[18] and "a power reversal"[19] that "pries apart slavery's domination.[20] It is of course true that many writers bury subversive plots or elements beneath more ostensibly orthodox ones.[21] And I would certainly class Brent's liaison with Sands, her self-imprisonment in the garret, and her letter-writing in this category, particularly as all of these activities so self-consciously rupture and parody the narrative conventions of romance, slave narratives, and epistolary fiction. But I would also question describing a black slave woman's "desperate" plunge into an affair with a free white man an "act of *subversion*," or her desperate self-imprisonment an "*assault* on her master's domination." In what sense is this miserable, wasting, wasted seven-year period a form of "*effective combat*"? Do her letters really effect a "*power reversal*"? Do they "*pry apart*" the social system?

Identifying Brent's agency solely with the rebelliousness of these acts assumes that their liberatory meanings override their self-defeating or submissive ones: the sense of a "desperate" plunge in Linda's affair, of self-imprisonment and living death in the coffin-like garret, of false choices. Where does the authority for such a judgment come from? And from what kind of position? Not only do such conclusions risk suggesting that power is easily subverted and reversed, but they also risk occluding the very impasse this narrative represents. Jacobs is at great pains to dramatize Brent's *inability* to "subvert" her status, "*assault*" her master's domination, wage "*effective combat*," or "*reverse*" the power structures that bind her.

This inability is the lived meaning of slavery for Linda Brent. It is this narrative's strongest indictment. Defining agency, broadly speaking, as the act of writing misses the point.

One of the more remarkable (and lucky) features of Brent's struggle with Dr. Flint is the fact that he does not rape her, although clearly he could: "do you know that I have a right to do as I like with you,—that I can kill you, if I please?" (39). Flint insists instead that Linda voluntarily submit to his coercion. He demands not simply her body but also her consent; he wants her to legitimate his domination over her. This Linda refuses to do. "You have no right to do as you like with me," she answers Dr. Flint (39). Linda exercises agency here by refusing to consent, just as elsewhere she does so by refusing to act. Insofar as we attempt to locate Brent's agency in specifically rebellious acts, making any meaningful rebellion of hers tantamount to *acting*, her refusal of consent and self-justification, which often takes the form of seeming to refuse to "act," may remain invisible. Defining agency more narrowly, then, as certain kinds of acts, may also miss the point.

The problem of locating and perhaps even of restoring Brent's agency becomes particularly troubling when we recognize, as I think we must, that we, as readers, are implicated in the problem we are analyzing. Narration, or writing, has no fixed status in Jacobs's text. It derives its meaning from the human interactions it mediates: our own, in this case. This raises an important methodological question for recuperative work: what will it mean for us to recover or recuperate Jacobs's agency when we, as readers, are problematically and unavoidably (albeit also variously and differently) implicated in the process of its construction?

Structurally, in fact, the reader parallels Dr. Flint. The narrative presents just two representations of writing: first, the "bit of paper" that "frees" Linda but sends her reeling with an even stronger sense of unfreedom; and, second, her fraudulent letters to Flint. As the addressee of Brent's letters, Flint therefore is the narrative's only represented reader. He parodies the convention of an implied reader who is also an ideal reader. But because he is the text's *only* representation of a reader, the reader is practically forced to ask: How ideal am I? How competent? What forms of authority and power do I bring to this text? How do I inscribe it with those as I read? The letter-writing exchange, interestingly enough, parallels the act of reading this text. And this exchange is pointedly nondialogic. It parodies writing as a form of communication, as a coming together of writer and reader, as the frequently invoked writer-reader "contract."

NARRATIVE CONTRACTS

The assumption that literature involves reader/writer contracts is so commonplace that Northrop Frye can call it an "accepted postulate" that "the contract agreed upon by the reader before he [sic] can start reading, is the same thing as a convention."[22] But just as the term "convention" has been denaturalized as a set of particular forms of knowledge and historically situated contingencies that vary enormously from one "interpretive community" to another,[23] so the idea of the literary contract needs rethinking. Do narratives really work like contracts between writers and readers? And if so, what grounds them and makes them binding? How are they broken? How are they adjudicated and enforced? By whom? With what authority? In what sense has the idea of the literary contract evolved from social and legal ones? In what ways does it allude back to them to ground and legitimate itself?

Jonathan Culler's discussion of the novel in *Structuralist Poetics* illuminates how theories of narration may draw on social and legal contracts. Culler argues that narrative is shaped by thematic and structural contracts, specifically by the narrative movement between implicit and broken contracts.[24] His account of the novel as "communication about a world," between a narrator and imaginary reader who "share the same world to which the language of the novel refers" (195–96) reiterates what I am taking to be a prevailing—if not always acknowledged—model. According to Culler, the novel shares, across an array of subgenres and stylistic/structural innovations, an essentially conversational dynamic. Readers deploy a wide range of strategies of "recuperation" to identify, imagine, or construct narrators, so as to answer the dialogic question of who is speaking to whom, such that even the most unlikely and radically innovative texts resemble conversations.

This insistence on conversational models (less Culler's own, perhaps, than his diagnosis of critical and theoretical pieties) helps us to grasp the homology between a conversational fictional model and a contractarian social one. As we have seen, contracts depend, at the moment of contracting, on a consensual exchange between equals. But the fact of inequality poses a pressing dilemma, one that contract theory resolves through the double fiction that we are always already equals (because our apparent inequalities are themselves the products of previous contracts), and that the contract itself, as the medium of transaction between the two parties, not only regulates an exchange between parties, but is also the medium of their transformation—however momentary—into equals. Maintaining that novels mediate between parties who "share the same world to which the language of the novel refers" generates a homologous dilemma. Novels in fact are often written explicitly in and about the gap or conflict between those worlds. And whereas both sides of a parallel double fiction are available to resolve this narrative dilemma, one view seems to have lost currency in recent years: namely, that we all do share the same world (because good literature is universal). But corresponding to the fiction that contract mediates the transformation *into* equals of contracting parties is the idea that narrative not only mediates between nonequals, but mediates a transformation whereby the narrator and reader are equalized through the narrative "transaction." And I would argue that this fiction, unlike that of literary universality, is gaining currency.

Taken to its extreme, this occlusion of the divisions and differences between different readerships (historical and otherwise), can lead to seeing all narrative as an intrinsically oppositional practice. Ross Chambers, for example, describes narrative as a "transactional" or "contractual" practice that "mediates human relationships," "has the power to change human situations," and is therefore an "'oppositional practice' of considerable significance."[25]

Chambers calls the key mechanism of this transformation "seduction," the seduction practiced by the "situationally condemned" narrator who has to "earn the authority to narrate in the very act of storytelling" (214). Like classic social contract theory, the claim that narrative equalizes social relations seems revolutionary, but also like classic social contract theory, it obviates the need for any explanation of persistent inequalities.

Even work that foregrounds the divisions and differences of different readerships may take for granted that they are breached. Important work on Jacobs, for example, has examined her use of literary conventions to break social contracts. According to Valerie Smith, slave narrators "not only grant themselves significance and figurative power over their superordinates, but in their manipulation of received literary conventions they also engage with and challenge dominant ideology."[26] Jacobs found no available literary form for the story she needed to tell: as a woman she broke with many of the conventions of the traditional slave narrative; as a black slave she broke the taboos of nineteenth-century sentimental women's writing. Consequently, Smith compellingly argues, she uses silence as a protest and indictment: "By consigning to the narrative silences those aspects of her own sexuality for which the genre does not allow, Jacobs points to an inadequacy in the form."[27] "*Incidents*," Yellin observes, "transforms the conventions of literature. . . . formal problems suggest that new forms were needed, new characters, new narrative voices, if literature was to express the fullness of Jacobs' new point of view and her new content."[28] Hazel Carby's reading of *Incidents* illuminates its challenge to the conventions of true womanhood: "the narrative of Linda Brent's life," Carby points out, "stands as an exposition of her womanhood and motherhood, contradicting and transforming an ideology that could not take account of her experience."[29]

These readings convincingly delineate the narrative strategies Jacobs developed to address her situation as a fugitive slave woman and author. They also shift the ground from narrated acts to problems of narration and draw attention to the important ways that literary conventions index social ideologies: breaking with patterns of slave narratives, Brent's story does not end with freedom; reversing patterns of nineteenth-century women's literature, Brent prefers a loss of sexual purity and virtue to death; her sexual struggle does not resolve social conflict, nor does it enable her—through marriage—to change her class status.

But these readings also raise an important question. Don't modern readers pose the same problems of authority and legitimation that obviated Jacobs's use of available conventions? How do contemporary readers recognize a "subversive" plot that, presumably, slipped past other readers: contemporaneous and antagonistic? If contemporary feminist scholars can recognize the unsaid meanings of silences that other readers failed perhaps even to notice, have those now-spoken silences, then, lost their power to indict? Does this new understanding signal the arrival of the "new forms" that Jacobs suggested would be needed? How, in short, can a recuperative reading recover these silences, indictments, and subversions without assuming its own position of historical and epistemological privilege? "Sympathy" with the narrator might seem to be an obvious answer, but as feminist readings like Nelson's and Carby's point out, assumptions about "sympathy" and "identification" are part of what Jacobs puts under interrogation here.

In place of sympathy or identification, a critic like Chambers might suggest that "seduction" is the answer. Some texts are simply more seductive to some readers at some moments. The question, for Chambers, is merely a matter of mutual attraction, a kind of successful coming together, if you will, of reader and writer through the "contractual" mediations of the text. Chambers, however, does not account for how categories like gender or race inflect this formula. What kind of charge, after all, would "seduction" carry in the context of a black slave woman's story, addressed to Northern white women, of her master's failed seduction? In Jacobs's context, is a seductive contract really possible, let alone in her interest? Can she enter contracts—literary or social—on her own behalf at all?

Where the feminist critics I cite above have focused, in the main, on Jacobs's rupture of literary conventions and social contracts, Houston Baker makes a case for Jacobs's use of contract. Baker contends that the slave narrator's challenge was to master the "economics of slavery" (*Blues*, 26) through the "ironic transformation of property by property into humanity" (*Blues*, 36), a transformation enacted discursively. The slave narrator must "negotiate the economics of slavery" (*Blues*, 37) and free himself by engaging in acts that redefine him as an individual. As example, Baker offers Frederick Douglass's marriage certificate. "What Douglass's certificate of marriage . . . signifies," Baker argues, "is that the black man has repossessed himself in a manner that enables him to enter the kind of relationship disrupted, or foreclosed, by the economics of slavery" (*Blues*, 48).

Baker argues that, like Douglass, Brent negotiates through ironic economic exchanges with Sands that commodify herself and her children. Thus she becomes a possessive individual, or "at least provides necessary conditions for such a conversion to occur" (*Blues*, 54).[30] Although, Baker argues, "gender produces striking modifications in the Afro-American discursive subtext" (*Blues*, 50), "gender does not," he concludes, "alter a fundamentally commercial set of negotiations represented as liberating in the black narrative" (*Blues*, 54). Baker's example of Douglass's negotiation could hardly be more inflected *by* gender, however. It is marriage, after all, that engenders contractarian individuality. It establishes male possessive individuality through the exchange of women who mediate social relations not by being possessors of property but by being property. The entry into individuality available to Douglass necessitates a woman's exclusion from it, and would not be available *to* her.[31] While for Brent also, marriage is a relationship "foreclosed by the economics of slavery," it can only signify a deeper inscription into that economics, not a pathway out of it. As for her self-commodification via Sands, Jacobs, we might remember, expressly rejects the strategy of "ironic transformation of property by property into humanity" that Baker identifies with Douglass when she attempts to avoid her own purchase and self-possession. The efficacy of contract, in other words, like "seduction" on the narrative register, is inflected with Jacobs's gender. What may be "represented as liberating" for Douglass doesn't offer Jacobs any measure of freedom at all.

Gender, in other words, *does* alter those "negotiations represented as liberating in the black narrative," as Baker puts it. Douglass accepts, as Baker so deftly demonstrates, the available modes of freedom: mercantile freedom, freedom through literacy, freedom as a possessive individual. In so doing, Douglass fights his way into contractarian ideology and the rights that this entails. And Baker, quite rightly, celebrates this. But Brent, as we have seen, *refuses* available modes of freedom: mercantile freedom, freedom through marriage, freedom as a (self-)possessive individual. In so doing, Brent exposes her own categorical exclusion from that ideology and from those rights, an exposure that depends, in large part, upon her deconstruction of "negotiation" itself, narrative "negotiation" not excepted.[32]

NARRATIVE RESISTANCE

Robert Stepto describes African-American narrative as deploying a "discourse of distrust." In African-American storytelling texts, unreliability is located, Stepto argues, not with the narrator or author, but with the reader. And the reader is "told off" for being so untrustworthy: "It is usually in this way that most written tales express their distrust not just of readers but of official literate culture in general."[33]

Brent makes frequent reference to her implied readers: "the women of the North" (1). "You happy free women, contrast *your* New Year's day with that of the poor bond-woman" (16), she implores. She expresses her attitude toward this reader through her strategies of address, particularly the technique of presenting information a Northern white woman would be unlikely to know as if she is merely stating the obvious: "we all know that the memory of a faithful slave does not avail much to save her children from the auction block" (7); "the reader probably knows that no promise or writing given to a slave is legally binding; for, according to Southern laws, a slave *being* property, can *hold* no property" (6, italics in original). As Brent elsewhere suggests, however, these are just the sorts of things her Northern white reader would *not* know: how little value slaveowners placed on loyalty, what was or was not legally binding under the complicated slave codes of the South. Indeed, it is largely to try to *explain* such things that the narrative is written.

Why, then, pose as if this reader knows things she does not, feels things she doesn't feel, and understands things she apparently couldn't? Is Brent merely being (strategically) kind? Or diplomatic? Is she pretending to bow and scrape so as to put the reader at ease? Saving the reader embarrassment at her own ignorance? Stepto suggests that when the (white) reader (of the African-American text) is "told off" it is for his or her own good. The "instructional nature" of the "discourse of distrust" resides in teaching the reader how to reliably read the African-American tale and become a more "competent" reader.[34]

Brent's strategies of address do not follow this formula. She does not go to the trouble of "telling off" her reader and expecting—or even inviting—her to change. Instead, she invites the implied reader to take herself as already ideal and competent, even in the face of massive evidence to the contrary. Rather than "tell her off," Brent encourages her reader to congratulate herself for moral gestures this reader is spared from having to make.[35] Whereas Chambers argues that narrative "has the power to produce change, and first and foremost to change the relationship between narrator and narratee" (74), Jacobs's presumption seems to be that narration lacks this power, that the reader will not change, and that the mechanics of the narrative encounter are insufficient to the task of moral transformation. In place of a "discourse of distrust" she substitutes a profoundly more skeptical distrust of discourse. The inadequacies of literary form and convention she points to turn out to be inadequacies in her reader, inadequacies that she does not trust—or even ask—her narrative itself to ameliorate.

What we might call Jacobs's radical narrative skepticism is evident not only in her ironic treatment of "transactional" discourse, her mockery of the reader's capacity for change and of the narrative's capacity to change its readers, but also in her treatment of silence as a gendered form of kindness, respect, and fineness—or "delicacy"—of feeling. Her kindest white friends, for example, are represented as exhibiting the "delicate silence of womanly sympathy" (162) and as being careful "not to say anything that might wound my feelings" (161). Her daughter, Ellen, is praised "for the delicacy she had manifested towards her unfortunate mother" in not speaking aimlessly of painful subjects (189). Even more important, silence is racially coded. Whereas white silence is presented as shameful and cowardly, black silence is valued, privileged, and protected. Whereas whites are called upon to speak out against the outrages of the Fugitive Slave Law—"Why are ye silent, ye free men and women of

the north? Why do your tongues falter in maintenance of the right?"
(30)—the ability to keep silent is an index, among blacks, of trust-
worthiness and reliability. Brent's children's good character, for example, is established by their ability to maintain a "prudent," "cautious," and "cunning" silence about their mother's presence in the
garret above them. There is much to suggest that we take Brent at
her word when she insists, on the very first page, that "it would have
been more pleasant to me to have been silent about my own history" (1) and repeats, on the very last page, that "it has been painful
to me to recall the dreary years I passed in bondage" (201).

But of course recalling those years is just what she does by telling both her own story and the history of her family. "What tangled
skeins are the genealogies of slavery!" (78) she declares. And much
of our work as readers involves putting together the complicated
puzzle of Brent's family history. The shifting status of "free" blacks
is evoked from the first page of the narrative, when Brent describes
the family background of her maternal grandmother, the daughter
of a white South Carolina plantation owner and a black slave who
is freed at the planter's death and leaves slavery with her children,
only to see them captured again during the revolutionary war, "carried back, and sold to different purchasers" (5).

Racial status and gender politics come together in her family's
sexual history. Three generations of women have all had children
by white men, whether through rape, coercion, or, as in Brent's case,
strategy. The puzzle in this history is Brent's maternal grandmother, the "Aunt Marthy" who judges Linda so harshly for her liaison
with Sands. Both of Brent's parents are termed "mulattoes," imply-
ing that both have mixed parents. Brent's aunts and uncles are extremely light; in fact Benjamin is described as "nearly white" and
escapes slavery by passing (6). Aunt Marthy, this suggests, may also
have had her children, including Brent's mother, by a white slave-
owner. A narrative silence surrounds this grandfather, in spite of the
extensive attention otherwise devoted to establishing family history. How is this peculiar silence explained? Only through Brent's very
odd claim to "not remember all the particulars." This silence is less
a memory lapse than it is a denial—to the reader—of information
that would support her own claims of "tangled skeins" but which
might titillate her readers at her grandmother's expense, shame her
grandmother, or expose another family member to ridicule or deri-
sion. This use of silence suggests that thinking about freedom "not
in the usual way" may entail imagining what it would be like not

to have to give an account of yourself or your family to others, what it would be like to be freed from the juridical, attestory, or seductive position characteristic of slave narratives.

Of course, Jacobs's options for representing and engaging in communicative exchanges are not limited to those between narrators and readers. Internal dialogues, William Andrews has argued, play an important role in exposing the power relations that inflect the production and reception of slave narratives. I agree with his claim that "dialogue in slave narratives tells us something about the negotiation of power that goes on in discourse, whether between a master and a slave or a black autobiographer and a reader."[36] But I question his celebration of dialogue as a "liminal phase" of indeterminacy, power, and "freedom, even for slaves that would seem to be most powerless" (93). Andrews contends that *Incidents* is the most "'dialogized'" of antebellum black autobiographies," and that Brent's "repeated 'dialogic' struggles with Flint testify to the power she could and did exercise against his attempts to manipulate and dominate her" (93, 95).

But what is the nature of Jacobs's reconstructed dialogues? In whose favor *are* they resolved? There are eight passages that, broadly speaking, might be called dialogues between Linda Brent and Dr. Flint, but of these, only three can properly be called reconstructed dialogues; most of Brent's responses are summarized, not rendered in direct speech. Moreover, many of these dialogues end in violence. In one, Dr. Flint learns that Linda is pregnant again and cuts off all her hair and beats and harangues her until she faints at his feet (77); in another, he learns that Sands has tried to buy Linda and the children and hurls Benjamin across the room, nearly killing him (81). All the remaining "dialogues" end in unresolved silence. A number of times, Brent refuses to consent to Flint's desires. When he demands that she go to the cottage he has built for her, she replies, "'I will never go there. In a few months I shall be a mother'" (56). Again, later, "'No, sir'" (83). In each of these instances Brent acts out a performance of not responding, of being outside of attestory or seductive roles.

Moreover, in almost every instance Brent addresses her responses *not* to Flint at all, but to the reader. Following, for example, a lengthy expostulation by Flint on why Brent should submit herself to him, Brent asks, "Reader, did you ever hate?" (40). In having Brent address her reader—a reader she has already represented as a failed listener—rather than her interlocutor, Jacobs establishes a discursive triangle that makes any dialogue, in Andrews's sense, clearly impossible, given that the participants—Brent, Flint, and the reader—do not exist on the same plane, let alone within the same temporal register. While Brent may speak, she does so in a way that avoids exchanges or direct response.

There are two instances in which, as Andrews claims, Brent answers Flint back: telling him, in one, that he has no right to do as he likes with her (39) and stating, in the other, that she has sinned against God and herself but not against him (58). Here the "verbal battle" is over Flint's demand that Brent not only become his mistress, but perhaps more important, that she consent to being so. In this, Flint implies that she could also *not* consent, that she has, in other words, real consent to either give or refuse. When she does refuse, she exposes Flint's rhetoric—he never means her to have real consent either to give or to withhold—and makes any further conversation between them impossible. That is why their exchanges can only end in violence, silence, or in turning to the reader. Even when she is being most seemingly "dialogic," then, Brent is also exposing and attempting to refuse her categorical disadvantages within the verbal exchange. This refusal of dialogue is continuous with her refusal of consent and it is part of her larger effort to avoid all contracts and exchanges in which she is definitionally disadvantaged.

But if Jacobs was so resistant to narrative, dialogic, or contractual exchanges, one might ask, why did she write and publish her story? Surely writing for publication means entry into a whole range of contractual practices, both market and metaphoric. The answer to that very important question lies in two seemingly contradictory but mutually constitutive moments. On the one hand, there is her sense that any contract between whites and blacks is an impossible relation, expressed in the precept that "promises made to slaves, though with kind intentions and sincere at the time, depend on many contingencies for their fulfillment" (134). On the other hand, she hopes that contractual exchanges—of all types—will offer some kind of self-empowerment, expressed in her avowal that "never should I know peace till my children were emancipated with all due formalities of law" (138).

For Brent, then, as I believe for us, contracts remain compelling. There are many good reasons for this. Not only do they represent power, or at least its possibility, but they also represent an ideal of equal and equalizing social and civic relations. Perhaps it should not be surprising that Jacobs seems, at times, to cling to contracts. She is, as I have suggested, at a terrible impasse. Narration fails her as a mode of social transformation, yet remains one of her few available tools. Contracts fail to alter her status or provide her real freedom, yet they remain her only meaningful hope for both protection and change.

Where does this leave her readers and critics, particularly those who turn to this text, as I believe we still should, as an exemplar of resistance and rebellion? There seems to be little in our critical repertoire that could ameliorate this impasse. We could, of course, argue that Brent's ambivalence about narrative, writing, and dialogue is only a feature of her particular historical situation and that better, more sympathetic readers would render it superfluous. But given the extent to which Jacobs parodies—even as she seems sometimes to invite—the collapse of ideal and implied readers, this solution risks obscuring the tragic conditions that make Jacobs ambivalent and wary in the first place. Although Brent does eventually get out of her miserable attic hideaway, Jacobs does not escape the impasse this narrative so brilliantly renders. And that is the narrative's point. Her inability to do so suggests that we need to take further—or future—action on her behalf.

Brent's efforts to avoid consent or participation in her own nearly overwhelming disempowerment lead her to refusals of engagement or contract that can look like passivity, like an unwillingness to fight back. But what counts as fighting back is partly what's at stake here. Many forms of "verbal battle," we must remember, insofar as they are already coded as juridical and attestory, are objects of Brent's rebellion rather than its tools. One of the costs of refusing to consent and of trying to place limits on the universality of contract may be this much self-constriction and restraint, a self-constraint, in this case, as deliberately, if as tragically, chosen as the garret in which she imprisoned herself.

NOTES

This essay appeared in a longer version in *The Yale Journal of Criticism* 6, no. 1 (Spring 1993): 93–119, under the title "Narrative Contracts and Emancipatory Readers: *Incidents in the Life of a Slave Girl*." I am grateful to the journal's anonymous reader, as well as to Houston A. Baker, Jr., John Brenkman, Richard Brodhead, Lynn Enterline, Lynne Huffer, Nina Miller, Julie Rolston, and Louise Yelin, for helpful comments.

1. Harriet A. Jacobs, *Incidents in the Life of a Slave Girl, Written by Herself*, ed. Jean Fagan Yellin (Cambridge: Harvard University Press, 1987). All future references to the text, or to Yellin's introduction to it, are to this edition and will be cited parenthetically.

2. Sondra R. Herman, "Loving Courtship or the Marriage Market? The Ideal and Its Critics, 1871–1911," *American Quarterly* 25 (May 1973): 235–52. This repudiation of the marriage ideal, in the context of a narrative about slavery, freedom, and agency, is a particularly bold move on Jacobs's part. Marriage, as Eugene Genovese points out, was the centerpiece of slaveholders' defense of slavery. See Eugene D. Genovese, *The World the Slaveholders Made* (New York: Vintage, 1971), 195–97ff. The health of the domestic, nuclear family was also, as *Uncle Tom's Cabin* so vividly demonstrates, a principal ground of antislavery arguments.

3. See also Carla Peterson, "Capitalism, Black (Under)development, and the Production of the African-American Novel in the 1850's," *American Literary History* 4, no. 4 (Winter 1992): 559–83. Peterson, whose article appeared after my own was completed, discusses the difficulties faced by black Americans who sought to transform themselves from property into possessive individuals. On the status of black Americans as objects of property rather than possessors of it, the lingering implications and consequences of this history, and the "deadening power" of contracts, see Patricia J. Williams, "On Being the Object of Property," *Signs* 14, no. 1 (1988): 5–24. While Williams's description of contracts in some ways runs counter to my own, my reading of Brent's vision of freedom is nevertheless indebted to Williams's provocative self-recuperation.

4. Carole Pateman provides an excellent discussion of this political-philosophical premise. See *The Sexual Contract* (Stanford: Stanford University Press, 1988) and *The Disorder of Women: Democracy, Feminism and Political Theory* (Stanford: Stanford University Press, 1989). Future references are to *The Sexual Contract* and will be cited parenthetically.

5. The historical relationship between slavery and contract is an extremely complicated one (and might well be the topic of a different essay on Brent's relation to contract).

6. For a different reading of Jacobs's relation to the liberal, domestic ideologies inscribed in the female spheres of home, family, motherhood, and marriage, see Claudia Tate, *Domestic Allegories of Political Desire: The Black Heroine's Text at the Turn of the Century* (New York: Oxford University Press, 1992).

7. See also Dana Nelson, *The Word in Black and White: Reading "Race" in American Literature, 1638–1867* (New York: Oxford University Press, 1992), 140–41. Nelson, whose book appeared after this essay was completed, argues that *Incidents* "critiques and redefines the 'sympathetic' framework for understanding that featured prominently in both domestic and abolitionist texts of the period."

8. John Blassingame, *The Slave Community* (New York: Oxford Univer-

sity Press, 1972), 233–34, as quoted by Jean Fagan Yellin, "Written by Herself: Harriet Jacobs' Slave Narrative," *American Literature* 53, no. 3 (Nov. 1981): 480 n. 2.

9. See Yellin, "Written by Herself," 479–86.

10. I discuss this problem further in "Narrative Contracts and Emancipatory Readers." See also Henry Louis Gates, Jr., *The Signifying Monkey: A Theory of African-American Literary Criticism* (New York: Oxford University Press, 1988), and *Figures in Black: Words, Signs, and the Racial Self* (New York: Oxford University Press, 1987); Robert B. Stepto, *From Behind the Veil: A Study of Afro-American Narrative* (Urbana: University of Illinois Press, 1979); James Olney, "'I Was Born': Slave Narratives, Their Status as Autobiography and as Literature," in *The Slave's Narrative*, ed. Charles T. Davis and Henry Louis Gates, Jr. (New York: Oxford University Press, 1985); William L. Andrews, *To Tell a Free Story: Toward a Poetics of Afro-American Autobiography, 1760–1865* (Urbana: University of Illinois Press, 1986); and Houston A. Baker, Jr., "Autobiographical Acts and the Voice of the Southern Slave," in *The Slave's Narrative*, ed. Davis and Gates.

11. One interesting passage in Brent's narrative details her efforts to teach a fellow slave to read (72–73). In an ironic twist on white antebellum anxieties, Brent intimates that literacy will not endanger or empower slaves, but will merely make them better Christians, even less threatening than their illiterate brethren. I am grateful to Houston Baker for bringing this passage to my attention.

12. Minrose C. Gwin, "Green-eyed Monsters of the Slavocracy: Jealous Mistresses in Two Slave Narratives," in *Conjuring: Black Women Writers and Literary Tradition*, ed. Marjorie Pryse and Hortense J. Spillers (Bloomington: Indiana University Press, 1985), 39–52.

13. Valerie Smith, *Self-Discovery and Authority in Afro-American Narrative* (Cambridge, Mass.: Harvard University Press, 1987), 28.

14. Yellin, "Introduction," xxix.

15. On the feminist recuperative project of reading such silences, see my "Reading Feminist Readings: Recuperative Reading and the Silent Heroine of Feminist Criticism," in *Listening to "Silences": New Essays in Feminist Criticism*, ed. Shelley Fisher Fishkin and Elaine Hedges (New York: Oxford University Press, 1994).

16. Andrews, *To Tell a Free Story*, 252.

17. Smith, *Self-Discovery*, 29.

18. Houston Baker, *Blues, Ideology, and Afro-American Literature: A Vernacular Theory* (Chicago: University of Chicago Press, 1984), 53. Future references will be cited parenthetically.

19. Yellin, "Introduction," xxvi.

20. Andrews, *To Tell a Free Story*, 259.

21. See Elaine Showalter, "Literary Criticism," review essay, *Signs* 1 (Winter 1975): 435–60.

22. Northrop Frye, *Anatomy of Criticism: Four Essays* (New York: Atheneum, 1968), 76.

23. Stanley Fish, *Is There a Text in This Class? The Authority of Interpretive Communities* (Cambridge, Mass.: Harvard University Press, 1980).

24. Jonathan Culler, *Structuralist Poetics: Structuralism, Linguistics, and the Study of Literature* (Ithaca: Cornell University Press, 1975), 193, 214. Future references will be cited parenthetically. For particularly useful discussions of contract in literature, see Nancy Armstrong, *Desire and Domestic Fiction: A Political History of the Novel* (New York: Oxford University Press, 1987), and Tony Tanner, *Adultery in the Novel: Contract and Transgression* (Baltimore: Johns Hopkins University Press, 1979).

25. Ross Chambers, *Story and Situation: Narrative Seduction and the Power of Fiction* (Minneapolis: University of Minnesota Press, 1984), 4, 7, 212. Subsequent references will be cited parenthetically.

26. Smith, *Self Discovery and Authority*, 2.

27. Ibid., 42.

28. Yellin, "Introduction," xxiv; "Text and Contexts of Harriet Jacobs' *Incidents in the Life of a Slave Girl, Written by Herself*, in *The Slave's Narrative*, ed. Davis and Gates, 277.

29. Hazel V. Carby, *Reconstructing Womanhood: The Emergence of the Afro-American Woman Novelist* (New York: Oxford University Press, 1987), 49. See also Tate, *Domestic Allegories*.

30. Carla Peterson and Claudia Tate also argue that Brent willingly engages in acts of self-commodification. See Peterson, "Capitalism," 571, and Tate, *Domestic Allegories*, 30.

31. Claudia Tate, however, argues that *Incidents* represents marriage as "an ideal, though unrealizable, sign of liberation" (*Domestic Allegories*, 32).

32. See also Houston A. Baker, Jr., *Workings of the Spirit: The Poetics of Afro-American Women's Writing* (Chicago: University of Chicago Press, 1991). In his more recent discussion of *Incidents in the Life of a Slave Girl*, Baker considers how scenes of silencing in Brent's tale work to gender her narrative position, particularly in her treatment of her own "historicized body" as a "willed object of exchange" (20–21).

33. Robert B. Stepto, "Distrust of the Reader in Afro-American Narratives," in *Reconstructing American Literary History*, ed. Sacvan Bercovitch (Cambridge, Mass.: Harvard University Press, 1986), 309.

34. Ibid., 309–10.

35. For a contrary reading of Brent's addresses to her reader, see Beth Maclay Doriani, "Black Womanhood in Nineteenth-Century America: Subversion and Self-Construction in Two Women's Autobiographies," *American Quarterly* 43, no. 2 (June 1991): 199–222.

36. William L. Andrews, "Dialogue in Antebellum Afro-American Autobiography," in *Studies in Autobiography*, ed. James Olney (New York: Oxford University Press, 1988), 91. Future references will be cited parenthetically.

FIFTEEN

A Provoking Agent: The Pornography and Performance Art of Annie Sprinkle

LINDA WILLIAMS

> My feminist mother used to come into my room and joke
> whether I would grow up to be a whore or an artist. She was
> exactly right!
>
> —Annie Sprinkle

Annie Sprinkle's is a peculiarly American success story. Beginning her professional performance career as a masseuse, soon after that becoming a whore, Sprinkle next expanded into burlesque and live sex shows, then to writing sex magazines and performing in pornographic films and videos (where she eventually became a director). In a later stage of her career she moved to such avant-garde venues as the Franklin Furnace, Performing Garage, and Highways. In her one-woman show entitled *Post-Post Porn Modernist,* she performs a parodic show-and-tell of her life as a sexual performer—a show that includes inviting audience members to shine a flashlight at her cervix through a speculum. In 1990, the municipal vice squad in Cleveland forced her to omit the speculum component of her act. It is a fascinating comment on American culture that when Annie Sprinkle performed live sex shows in that same city years earlier she was never visited by the vice squad.[1]

Performance artists, especially women performers whose gendered and sexed bodies serve as the basic material of the performance, are often vulnerable to vice squads, or to censorship by the National Endowment for the Arts, because their art and thought occurs through the body. Defenders of performance art have thus often found it necessary to distinguish this art from pornography.[2] While I agree that this art is not pornography, I am suspicious of attempts to draw the line too vigorously between performance art on the one hand and pornography on the other.[3] My tactic in this essay, therefore, will not be to establish the precise moment when Annie Sprinkle became a performance artist, not to argue, as Chuck Kleinhans has done, that Sprinkle has always been a performance artist,[4] but rather to show how her myriad sexual performances tend to blur the boundaries between the two. This, I will argue, is the particular genius, as well as the limitation, of Annie Sprinkle's postmodern feminist agency.

Annie Sprinkle's work demonstrates that the political context in which we ponder the question of art and obscenity is no longer one in which a secure category of sexual obscenity can be safely confined to the wings of sexual representation. For as both gender and sexual identities have become more politicized, and as "speaking sex" has become as necessary to gay, lesbian, bisexual, transsexual, and sadomasochistic activists as it has to Jesse Helms, drawing clear lines between what is dirty and what is clean, what is properly brought on scene and what should be kept off (ob) scene, no longer seems the crux of a feminist sexual politics.[5]

A recent reviewer of *Post-Post Porn Modernist* claims, mistakenly I think, that Sprinkle's performance "strips away all porn," as if vehement denial of all pornographic elements purifies the art.[6] Such a claim relies on the kind of hierarchical binary between art and pornography, and between artist and whore, that Annie Sprinkle's art *and* pornography challenge. The phenomenon of Annie Sprinkle forces us to ask: What is the political value, in terms of women's agency, of not drawing a firm line between obscene pornography on the one hand and legitimate art on the other?

As the quotation that forms the epigraph to this essay suggests, Annie Sprinkle has a way of defusing, of going beyond, rather than directly confronting, familiar oppositions. In this quotation the feminist mother poses the question of her daughter's vocation as an opposition: Will her daughter be an artist *or* a whore? Without confronting the mother directly, the "postfeminist," "postporn" daughter counters her either/or with a destabilizing agreeability: "my mother was right!" The daughter unsettles the opposition: she is neither artist *nor* whore but artist *and* whore.

Can Annie Sprinkle's performance of the postmodern, "postfeminist" sexual role of "woman" accomplish the feminist goal of being *for women*? Does this role represent a new permutation of feminist agency that moves beyond some of feminism's most troubling binary oppositions—beyond, for example, the opposition that posits pornography as inimical to women; beyond the opposition that posits pornography as inimical to art; beyond the opposition that posits women as powerless victims of male sexual power and thus as colonized in their desires? Or, is Annie Sprinkle more simply a symptom of a "postfeminism" that has been accused, most recently by Tania Modleski, of being an end to feminism, even a reversion to prefeminism?[7]

How, in other words, shall we interpret this postfeminist sensibility emerging so agreeably from the "depths" of a misogynist mass culture? Like Modleski I reject postfeminism if it is taken to mean that the goals of feminism are either irrelevant or already achieved. However, I understand the political and social realities that have led many women to reject the term "feminism," to claim to be beyond it, when to my way of thinking they are still embedded within its struggles. One of the reasons for this rejection has been the association of feminism with a self-righteous understanding of what *is* good for women, of which side of any binary a "proper" feminism belongs.

Sex workers, we know, have often found themselves on the "wrong" side of these binaries. Sex workers have all too often been regarded by feminists as objectified victims of an aggressive, sadistic, masculine sexuality rather than as sexual agents themselves. Antipornography feminists in particular have gone so far as to define pornography as "the graphic sexually explicit subordination of women" in which women are dehumanized sexual objects who are "presented as whores by nature."[8] To the Dworkin-MacKinnon antipornography faction, agency can only be located, as Marianne Hirsch has put it in chapter 13 of this volume, "in resistance and contestation." Yet in Annie Sprinkle we encounter a whore-turned-pornographer-turned-performance-artist with more of a stake in the "post" than in the "anti"s that constitute so much feminist position taking on this subject. For these reasons, I suggest that we take seriously the whore side of Annie Sprinkle's performances by examining, first, her early work as a whore and then how this persona informed her later work as a pornographer and performance artist. My hope is that this examination may help us to clarify the nature of a postfeminist sexual agency that has brought obscenity so aggressively on scene.

Another hope is that the case of Annie Sprinkle might be used to clarify a larger argument on the essentialist or nonessentialist meaning of the name "woman." In *Am I That Name?* Denise Riley, for example, has argued the value of a poststructuralist refusal of the name "woman" as reducing women to fixed identities that then work to reduce women's agency.[9] Feminism does not need the fixed-category woman, Riley argues. On the other hand, Tania Modleski has argued the importance of keeping the name "woman" as an essential category.[10] Modleski points out that Riley's title, a quotation from *Othello* in which Desdemona asks Iago if she is the name her husband has given her, ignores the fact that the name Othello actually gave Desdemona was not "woman" but "whore." Riley's point is that the name "woman" has become an essentialist trap. Her post-structuralist argument is that women lose agency if reduced to the singularity of this name. Modleski, however, suggests that Riley's elision of the other name, "whore," is an example of why the feminist use of the name "woman" is politically important. "Although women have had to take up the term 'women' emphatically to rescue it from opprobrium, they have done so in opposition to patriarchy's tendency to 'saturate' us with our sex."[11]

My interest in Annie Sprinkle is that she represents a fascinating test case of how one kind of feminist agency can arise out of this saturation. For Annie Sprinkle the postmodern, postfeminist, postporn performance artist has not eschewed the term "whore" nor the sexual saturation of "woman." Rather, her sexual performances, firmly rooted within the specific conventions of pornography and the persona of whore, are provocative instances of agency that draw upon the performative traditions of the sexually saturated woman, yet do not simply duplicate them. By performing sex differently, though still within the conventional rhetoric and form of the genre, Annie Sprinkle's pornography demonstrated a provocative feminist agency that would contribute to her later feminist performance work.

FROM MASSEUSE TO WHORE

Let's begin with Annie Sprinkle's first sexual performances, the ones she writes about in her early sex magazines, then later in her book *Annie Sprinkle: Post Porn Modernist* (not to be confused with her performance piece *Post-Post Porn Modernist*), and in her interview in *Angry Women*. These writings are all versions of Annie Sprinkle's life story, which she has been writing and performing since the early seventies. In every version of this story, Annie Sprinkle tells us that she did not know she was a prostitute until she was linguistically hit over the head—or in Althusser's terms "hailed" or "interpellated"—by this term. "I was working in a massage parlor. For 3 months I worked and didn't even know I was a hooker—I was having such a good time! The men I saw were referred to as 'clients' or 'massages.' But finally, after about 3 months one woman used the word 'trick' and I realized, 'Ohmigod—they're *tricks!* Oh shit—I'm a *hooker!'*"[12]

At first she believed the performance for which she was paid was the massage. The money "was for the massage plus a tip," while the sex "was just something I threw in for fun!"[13] "I just thought of myself as a horny masseuse. I liked having sex with the guys after I gave them a brief massage. When it finally did occur to me that I was a hooker, and I got over the initial shock, I enjoyed the idea."[14]

We could interpret this reasoning as the false consciousness often attributed to sex workers by antipornography feminists. But false consciousness assumes the existence of a "true" or authentic consciousness betrayed by the persona of the "happy hooker." It is this idea of an "authentic," "true" self that Annie Sprinkle's account of her experience contradicts. For she only recognized herself as a whore—one who performs sex for money—in the word "trick." She never chose to become a whore. She simply found herself "hailed" by an entire system of signification.[15] But her inability to choose does not necessarily mean that she was discursively constructed by a misogynist system over which she had no control or that she was the victim of misogynist false consciousness. In what sense, then, *can* we speak of Annie Sprinkle's agency in the deeds that make her first a whore and then, later, an artist?

The answer involves the thorny question of how and in what way there can be agency—the ability to "act otherwise," as Ellen Messer-Davidow puts it in chapter 1 in this volume—in the absence of a subject who preexists the discourses in which he or she is situated. In other words, if there is no subjectivity prior to discourse, then what hope is there for a woman's ability to "act otherwise" if she doesn't act *against* the system that constructs women as whores and objects of pornography?

The feminist theorist Judith Butler offers one answer to this problem when she writes that "the question of agency is not to be answered through recourse to an 'I' that preexists signification."[16] Rather, Butler argues, agency needs to be reformulated as a question of how agents construct their identities through *resignification*. The rules that enable and restrict the intelligible assertion of an "I"— rules that Butler reminds us are structured by gender hierarchy and compulsory heterosexuality—operate through repetition. Signification itself is *"not a founding act, but a regulated process of repetition."* Agency is "located within the possibility of a variation on that repetition." In other words, there is no self prior to the convergence of discursive injunctions to be something (whore, mother, heterosexually desirable object, etc.). There is only, Butler writes, "a taking up of the tools where they lie."[17]

For Annie Sprinkle these tools were initially the remarkable opportunity for repetition in the sexual acts performed by a whore. If, as Butler argues, the self is constructed out of the repetition of performances, and if agency occurs within the possibility of variation, then Annie Sprinkle's repetitious performance of sex acts have been the locus of her construction of self throughout her career. In this first series of sexual performances in which she first wasn't, and then was, hailed a whore, we can see the discovery of an agency that is not opposed to, but rooted in, the discourse that constructs her. Her agency could be said to consist in the fact that, in the repetition of the performance of sex, first for free, then for money, she realizes that "whore" does not fully name who she is. Annie Sprinkle neither denies that she is a whore nor fights the system that so names her. Rather, she accepts the nomination. But in that acceptance she also sees room for what Butler calls "subversive repetition," which becomes an articulation of something that is not named in "whore": her own desire, surprisingly new pleasures. There is no other scene of Annie Sprinkle's agency; the scene of the ob-scene is the place where she is able both to "act otherwise" and still to "be herself."

A whore performs sex for pay, usually for a single customer. The sexual performances must please the customer; they do not necessarily please the performer, who may or may not be caught up in their art or excitement. Because the performer is so restricted in the nature of the performance, remarkably little is said about the quality of performance within the customer-whore transaction. Though it is often acknowledged that this performance can be either perfunctory or inspired, it is not an area of performance that is taken very seriously by the traditions of Western art. It is, however, taken seriously in an Eastern, tantric tradition to which Sprinkle has been recently drawn, as well as in the narratives of pornographic films and videos, which are almost obsessively about the qualities (and the quantities) of sexual performance. Sprinkle's merging of these two traditions constitutes a large degree of her originality in her later work for Femme Productions and in *The Sluts and Goddesses Video Workshop: Or How to Be a Sex Goddess in 101 Easy Steps* (produced and directed by Maria Beatty and Annie Sprinkle, 1992).

All of Annie Sprinkle's performances begin by taking this performance of sex for the pleasure of a customer or viewer very seriously and by linking this performance to the fundamental contract by which the whore agrees to please the john by showing him her "secrets." When Sprinkle describes herself as a "hooker with a heart of gold" she does so without mockery, without intention of demeaning the profession of whore, and without intention of subverting the whore's basic function of performing sexual acts that give pleasure.[18] She does not rail against the basic dichotomy that divides women into good girls and whores.[19] The art of her performance consists in what she can do by way of subversive repetition within this basic contract, not in refusing or opposing it but in finding new pleasures cultivated and satisfied within it. In the whore phase of Annie Sprinkle's career, these subversive repetitions consist of an ever-widening range of sexual acts—"perversions" that expand the notion of what sexual performance is—and sexual objects—performing sex with persons who are not conventionally regarded as acceptable objects of desire—dwarfs, burn victims, transsexuals, persons with AIDS, amputees—but who allow her to explore her desires and pleasures in new ways.

FROM WHORE TO PORNOGRAPHER

Deep Inside Annie Sprinkle, the 1981 porno film that Sprinkle wrote and directed, is consistent with her early writings as well as with her later performance work in its first-person direct address in the persona of the whore speaking to the client. "Hi, I'm Annie Sprinkle. I'm glad you came to see me. I want us to become very intimate. . . ." Intimacy here consists, as in the discourse of the whore, in showing and telling sexual secrets that please. Yet intimacy with a flesh-and-blood client is the one thing that is not possible within porno film and video; the whore-client relation of proximity is necessarily replaced, and in a sense compensated for, by the ideal visibility of sexual performers who are not physically present with the spectators viewing the film. Yet the woman who performs with another performer for the camera remains a kind of whore, replacing sexual performance with and for the pleasure of one person with sexual performance for an audience of many. In most contemporary feature-length hard-core film and video, this shift to the audience of many entails the abandonment of the female sexual performer's address to the client.[20]

Annie Sprinkle, however, maintains the paradoxical, quasiparodic rhetoric of intimate address to the client who is no longer really there in the introduction of each of this film's numbers. Her pornography thus makes a point of retaining the literal voice of the whore whose name is inscribed in the Greek word *pornographos,* literally, whore-writing: the *graphos* (writing or representations) by *pornei* (whores). This word deserves some explanation.

Though Andrea Dworkin has made much of the word's continuity from antiquity,[21] in actual fact our contemporary notion of pornography, as writing of images depicting sexual activities with the aim of arousal, bears little relation to the meaning of the word in antiquity. Holt N. Parker, a classicist, writes that *pornographos* was simply a subcategory of biography—tales of the lives of the courtesans—which may not contain any obscene material at all.[22] Parker notes, however, that another subspecies of literature—*an-aiskhuntographoi*, literally writers of shameless things—more properly corresponds to the erotic content of contemporary pornography.[23]

The writing of these manuals was ascribed to women, not because of any proven female authorship but because the pleasures of sex, which to the Greeks meant pleasures that rendered participants ecstatically out of control and thus out of possession of themselves, were conceived in antiquity as feminine. Active, in-control sexuality was associated with the free man who "penetrated, who moved, who fucked" and who could also abstain from doing so if he chose. Women, on the other hand, like slaves and boys, were the passive penetrated, who did not move, who were fucked, and who had no power to abstain. Thus, while women were the authorities on shameless things, they had no real authority or agency in speaking them because they lacked the ultimate cultural value of self-control.[24]

Parker borrows Joanna Russ's formulation of the classic double bind applied to this literature: "No proper woman writes about sex; therefore the writing is not by a woman. And if she does write, she's not a proper woman."[25] Since this class of writing about shameless things most closely corresponds to the kind of advice-giving that Annie Sprinkle, speaking from her whore persona, offers in *Deep Inside Annie Sprinkle*, it is worth considering whether this same double bind erasing women's sexual agency still operates today.

In traditional pornography, "whores" (whether literally so or simply women who because they speak of sex are automatically "shameless") write of their experience of sex for the pleasure of men. These experiences must be presented as pleasurable for the genre to function. A whole generation of feminist performance artists has aggressively and angrily broken the contract to provide pleasure and thus grounded their performance art in attacks on pleasure that sometimes use the tools of an aggressive, nonpleasurable obscenity. Annie Sprinkle differs from these performers in that she does not rupture the whore's contract to provide pleasure. Instead, she goes back to its roots. In taking on the persona and address of the whore hailed by misogynist culture, Sprinkle opens up a field of acting otherwise through subversive repetitions of the role. Moving-image pornography, like prostitution, offers the perfect occasion for repetition since it requires some variation of sexual performances to relieve the monotony of the seven-to-ten numbers conventionally offered by the feature-length form.

In her 1981 film, Annie Sprinkle, self-designated "porn star," tells the conventional pornographic narrative of her sexual evolution from shy, nonglamorous, nonsexual "Ellen" to the sexually fulfilled exhibitionist Annie. The basic structure of this narrative, which is full of advice about what positions are the most pleasurable, thus assumes the educative function that extends back to the sex manuals of antiquity. What is different in Annie Sprinkle's "whore writing," however, is that she injects elements into this narrative that disrupt the active male, passive female paradigm of conventional pornography.

She begins by displaying a scrapbook with photos that are the "real" pictures of herself as an awkward girl growing up. While the photos do not suggest that this is the true woman while the fetishized Annie is false, neither do they suggest, as conventional whore-writing does, that the "true" woman is the fetishized desirable one. Instead, they suggest the very constructedness of the woman's identity and Annie's ability to manipulate the codes of glamour. The film also introduces an uncommon note of social reality with a briefly shown photo of Mom and Dad and the mention of their efforts to accept her role in the "sex business."[26]

Having established that the persona who addresses us is not "naturally" glamorous and sexy, Annie next asks her absent client-viewer if "he" would like to see "what I would love to do to two husky men right now." Happening across two husky naked men arm-wrestling before a fireplace, she admires their bodies, kisses their muscles, and inserts herself between them to initiate a three-way number that ends with two conventional porno "money shots"—e.g., external, and therefore visible, ejaculation by the males.[27] This threesome is perfectly conventional for 1980s porn. What isn't conventional is the homoerotic context of the display of glistening male muscles, Annie's verbally articulated delight in their bodies, and her active control of the situation ("what I would like to do").

Moving on to the next number, still addressing an absent "client," Annie asks if he likes "big tits." "You may have noticed that I have rather large ones. . . ." She then introduces Sassy, a "girlfriend who loves big tits." The number with Sassy is positioned as the conventional "lesbian" duo interrupted and completed by a male intruder. What isn't conventional is Sassy's very short stature—her mouth comes to Annie's breasts—Annie's use of her breast to stimulate Sassy's clitoris, and Sassy's sustained, body-shuddering (performance of) orgasm, which takes place before the man arrives.

The third number introduces anal intercourse performed on Annie and ending in a conventional "money shot." What is different in this number is its beginning in Annie's verbal celebration of anal eroticism, in this case her pleasure taken in a man's ass: "You ever wonder why I keep my middle nail short? Now take this ass for example. . . ." Without our ever seeing the man's face, Annie continues her "dirty talk" instructions for fingering a man's ass while performing the deed. Only after she has completed her play with his anus does his play with hers commence.

Annie's "objectification" of the men's ass and her instructions on how to give anal pleasure to a man are unconventional preludes to her own, more conventional, anal penetration. It is possible to see them as simple table-turning: the objectified woman fragments and objectifies the male body in turn. But perhaps more challenging to the conventional porno form is the fact that here too Annie maintains the first-person address to a hypothetical client, speaking to the camera and thus raising new questions about the gendered nature of her address. Is she telling and showing a hypothetical "him" how to finger another man's ass? If so, the film transgresses "normal" heterosexual taboos against males penetrating males. Is she telling and showing "him" how *she* likes to finger a man's ass? If so, the pleasure depicted casts her in the role of active penetrator and him in the role of penetrated, again a switch in expectations for the conventionally posited heterosexual male viewer. Or, is she perhaps telling and showing a hypothetical "her" how to finger a man's anus? After all, this is eighties porn and women are included in its address. If so, the original rhetoric of the female-whore addressing the male-client breaks down. Any way you look at it, Annie has played with the conventions of who gives pleasure to whom.

The fourth number is even less conventional; it constitutes one of Annie's specialties and at least one source of her name. We could call it the female money shot. Annie performs it after cunnilingus with a male partner. This partner later performs his money shot as the conventional climax to intercourse while Annie does hers earlier and for a rather prolonged time. This exhibitionistic display of female pleasures that are usually, in post-seventies moving-image

pornography, internal and invisible may seem grounded on a competitive, male "anything you can do, I can do better" model. "You
want visible proof of my orgasms measured against the standards of
yours?" Annie seems to say, "Well, here they are!"

We have seen that Annie Sprinkle's performances take as their
starting point the role of the whore whose first commitment is to
deliver the goods: the performance of "sex" in a culture in which such
performances can be bought. I have argued in *Hard Core* that contemporary hard-core film and video pornography particularly locates the
climactic pay-off of those goods in the invisible interior of women's
bodies. The genre's "frenzy of the visible" is thus a contradictory
desire to see the involuntary, convulsive proof that a woman's pleasure is taking place measured against the standard of a male "norm."

"Normally," pornography does not see and measure the woman's
pleasure in the same quantitative way as the man's. However, since
visual pornography wants to show visual evidence of pleasure, the
genre has given rise to the enduring fetish of the male money shot.
One of the first "corrections" of the new pornography by and for
women was to eliminate this convention. The films of the Femme
production group offered clean sheets, handsome men, and no money
shots. Annie Sprinkle's directorial contribution to this effort—a half-
hour segment of *Rites of Passions* (Annie Sprinkle and Veronica Vera,
1987) called *The Search for the Ultimate Sexual Experience*—con-
formed to this standard as well. But suppression of the masculine
standard for the exhibition of pleasure is only one strategy of acting otherwise. Annie Sprinkle's strategy in this earlier work, as well
as later in *The Sluts and Goddesses Video Workshop: Or How to
Be a Sex Goddess in 101 Easy Steps*, where she also exhibits another female money shot along with a six-minute orgasm, would seem
to be to imitate the male standard of the pornographic evidence of
pleasure so spectacularly as to destabilize and denaturalize its "normal" meaning.

Anyone with some experience of hard-core film and video must
marvel at the nature of these orgasmic performances. We might say,
in an adaptation of Luce Irigaray's terms, that recognizing the extent to which orgasm is one of the basic goods of porno, Annie Sprinkle decided to market her goods with a difference. This difference
is a degree of discrepancy and deformation produced in repetitions
that destabilize the very sense of what the goods are.[28] At the Society for Cinema Studies panel on Annie Sprinkle (May 1992), I argued
that Sprinkle had performed a female version of a money shot. However, a fellow panelist, Chuck Kleinhans, insisted that I had miscon-

strued golden showers for female ejaculation. Another panelist, Chris Straayer, perceived the liquid to be ejaculate but argued a different significance than I had: a liberatory return of the repressed female ejaculation.[29]

The debate suggests how insistently pornography catches up its viewers in the impossible question of the ontological real of pleasure. Each of us had a fantasy of this real corresponding to our ideological investments in pleasure. I saw Sprinkle playing with the conventions of the hard core "frenzy of the visible" and exhibiting agency in the parody of masculine money shots; Kleinhans saw a greater affirmation of agency in the greater taboo of golden showers; Straayer saw even greater agency in the exhibition of a self-sufficient female sexuality in female ejaculation. The important point, however, is not to fix the truth of what the female body experiences, but rather the variety of different truths that can be constructed and the fact that they are constructed here by a female pornographer who is clearly in control. Annie Sprinkle shows the extent to which even the whore locked in the contract to please the customer, making confession of the "shameless things" of sex, can speak differently—not necessarily more truthfully—of these things.

In a broader sense, however, we might consider the basic marketing of the "shameless goods" of Annie Sprinkle herself. Sprinkle is the fetishized woman par excellence. Though she later metamorphoses into an oscillation between the two equally valued states of slut and goddess, in this earlier pornography the self-conscious masquerade of femininity is of the whore who aims to please. But as we have seen, there is enough exaggeration in this persona to alert us to an element of parody. The gap-toothed, big-breasted, slightly chubby woman who addresses us in her sexiest voice and who has already shown us the pre-whore, pre-porn body out of which this new persona was constructed, presents herself as an effect of performance and invites us to admire a performance the final truth of which is always elusive.

The separation between the performed imitation of the sex goddess and the "original" on which that imitation is based creates an effect not unlike that of the male performer in drag. Although Sprinkle "is" a woman and doesn't perform otherwise, her fetishized femme appearance is presented as a performative achievement. Judith Butler writes that "in imitating gender, drag implicitly reveals the imitative structure of gender itself."[30] Sex and gender are denaturalized in drag by a performance that avows their distinction and dramatizes the cultural mechanism of their fabricated unity.

In a documentary about tantric sexual seekers, *Sacred Sex* (Cynthia Connop, 1992), Annie Sprinkle tells us in an interview that in her *Post-Post Porn Modernist* performance piece she takes on the persona of a "porno bimbo character." This could sound as if she performs a demeaning imitation of such a character, as if the parodic repetition criticizes the inauthenticity of the original. However, in neither of the performances of this role does Annie Sprinkle assume that there is a "proper" or "normal" female identity from which this construction diverges. Her parody of gender and desirability thus reveals, as Butler puts it about drag, "that the original identity after which gender fashions itself is an imitation without an origin."[31]

Parody causes laughter. But *this* laughter does not chide the imitative failure of this character with reference to a better, "truer" woman. It might be appropriate, then, to speak of Annie Sprinkle's parody—her subversive repetitions of sexual performances, her "porno bimbo character" played to the hilt—as more properly a form of pastiche. The term has been invoked in a manner critical of postmodernism by Fredric Jameson, who argues that our contemporary postmodern condition is replete with parodies that have lost their ability to criticize and hence their ability to laugh. Such parodies degenerate to mere pastiche: imitations that mock the very notion of an original. Jameson argues that without the feeling that there exists something normal compared to which what is being imitated is comic, pastiche becomes blank parody, "parody that has lost its humor."[32] It is precisely this notion of "norm" and "original," however, that is at issue in a postmodern world of sexual identities and representations.

Laughter at sexual pleasures that diverge from some "norm" is a familiar feature of contemporary culture. All the more reason, then, to welcome the pastiche with humor that does not posit a corrective norm but that continuously plays with the terms of norm and perversion. This is what Annie Sprinkle does best. Sprinkle is proof, as Judith Butler puts it, that "the loss of the sense of 'the normal' . . . can be its own occasion for laughter, especially when 'the normal,' 'the original' is revealed to be a copy . . . an ideal that no one *can* embody."[33]

FROM PORNOGRAPHER TO PERFORMANCE ARTIST (A SKETCH)

These, then, are some examples of the strategy of the "post"—postmodern, poststructuralist, postfeminist—in the early work of Annie Sprinkle. While this work is not yet performance art and not yet post-porn, we can see in it the seeds of an art that is beyond, but never against, pornography. Annie Sprinkle's personae will go on to include the sex educator, the sex therapist, the sexual fairy godmother and the sex goddess—all personae that are reworked into the *Post-Post Porn Modernist* theater piece. In each permutation, Sprinkle never denies or criticizes her whore-porn origin. For example, in *The Sluts and Goddesses Video Workshop: Or How to Be A Sex Goddess in 101 Easy Steps*, Sprinkle becomes a "legitimate" sex educator proffering more knowledge than pleasure. Yet the interest of the tape is its combination of clinical knowledge and raunchy enjoyment, the participatory hands-on, pornographic nature of this particular sex educator's show-and-tell. Once again Sprinkle has gone to the roots of the form—sex-manual advice on the best positions— and transformed it without directly opposing it.

If, as the classicists tell us, pornographic sex manuals by putative women for the pleasure of men are the true origins of what we call pornography, then this "workshop" exclusively by and discursively addressed to women, yet still imbued with all the naughtiness of conventional pornography, is its reappropriation. This reappropriation is certainly not free of the conventions of pornographic sex manuals for men. In this video, for example, Sprinkle repeats her performance of the female money shot and goes on to measure the duration of an orgasm with a graphic insert of a digital clock (five minutes and six seconds).

This image of the sex educator flexing her orgasmic muscles is still similar to the whore-pornographer in *Deep Inside Annie Sprinkle*. In both cases duration and ejaculation are emphasized. In both cases a parody pastiche of masculine conventions dominates. Yet in this video, orgasm is no longer performed for the pleasure of a discursively addressed male viewer. Other women in the video facilitate the orgasm and function as audience cheerleaders. In the *Post-Post Porn Modernist* performance piece, the orgasm is a solo and the point is the self-sufficiency of the female body.

We have seen that Annie Sprinkle's spectacular orgasms are the constant feature of each one of her pornographic-educative-art performances. We have also seen the ways in which these orgasms take on new meanings in different contexts. The point about these orgasms is not whether they are real or performed, showered with ejaculate or urine, parodic or sincere, since with Annie Sprinkle there is never an either/or but always a this/and. These orgasms can be taken as indices of a very different sexual agency than that which obtained for the whore writers of antiquity. For the Greeks, the woman's pleasure, quantified as inherently greater than the male's, was out of control and in excess, while the masculine pleasure of penetrator was capable of control and not in excess.[34]

The female body remains today the one that is more "saturated" with sex. The insatiable, "excessively" pleasuring woman remains caught in the familiar double bind by which her knowledge of sex invalidates other forms of authority—we can think, for example, of Arlen Specter and the United States Senate Judiciary Committee's dismissal of Anita Hill's charges against Clarence Thomas as sexual fantasy. Nevertheless, despite the real operation of this harmful double standard, the sphere of the sexual now occupies so great an area of social concern and social power that participation in sexual pleasure no longer automatically signifies the same powerlessness for women as it did for the Greeks. This is why it is important not to conflate today's pornography with that of the ancients, or indeed, with that of any other time. This is why sex-positive Annie Sprinkle and her spectacular orgasms and ejaculations can suggest quite another strategy for "acting otherwise."

I make no claim here for the resisting, subversive potential of Annie Sprinkle's strategies outside the realm of the sexual. Agency in sexual performance speaks only to certain of the concerns of women. Annie Sprinkle herself speaks only to certain women, especially to those who have rejected the kind of orthodox, moralistic feminism that has presumed to know which sexual pleasures and performances are good for women. But Annie Sprinkle shows that within the realm of the sexual, performances of bosom ballets, female money shots, and six-minute orgasms can sometimes work wonders. For sexuality today is a thoroughly commodified arena of self-help and self-fulfillment requiring levels of self-control and agency that would have baffled the Greeks. While it was once the case that a mind/body split relegated men to the realm of the spirit, women to the realm of the body, placing the blame for male lust on women, today sexual pleasure is far too important a commodity for women not to seek their own agency and pleasure in it. Sex-positive Annie Sprinkle—masseuse, whore, pornographer, sex educator, and performance artist—shows how agency inheres in a strategic "stylized repetition of acts."[35]

NOTES

The quotation that forms the epigraph to this chapter is from Annie Sprinkle, *Love Magazine* 83: 4963. My essay appears in a slightly different form in the anthology *Dirty Looks: Woman, Pornography, Power*, ed. Pam Church Gibson and Roma Gibson (London: British Film Institute, 1993).

1. Cindy Carr, "War on Art: The Sexual Politics of Censorship," *The Village Voice*, 5 June 1990, 28.

2. The art critic Linda Burnham writes, for example, "I went to Cleveland for this performance [Annie Sprinkle's performance at the Cleveland Performance Art Festival], and performance art critics don't come any more credentialed than I do, and I declare it: Annie Sprinkle is a performance artist and this performance was art, not pornography." *High Performance* 1990, 13. See also Linda Montano, "Summer Saint Camp 1987," *The Drama Review* 33, no. 1 (Spring 1989): 94–103.

3. This drawing of lines, like the drawing of lines between the erotic and the pornographic, almost always depends on who you are and what turns you on (or off): pornography, as Robbe-Grillet once said, is the eroticism of the "other."

4. Chuck Kleinhans, "When did Annie Sprinkle Become an Artist? Female Performance Art, Male Performance Anxiety, Art as Alibi, and Labial Art," paper given at Society for Cinema Studies, May 1992.

5. Linda Williams, "Pornographies On/Scene, or 'Diff'rent Strokes for Diff'rent Folks," in *Sex Exposed: Sexuality and the Pornography Debate*, ed. Lynne Segal and Mary McIntosh (London: Virago, 1992), 233–65. In this article I suggest that the word "obscene," which literally means off scene, no longer functions to refer to genuinely hidden things, sexual or otherwise. In our contemporary sexual politics the more proper term is on/scene.

6. Quoted in the documentary film *Sacred Sex* (Cynthia Connop, 1992).

7. Tania Modleski, *Feminism without Women: Culture and Criticism in a "Postfeminist" Age* (New York: Routledge, 1991), 8.

8. These are excerpts from the Minneapolis Ordinance authored by Andrea Dworkin and Catharine MacKinnon, in Appendix 2 of *Women against Censorship*, ed. Varda Burstyn (Vancouver: Douglas and MacIntyre, 1985), 206.

9. Denise Riley, *Am I That Name? Feminism and the Category of "Women" in History* (Minneapolis: University of Minnesota Press, 1988).

10. Modleski, *Feminism without Women*, 16–17.

11. Ibid.

12. Quoted in Andrea Juno and V. Vale, *Angry Women*, Re/Search no. 13 (San Francisco: Re/Search Publications, 1991), 24.

13. Ibid., 26.

14. Annie Sprinkle, *Annie Sprinkle: Post Porn Modernist* (Amsterdam: Torch Books, 1991), 13.

15. See Louis Althusser, "Ideology and Ideological State Apparatuses (Notes Towards an Investigation)," in *Lenin and Philosophy and Other Essays*, trans. Ben Brewster (London: New Left Books), 122–73.

16. Judith Butler, *Gender Trouble: Feminism and the Subversion of Identity* (New York: Routledge, 1990), 143.

17. Ibid., 145.

18. Quoted in Juno and Vale, *Angry Women*, 26.

19. This is why she is out of place in an anthology called *Angry Women*.

20. Many stag films, however, retain this discursive address. See Linda Williams, *Hard Core: Power, Pleasure and the Frenzy of the Visible* (Berkeley: University of California Press, 1989), 58–92.

21. Andrea Dworkin, *Pornography: Men Possessing Women* (Chicago: University of Chicago Press, 1979), ix.

22. Holt N. Parker, "Love's Body Anatomized: The Ancient Erotic Handbooks and the Rhetoric of Sexuality," in *Pornography and Representation in Greece and Rome*, ed. Amy Richlin (New York: Oxford University Press, 1992), 91.

23. Ibid.

24. Ibid., 99.

25. Ibid., 93.

26. It is worth noting that this shot of Mom and Dad is held briefly so that their faces are not discernible, apparently out of consideration for their feelings.

27. I discuss the form and function of this money shot in chapter 4 of *Hard Core*.

28. Irigaray suggests that women as commodities to men should refuse, as "goods," to go to market. However, she also raises another possibility—which she goes on to reject—that the goods might "go to market on their own . . . enjoy their own worth among themselves, to speak to each other, to desire each other, free from the control of seller-buyer-consumer subjects." Luce Irigaray, *This Sex Which Is Not One*, trans. Catherine Porter and Carolyn Burke (Ithaca: Cornell University Press, 1985), 197. I have suggested in *Hard Core* that the Femme Productions group of female pornographers, to which Annie Sprinkle belongs, represents a form of the "goods" getting together to market themselves differently (248–50). I am suggesting here that Annie Sprinkle's marketing offers a subtle revision of what these goods are.

29. Kleinhans's argument ("When Did Annie Sprinkle Become an Artist?") was based on his perception that liquid emerged from the urethra and not, as I thought, the vagina. Kleinhans maintained that Sprinkle tells us we are seeing ejaculation for legal reasons, since urination is legally actionable in some localities. Straayer's talk, "The Seduction of Boundaries: Feminist Fluidity in Annie Sprinkle's Art/Education/Sex," has been published in the anthology *Dirty Looks*, ed. Gibson and Gibson.

30. Butler, *Gender Trouble*, 137.

31. Ibid., 138.

32. Fredric Jameson, "Postmodernism and Consumer Society," in *The Anti-Aesthetic: Essays on Postmodern Culture*, ed. Hal Foster (Port Townsend, Wash.: Bay Press, 1983), 114.

33. Butler, *Gender Trouble*, 138–39.

34. See Williams, *Hard Core*, 153, 230–31, 278–79.
35. Butler, *Gender Trouble*, 140.

Contributors

Sandra Lee Bartky, Professor of Philosophy and Women's Studies at the University of Illinois at Chicago, wrote *Femininity and Domination: Studies in the Phenomenology of Oppression* (1990). Her current project is "Sympathy and Solidarity: On a Tightrope with Scheler," forthcoming in *Feminists Rethink the Self*, edited by Diana Meyers.

Judith Kegan Gardiner, author of *Rhys, Stead, Lessing, and the Politics of Empathy* (1989) and an editor of *Feminist Studies*, is Professor of English and Women's Studies at the University of Illinois at Chicago. She is rethinking humanist feminism in her book in progress, *Breaking Set and Building Stories: Readings in Culture and Women's Fiction*.

Valerie Hartouni is Assistant Professor of Communication and Women's Studies at the University of California, San Diego. She is author of numerous articles that treat as problems of discourse and culture the controversies surrounding the new technologies of human genetics and reproduction. Her book *Reproductive Technologies and the Negotiation of Public Meanings* is forthcoming.

Susan Hekman is Professor of Political Science at the University of Texas at Arlington. Her book *Gender and Knowledge* was published in 1990. She is presently at work on a book on feminist moral theory, *Moral Voices, Moral Selves*, that will be published in 1995.

Marianne Hirsch is Dartmouth Professor of French and Comparative Literature at Dartmouth College. Most recently, she is the author of *The Mother/Daughter Plot: Narrative, Psychoanalysis, Feminism* (1989) and coeditor of *Conflicts in Feminism* (1990). She is completing a book entitled *Family Frames: Narrative and Photography in the Postmodern.*

Miriam M. Johnson, Emerita Professor of Sociology at the University of Oregon, is author of *Strong Mothers, Weak Wives: The Search for Gender Equality* (1988). Her article "Functionalism and Feminism: Is Estrangement Necessary?" appears in *Theory on Gender/Feminism on Theory,* edited by Paula England (1993).

Carla Kaplan is Assistant Professor of English and Women's Studies at Yale University. Her essay "Reading Feminist Readings: Recuperative Reading and the Silent Heroine of Feminist Criticism" appears in *Listening to "Silences": New Essays in Feminist Criticism,* edited by Elaine Hedges and Shelley Fisher Fishkin (1994). She is completing a book entitled *The Erotics of Talk: Women's Writing and Feminist Paradigms.*

Katie King is Associate Professor of Women's Studies at the University of Maryland, College Park. Her previous essays have been on feminist theory, lesbian and gay studies, and the apparatus of literary production. She is finishing a book, *Theory in Its Travels: Conversations in U.S. Feminism,* and proselytizing a field she calls "Feminism and Writing Technologies."

Patricia S. Mann is Assistant Professor of Philosophy at Hofstra University. She serves on the editorial boards of *Social Text* and *Hypatia* and has published many articles on contemporary social and political issues as well as a book, *Micro-Politics: Agency in a Postfeminist Era* (1994).

Ellen Messer-Davidow, Associate Professor at the University of Minnesota, teaches in the departments of English, Women's Studies, and Cultural Studies. Her most recent book, edited with David R. Shumway and David J. Sylvan, is *Knowledges: Historical and Critical Studies in Disciplinarity* (1993). She is currently finishing *Disciplining Feminism: Episodes in the Discursive Production of Social Change.*

Julie Nelson-Kuna, former director of the eating disorders program at Mercy Center, is a graduate student in the Department of Psychology at the University of Illinois at Chicago. She is completing her thesis on treatment of bulimia, and her current research is in smoking cessation.

Stephanie Riger is Professor of Psychology and Women's Studies at the University of Illinois at Chicago where she directs the Women's Studies Program. Her recent publications include "Epistemological Debates, Feminist Voices: Science, Social Values, and the Study of Women," *American Psychologist* (1992), which received the Distinguished Publication Award from the Association for Women in Psychology. She is coauthor, with Margaret T. Gordon, of *The Female Fear: The Social Cost of Rape* (1989). Her current research examines the quality of the working environment for women in corporate and academic settings.

Chéla Sandoval is a teacher of Cultural Studies for the Department of Chicano Studies and English at the University of California, Santa Barbara. Sandoval has contributed to *Signs, Haciendo Caras,* and *The Oxford Companion to Women's Writing in the United States.* She is the author of "U.S. Third World Feminism," published in *Genders* (1991). At present she is working on a book entitled *Oppositional Consciousness in the Postmodern World.*

Patrocinio P. Schweickart is Professor of English and Women's Studies at the University of New Hampshire. She is the 1984 winner of the Florence Howe Award of the Women's Caucus of the Modern Language Association. With Elizabeth A. Flynn, she edited *Gender and Reading* (1986), and she is author of "Reading, Teaching and the Ethic of Care," in *Gender in the Classroom: Power and Pedagogy* edited by Susan L. Gabriel and Isaiah Smithson (1990). She is the current editor of the *National Women's Studies Association Journal.*

Patricia Stamp is Associate Professor, Division of Social Science, York University, Toronto, Canada, and author of *Technology, Gender, and Power in Africa* (1990). She is now researching and writing on local government in Africa and Asia, and women, democracy, and development in Africa and South Asia.

Margaret Strobel, Professor of Women's Studies and History at the University of Illinois at Chicago, is working on a history of the Chicago Women's Liberation Union. She is on the editorial board of the *Historical Encyclopedia of Chicago Women.* Her earlier research dealt with African women; and with gender, race, and empire in her book *European Women and the Second British Empire* (1991).

Linda Williams is Professor of Film Studies and Women's Studies at the University of California, Irvine. Her most recent book is *Hard Core: Power, Pleasure, and "The Frenzy of the Visible"* (1989). She is currently working on a study of movies that move audiences to strong responses.

Index

abolitionism, 284

abortion: choices for, 135–38, 140, 145, 148; illegal, 54, 57; and moral issues, 137–39; opposition to, 136, 141; and popular culture, 143–45; referral service for, 58. *See also* birth control methods

abstractions, 103–4

academic feminism, 8, 12–13, 25, 109. *See also* feminism

acquired immunodeficiency syndrome (AIDS), 99. *See also* AIDS activism

action: and affectivity, 37–38; and articulatory practices, 34–35, 41–46, 52; beyond personal transformation, 52–53, 55–63, 66, 229; and community, 11; and consciousness-raising, 52; definitions of, 170–71, 178; hostility to, 42; and language, 30, 33–34, 42; mechanisms for, 53; and production of social system, 29–30; and social change, 46; and subordination, 169; types of, 170–72. *See also* agency; choice

activity, 2–3, 10

ACT-UP, 11, 95, 97–99

adolescence: and agency, 254, 264–66, 276; narratives of, 254–55, 257–61; and resistance, 256, 259; sexual harassment during, 286

adoption, 116–17, 120, 160. *See also* reproductive technologies

Aeschylus, 117, 122–23

affect-attunement: in CR groups, 38–41, 43, 52; definition of, 14, 53; and language, 33–34; process of, 32–34

affectivity, and action, 37–38

Africa: age-grade organizations in, 75; and agency, 69; aid projects for, 72–73, 76–77, 83; colonialism in, 75–76, 78; communal practices in, 71, 73–75; feminist discourse in, 70, 83; gender relations in, 71, 80; identity in, 71, 77; stereotypes of women in, 71–72, 88; traditions in, 158. *See also* Kenya; Kikuyu

African-Americans: community building of, 15–16; and definition of mothering, 153, 157; and HIV transmission, 102; and identity, 8; narratives of, 280–301; and use of silence, 294–95. *See also* ethnicity; race

age-grade organizations, 75

agency: in adolescence, 254, 264–66, 276; and autobiography, 250, 254, 274; versus communion and cooperation, 170–72, 175; comprehension as precondition for, 234–35; and constituting subject, 195–97, 201–4; debates on, 106–7, 109; versus determinism, 26–28; development of, 62, 268, 273–74; dimensions of, 134–37, 141; and discontinuities, 261–62; and emotions, 269, 273; and feminist theory, 9, 169–70, 199–203; and Foucault's theories, 16, 179, 186; and gender, 2–14; and historical conditions, 97, 109; and identity, 1, 8; models of, 25–29; and power relations, 4, 10, 13; production of, 29–30, 35–43; psychological theories of, 169–77; relation of subject to, 196–97; and sexuality, 305, 309, 313, 316; and social change, 17, 25; social con-

Education Act of 1944 (U.K.), 266
efficacy beliefs, and gender, 5, 16, 174–75
egalitarianism, 74, 152, 157, 164. *See also* equality
Eisenstein, Hester, 40, 212–13
ejaculation (female), 312–13, 315
elderly, care for, 161–62
elections, in Kenya, 86
electronic networks, 46
elitism, and cultural production, 102
emotions: anger, in feminist discourse, 243; identification of, 269, 273; and self-efficacy theory, 175; and theories of depression, 171
empiricism, 194
Enlightenment, Age of, 7, 180, 182, 185–86, 188
environmentalism, 70, 81–82, 162
epic narrative versus modern literature, 181
epistemology of modernity, 197–99, 203, 206
epistolary fiction, 287
equality: discourses on, 204, 236; and social contract, 297–98; for women in public sphere, 159, 163. *See also* egalitarianism
equal rights, 43, 215–16
Equal Rights Amendment (ERA), 43
ERAP (Economic Research and Action Project), 45
Eskimo, and model of self, 25
essentialism: and AIDS activism, 100; definitions of, 200–201, 230, 304–5; dichotomies in, 197; and sexual identities, 101, 107
ethnicity: of CWLU membership, 54; and difference, 212–13; and factionalism, 87; and gender, 209; in Kenya, 70, 79–80; and politics, 85; and violence, 87. *See also* African-Americans; Hispanics; Kikuyu; Latinos; race
ethnic nationalism, 216
existentialism, 57, 149n4
expectations, 134–37, 145–46
expressive action, 170–72

factionalism, and ethnicity, 87

fairy tales, 2–5
false consciousness, 306
families: changes in, 153, 159–61, 250, 261–62; and childrearing, 143, 152, 158; definitions of, 119–21, 124, 126, 128–29, 161; middle-class, 2, 161; photographs of, 249–50, 254–63, 275; relationships in, 249–50, 254, 262; in slavery, 295; status of females in, 254, 258, 277; stepfamilies, 160–61; traditional ideal of, 77, 126, 134, 153, 157, 161. *See also* children; fatherhood; motherhood; parents
fantasy, and photography, 267
fatherhood: definitions of, 120–24, 126, 128–29; and divorce, 160; in Greek imagination, 122; and ideas of mothering, 161–62; motivations for, 147; prerogatives of, 118, 121–22, 124, 126; rights in, 116–18, 121–24. *See also* motherhood
FCF (Free Congress Foundation), 24, 46
feedback from teachers, 174–75
femininity, 3, 268
feminism: academic, 8, 12–13, 25, 109; activism in, 8, 13, 29; and antipornography movement, 304; characteristics of, 155–57; cultural, 95, 216; and cyborgean analysis, 142–44; definitions of, 12, 16, 100, 164, 229–48, 304; discourse on, 232, 242–43; failures of, 43–44; goals of, 8, 13, 190, 202, 230, 235–36; humanist, 9; in Kenya, 83–85; liberal, 156, 194–96, 234; Marxist, 234; materialist, 6–7, 9, 109; postfeminism, 137–45, 303–4; postmodern, 196, 199; poststructuralist, 108, 143, 304–5; projects of, 233; radical, 156, 195–96, 234; revival of (1960s), 155, 169, 175–76; roots of, 266; social constructionist, 195–97; and technology, 140; as text, 235–36, 241; and theories of human nature, 234; and views of motherhood, 154–55. *See also* feminist theory; second-wave feminism; socialist feminism; women's liberation movement
feminist theory: and agency, 9, 169–70, 199–203; and AIDS activism, 93–95; appropriations by, 106, 209, 214; bias-